RANMA 1/2

VOL. 22
Action Edition

Story and Art by
RUMIKO TAKAHASHI

English Adaptation by Gerard Jones
Translation by Kaori Inoue
Touch-Up Art & Lettering/Wayne Truman & Bill Schuch
Cover Design/Hidemi Sahara
Graphics & Layout/Sean Lee
Editor/Julie Davis

Managing Editor/Annette Roman
Editor in Chief/William Flanagan
Dir. of Licensing & Acquisitions/Rika Inouye
Sr. VP of Sales & Marketing/Rick Bauer
Sr. VP of Editorial/Hyoe Narita
Publisher/Seiji Horibuchi

RANMA 1/2 is rated "T+" for Older Teens. It may contain violence, language, alcohol or tobacco use, or suggestive situations.

For the purposes of publication in English, the artwork in this publication is printed in reverse from the original Japanese version.

Printed in Canada

Published by VIZ, LLC
P.O. Box 77010
San Francisco, CA 94107

VIZ
www.viz.com

Action Edition
10 9 8 7 6 5 4 3 2
First printing, April 2003
Second printing, April 2004

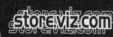

Ranma ½

VOL. 22

Action Edition

STORY & ART BY

RUMIKO TAKAHASHI

STORY THUS FAR

The Tendos are an average, run-of-the-mill Japanese family—at least on the surface, that is. Soun Tendo is the owner and proprietor of the Tendo Dojo, where "Anything-Goes Martial Arts" is practiced. Like the name says, anything goes, and usually does.

When Soun's old friend Genma Saotome comes to visit, Soun's three lovely young daughters—Akane, Nabiki, and Kasumi—are told that it's time for one of them to become the fiancée of Genma's teenage son, as per an agreement made between the two fathers years ago. Youngest daughter Akane—who says she hates boys—is quickly nominated for bridal duty by her sisters.

Unfortunately, Ranma and his father have suffered a strange accident. While training in China, both plunged into one of many "accursed" springs at the legendary martial arts training ground of Jusenkyo. These springs transform the unlucky dunkee into whoever—or whatever—drowned there hundreds of years ago.

From now on, a splash of cold water turns Ranma's father into a giant panda, and Ranma becomes a beautiful, busty young woman. Hot water reverses the effect...but only until next time.

Ranma and Genma weren't the only ones to take the Jusenkyo plunge—it isn't long before they meet several other members of the "cursed." And although their parents are still determined to see Ranma and Akane marry and carry on the training hall, Ranma seems to have a strange talent for accumulating extra fiancées, and Akane has a few suitors of her own. Will the two ever work out their differences, get rid of all these extra people, or just call the whole thing off? And will Ranma ever get rid of his curse?

CAST OF CHARACTERS

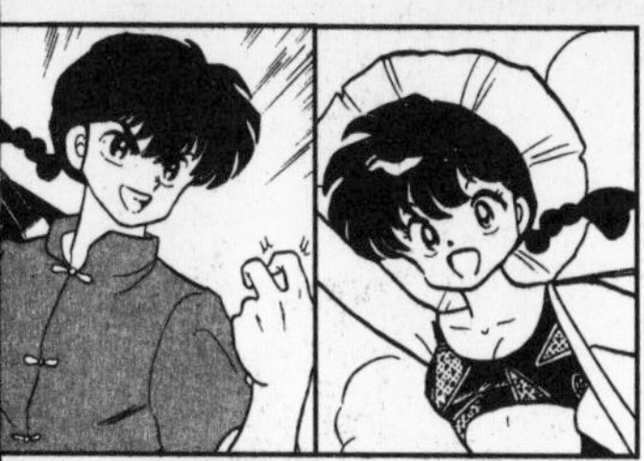

Ranma Saotome
Martial artist with far too many finacées, and an ego that won't let him take defeat easily. He changes into a girl when splashed with cold water.

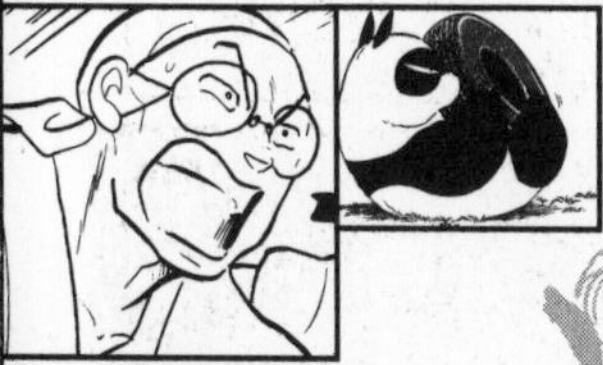

Genma Saotome
Ranma's lazy father, who left his home and wife years ago with his young son to train in the martial arts. He changes into a panda.

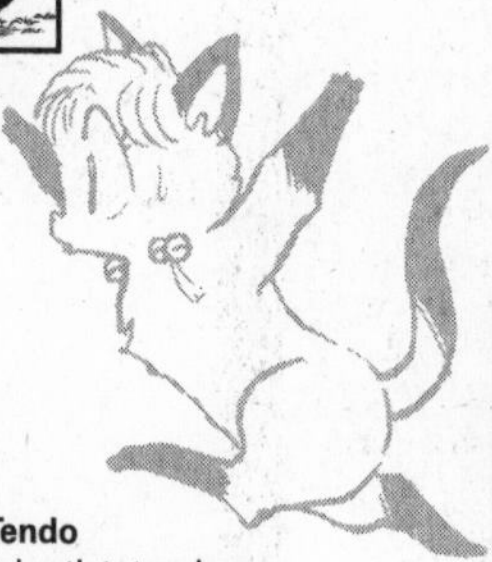

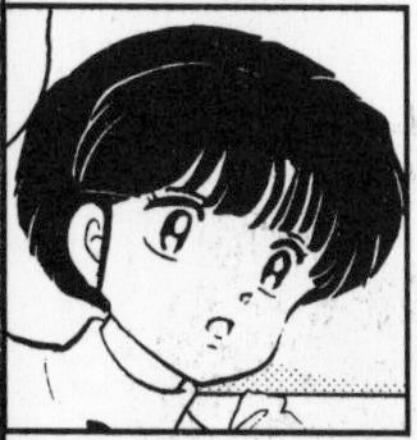

Akane Tendo
A martial artist, tomboy, and Ranma's fiancée by parental arrangement. She has no clue how much Ryoga likes her, or what relation he has to her pet black pig, P-chan.

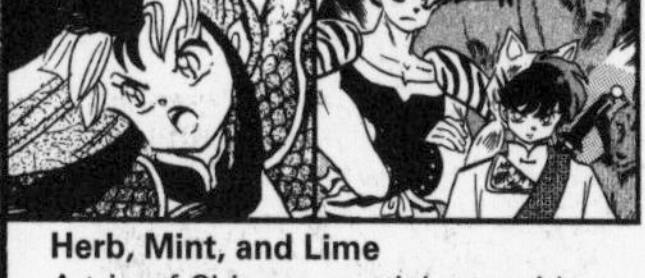

Herb, Mint, and Lime
A trio of Chinese martial arts with special powers.

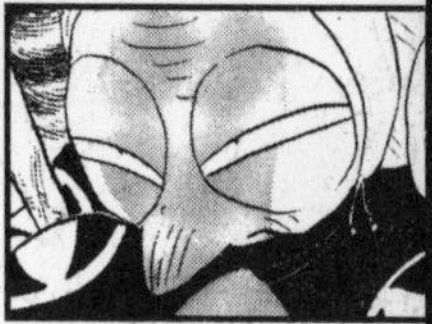

Cologne
Great-grandmother to Shampoo who's looking forward to getting a new grandson-in-law in Ranma.

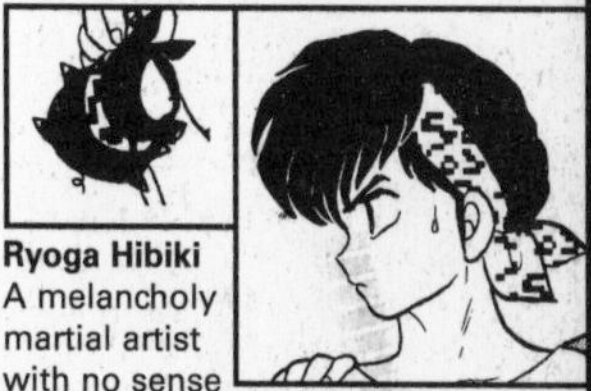

Ryoga Hibiki
A melancholy martial artist with no sense of direction, a crush on Akane, and a grudge against Ranma. He changes into a small, black pig Akane calls "P-chan."

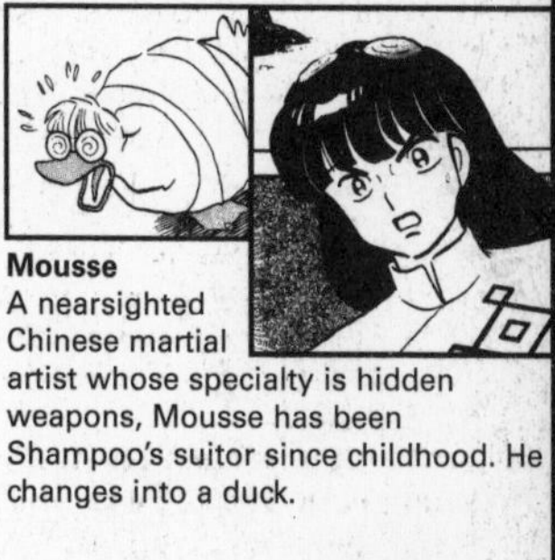

Mousse
A nearsighted Chinese martial artist whose specialty is hidden weapons, Mousse has been Shampoo's suitor since childhood. He changes into a duck.

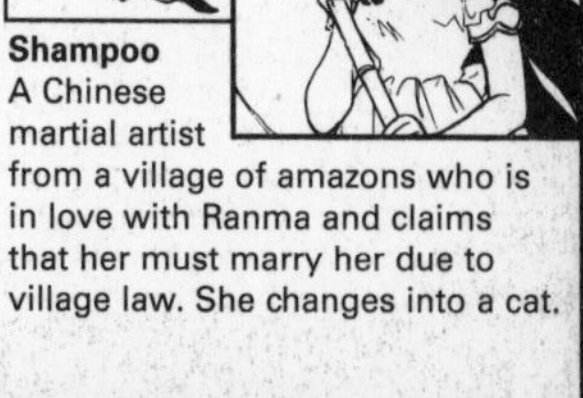

Shampoo
A Chinese martial artist from a village of amazons who is in love with Ranma and claims that her must marry her due to village law. She changes into a cat.

CONTENTS

Part 1

THE GUEST AT THE CAT CAFÉ

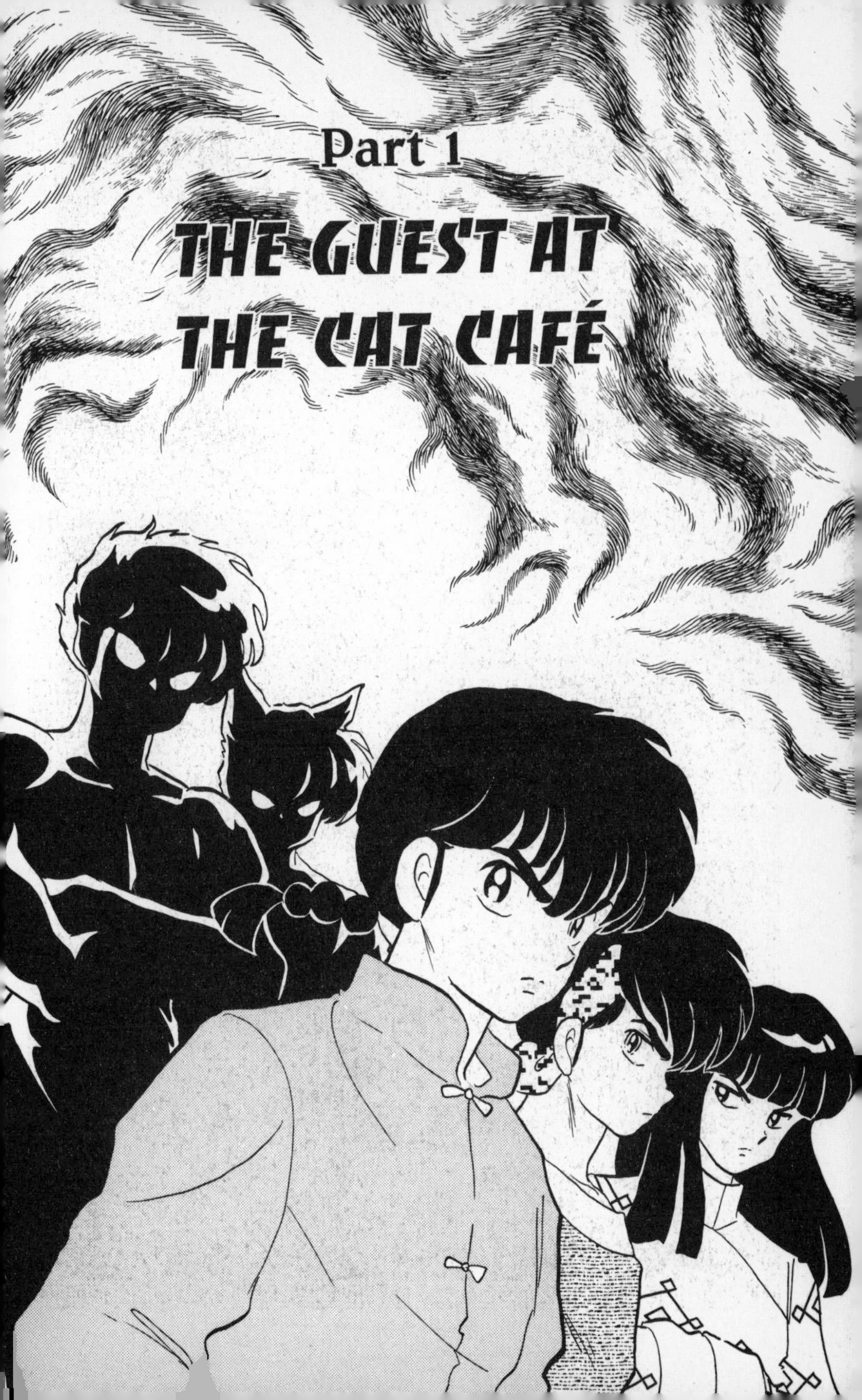

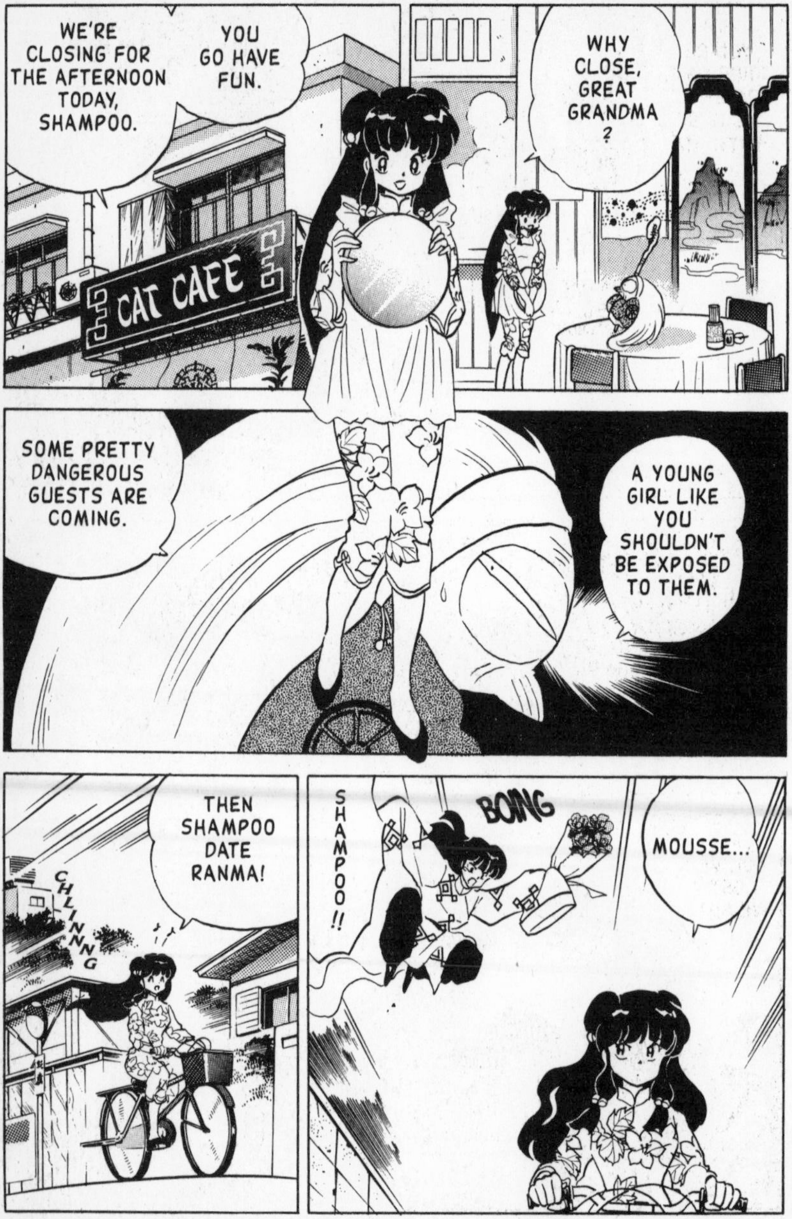
WE'RE CLOSING FOR THE AFTERNOON TODAY, SHAMPOO.
YOU GO HAVE FUN.
CAT CAFE
WHY CLOSE, GREAT GRANDMA ?
SOME PRETTY DANGEROUS GUESTS ARE COMING.
A YOUNG GIRL LIKE YOU SHOULDN'T BE EXPOSED TO THEM.
THEN SHAMPOO DATE RANMA!
CHLINNNG
SHAMPOO!!
BOING
MOUSSE...

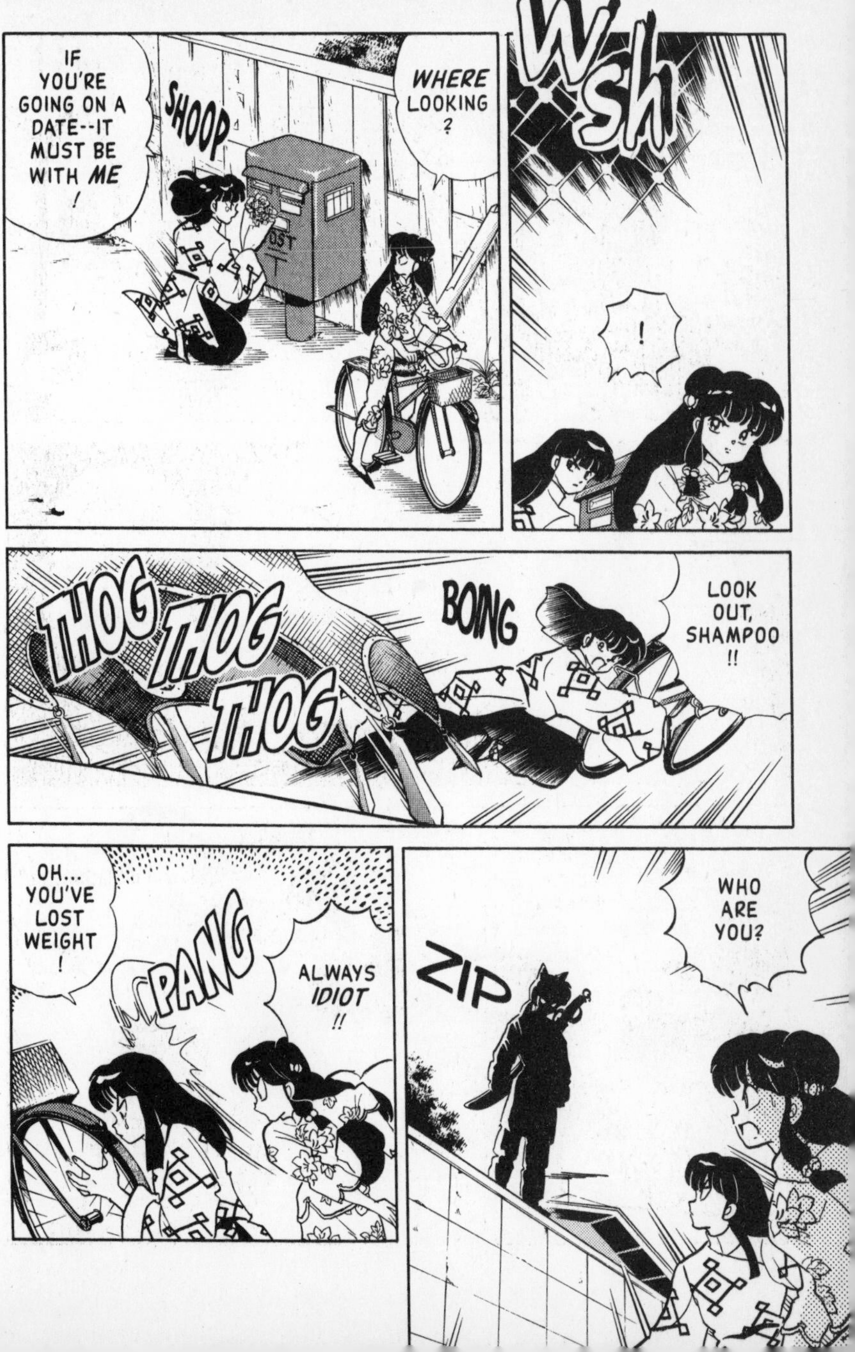

IF YOU'RE GOING ON A DATE--IT MUST BE WITH *ME* !
SHOOP
WHERE LOOKING ?
Wsh
!
THOG THOG THOG
BOING
LOOK OUT, SHAMPOO !!
OH... YOU'VE LOST WEIGHT !
PANG
ALWAYS *IDIOT* !!
ZIP
WHO ARE YOU?

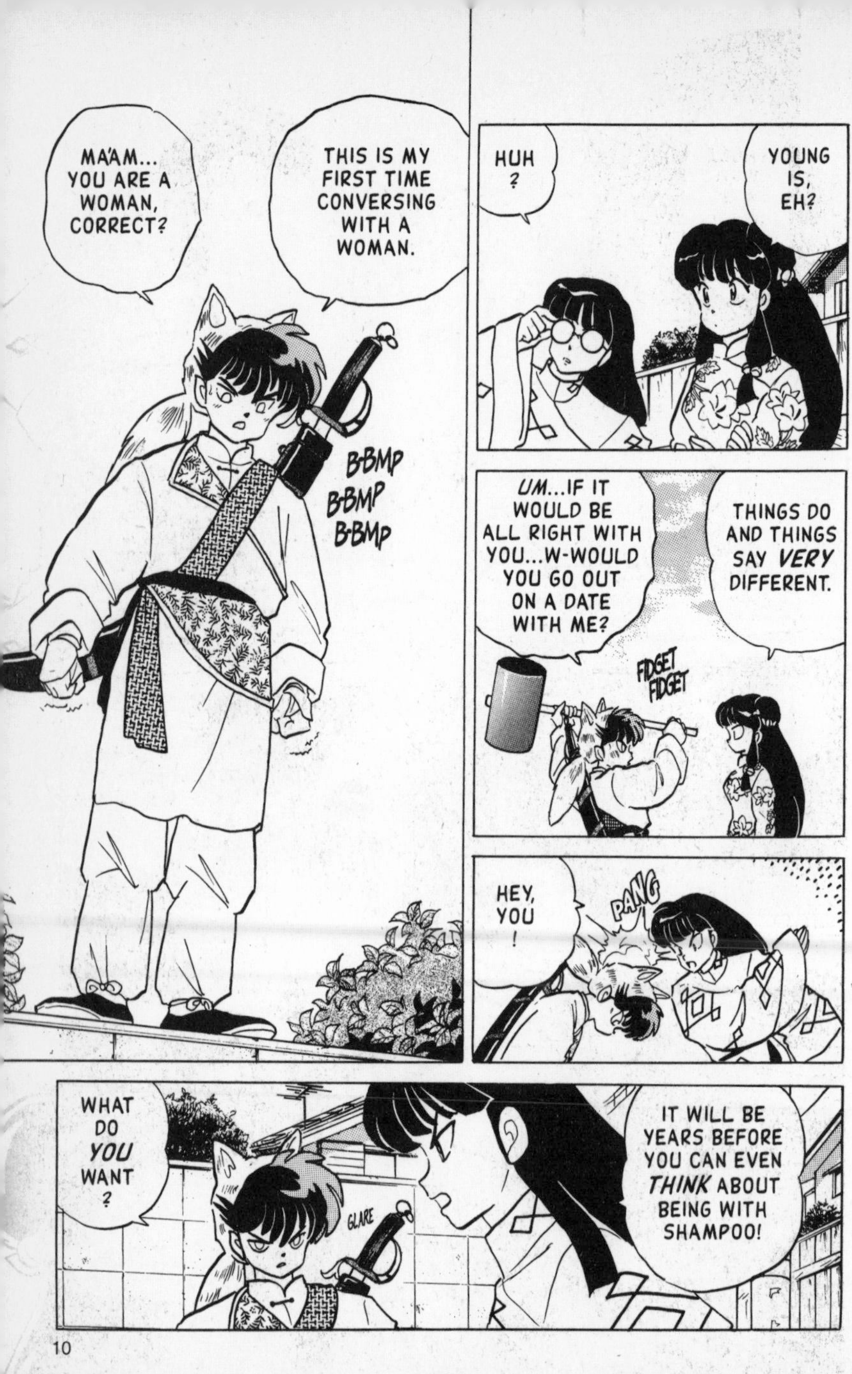
MA'AM... YOU ARE A WOMAN, CORRECT?
THIS IS MY FIRST TIME CONVERSING WITH A WOMAN.
B-BMP B-BMP B-BMP
HUH?
YOUNG IS, EH?
UM...IF IT WOULD BE ALL RIGHT WITH YOU...W-WOULD YOU GO OUT ON A DATE WITH ME?
THINGS DO AND THINGS SAY *VERY* DIFFERENT.
FIDGET FIDGET
HEY, YOU!
PANG
WHAT DO *YOU* WANT?
GLARE
IT WILL BE YEARS BEFORE YOU CAN EVEN *THINK* ABOUT BEING WITH SHAMPOO!

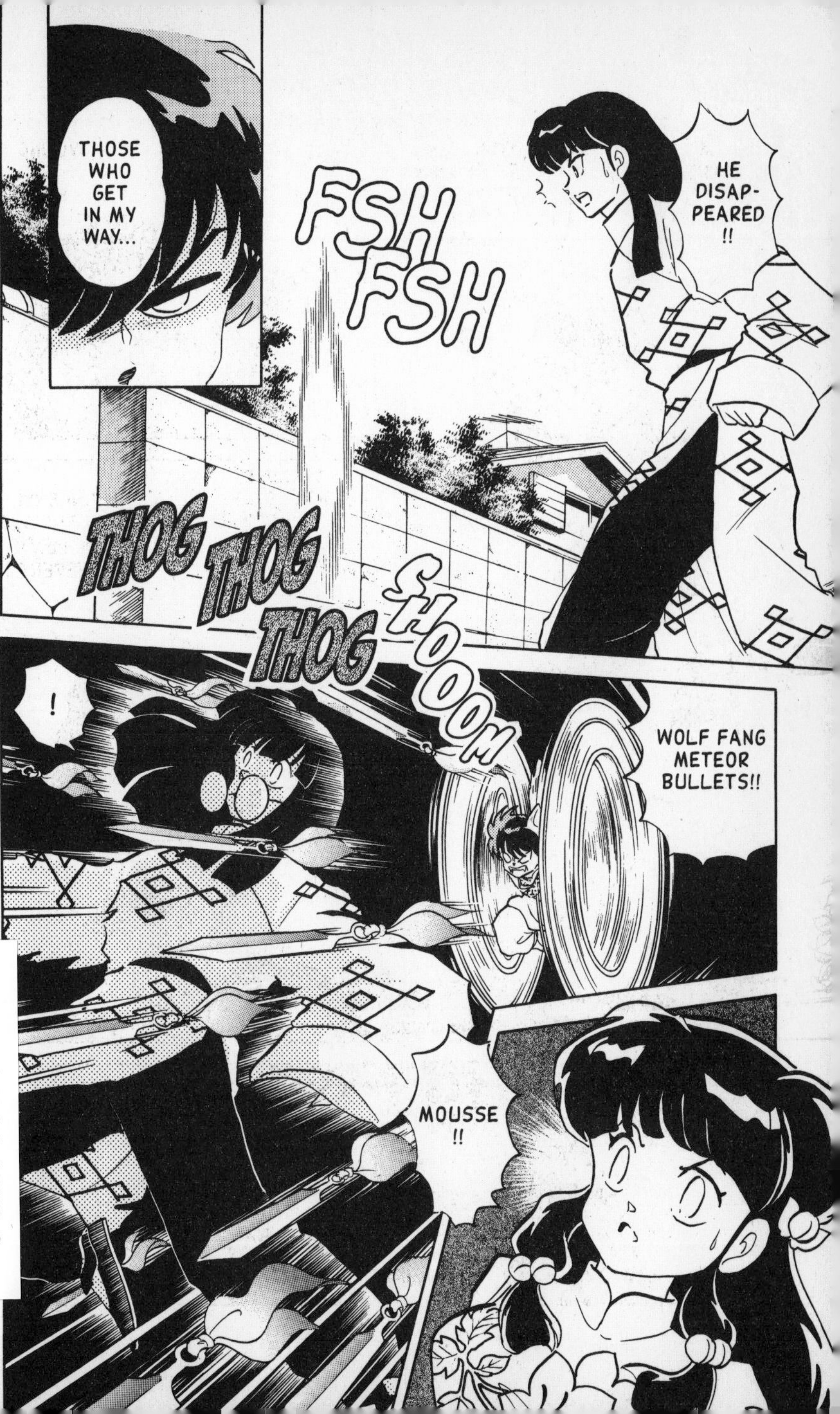
THOSE WHO GET IN MY WAY...
FSH FSH
HE DISAP- PEARED !!
THOG THOG THOG
SHOOOM
!
WOLF FANG METEOR BULLETS!!
MOUSSE !!

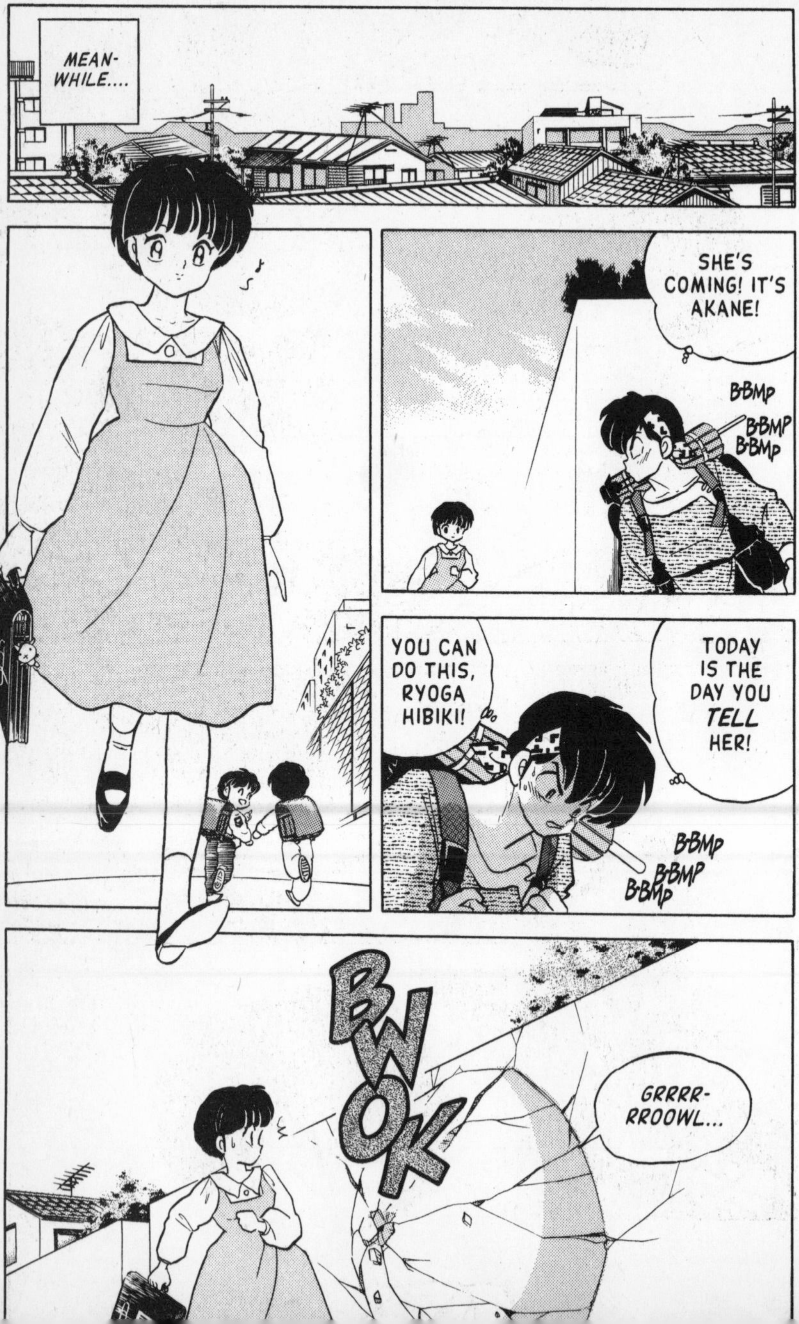
MEAN-WHILE....
SHE'S COMING! IT'S AKANE!
B-BMP
B-BMP
B-BMP
YOU CAN DO THIS, RYOGA HIBIKI!
TODAY IS THE DAY YOU TELL HER!
B-BMP
B-BMP
B-BMP
BWOK
GRRRR-RROOWL...

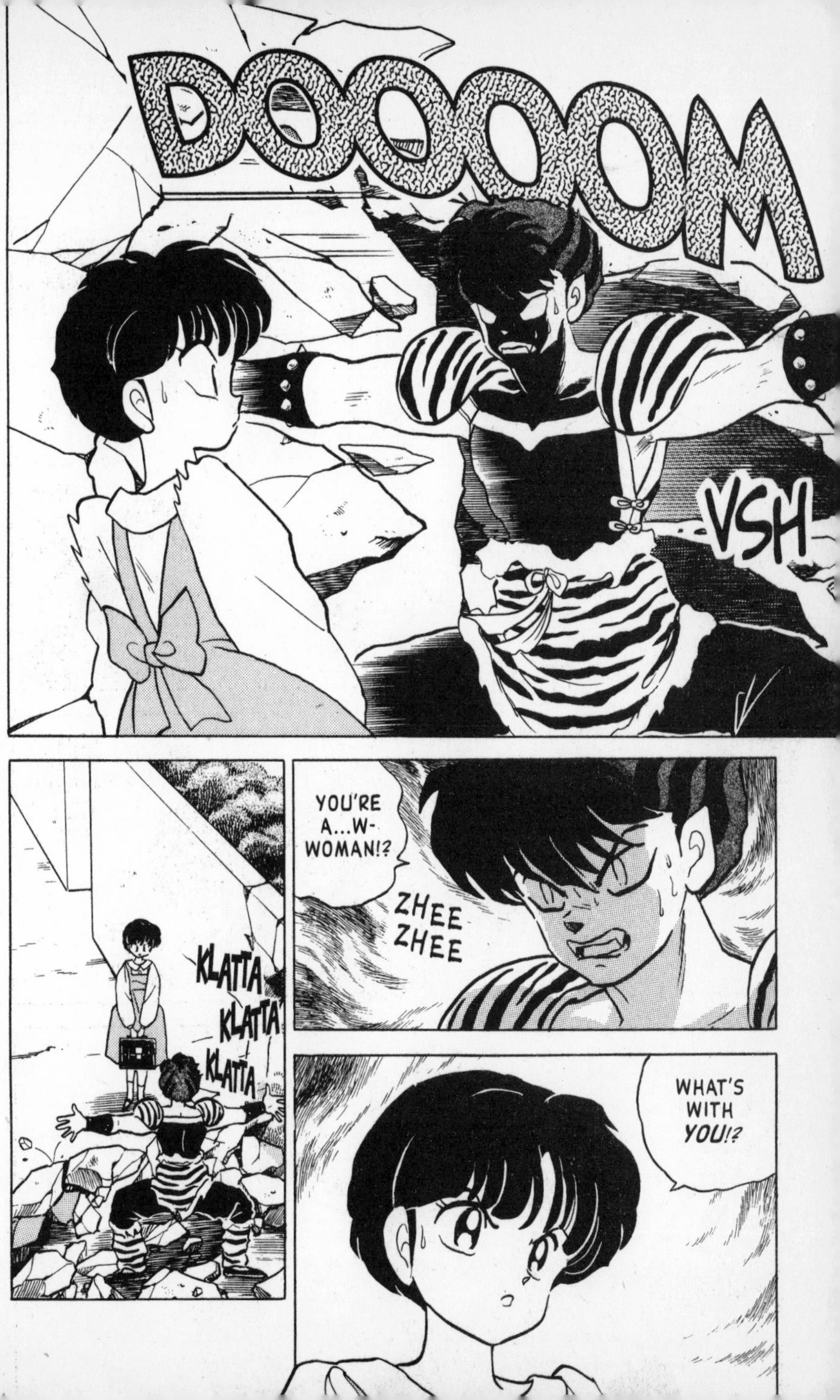
DOOOOOM
VSH
KLATTA
KLATTA
KLATTA
YOU'RE A...W-WOMAN!?
ZHEE ZHEE
WHAT'S WITH YOU!?

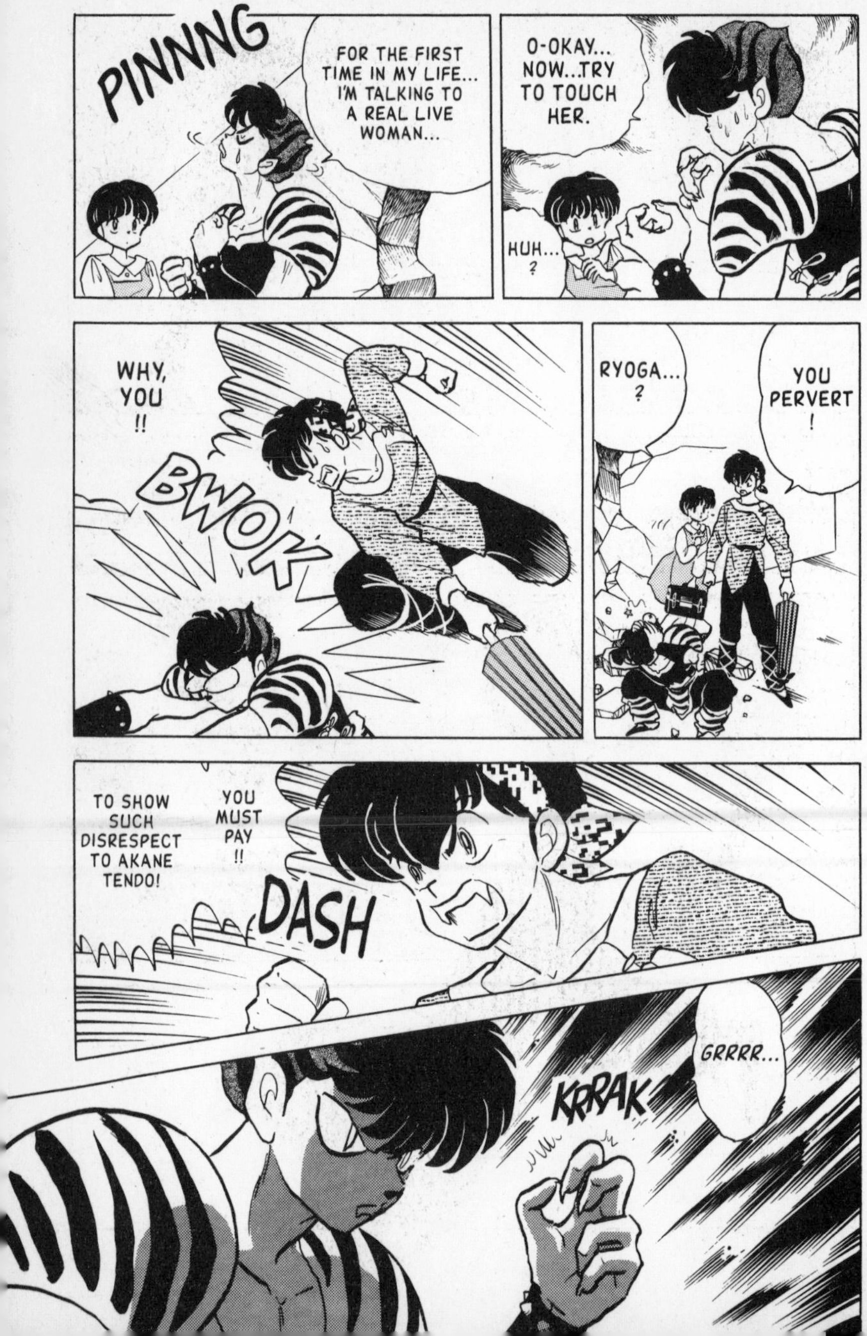
PINNNG
FOR THE FIRST TIME IN MY LIFE... I'M TALKING TO A REAL LIVE WOMAN...
O-OKAY... NOW...TRY TO TOUCH HER.
HUH...?
WHY, YOU!!
BWOK
RYOGA...?
YOU PERVERT!
TO SHOW SUCH DISRESPECT TO AKANE TENDO!
YOU MUST PAY!!
DASH
GRRRR...
KRRAK

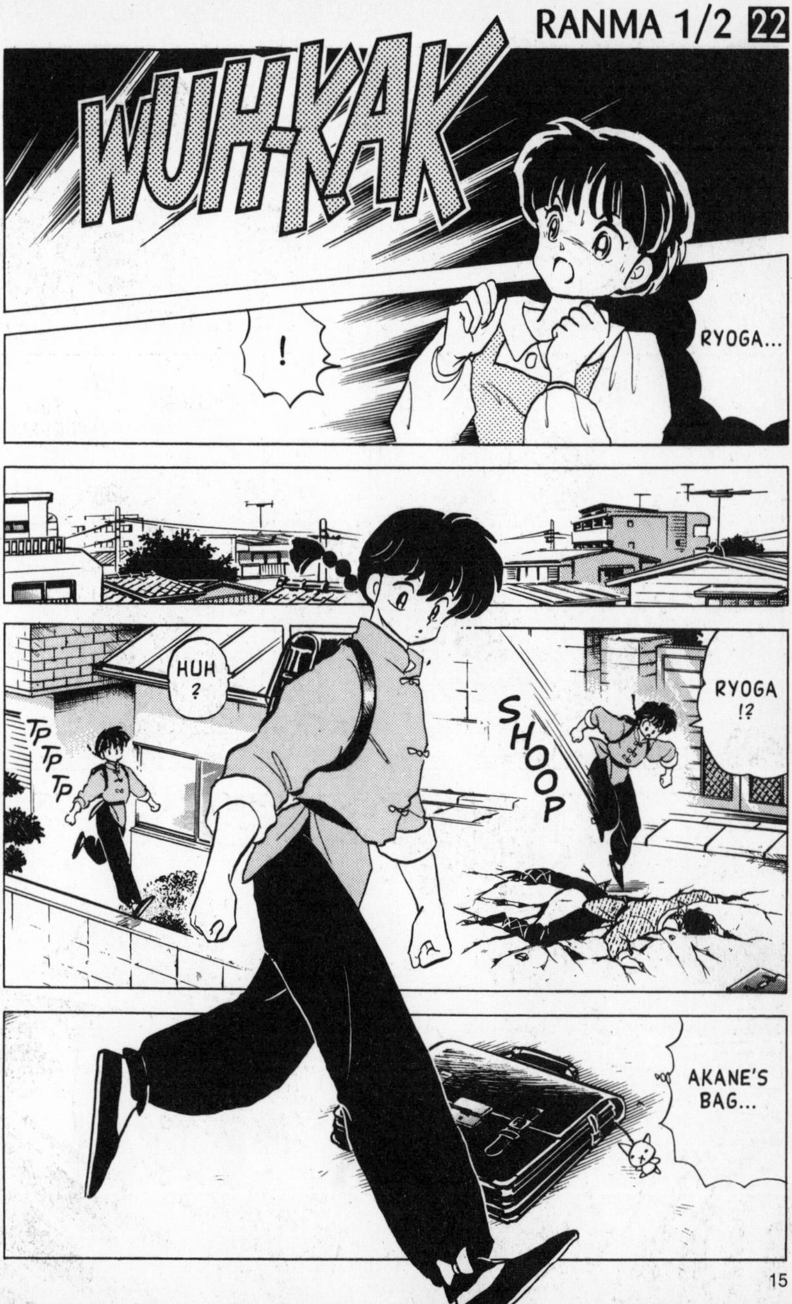
WUH-KAK
!
RYOGA...
HUH ?
TPTPTP
SHOOP
RYOGA !?
AKANE'S BAG...

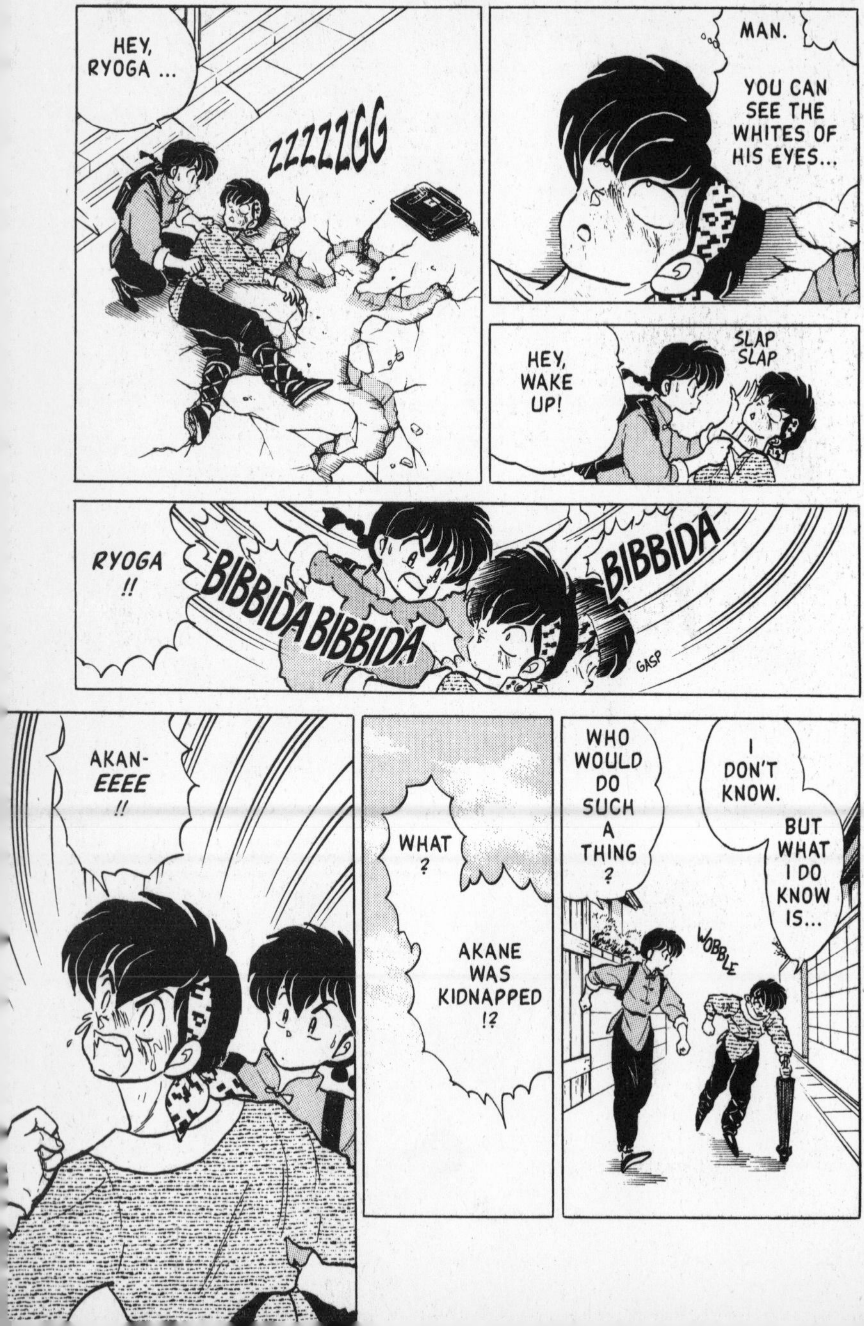
HEY, RYOGA ...
ZZZZZGG
MAN.
YOU CAN SEE THE WHITES OF HIS EYES...
HEY, WAKE UP!
SLAP SLAP
RYOGA !!
BIBBIDA BIBBIDA BIBBIDA
BIBBIDA
GASP
AKAN-EEEE !!
WHAT ?
AKANE WAS KIDNAPPED !?
WHO WOULD DO SUCH A THING ?
I DON'T KNOW.
BUT WHAT I DO KNOW IS...
WOBBLE

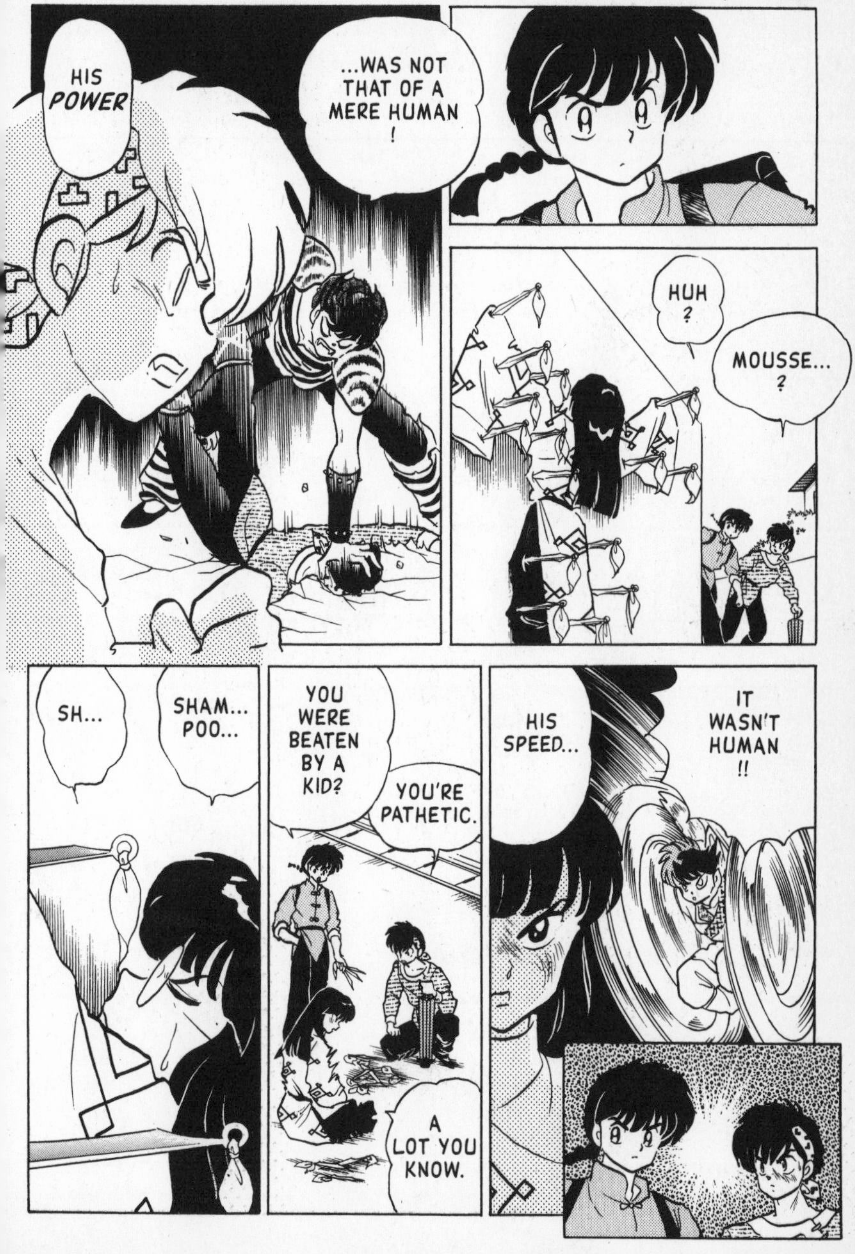
HIS POWER
...WAS NOT THAT OF A MERE HUMAN !
HUH ?
MOUSSE... ?
SH...
SHAM... POO...
YOU WERE BEATEN BY A KID?
YOU'RE PATHETIC.
A LOT YOU KNOW.
HIS SPEED...
IT WASN'T HUMAN !!

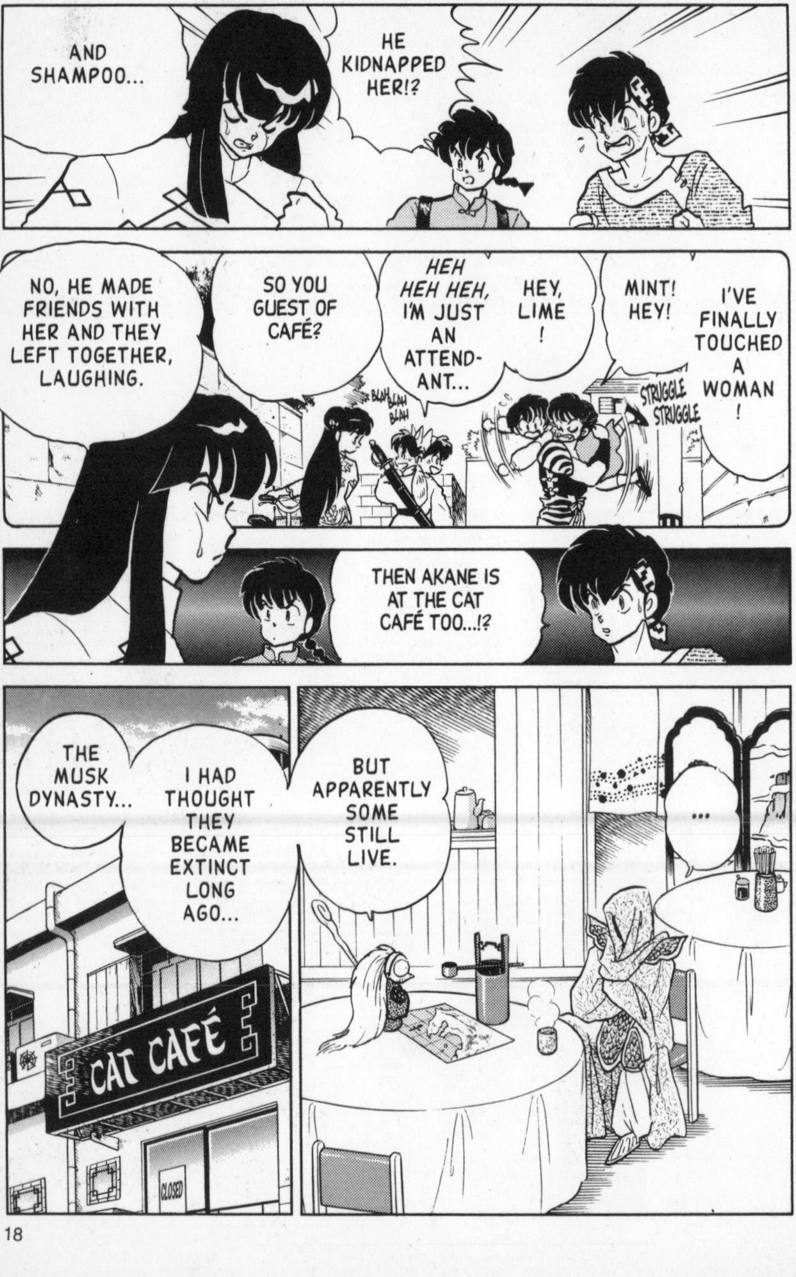
AND SHAMPOO...
HE KIDNAPPED HER!?
NO, HE MADE FRIENDS WITH HER AND THEY LEFT TOGETHER, LAUGHING.
SO YOU GUEST OF CAFÉ?
HEH HEH HEH, I'M JUST AN ATTEND-ANT...
HEY, LIME!
MINT! HEY!
I'VE FINALLY TOUCHED A WOMAN!
STRUGGLE STRUGGLE
THEN AKANE IS AT THE CAT CAFÉ TOO...!?
THE MUSK DYNASTY...
I HAD THOUGHT THEY BECAME EXTINCT LONG AGO...
BUT APPARENTLY SOME STILL LIVE.
...
CAT CAFÉ
CLOSED

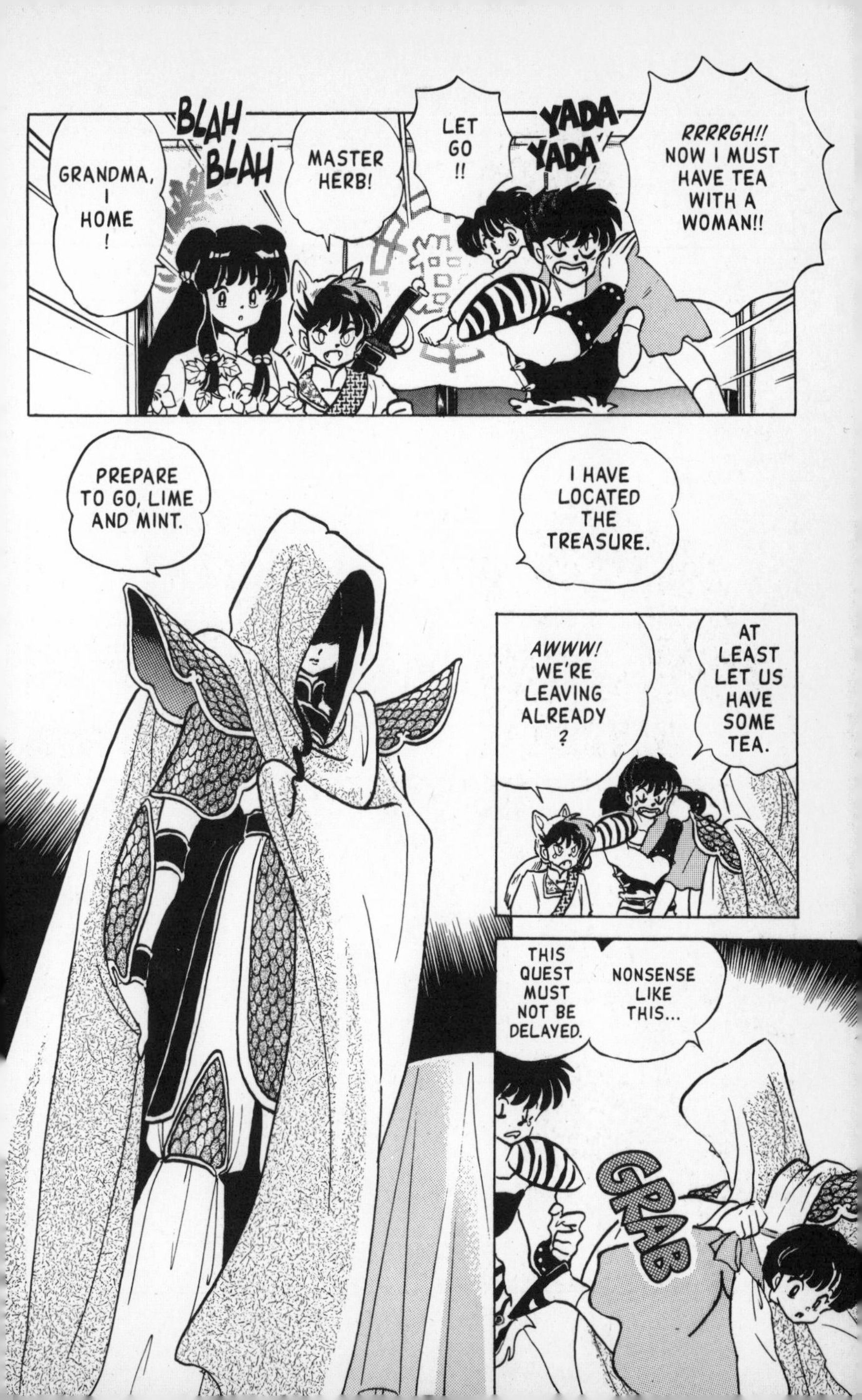
GRANDMA, I HOME!
BLAH BLAH
MASTER HERB!
LET GO!!
YADA YADA
RRRRGH!! NOW I MUST HAVE TEA WITH A WOMAN!!
PREPARE TO GO, LIME AND MINT.
I HAVE LOCATED THE TREASURE.
AWWW! WE'RE LEAVING ALREADY?
AT LEAST LET US HAVE SOME TEA.
THIS QUEST MUST NOT BE DELAYED.
NONSENSE LIKE THIS...
GRAB

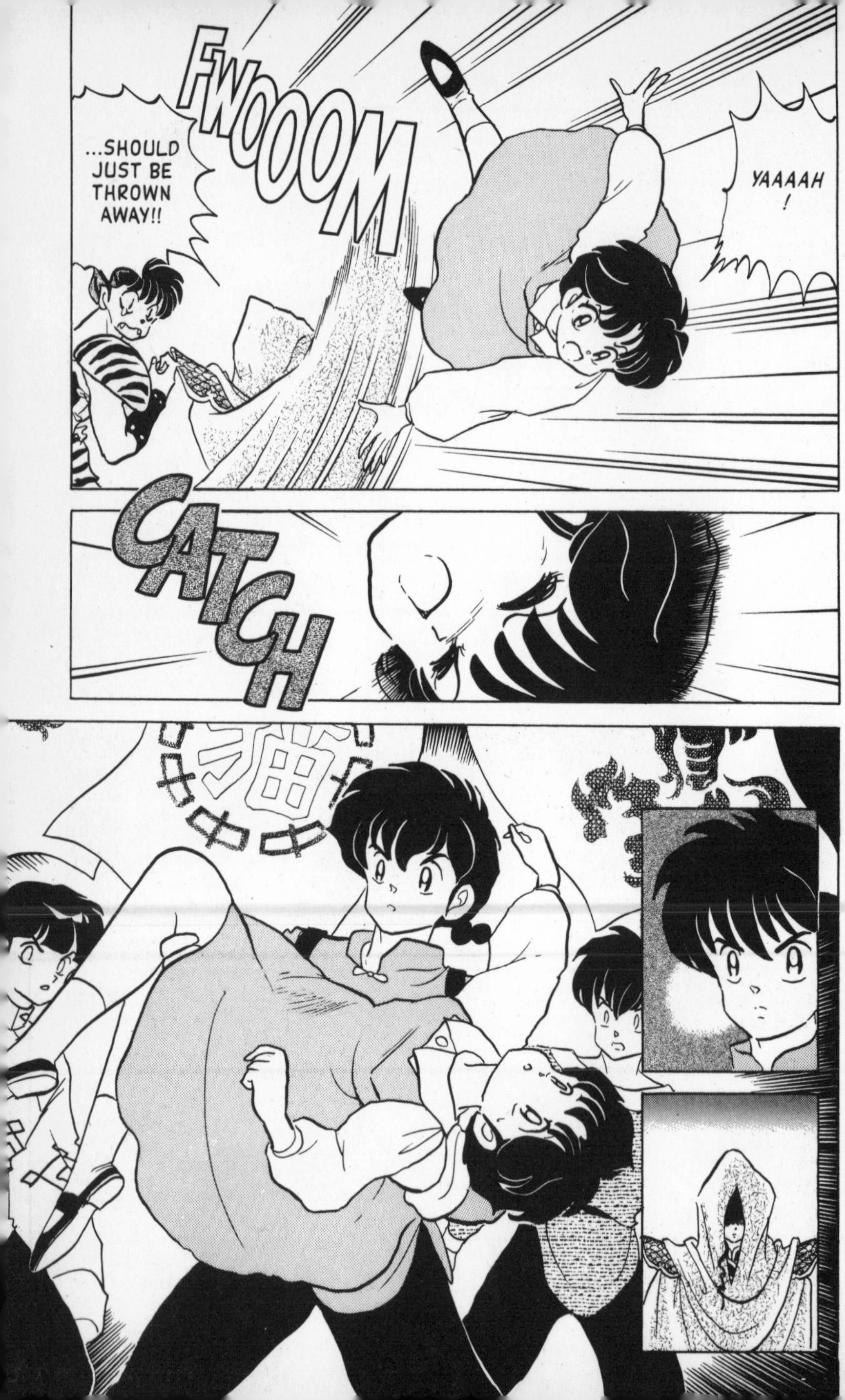
FWOOOM
...SHOULD JUST BE THROWN AWAY!!
YAAAAH !
CATCH

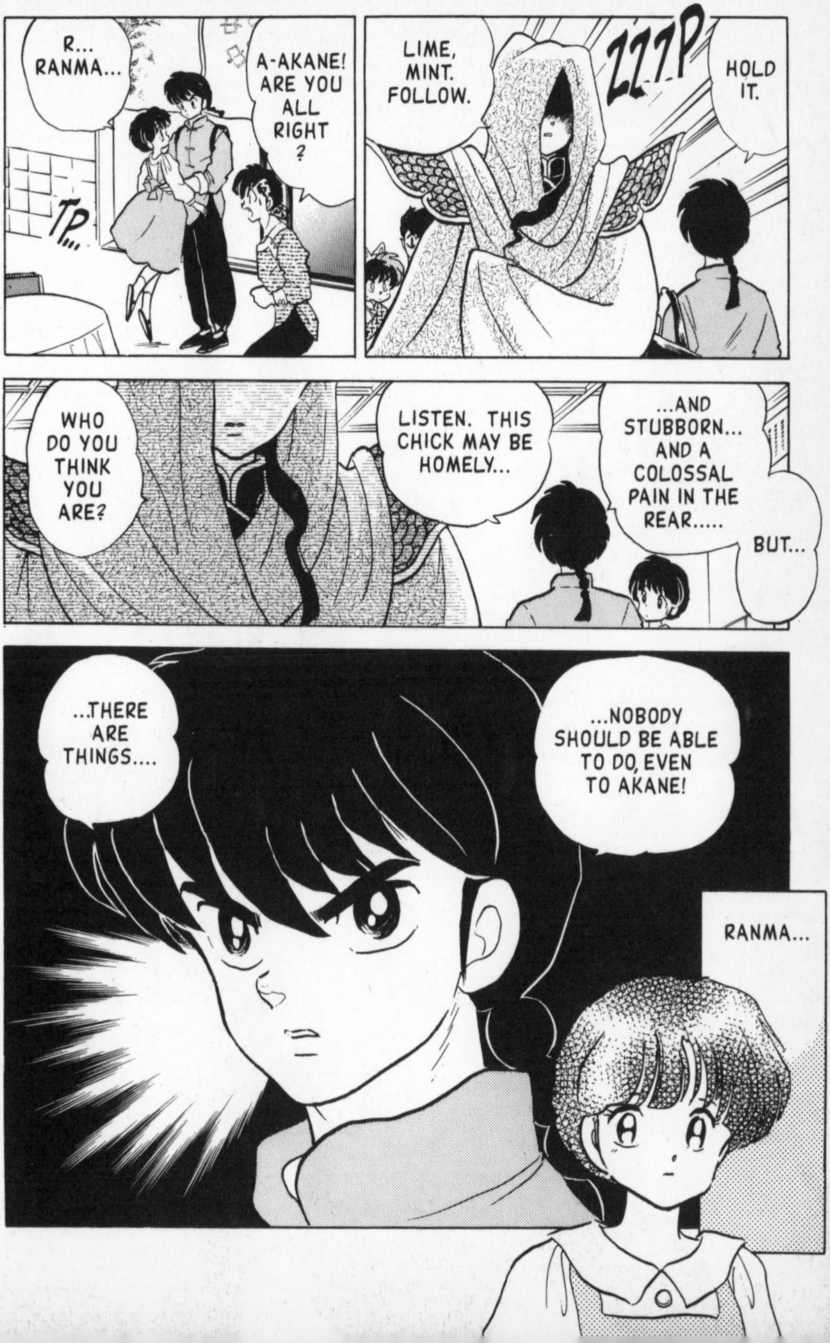
R... RANMA...
A-AKANE! ARE YOU ALL RIGHT?
TP...
LIME, MINT. FOLLOW.
ZZZP
HOLD IT.
WHO DO YOU THINK YOU ARE?
LISTEN. THIS CHICK MAY BE HOMELY...
...AND STUBBORN... AND A COLOSSAL PAIN IN THE REAR.....
BUT...
...THERE ARE THINGS....
...NOBODY SHOULD BE ABLE TO DO, EVEN TO AKANE!
RANMA...

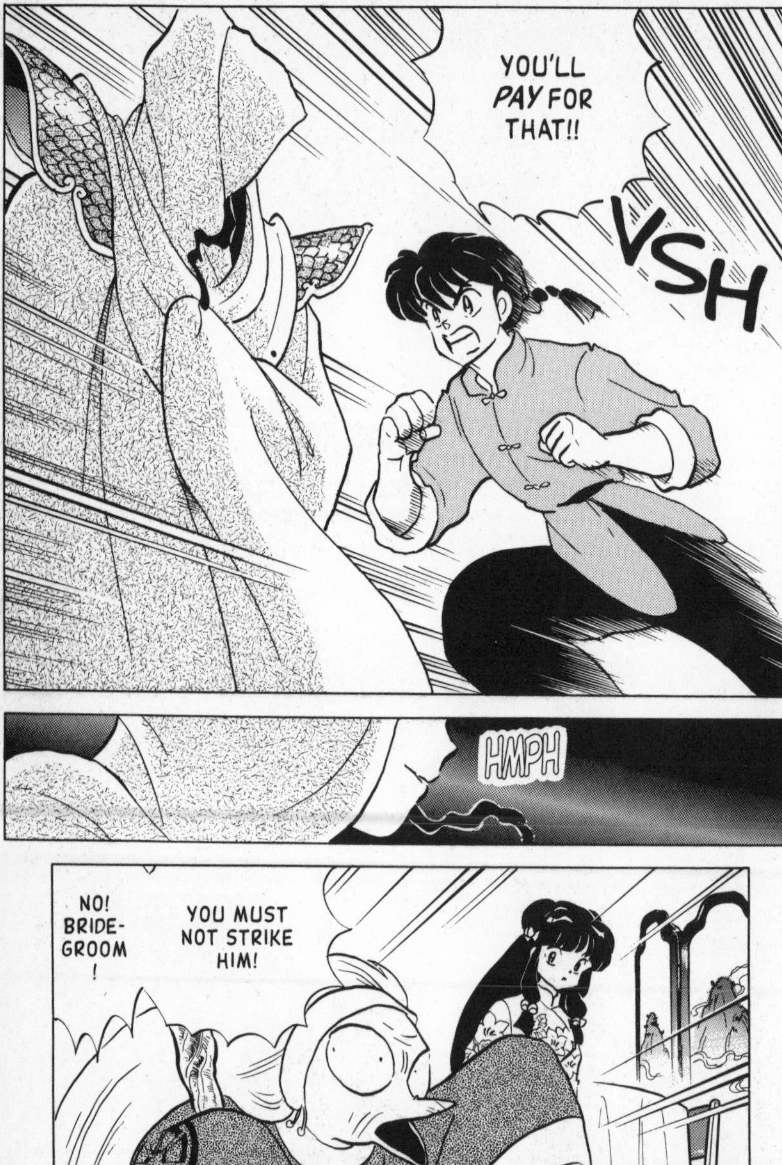
YOU'LL PAY FOR THAT!!
VSH
HMPH
NO! BRIDE-GROOM!
YOU MUST NOT STRIKE HIM!

Part 2

THE ANIMAL KINGDOM

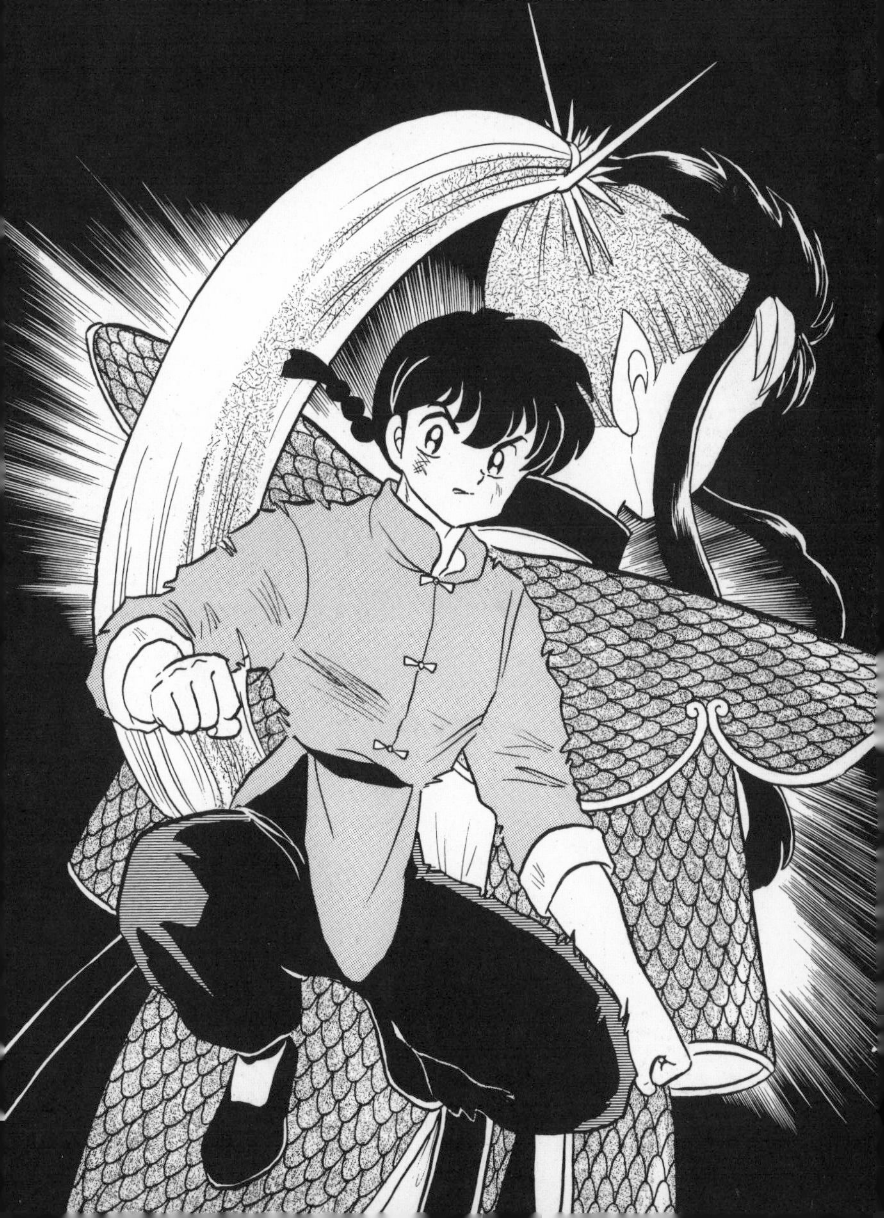

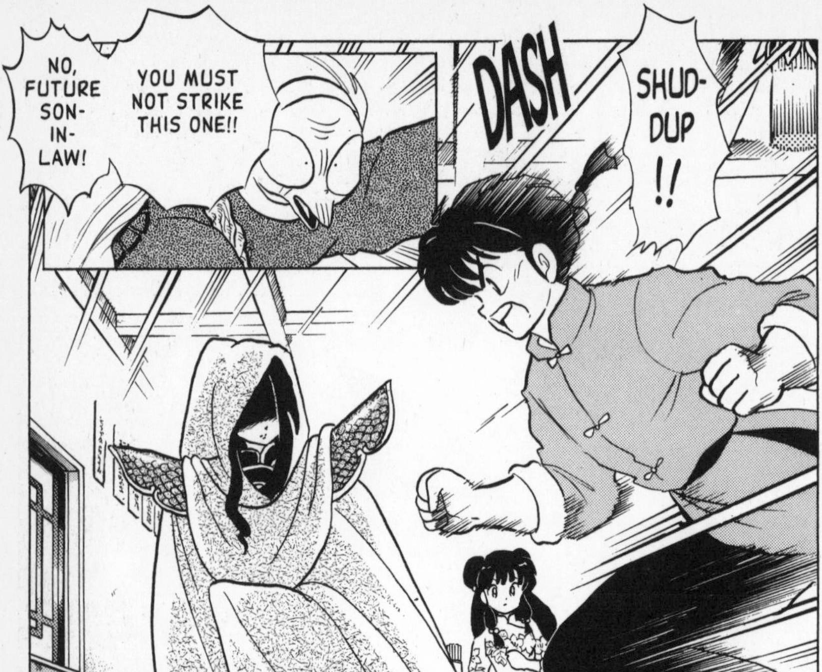
NO, FUTURE SON-IN-LAW!
YOU MUST NOT STRIKE THIS ONE!!
DASH
SHUD-DUP!!

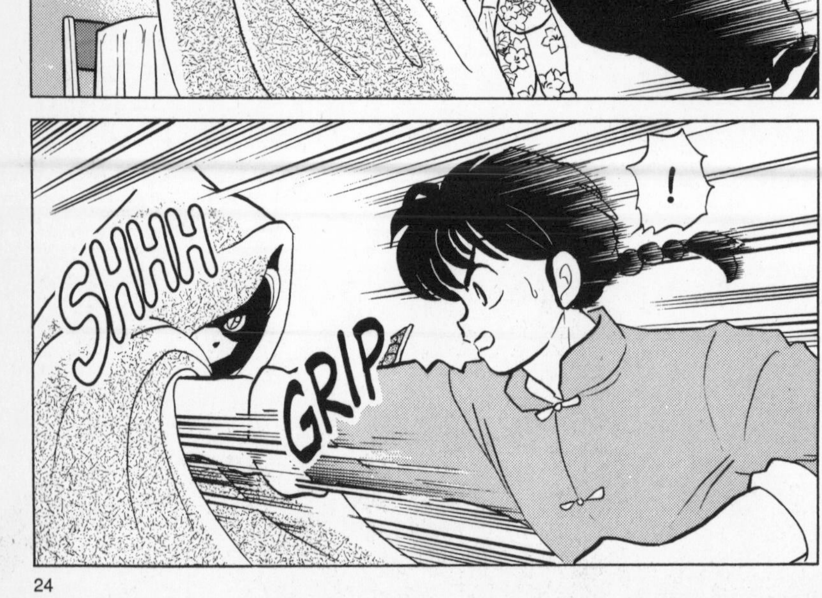
SHHH
GRIP
!

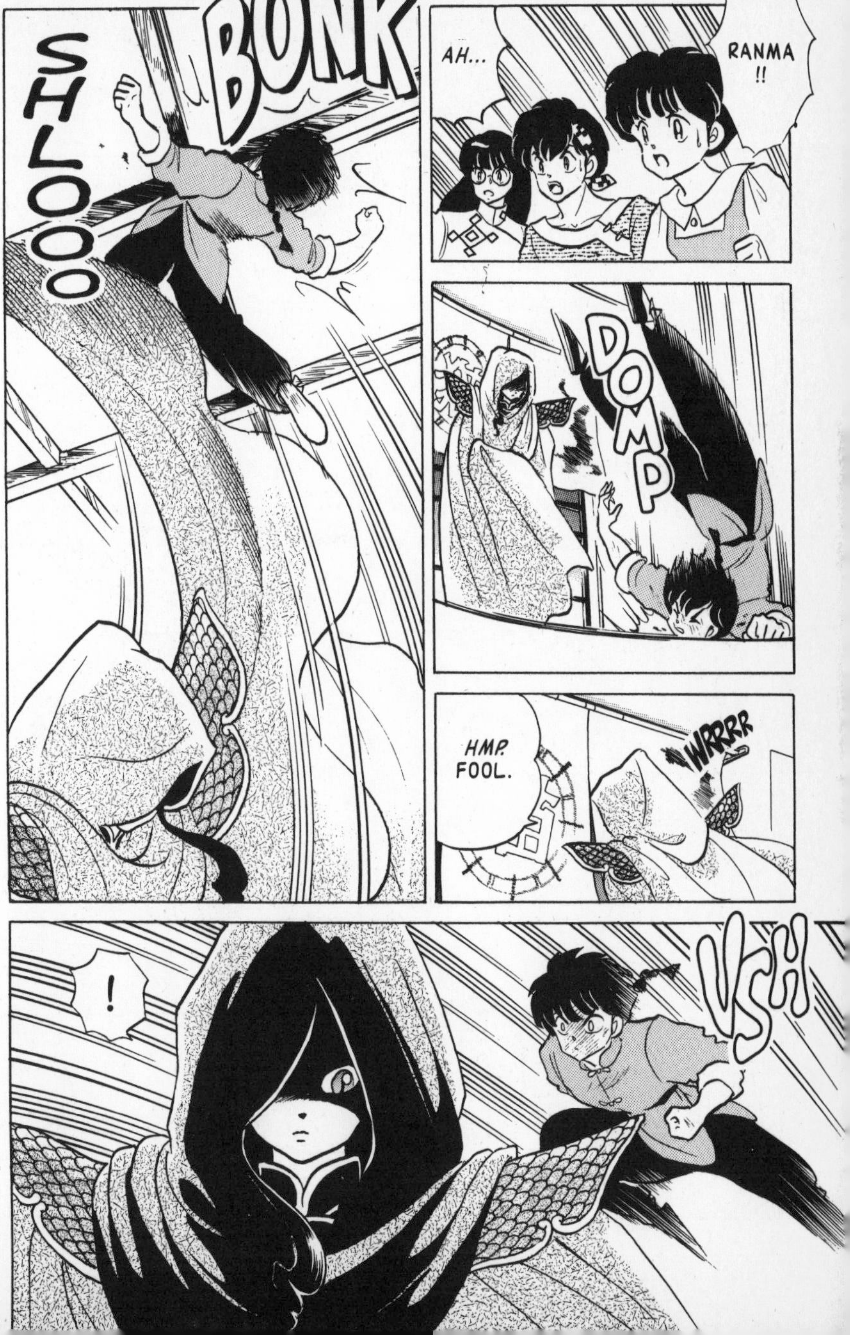
SHLOOO
BONK
AH...
RANMA !!
DOMP
HMP. FOOL.
WRRRR
!
VSH

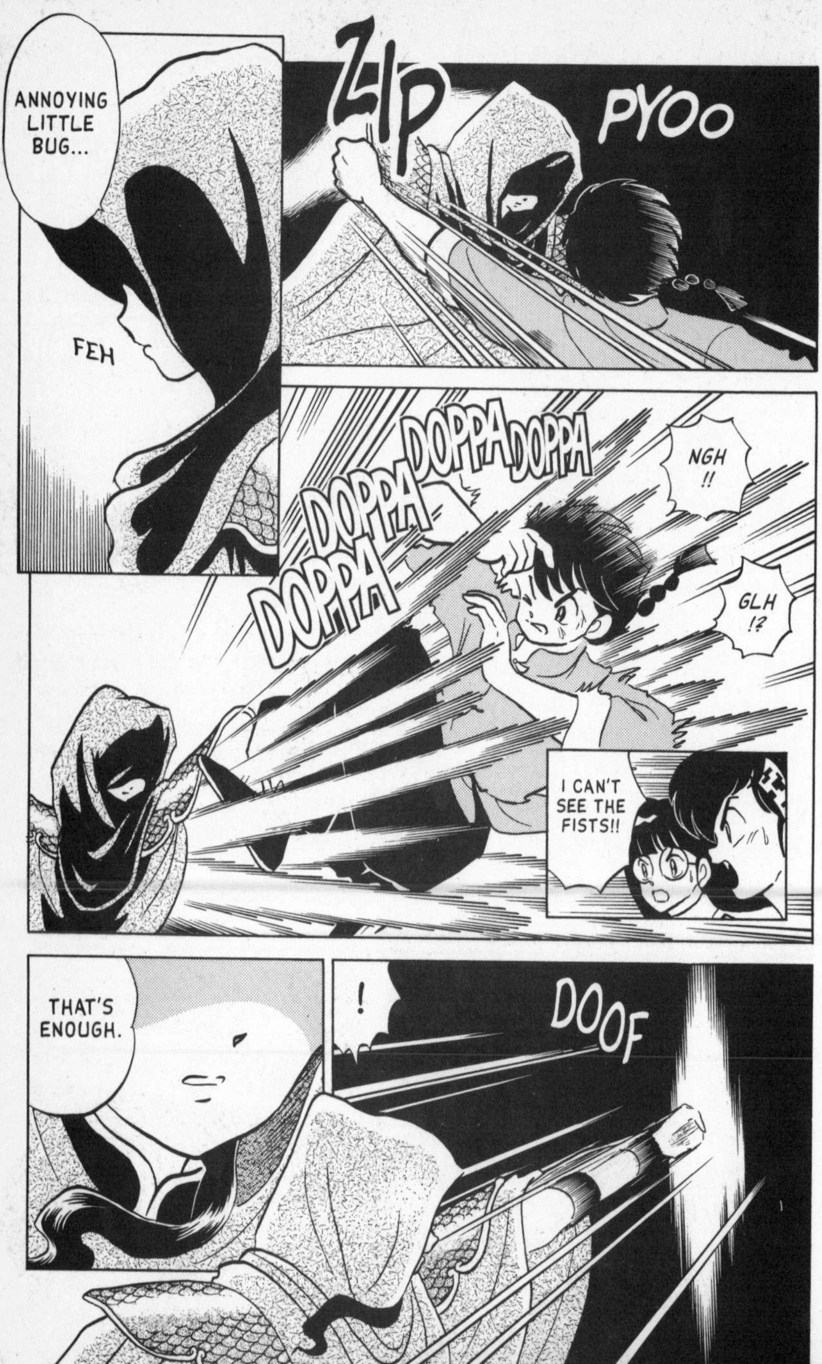
ANNOYING LITTLE BUG...
FEH
ZIP
PYOO
DOPPA DOPPA
DOPPA DOPPA DOPPA
NGH !!
GLH !?
I CAN'T SEE THE FISTS!!
THAT'S ENOUGH.
!
DOOF

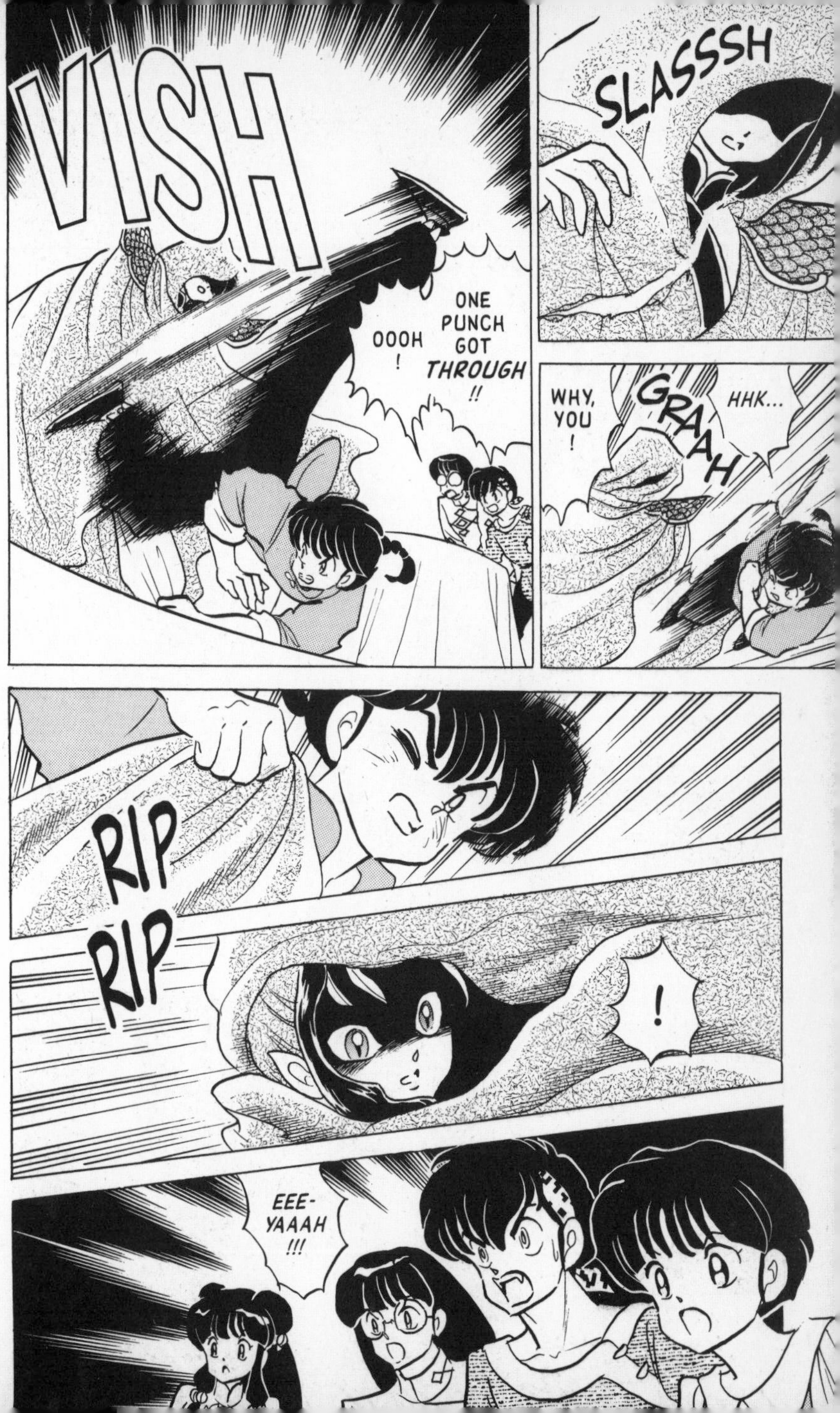
VISH
OOOH !
ONE PUNCH GOT THROUGH !!
SLASSSH
WHY, YOU !
GRAAAH
HHK...
RIP
RIP
!
EEE-YAAAH !!!

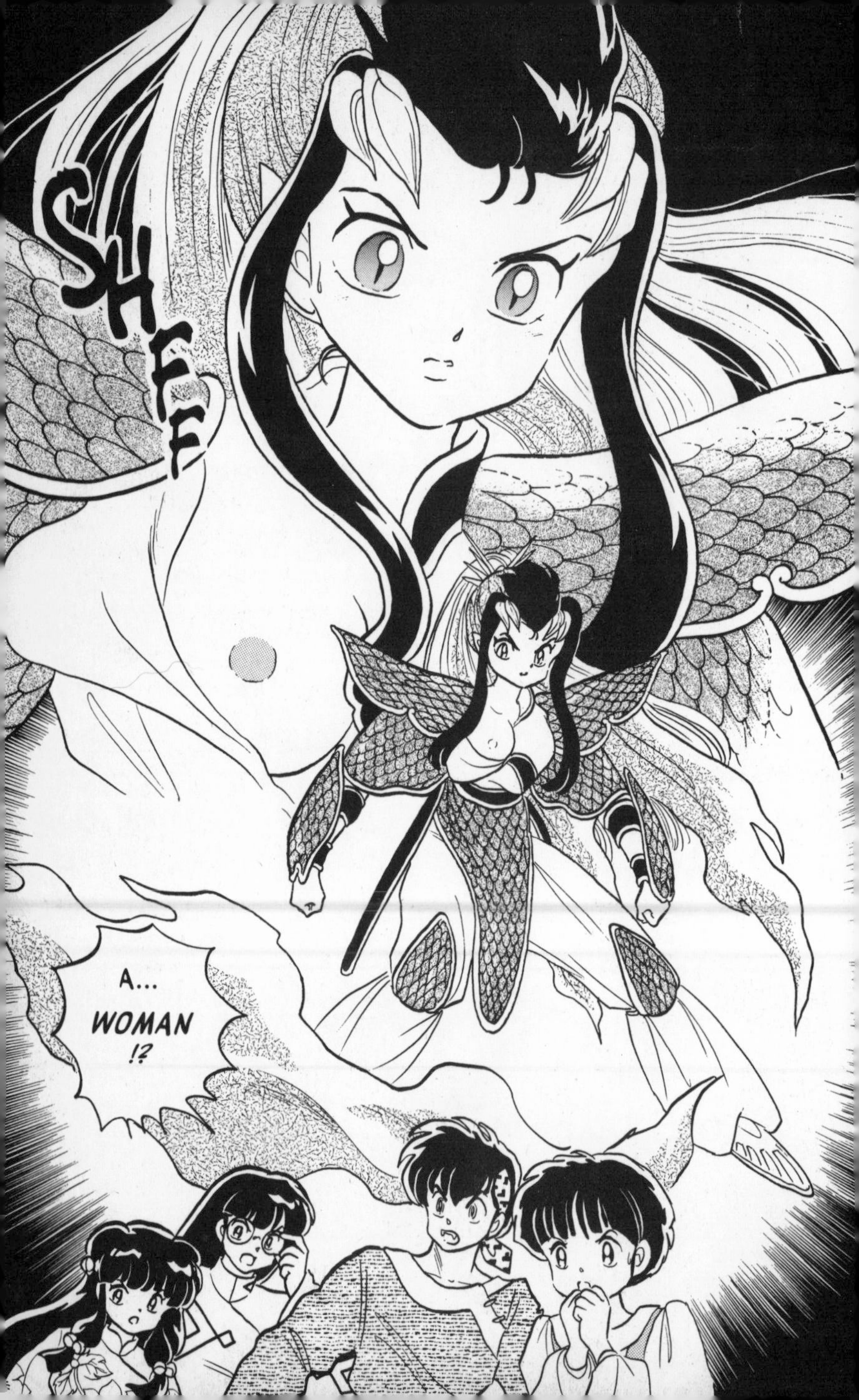
SHFF
A... WOMAN !?

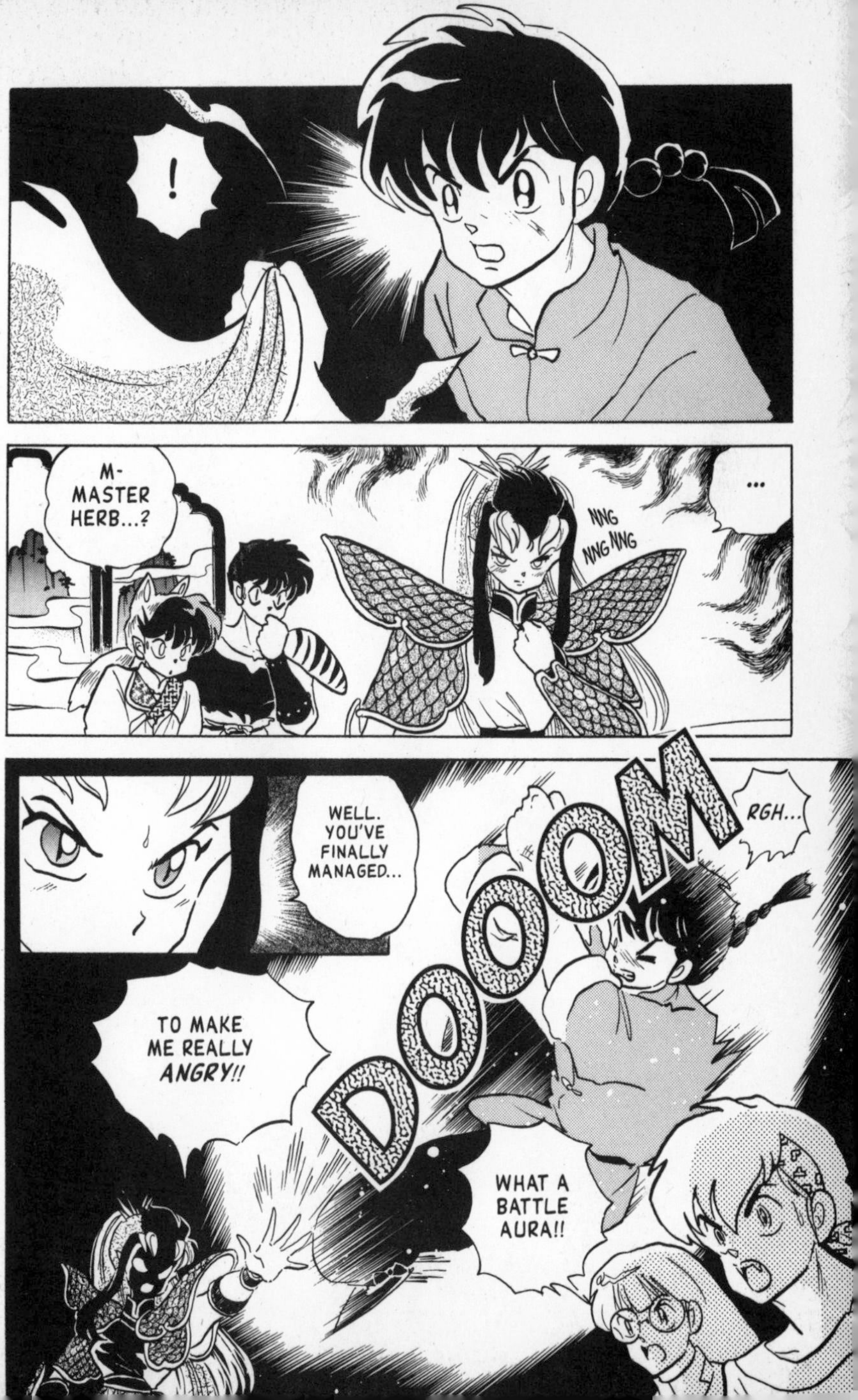
!
M- MASTER HERB...?
NNG NNG NNG
...
WELL. YOU'VE FINALLY MANAGED...
DOOOOOM
RGH...
TO MAKE ME REALLY ANGRY!!
WHAT A BATTLE AURA!!

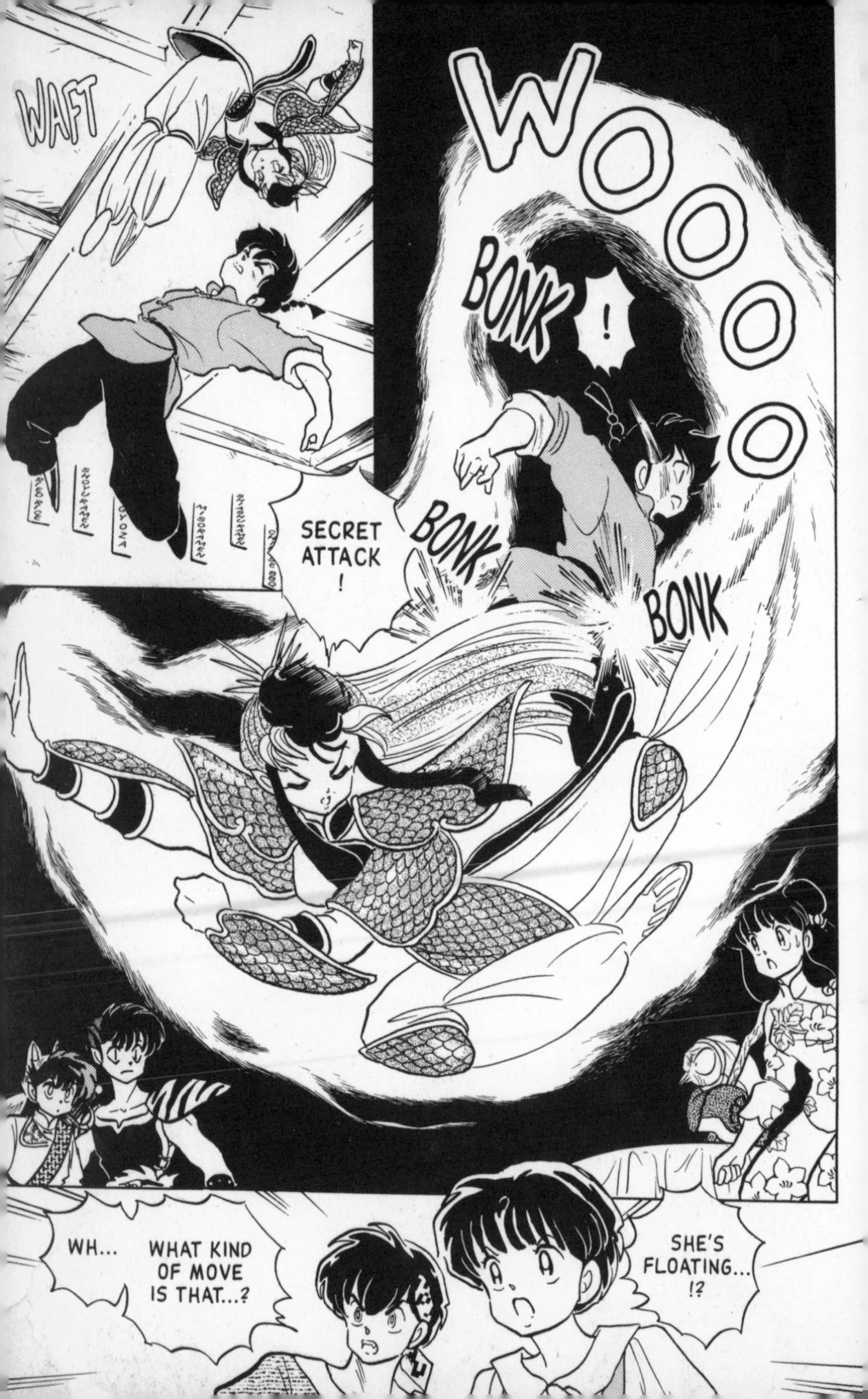
WAFT
WOOOOO
BONK
!
BONK
BONK
SECRET ATTACK !
WH... WHAT KIND OF MOVE IS THAT...?
SHE'S FLOATING... !?

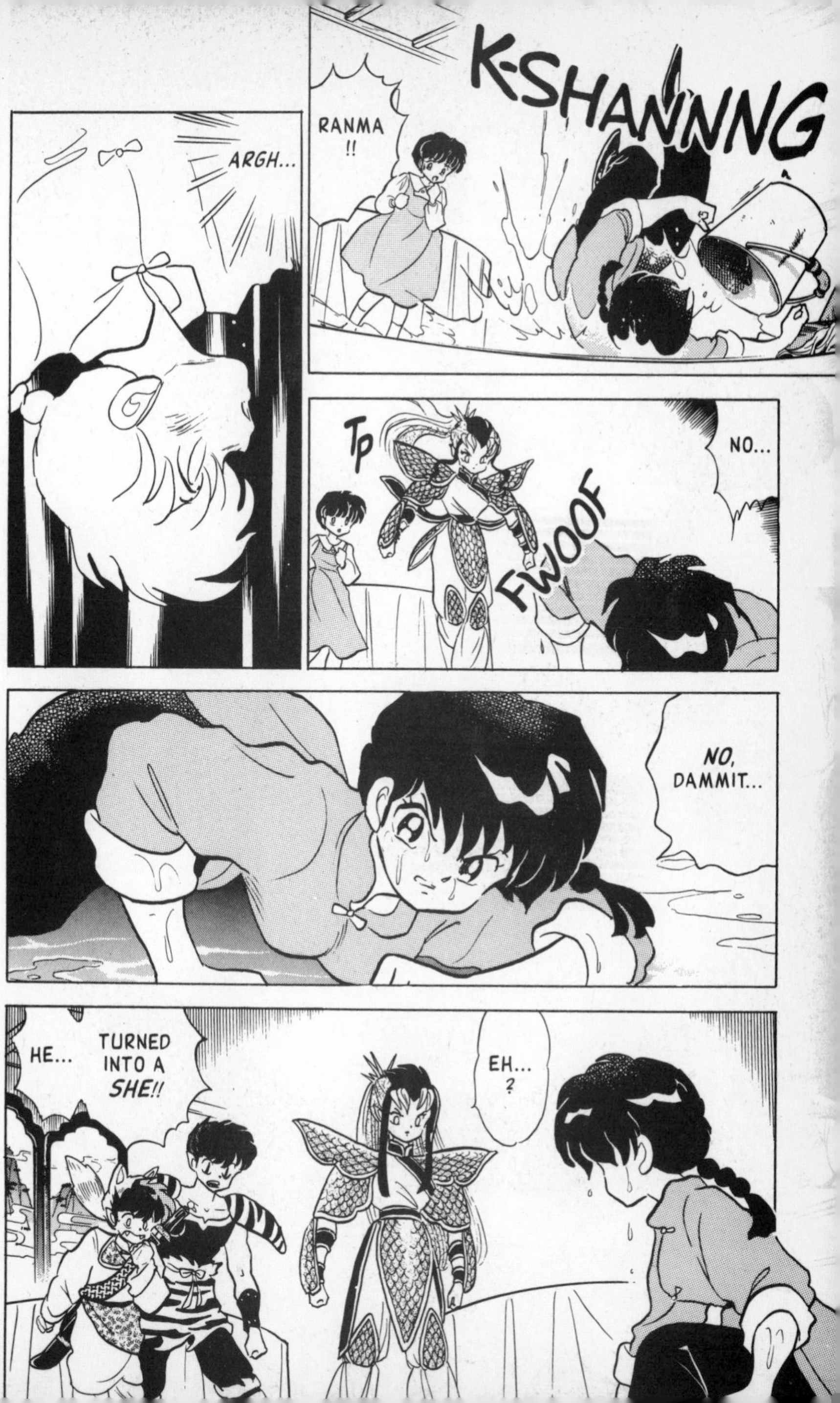
ARGH...
RANMA !!
K-SHANNNG
TP
FWOOF
NO...
NO, DAMMIT...
HE...
TURNED INTO A SHE!!
EH... ?

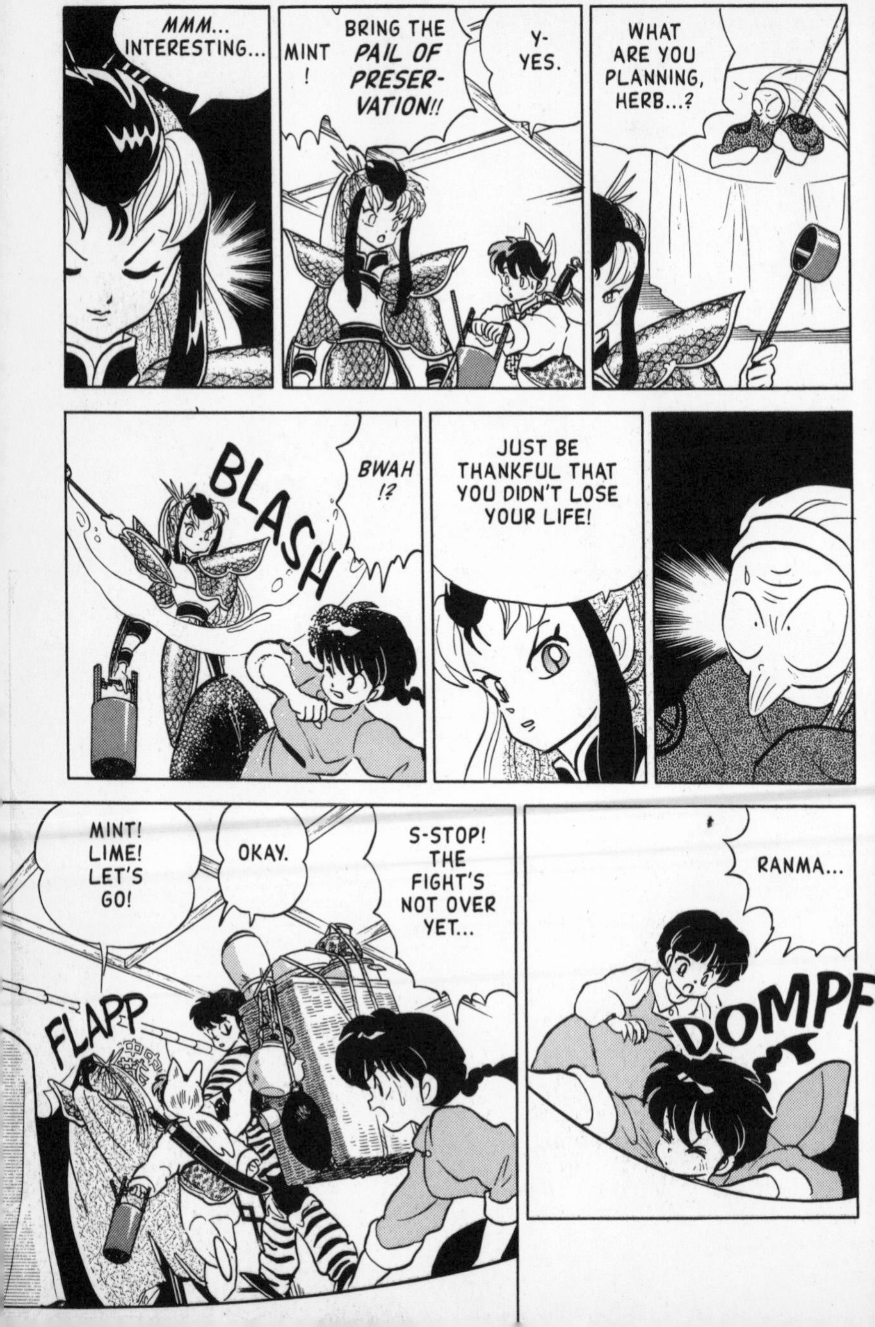
MMM... INTERESTING...
MINT!
BRING THE PAIL OF PRESERVATION!!
Y-YES.
WHAT ARE YOU PLANNING, HERB...?
BLASH
BWAH!?
JUST BE THANKFUL THAT YOU DIDN'T LOSE YOUR LIFE!
MINT! LIME! LET'S GO!
OKAY.
S-STOP! THE FIGHT'S NOT OVER YET...
FLAPP
RANMA...
DOMPF

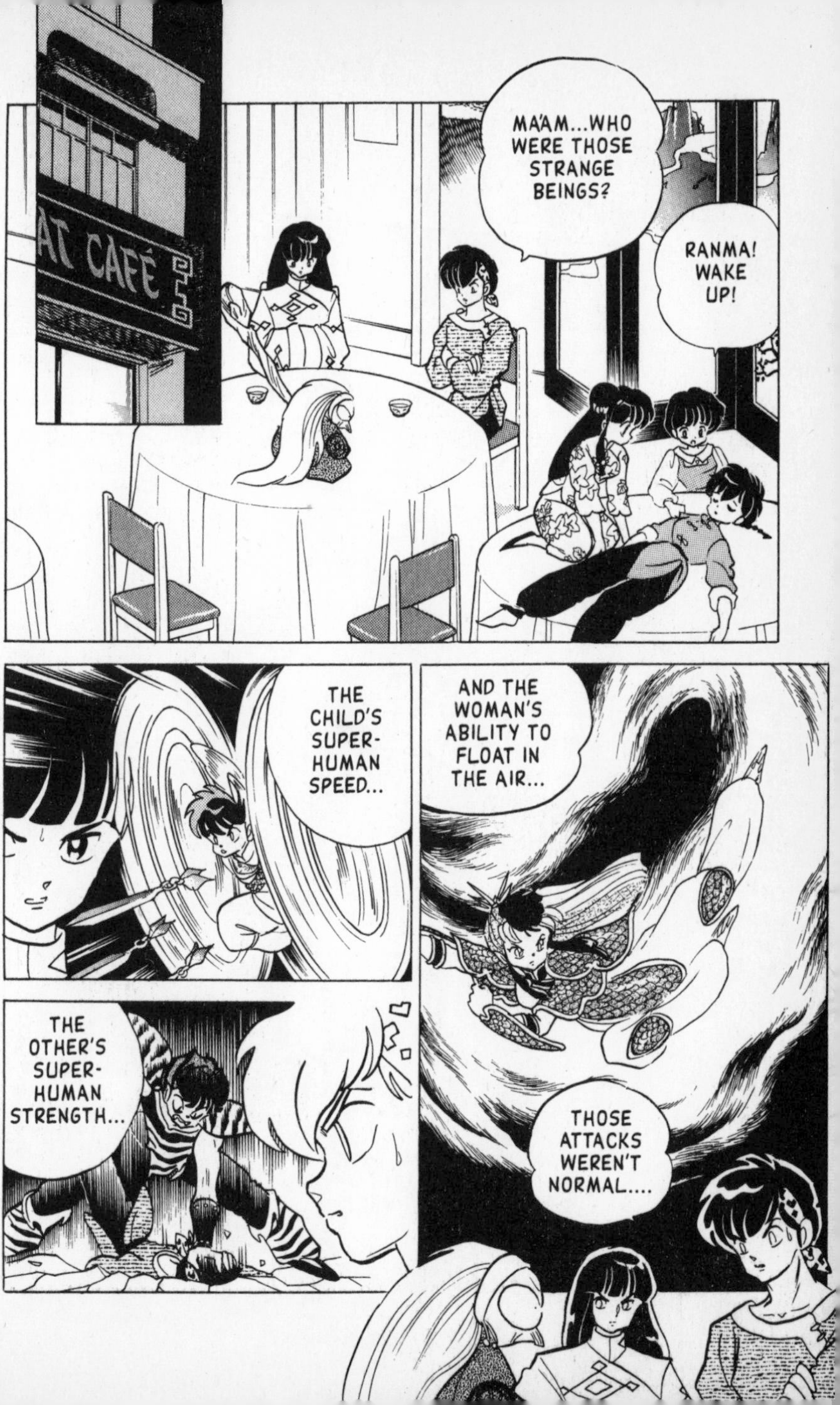
AT CAFÉ
MA'AM...WHO WERE THOSE STRANGE BEINGS?
RANMA! WAKE UP!
THE CHILD'S SUPER-HUMAN SPEED...
AND THE WOMAN'S ABILITY TO FLOAT IN THE AIR...
THE OTHER'S SUPER-HUMAN STRENGTH...
THOSE ATTACKS WEREN'T NORMAL....

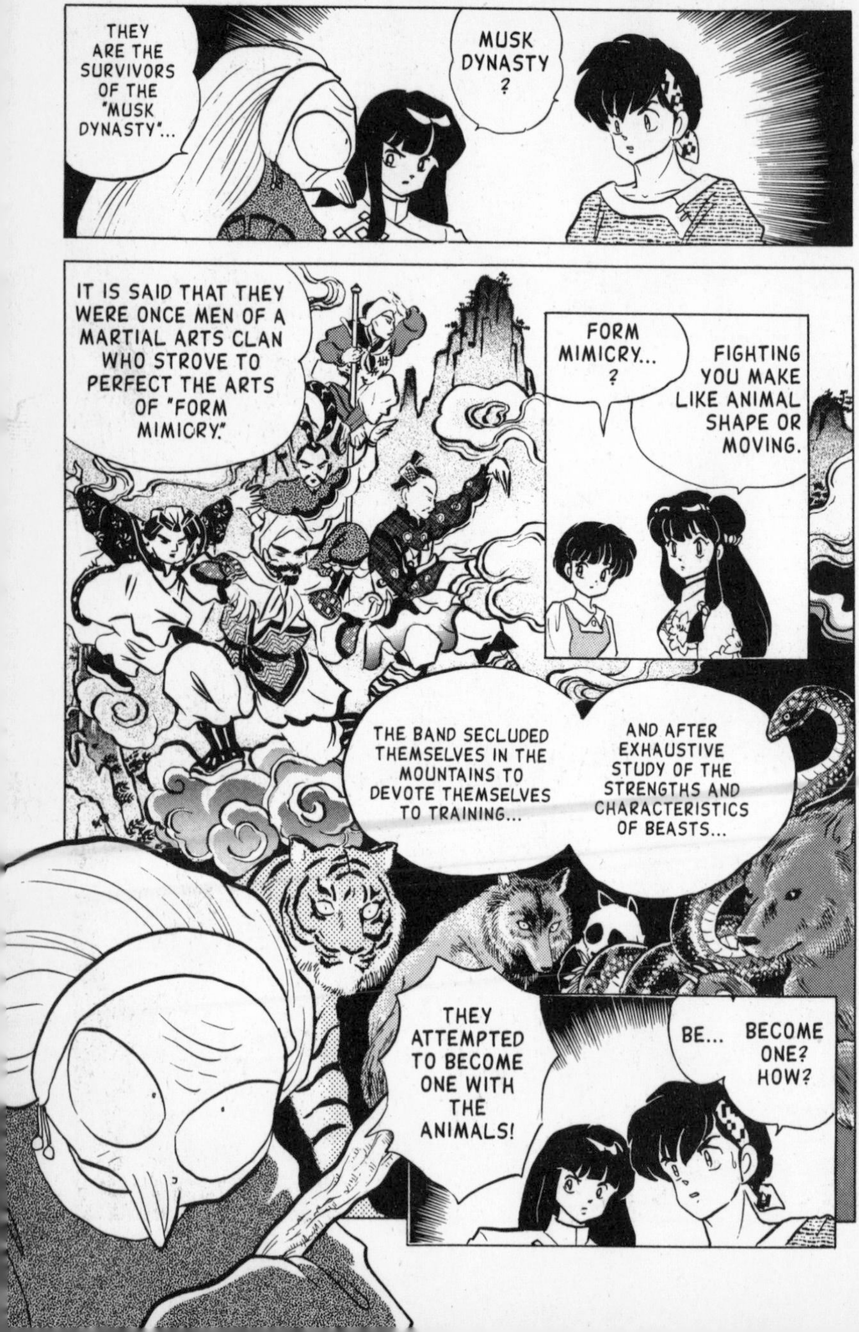
THEY ARE THE SURVIVORS OF THE "MUSK DYNASTY"...
MUSK DYNASTY ?
IT IS SAID THAT THEY WERE ONCE MEN OF A MARTIAL ARTS CLAN WHO STROVE TO PERFECT THE ARTS OF "FORM MIMICRY."
FORM MIMICRY... ?
FIGHTING YOU MAKE LIKE ANIMAL SHAPE OR MOVING.
THE BAND SECLUDED THEMSELVES IN THE MOUNTAINS TO DEVOTE THEMSELVES TO TRAINING...
AND AFTER EXHAUSTIVE STUDY OF THE STRENGTHS AND CHARACTERISTICS OF BEASTS...
THEY ATTEMPTED TO BECOME ONE WITH THE ANIMALS!
BE... BECOME ONE? HOW?

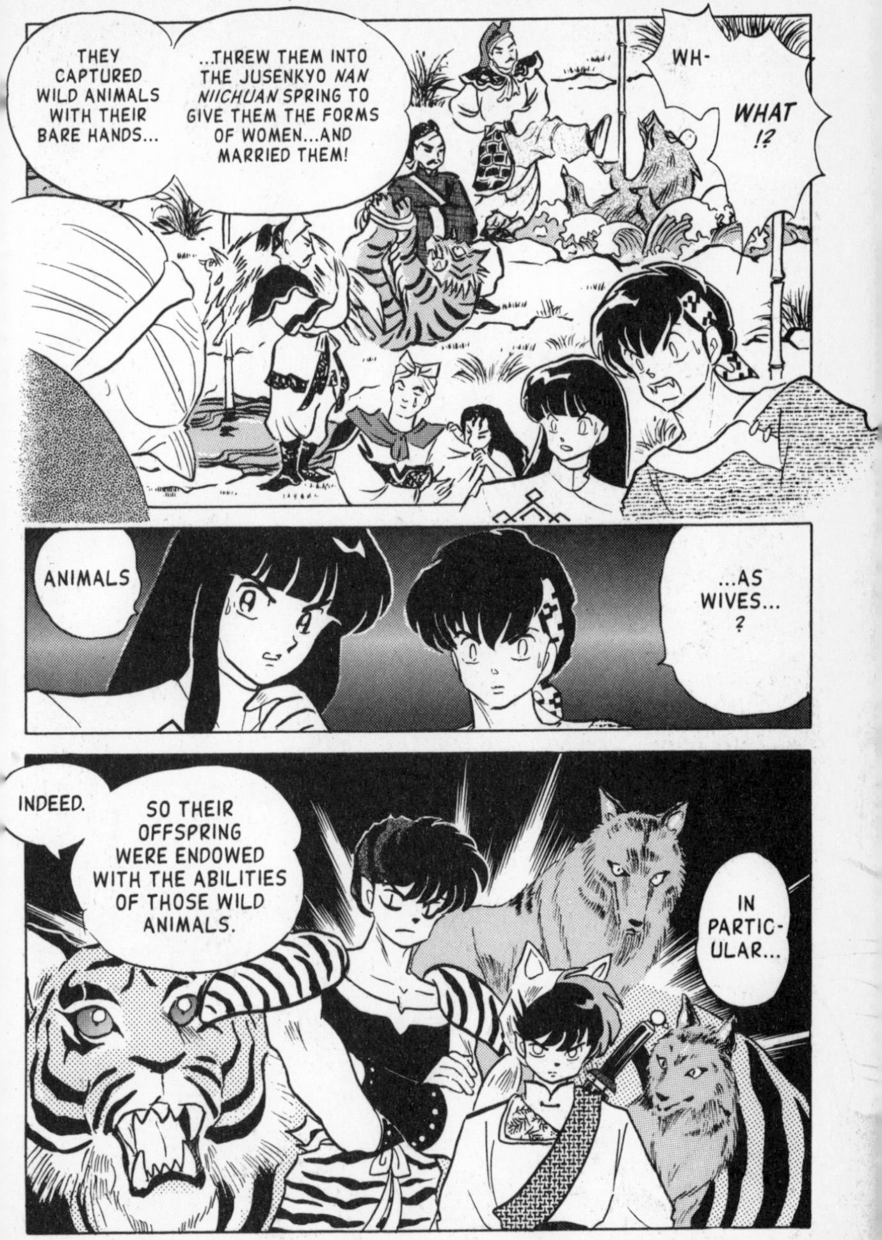
THEY CAPTURED WILD ANIMALS WITH THEIR BARE HANDS...
...THREW THEM INTO THE JUSENKYO *NAN NIICHUAN* SPRING TO GIVE THEM THE FORMS OF WOMEN...AND MARRIED THEM!
WH-
WHAT !?
ANIMALS
...AS WIVES... ?
INDEED.
SO THEIR OFFSPRING WERE ENDOWED WITH THE ABILITIES OF THOSE WILD ANIMALS.
IN PARTIC-ULAR...

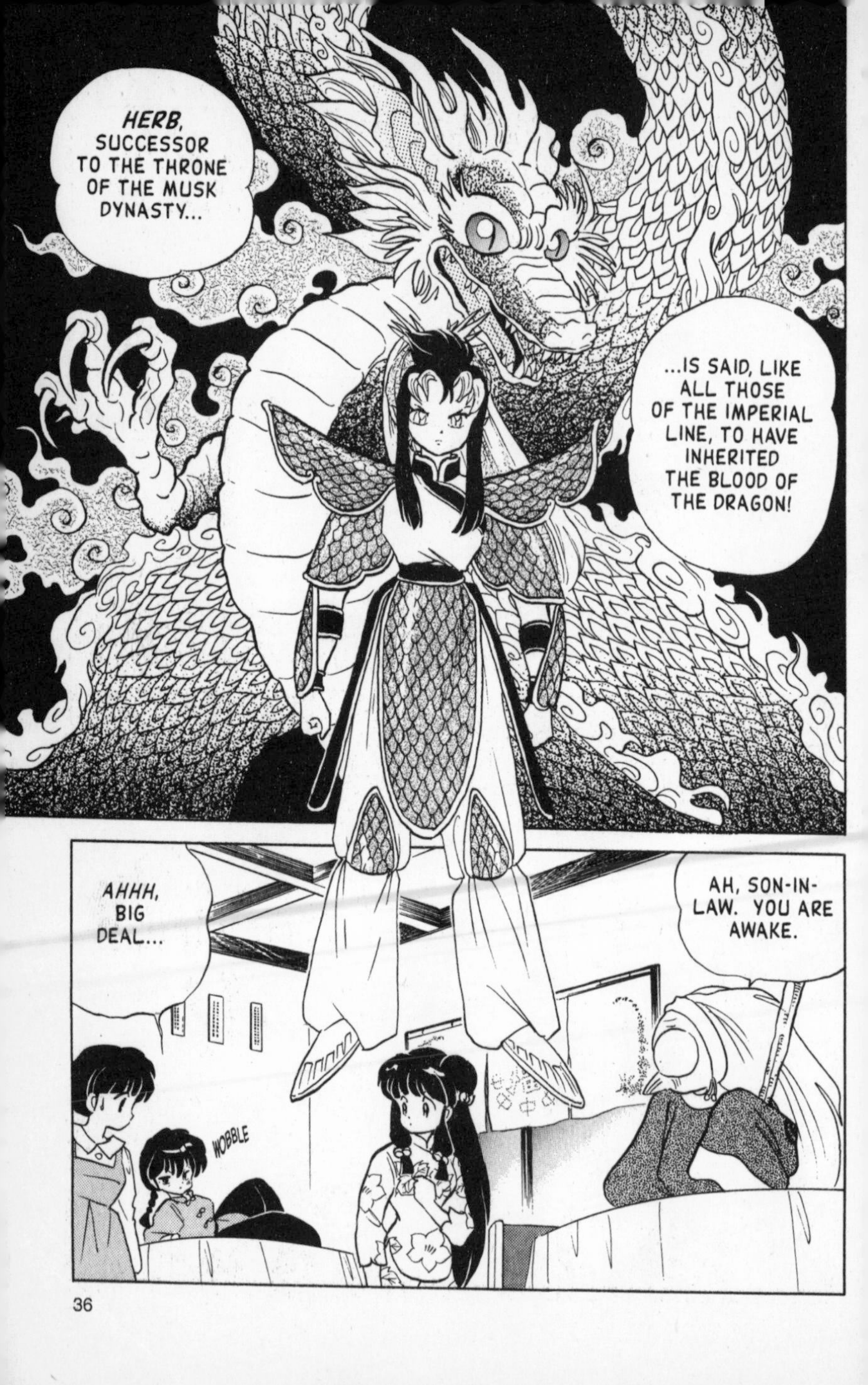
HERB, SUCCESSOR TO THE THRONE OF THE MUSK DYNASTY...
...IS SAID, LIKE ALL THOSE OF THE IMPERIAL LINE, TO HAVE INHERITED THE BLOOD OF THE DRAGON!
AHHH, BIG DEAL...
AH, SON-IN-LAW. YOU ARE AWAKE.
WOBBLE

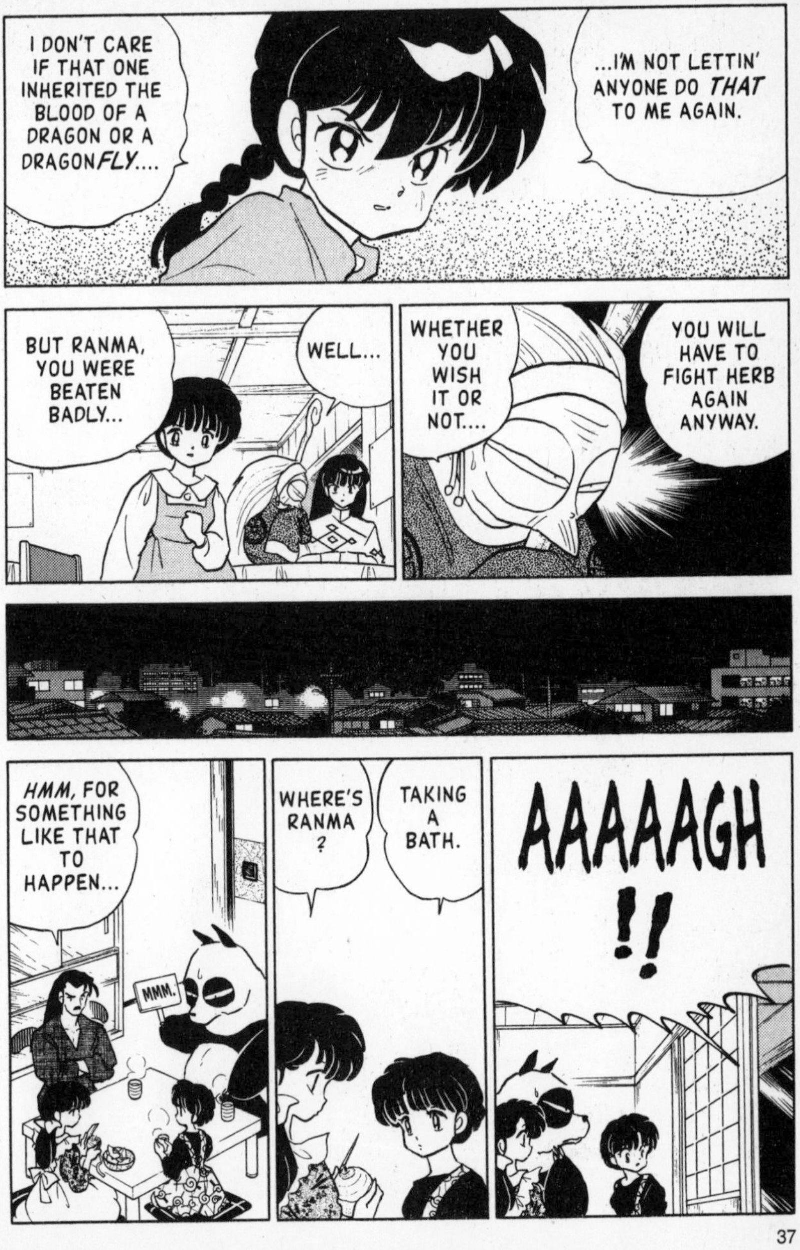
I DON'T CARE IF THAT ONE INHERITED THE BLOOD OF A DRAGON OR A DRAGON*FLY*....
...I'M NOT LETTIN' ANYONE DO *THAT* TO ME AGAIN.
BUT RANMA, YOU WERE BEATEN BADLY...
WELL...
WHETHER YOU WISH IT OR NOT....
YOU WILL HAVE TO FIGHT HERB AGAIN ANYWAY.
HMM, FOR SOMETHING LIKE THAT TO HAPPEN...
MMM.
WHERE'S RANMA ?
TAKING A BATH.
AAAAAGH !!

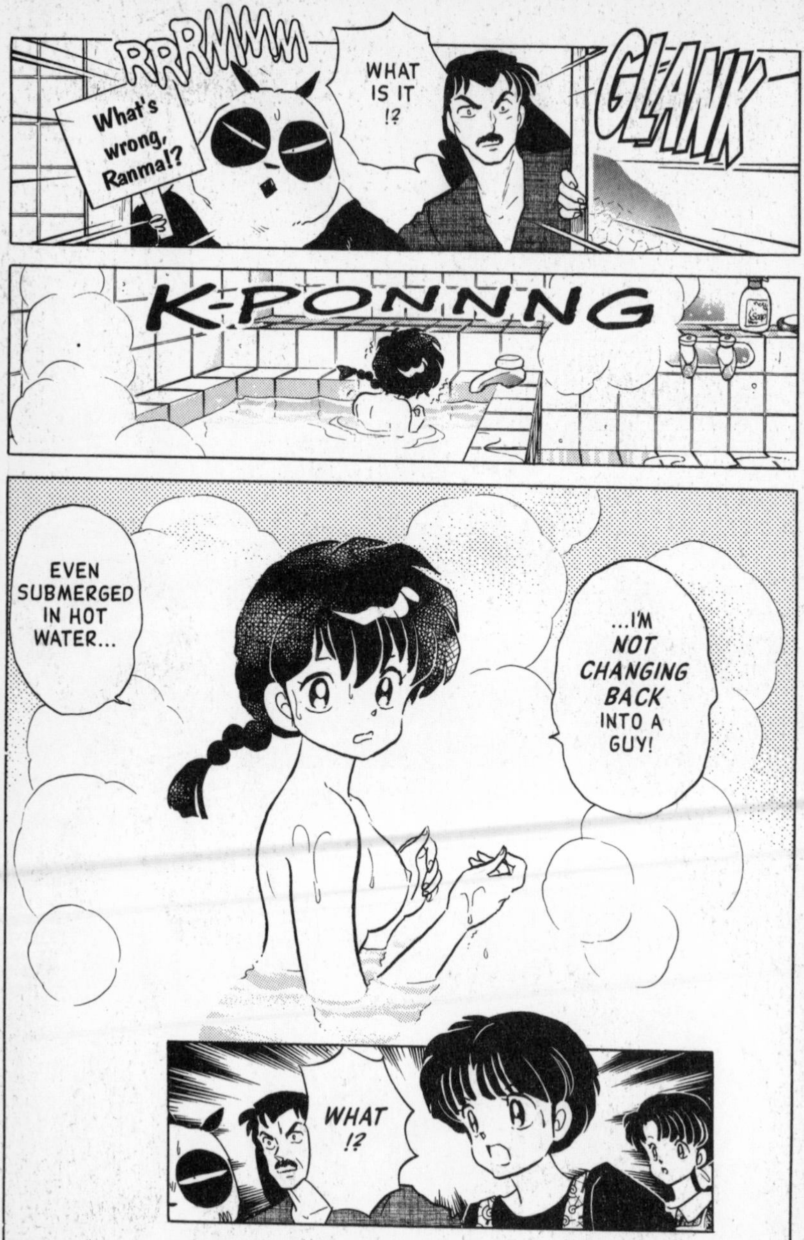
RRRMMM
What's wrong, Ranma!?
WHAT IS IT !?
GLANK
K-PONNNG
EVEN SUBMERGED IN HOT WATER...
...I'M NOT CHANGING BACK INTO A GUY!
WHAT !?

Part 3

THE LOST TREASURE

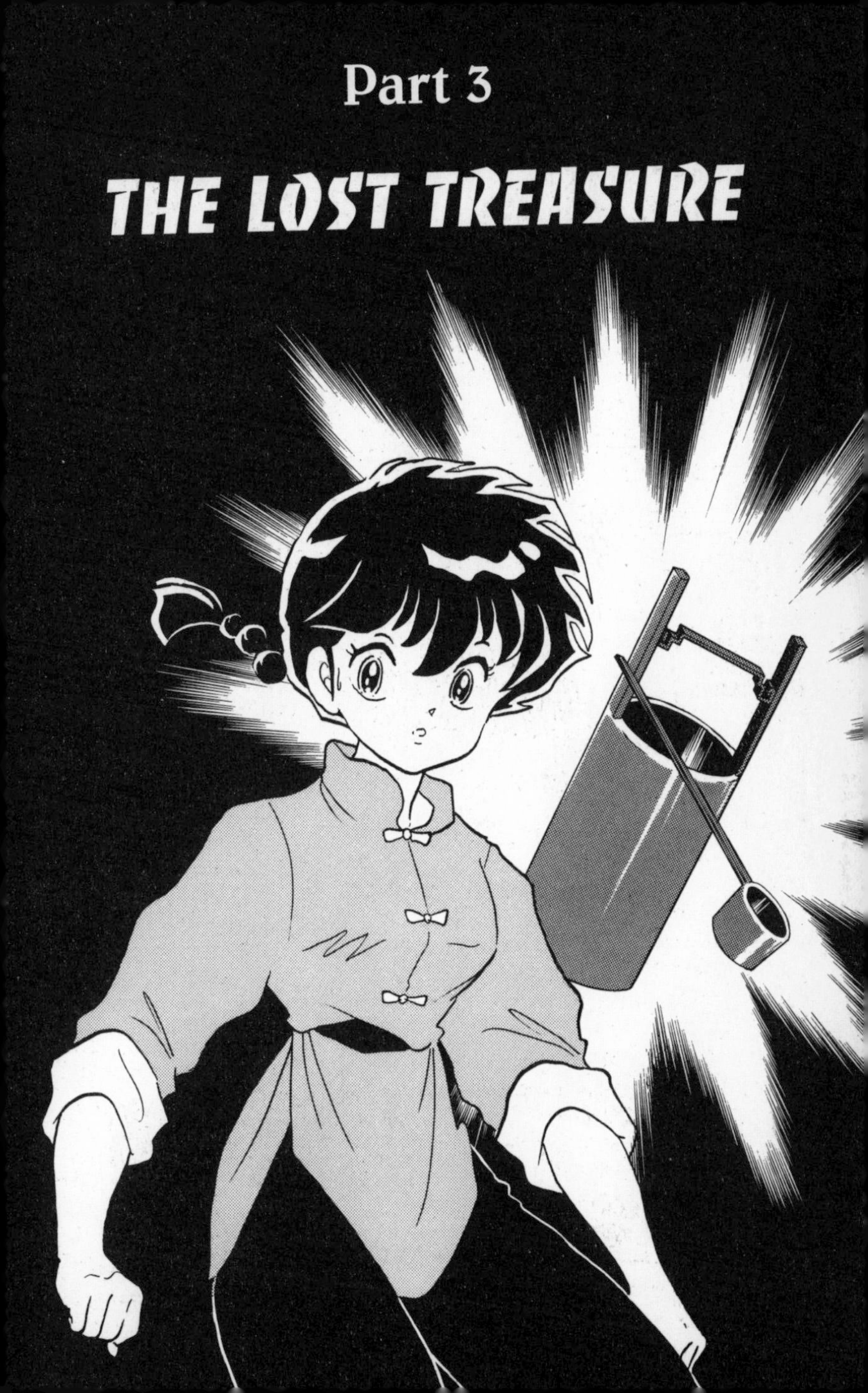

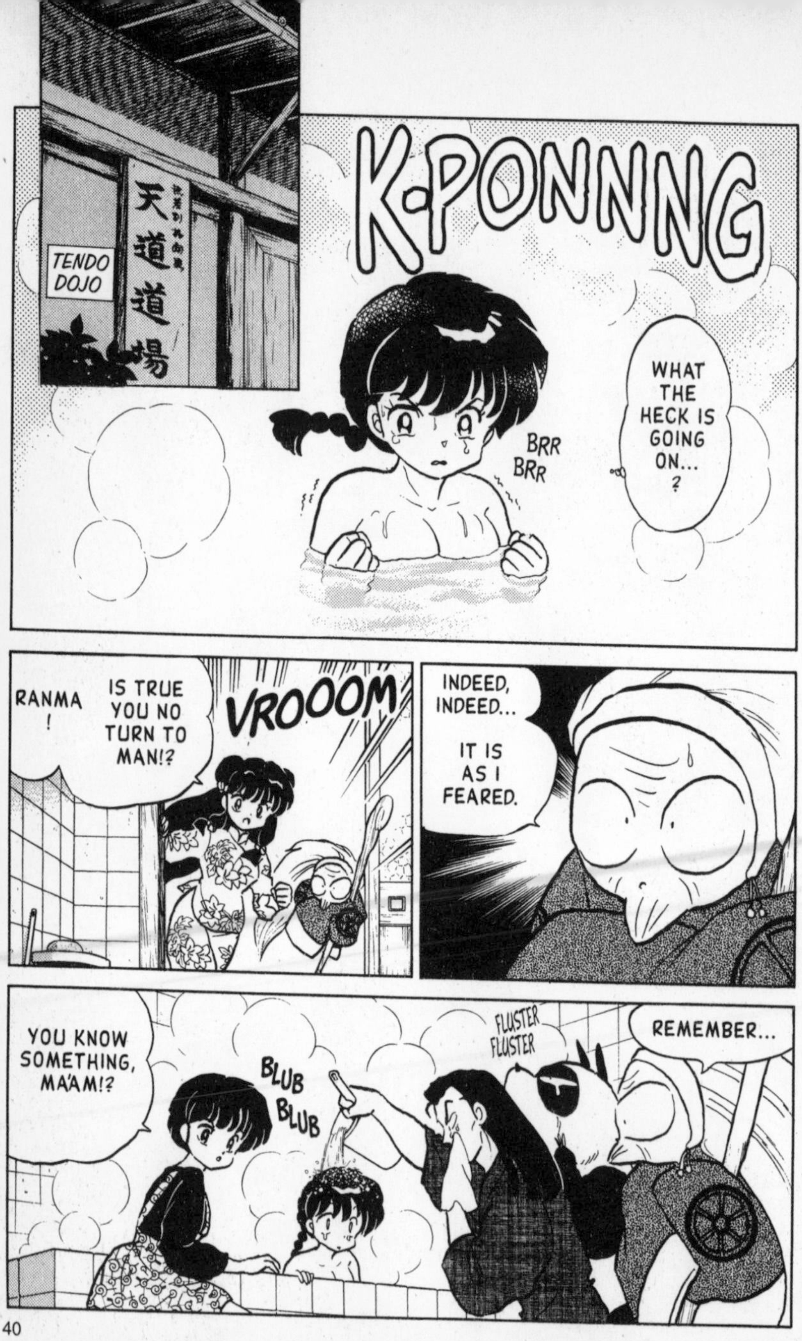
TENDO DOJO
天道道場
K-PONNNG
BRR BRR
WHAT THE HECK IS GOING ON...?
RANMA!
IS TRUE YOU NO TURN TO MAN!?
VROOOM
INDEED, INDEED...
IT IS AS I FEARED.
YOU KNOW SOMETHING, MA'AM!?
BLUB BLUB
FLUSTER FLUSTER
REMEMBER...

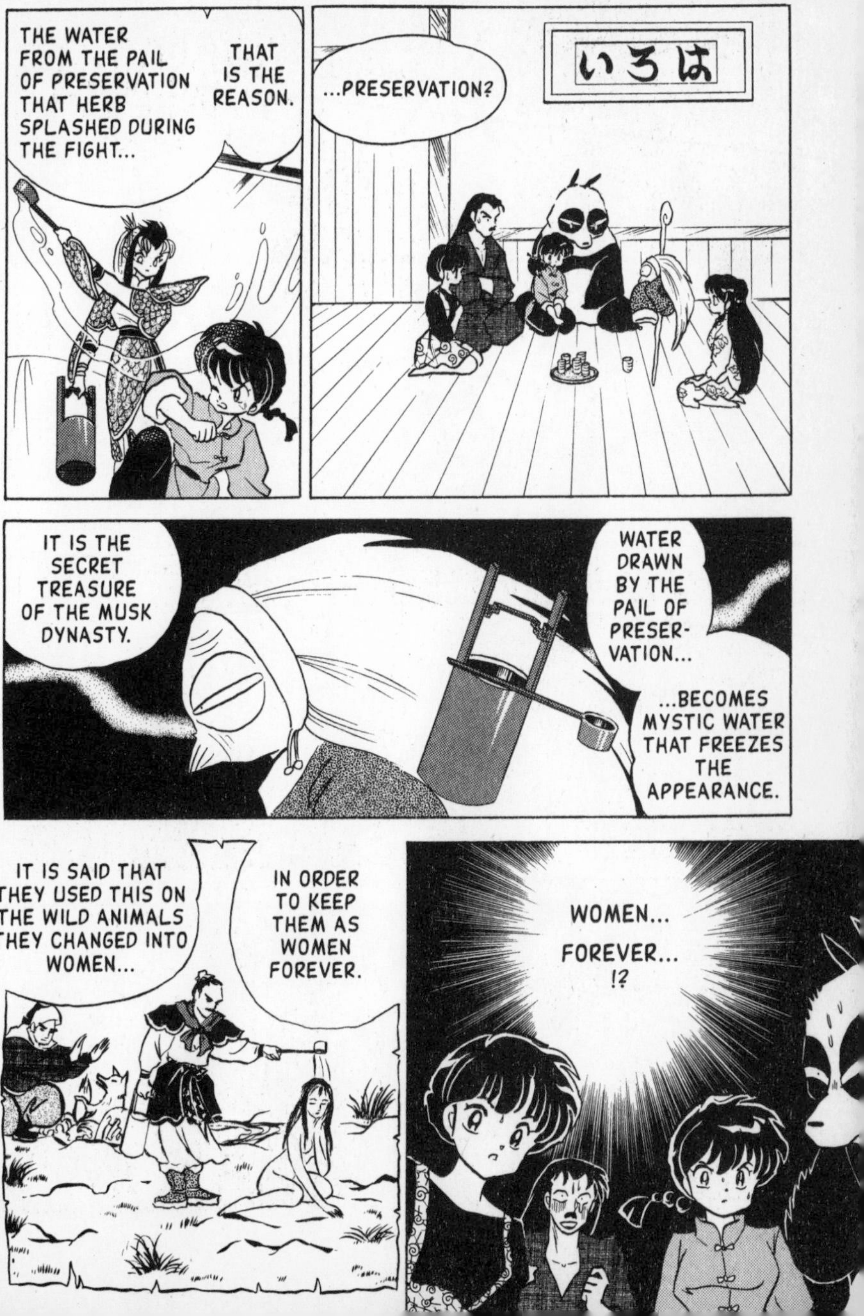
THE WATER FROM THE PAIL OF PRESERVATION THAT HERB SPLASHED DURING THE FIGHT...
THAT IS THE REASON.
...PRESERVATION?
いろは
IT IS THE SECRET TREASURE OF THE MUSK DYNASTY.
WATER DRAWN BY THE PAIL OF PRESER-VATION...
...BECOMES MYSTIC WATER THAT FREEZES THE APPEARANCE.
IT IS SAID THAT THEY USED THIS ON THE WILD ANIMALS THEY CHANGED INTO WOMEN...
IN ORDER TO KEEP THEM AS WOMEN FOREVER.
WOMEN... FOREVER... !?

ISN'T THERE ANY WAY TO FIX THIS?

THERE IS *ONE* WAY.

ANOTHER SECRET TREASURE OF THE MUSK DYNASTY WITH A POWER EQUAL TO THE PAIL OF PRESERVATION.

THE WATER POT OF LIBERATION!

IT IS SAID THAT WHEN BOILING WATER IS POURED FROM THE WATER POT OF LIBERATION...

THE EFFECTS OF THE PAIL OF PRESERVATION ARE NEGATED.

DURING WARS THROUGHOUT CHINA'S HISTORY, THE WATER POT OF LIBERATION CHANGED HANDS MANY TIMES...

AND IS PRESENTLY HERE IN JAPAN.

IT WAS THE QUEST FOR THAT LOST TREASURE THAT BROUGHT HERB AND THE OTHERS HERE TODAY.

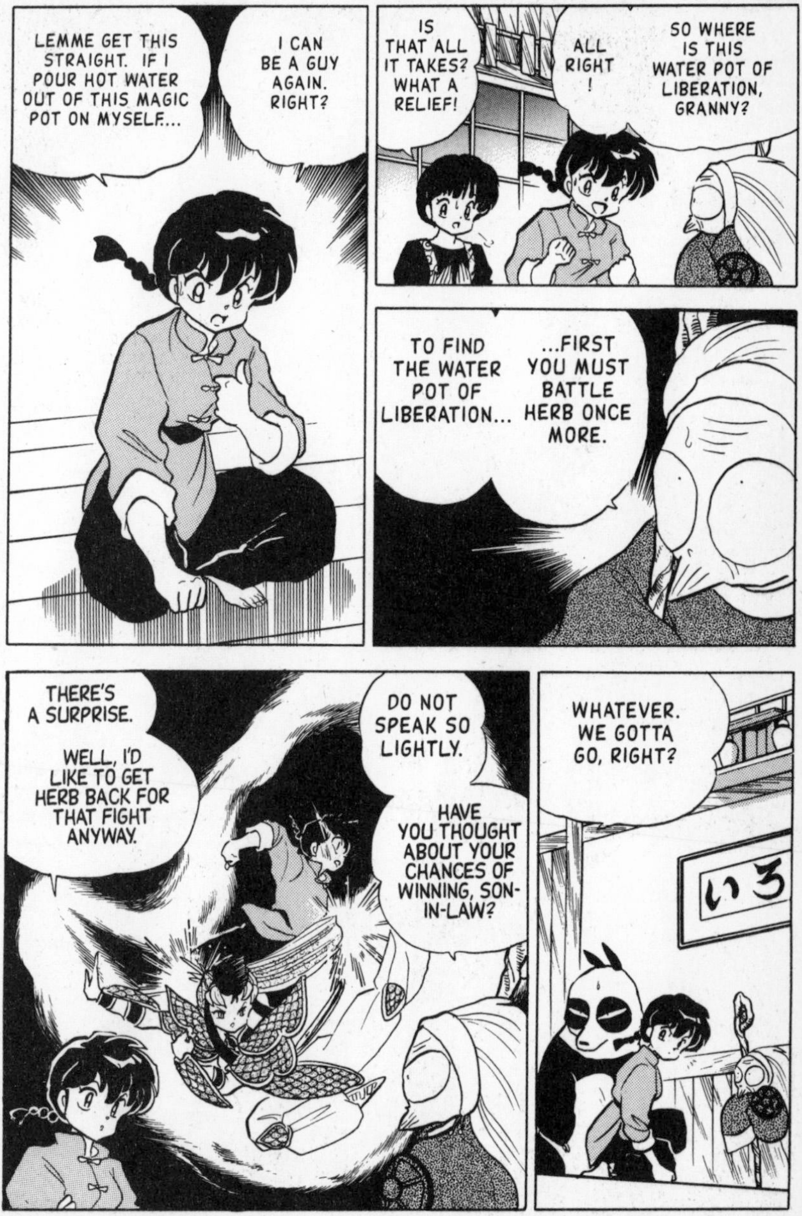
LEMME GET THIS STRAIGHT. IF I POUR HOT WATER OUT OF THIS MAGIC POT ON MYSELF...
I CAN BE A GUY AGAIN. RIGHT?
IS THAT ALL IT TAKES? WHAT A RELIEF!
ALL RIGHT!
SO WHERE IS THIS WATER POT OF LIBERATION, GRANNY?
TO FIND THE WATER POT OF LIBERATION...
...FIRST YOU MUST BATTLE HERB ONCE MORE.
THERE'S A SURPRISE.
WELL, I'D LIKE TO GET HERB BACK FOR THAT FIGHT ANYWAY.
DO NOT SPEAK SO LIGHTLY.
HAVE YOU THOUGHT ABOUT YOUR CHANCES OF WINNING, SON-IN-LAW?
WHATEVER. WE GOTTA GO, RIGHT?
いろ

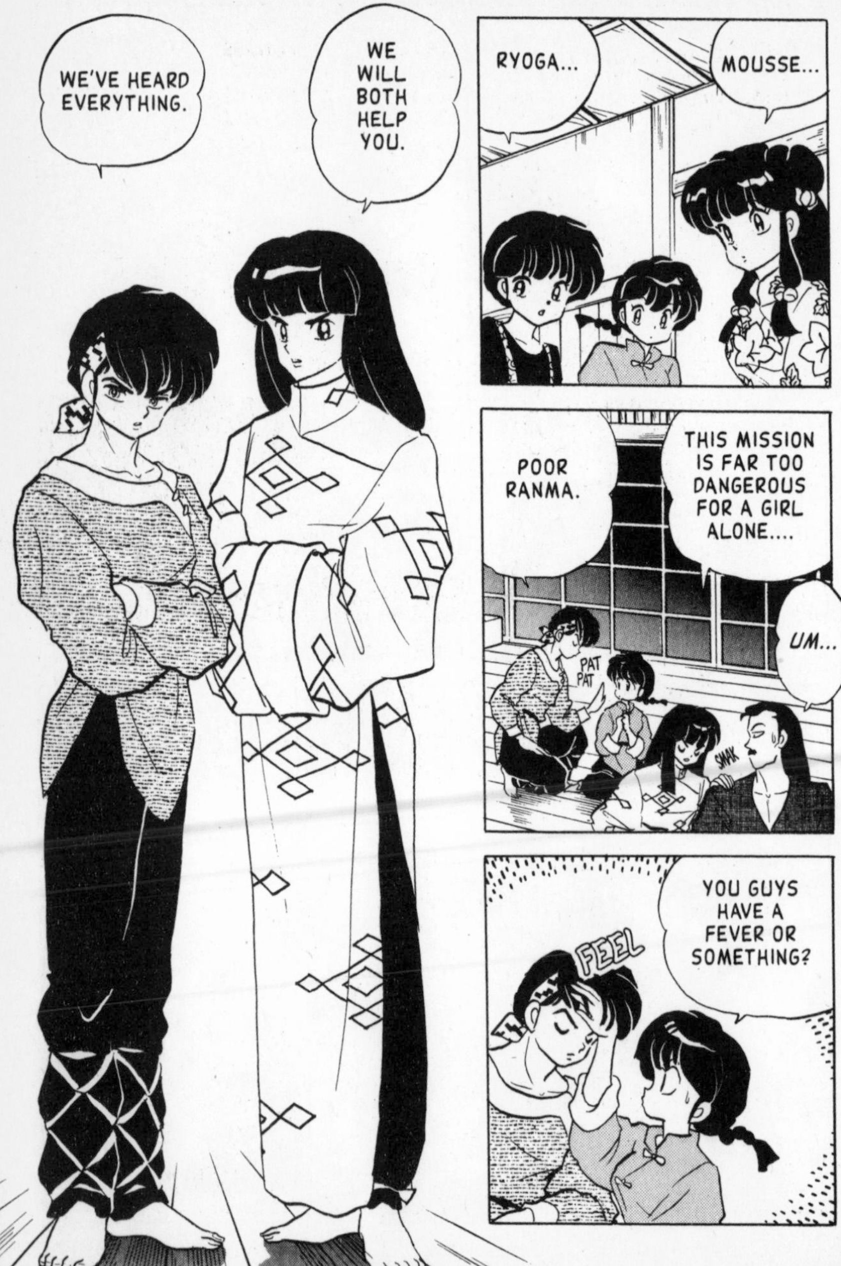
WE'VE HEARD EVERYTHING.
WE WILL BOTH HELP YOU.
RYOGA...
MOUSSE...
POOR RANMA.
THIS MISSION IS FAR TOO DANGEROUS FOR A GIRL ALONE....
PAT PAT
UM...
SMAK
FEEL
YOU GUYS HAVE A FEVER OR SOMETHING?

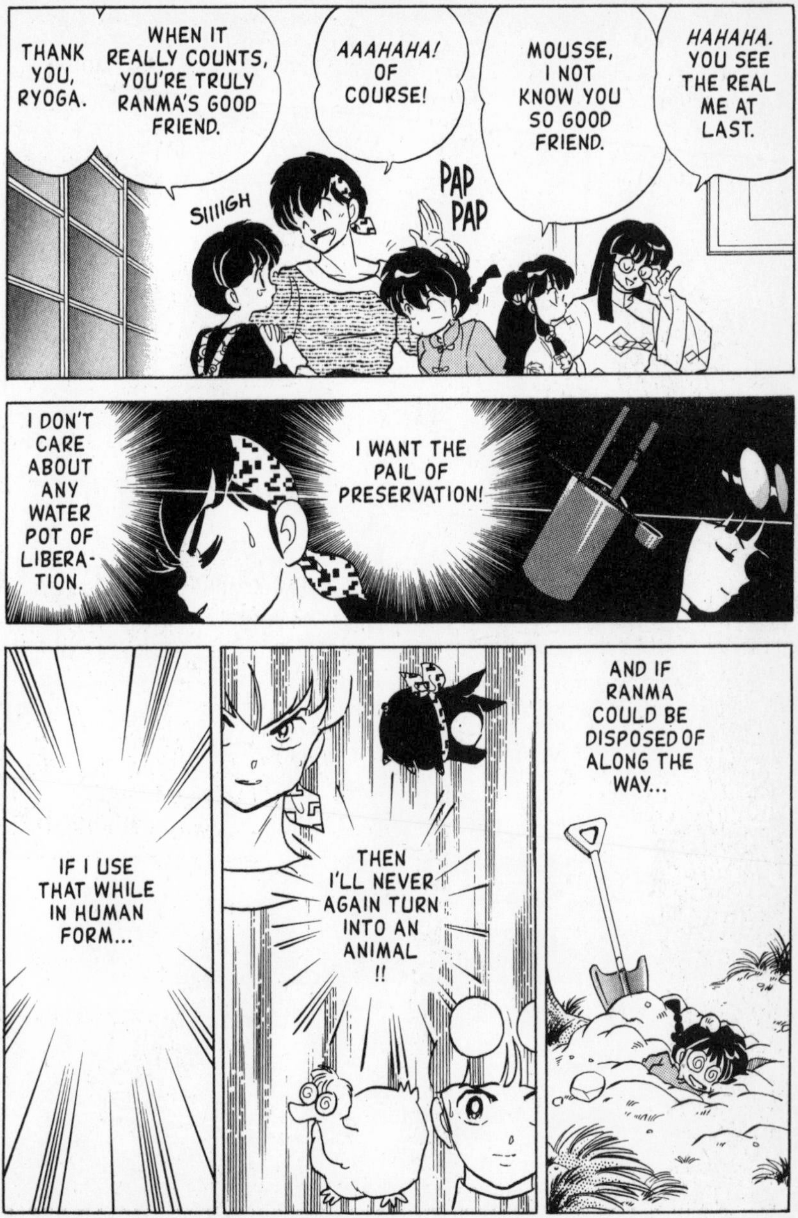
THANK YOU, RYOGA.
WHEN IT REALLY COUNTS, YOU'RE TRULY RANMA'S GOOD FRIEND.
SIIIGH
AAAHAHA! OF COURSE!
PAP PAP
MOUSSE, I NOT KNOW YOU SO GOOD FRIEND.
HAHAHA. YOU SEE THE REAL ME AT LAST.
I DON'T CARE ABOUT ANY WATER POT OF LIBERA-TION.
I WANT THE PAIL OF PRESERVATION!
IF I USE THAT WHILE IN HUMAN FORM...
THEN I'LL NEVER AGAIN TURN INTO AN ANIMAL !!
AND IF RANMA COULD BE DISPOSED OF ALONG THE WAY...

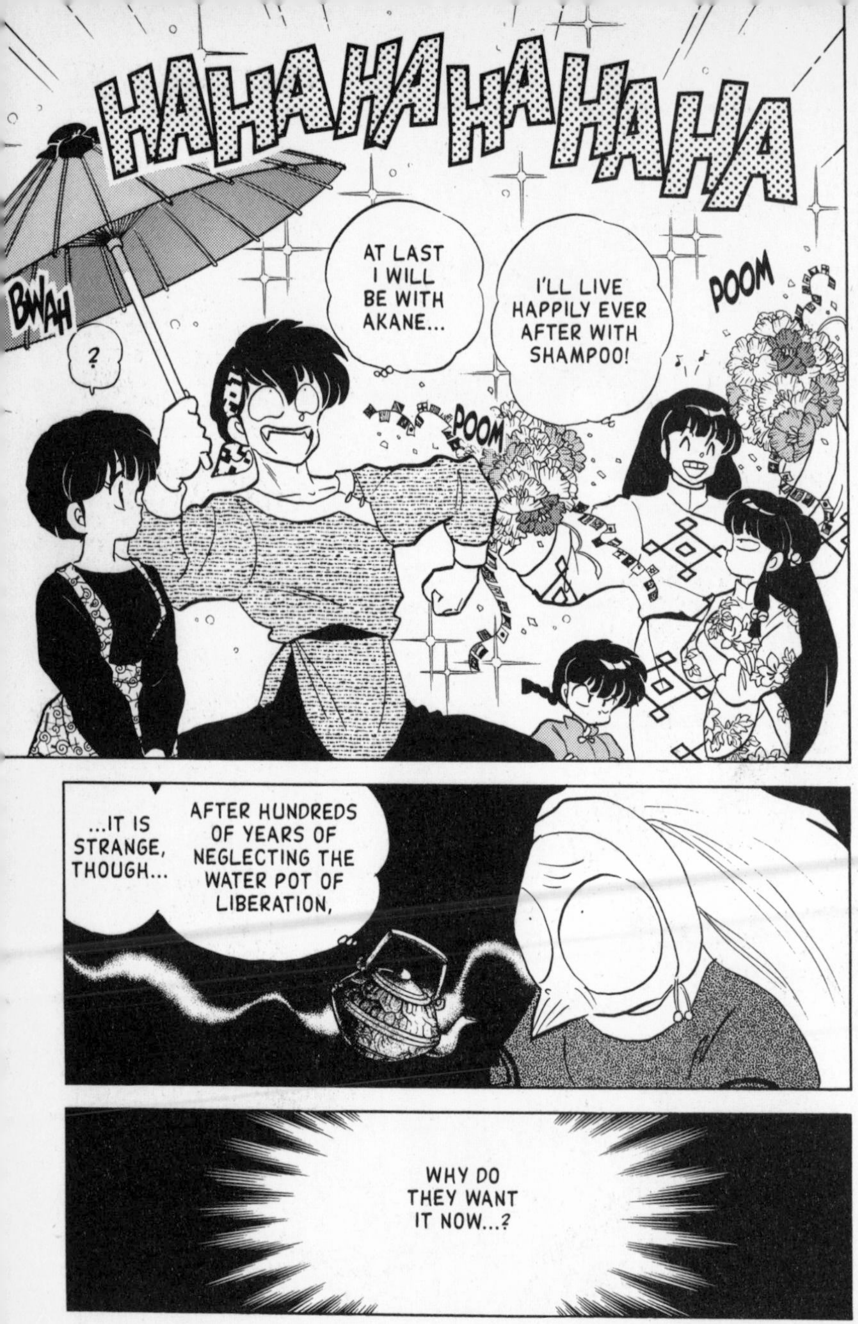
HAHAHAHAHAHA
BWAH
?
AT LAST I WILL BE WITH AKANE...
I'LL LIVE HAPPILY EVER AFTER WITH SHAMPOO!
POOM
POOM
...IT IS STRANGE, THOUGH...
AFTER HUNDREDS OF YEARS OF NEGLECTING THE WATER POT OF LIBERATION,
WHY DO THEY WANT IT NOW...?

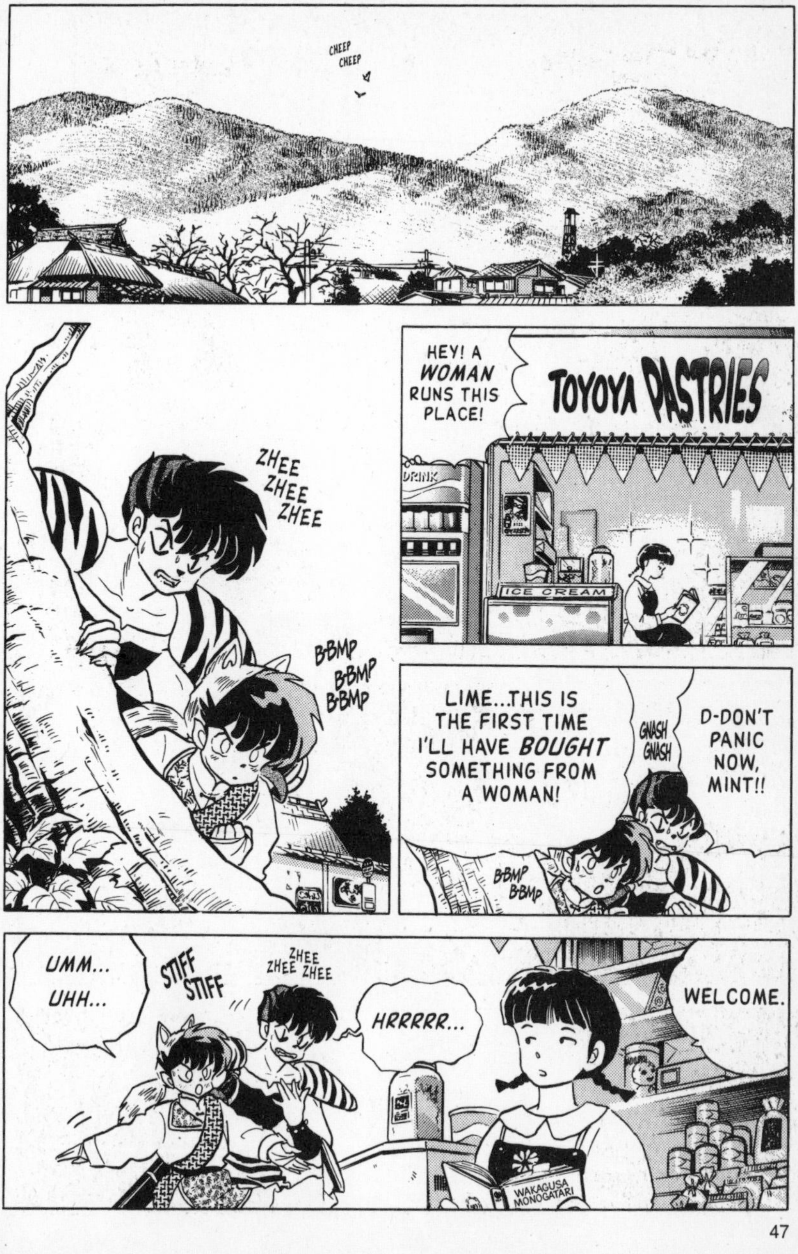
CHEEP
CHEEP
ZHEE
ZHEE
ZHEE
B-BMP
B-BMP
B-BMP
HEY! A *WOMAN* RUNS THIS PLACE!
TOYOYA PASTRIES
DRINK
ICE CREAM
LIME...THIS IS THE FIRST TIME I'LL HAVE *BOUGHT* SOMETHING FROM A WOMAN!
GNASH
GNASH
D-DON'T PANIC NOW, MINT!!
B-BMP
B-BMP
UMM... UHH...
STIFF
STIFF
ZHEE
ZHEE ZHEE
HRRRRR...
WELCOME.
WAKAGUSA MONOGATARI

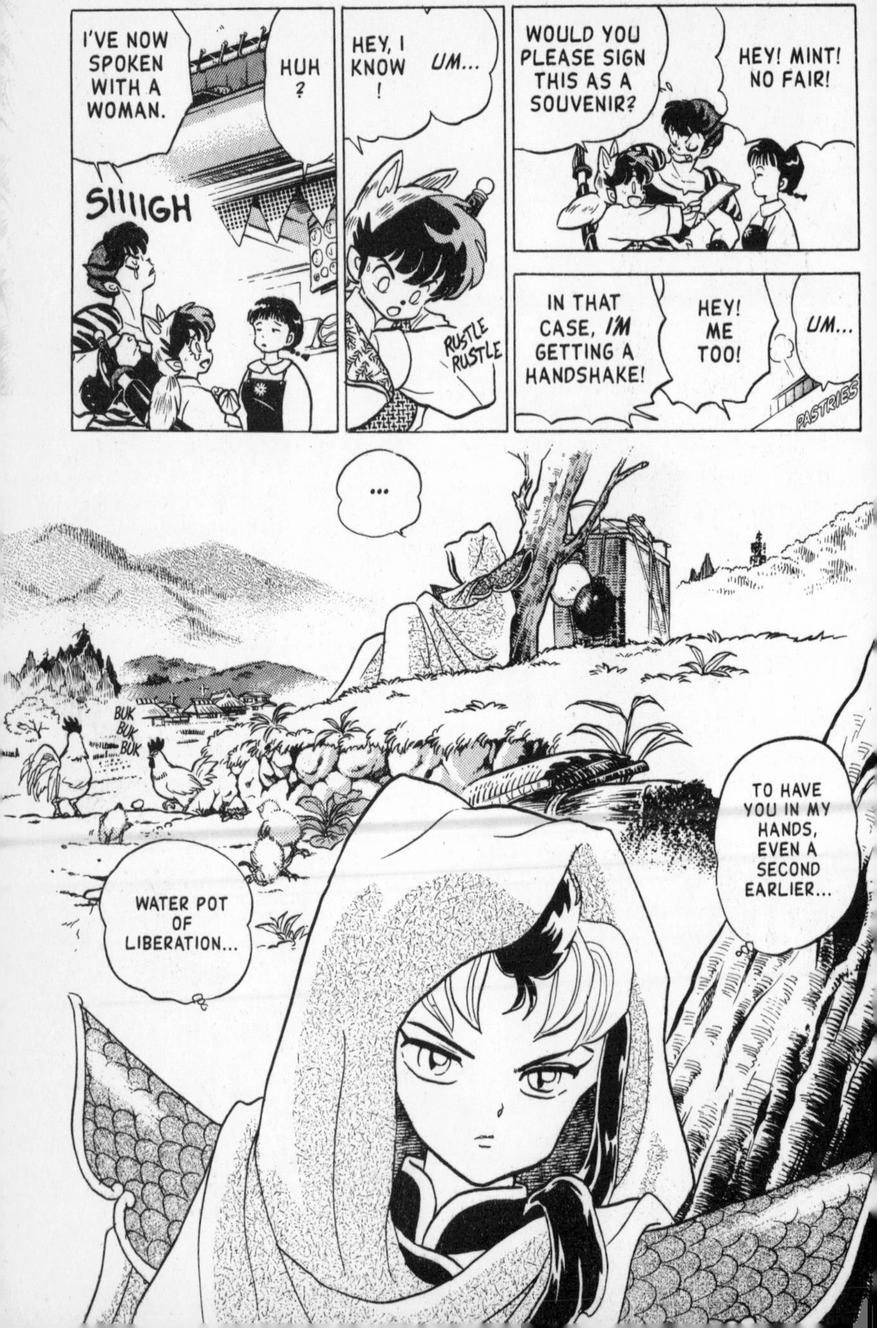

I'VE NOW SPOKEN WITH A WOMAN.
HUH ?
SIIIIGH
HEY, I KNOW !
UM...
RUSTLE RUSTLE
WOULD YOU PLEASE SIGN THIS AS A SOUVENIR?
HEY! MINT! NO FAIR!
IN THAT CASE, I'M GETTING A HANDSHAKE!
HEY! ME TOO!
UM...
PASTRIES
...
BUK BUK BUK
TO HAVE YOU IN MY HANDS, EVEN A SECOND EARLIER...
WATER POT OF LIBERATION...

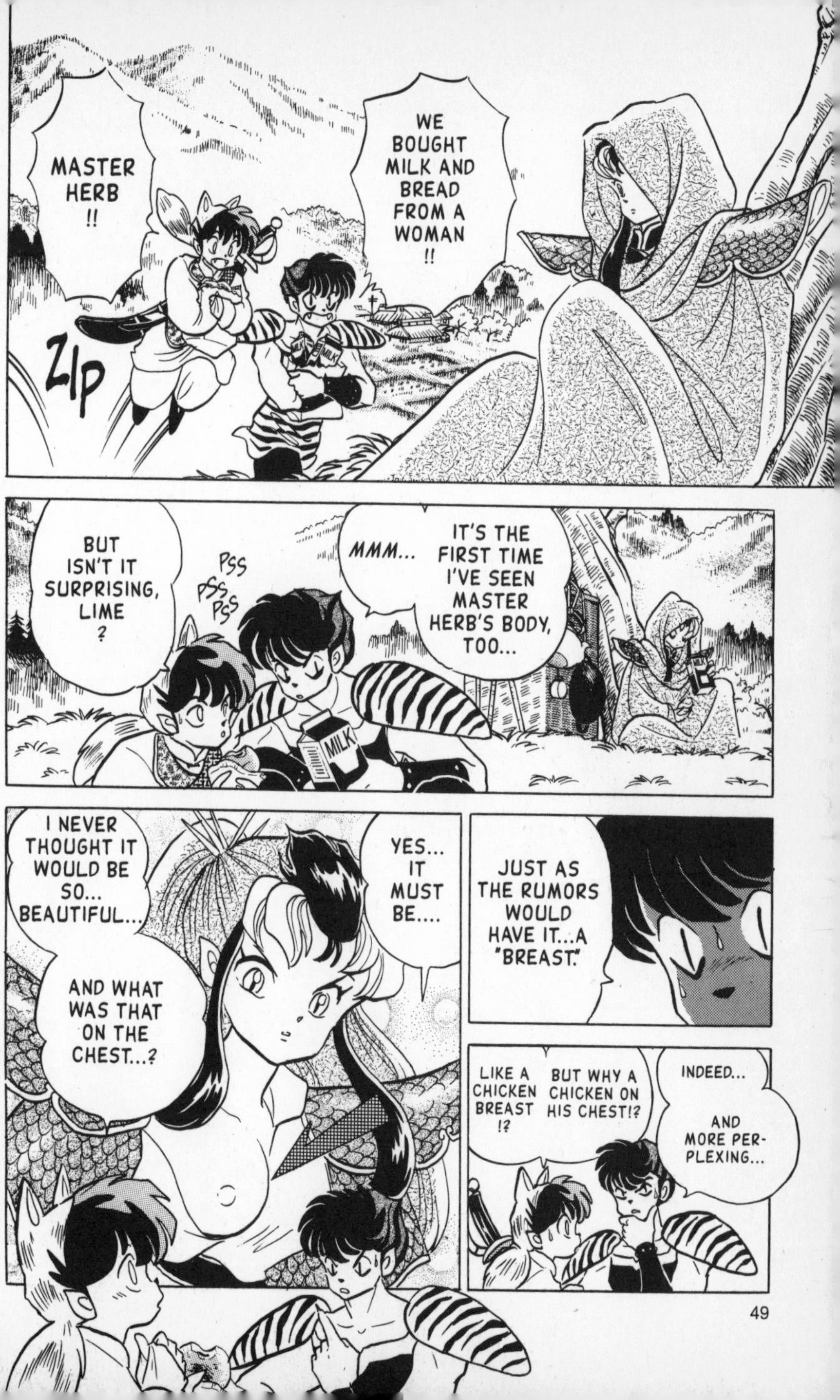
MASTER HERB !!
WE BOUGHT MILK AND BREAD FROM A WOMAN !!
ZIP
MILK
BUT ISN'T IT SURPRISING, LIME ?
PSS PSS PSS
MMM...
IT'S THE FIRST TIME I'VE SEEN MASTER HERB'S BODY, TOO...
MILK
I NEVER THOUGHT IT WOULD BE SO... BEAUTIFUL...
AND WHAT WAS THAT ON THE CHEST...?
YES... IT MUST BE....
JUST AS THE RUMORS WOULD HAVE IT...A "BREAST."
LIKE A CHICKEN BREAST !?
BUT WHY A CHICKEN ON HIS CHEST!?
INDEED...
AND MORE PER-PLEXING...

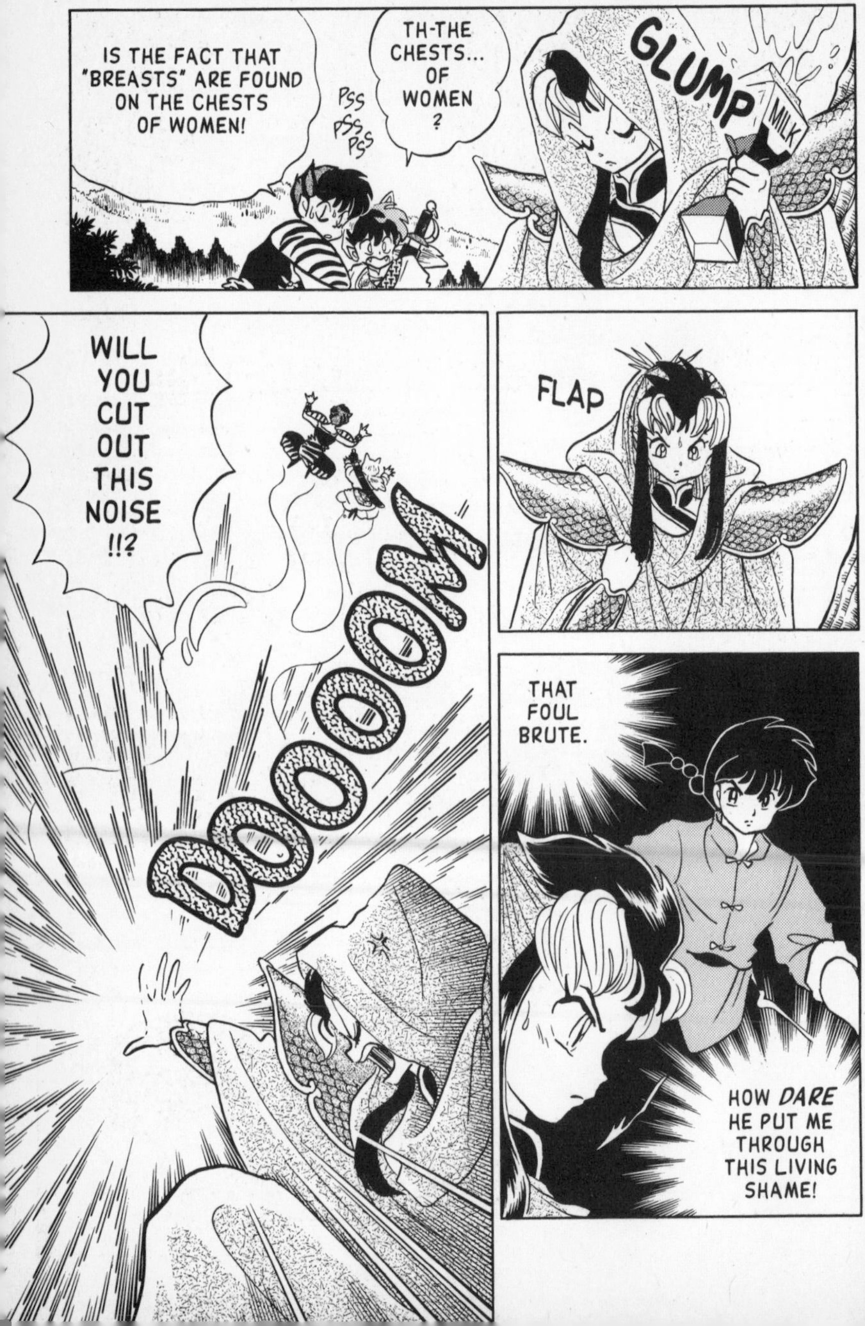
IS THE FACT THAT "BREASTS" ARE FOUND ON THE CHESTS OF WOMEN!
PSS PSS PSS
TH-THE CHESTS... OF WOMEN ?
GLUMP
MILK
WILL YOU CUT OUT THIS NOISE !!?
DOOOOM
FLAP
THAT FOUL BRUTE.
HOW *DARE* HE PUT ME THROUGH THIS LIVING SHAME!

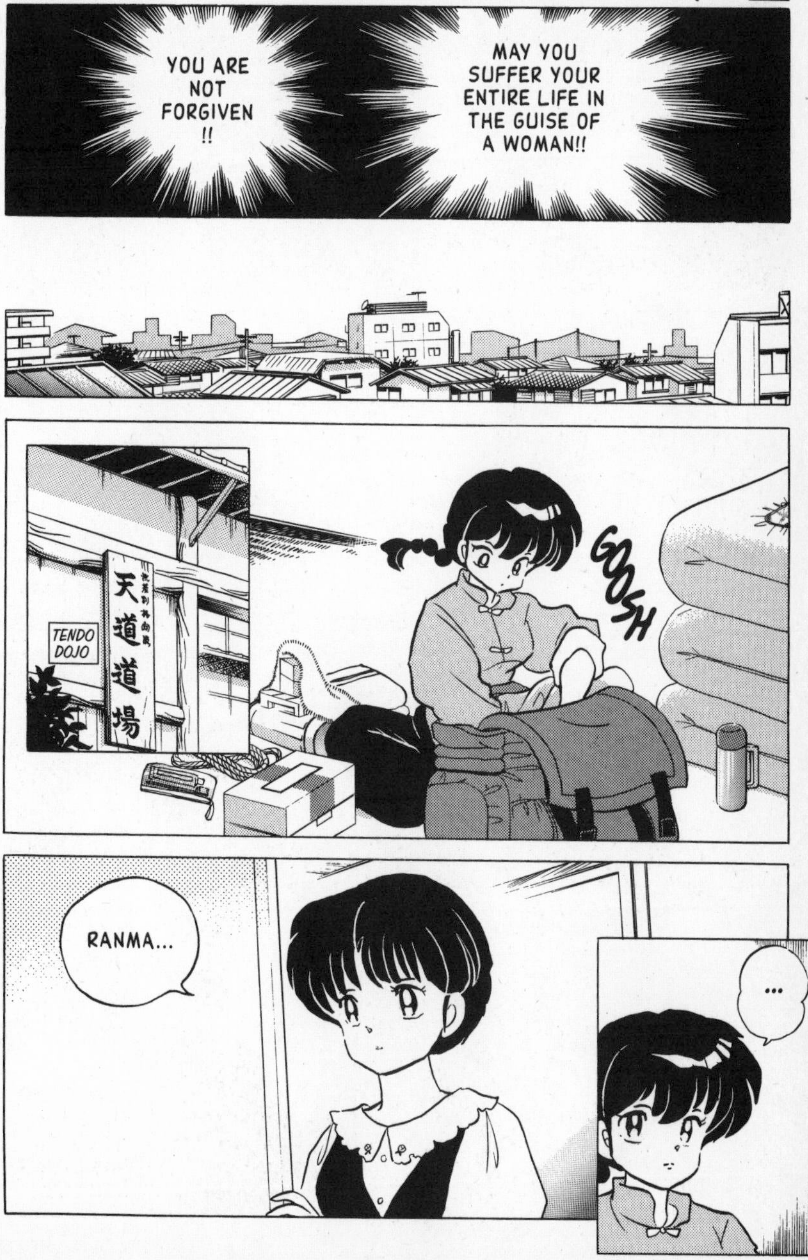
YOU ARE NOT FORGIVEN !!
MAY YOU SUFFER YOUR ENTIRE LIFE IN THE GUISE OF A WOMAN!!
TENDO DOJO
天道道場
GOOSH
RANMA...
...

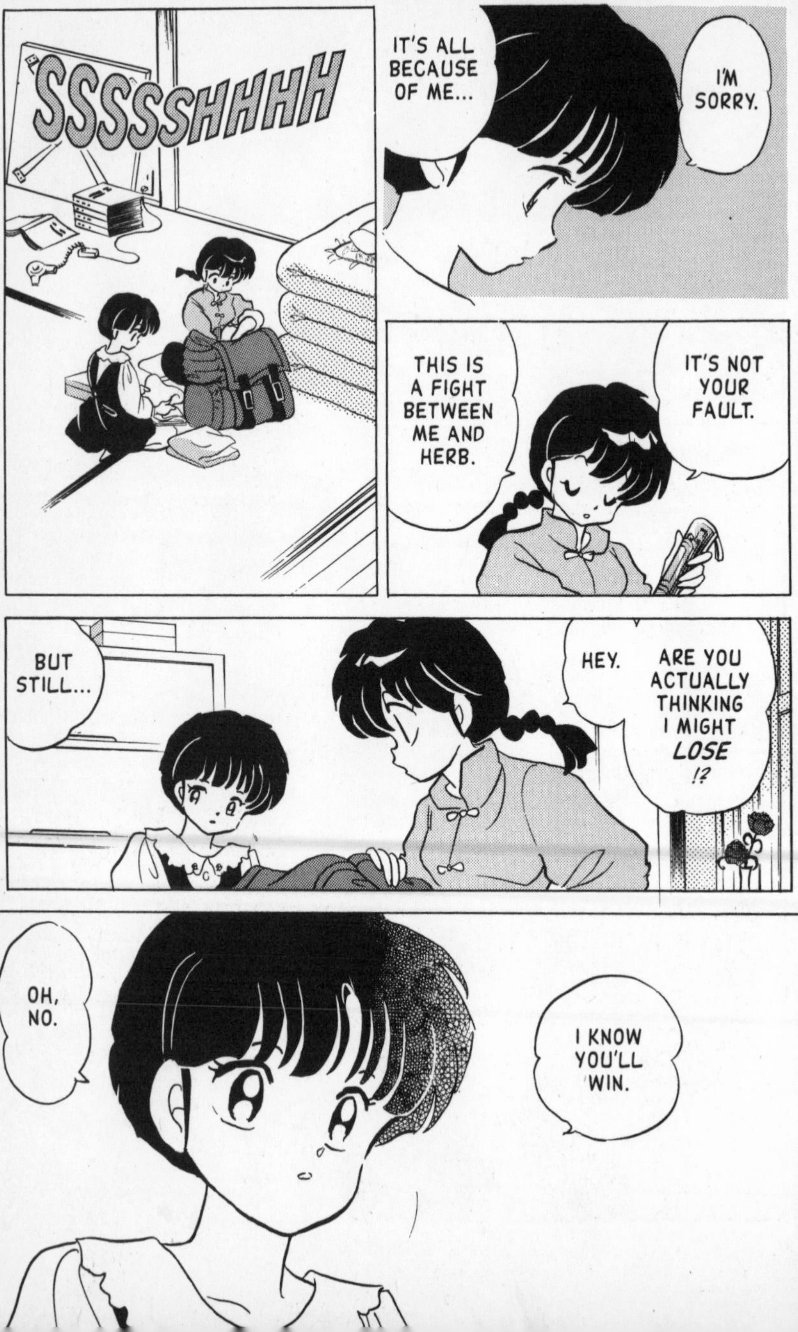
SSSSSHHHHH
IT'S ALL BECAUSE OF ME...
I'M SORRY.
THIS IS A FIGHT BETWEEN ME AND HERB.
IT'S NOT YOUR FAULT.
BUT STILL...
HEY.
ARE YOU ACTUALLY THINKING I MIGHT LOSE !?
OH, NO.
I KNOW YOU'LL WIN.

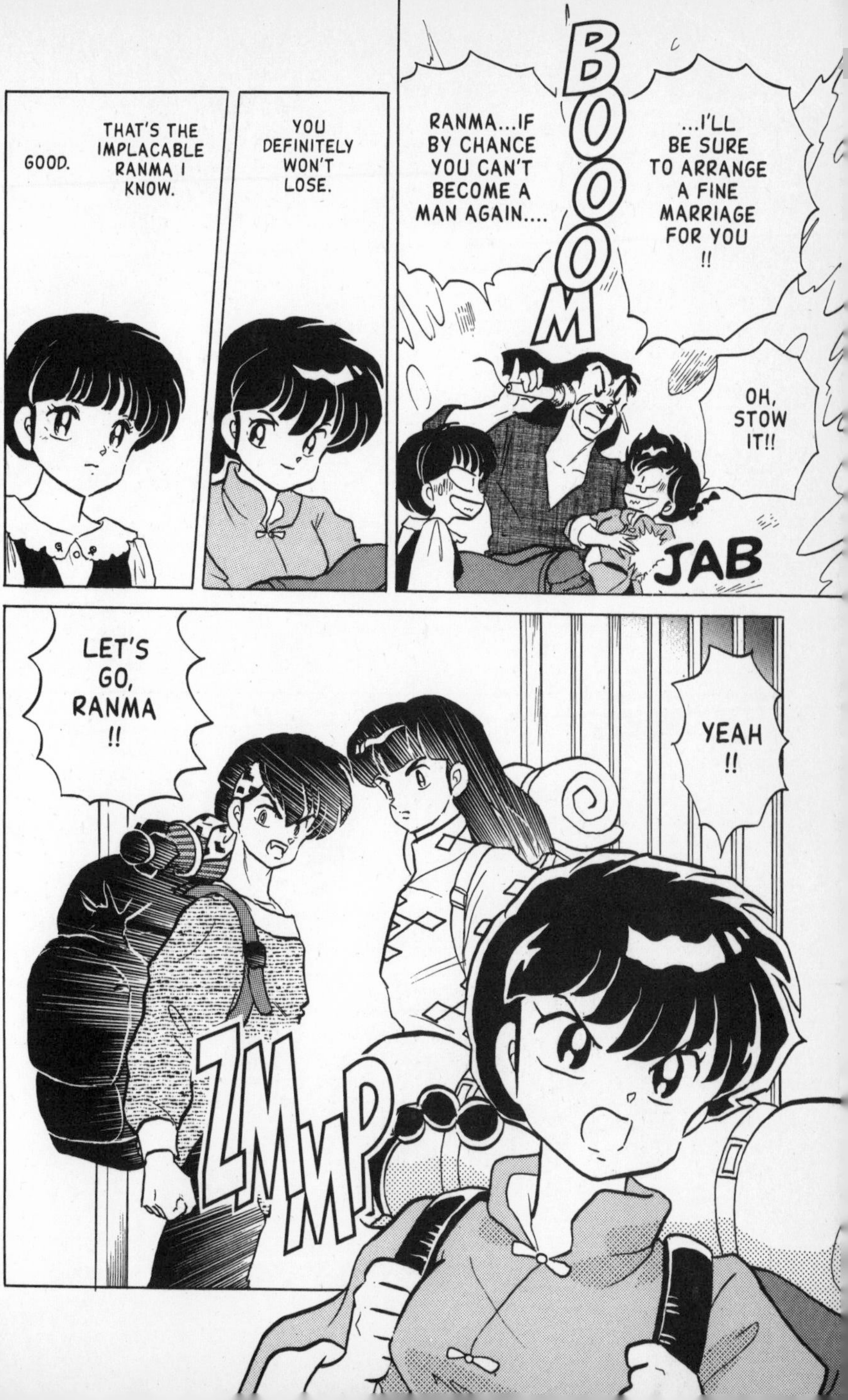
GOOD.
THAT'S THE IMPLACABLE RANMA I KNOW.
YOU DEFINITELY WON'T LOSE.
RANMA...IF BY CHANCE YOU CAN'T BECOME A MAN AGAIN....
BOOOOM
...I'LL BE SURE TO ARRANGE A FINE MARRIAGE FOR YOU !!
OH, STOW IT!!
JAB
LET'S GO, RANMA !!
YEAH !!
ZMMP

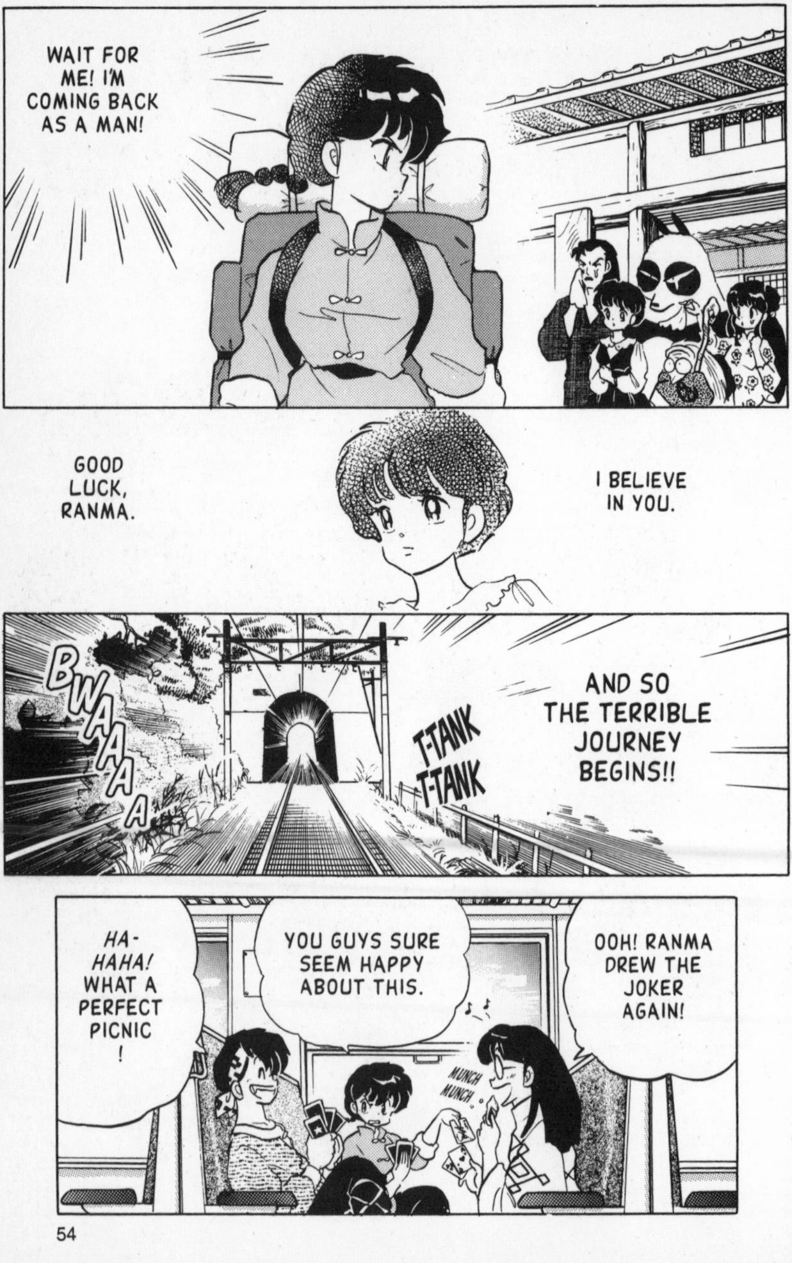
WAIT FOR ME! I'M COMING BACK AS A MAN!
GOOD LUCK, RANMA.
I BELIEVE IN YOU.
BWAAAAA
T-TANK T-TANK
AND SO THE TERRIBLE JOURNEY BEGINS!!
HA-HAHA! WHAT A PERFECT PICNIC!
YOU GUYS SURE SEEM HAPPY ABOUT THIS.
MUNCH MUNCH
OOH! RANMA DREW THE JOKER AGAIN!

Part 4

BATTLE OF THE HOT SPRINGS WOMEN!

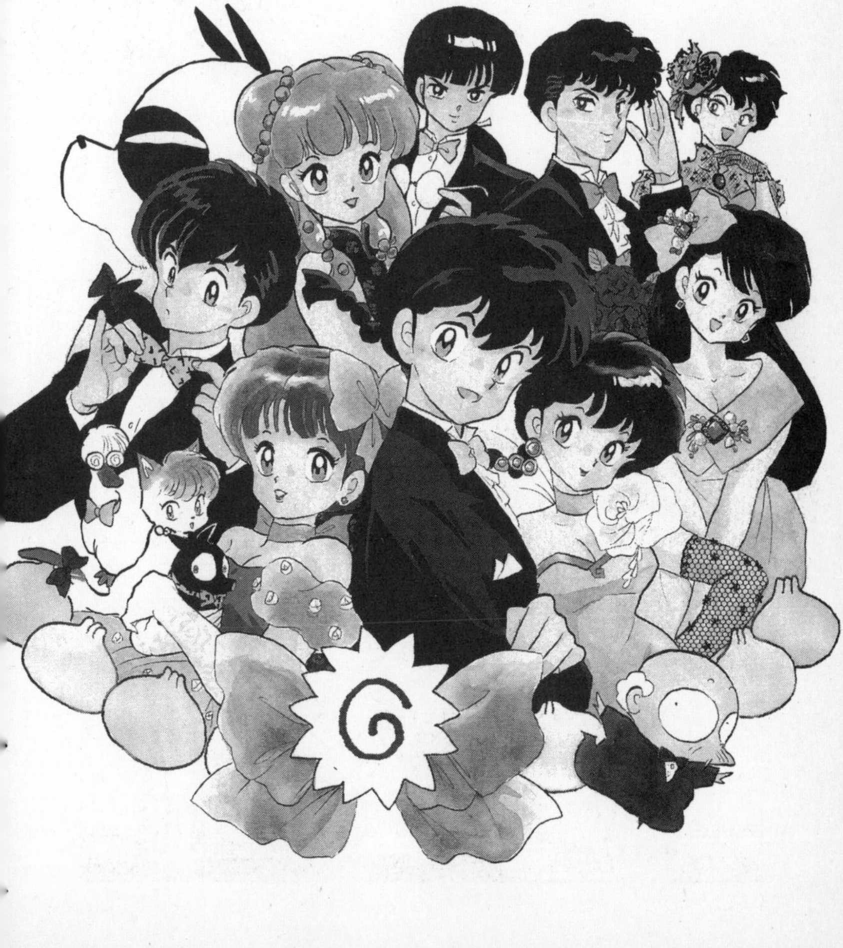

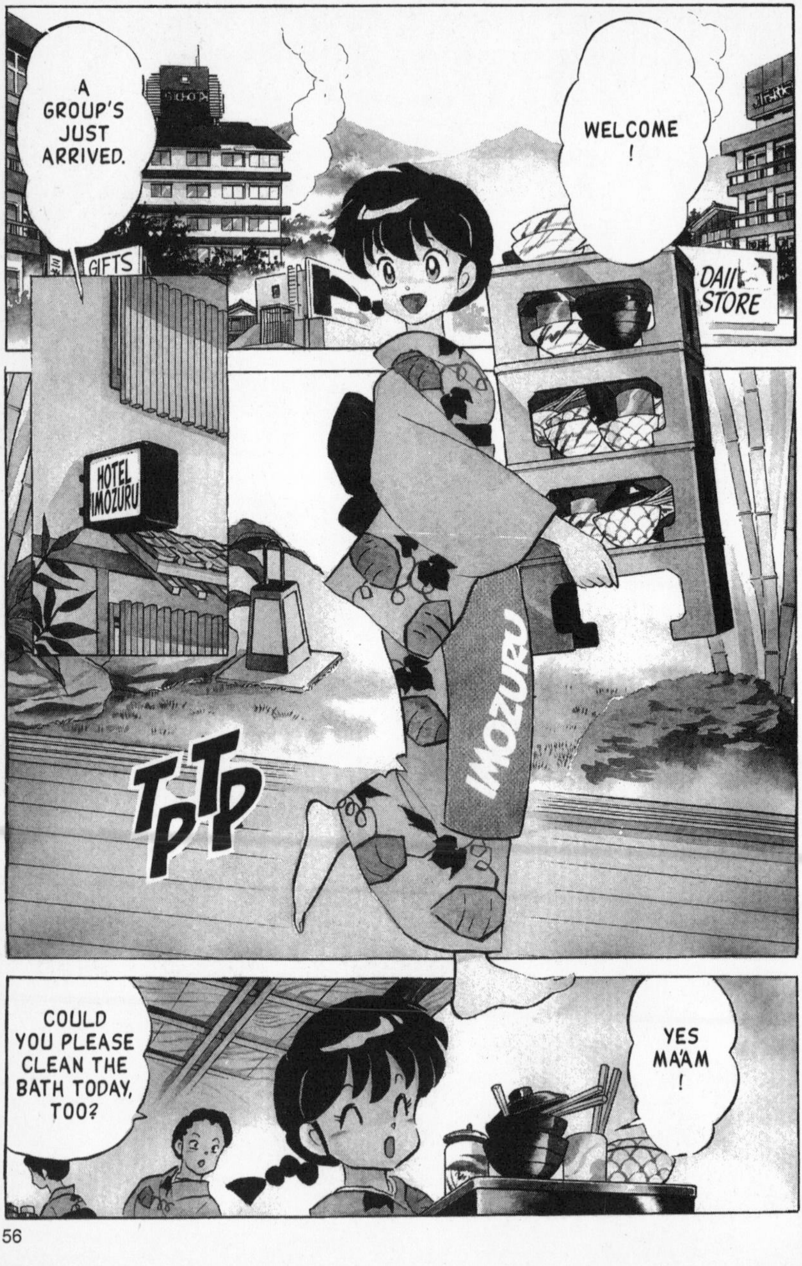
A GROUP'S JUST ARRIVED.
WELCOME!
GIFTS
DAII STORE
HOTEL IMOZURU
IMOZURU
TPTP
COULD YOU PLEASE CLEAN THE BATH TODAY, TOO?
YES MA'AM!

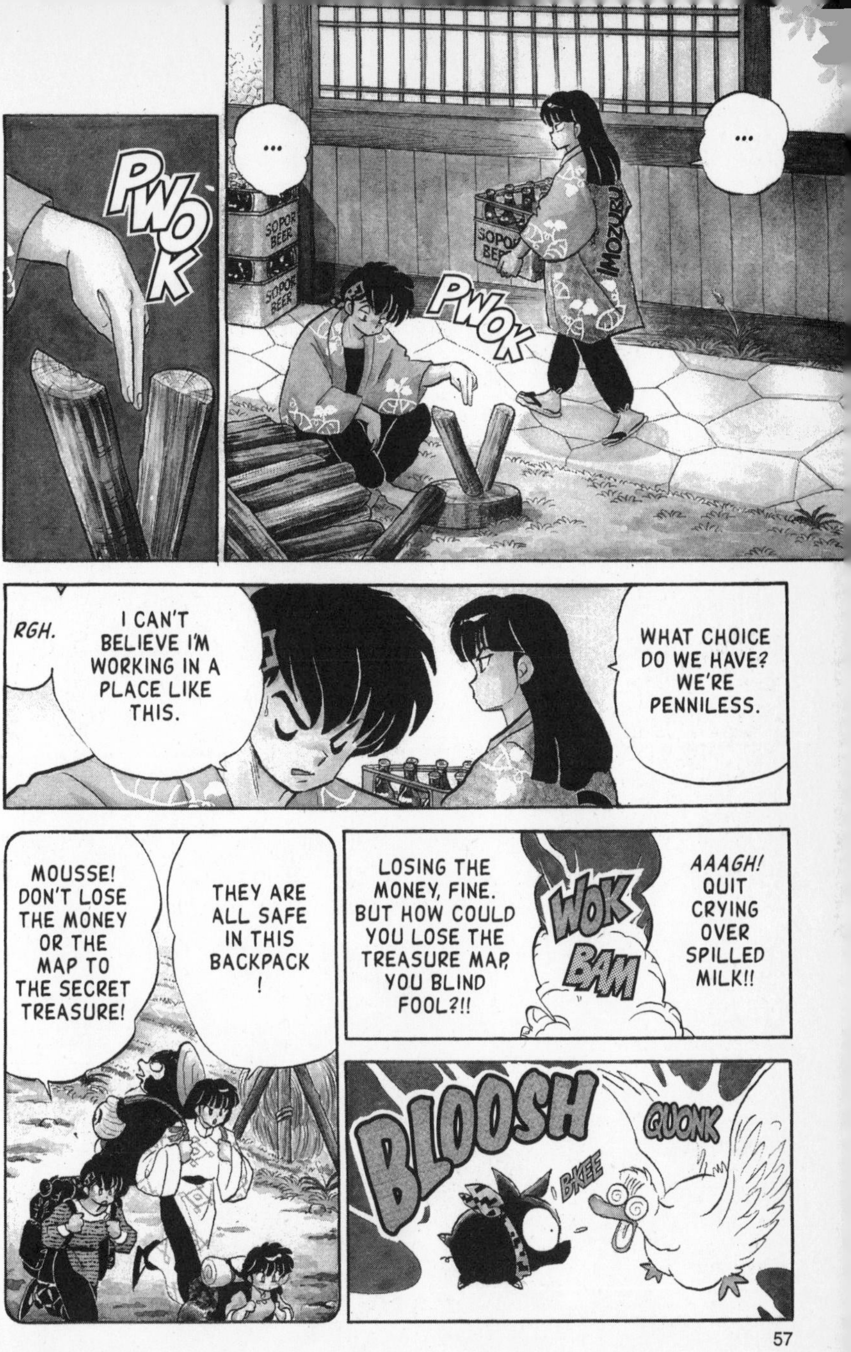
PWOK
...
...
SOPOR BEER
SOPOR BEER
SOPOR BEER
IMOZURU
PWOK
RGH.
I CAN'T BELIEVE I'M WORKING IN A PLACE LIKE THIS.
WHAT CHOICE DO WE HAVE? WE'RE PENNILESS.
MOUSSE! DON'T LOSE THE MONEY OR THE MAP TO THE SECRET TREASURE!
THEY ARE ALL SAFE IN THIS BACKPACK !
LOSING THE MONEY, FINE. BUT HOW COULD YOU LOSE THE TREASURE MAP, YOU BLIND FOOL?!!
WOK
BAM
AAAGH! QUIT CRYING OVER SPILLED MILK!!
BLOOSH
QUONK
BKEE

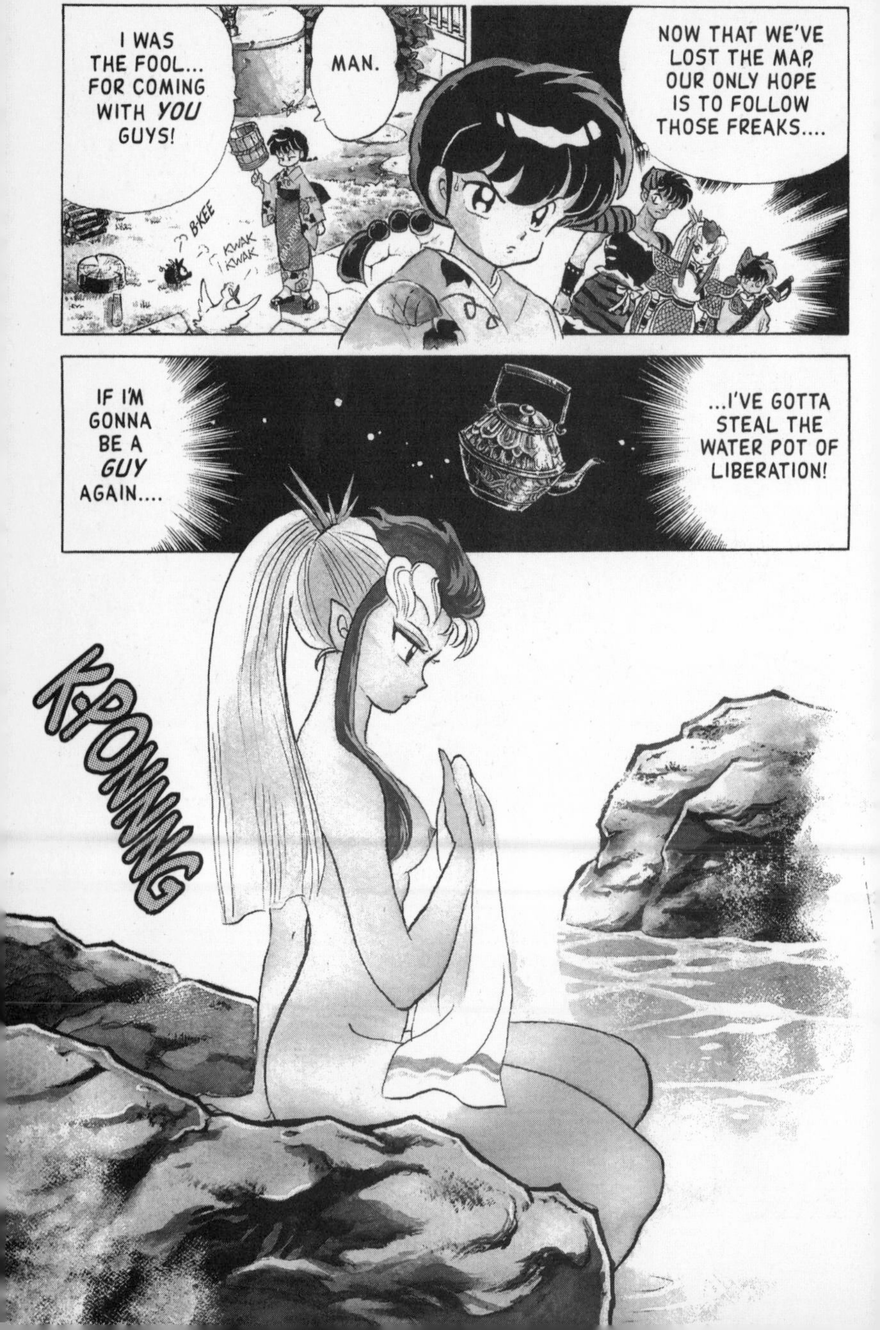
I WAS THE FOOL... FOR COMING WITH YOU GUYS!
MAN.
B'KEE
KWAK KWAK
NOW THAT WE'VE LOST THE MAP, OUR ONLY HOPE IS TO FOLLOW THOSE FREAKS....
IF I'M GONNA BE A GUY AGAIN....
...I'VE GOTTA STEAL THE WATER POT OF LIBERATION!
K-PONNNG

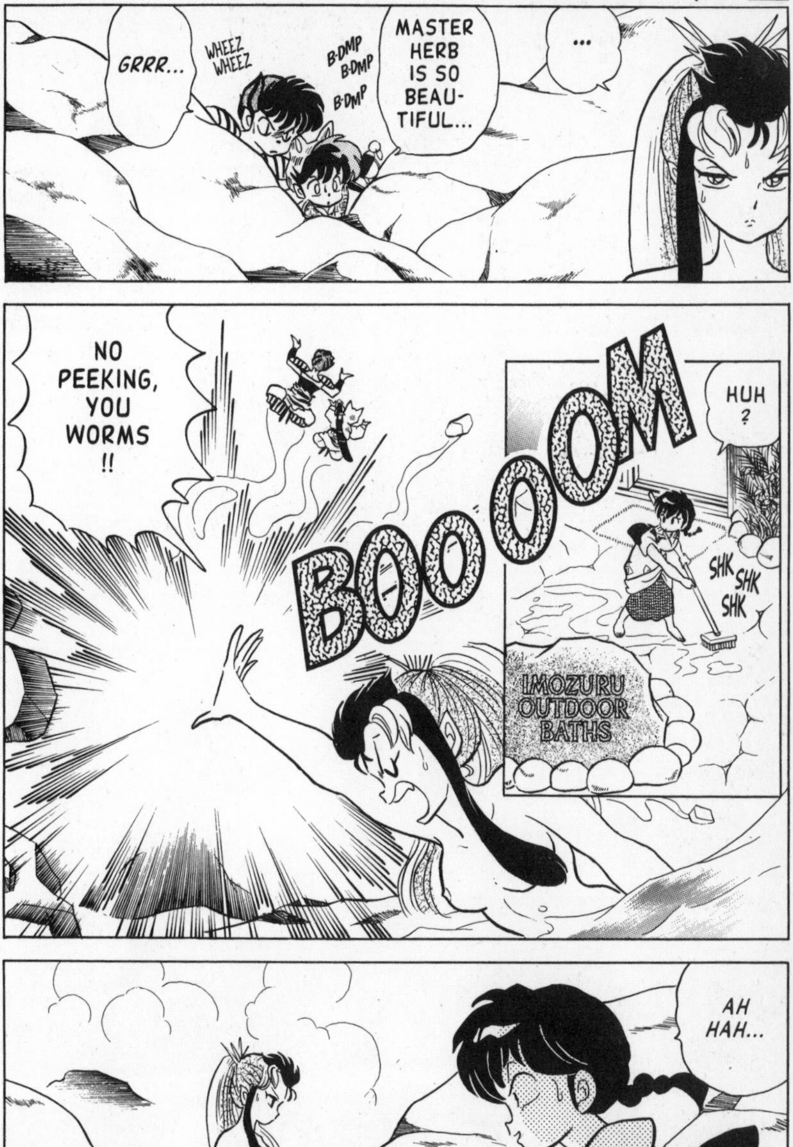
GRRR...
WHEEZ WHEEZ
B-DMP B-DMP B-DMP
MASTER HERB IS SO BEAU-TIFUL...
...
NO PEEKING, YOU WORMS !!
BOOOOOM
HUH ?
SHK SHK SHK
IMOZURU OUTDOOR BATHS
AH HAH...

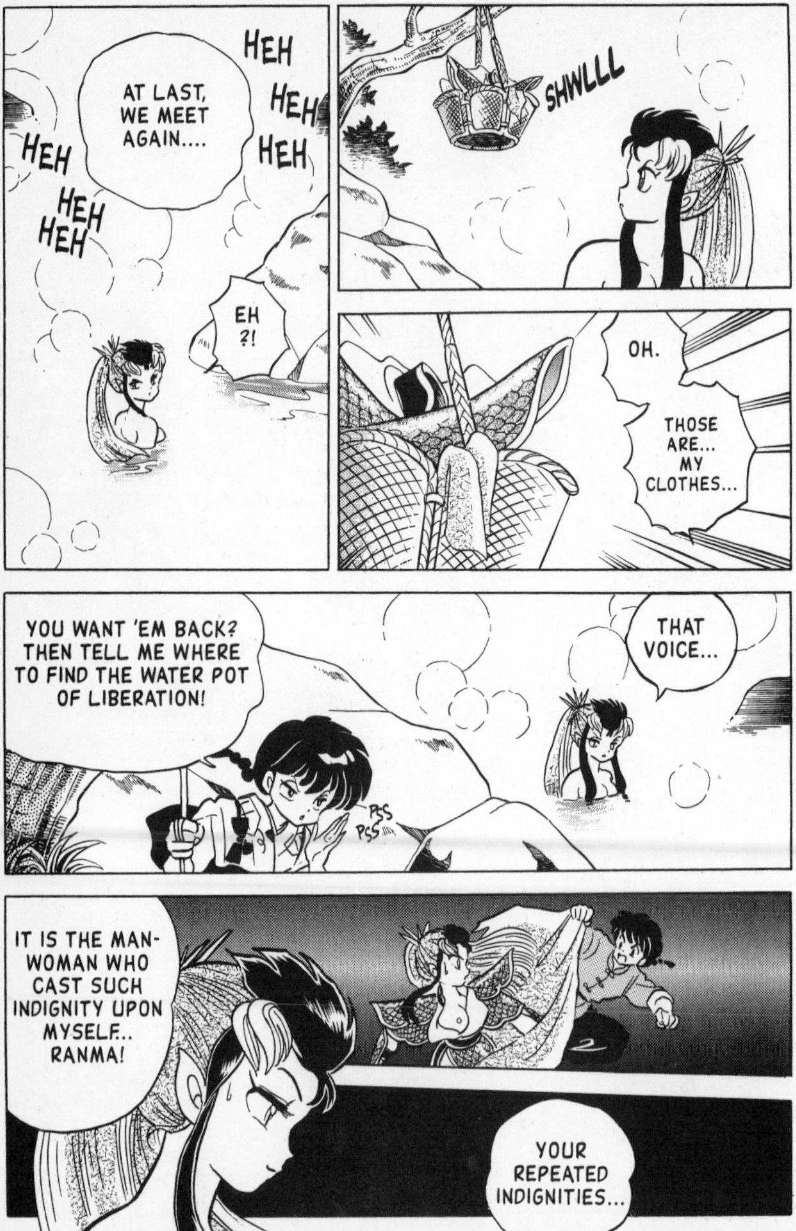

AT LAST, WE MEET AGAIN....
HEH HEH HEH
HEH HEH HEH
EH ?!
SHWLLL
OH.
THOSE ARE... MY CLOTHES...
YOU WANT 'EM BACK? THEN TELL ME WHERE TO FIND THE WATER POT OF LIBERATION!
PSS PSS
THAT VOICE...
IT IS THE MAN-WOMAN WHO CAST SUCH INDIGNITY UPON MYSELF... RANMA!
YOUR REPEATED INDIGNITIES...

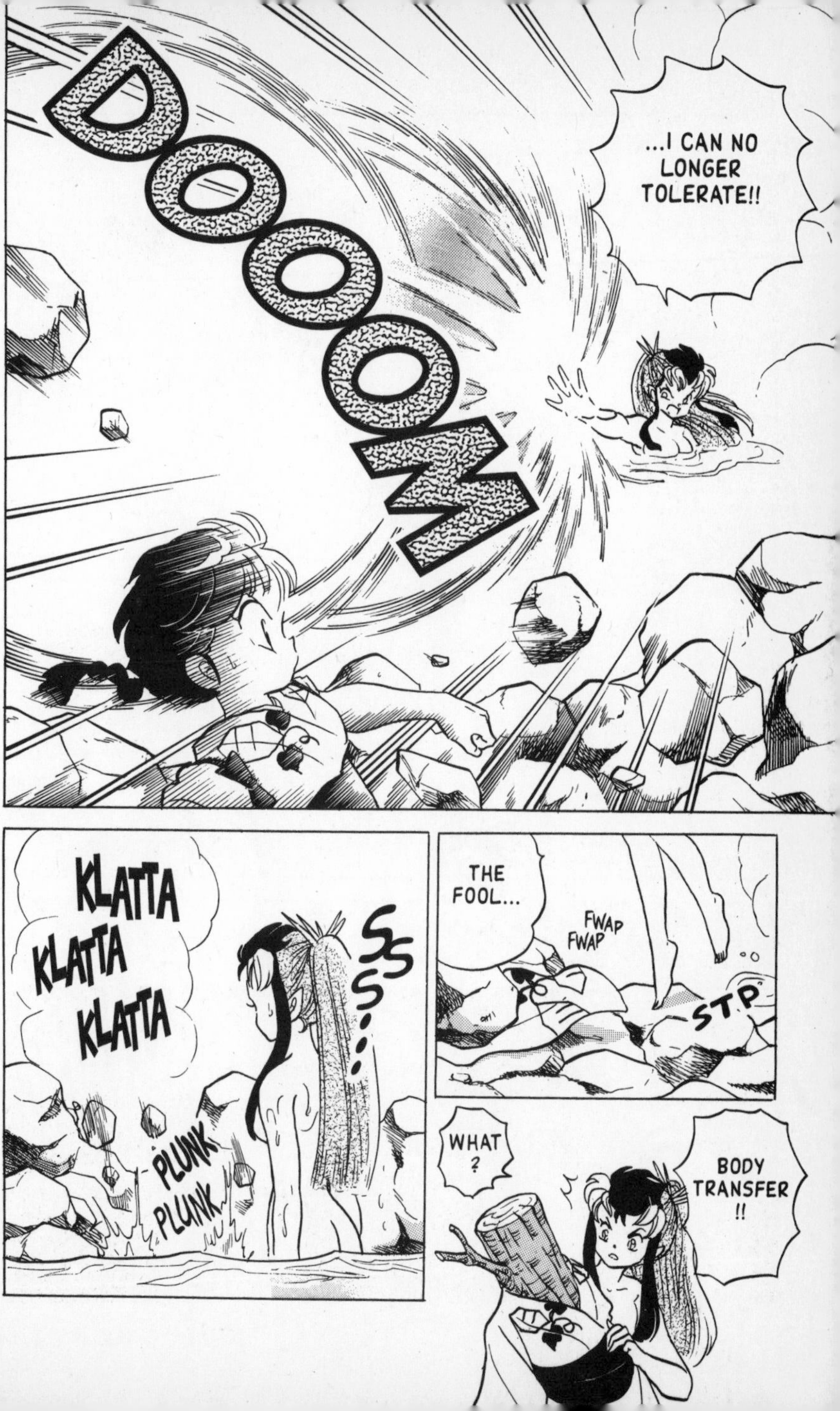
DOOOM
...I CAN NO LONGER TOLERATE!!
KLATTA
KLATTA
KLATTA
KLATTA
SSS...
PLUNK
PLUNK
THE FOOL...
FWAP
FWAP
STP
WHAT?
BODY TRANSFER!!

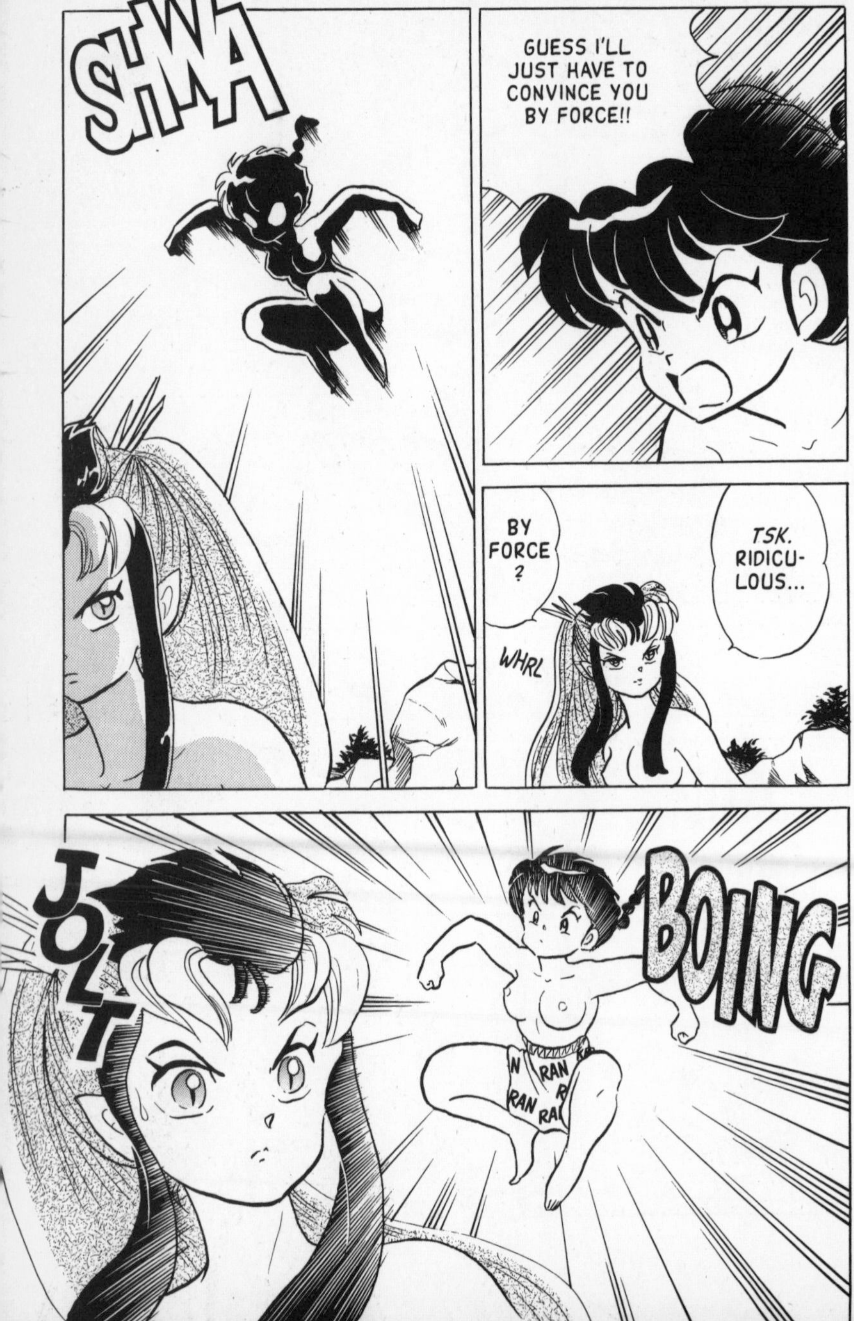
SHWA
GUESS I'LL JUST HAVE TO CONVINCE YOU BY FORCE!!
BY FORCE?
TSK. RIDICULOUS...
WHRL
JOLT
BOING

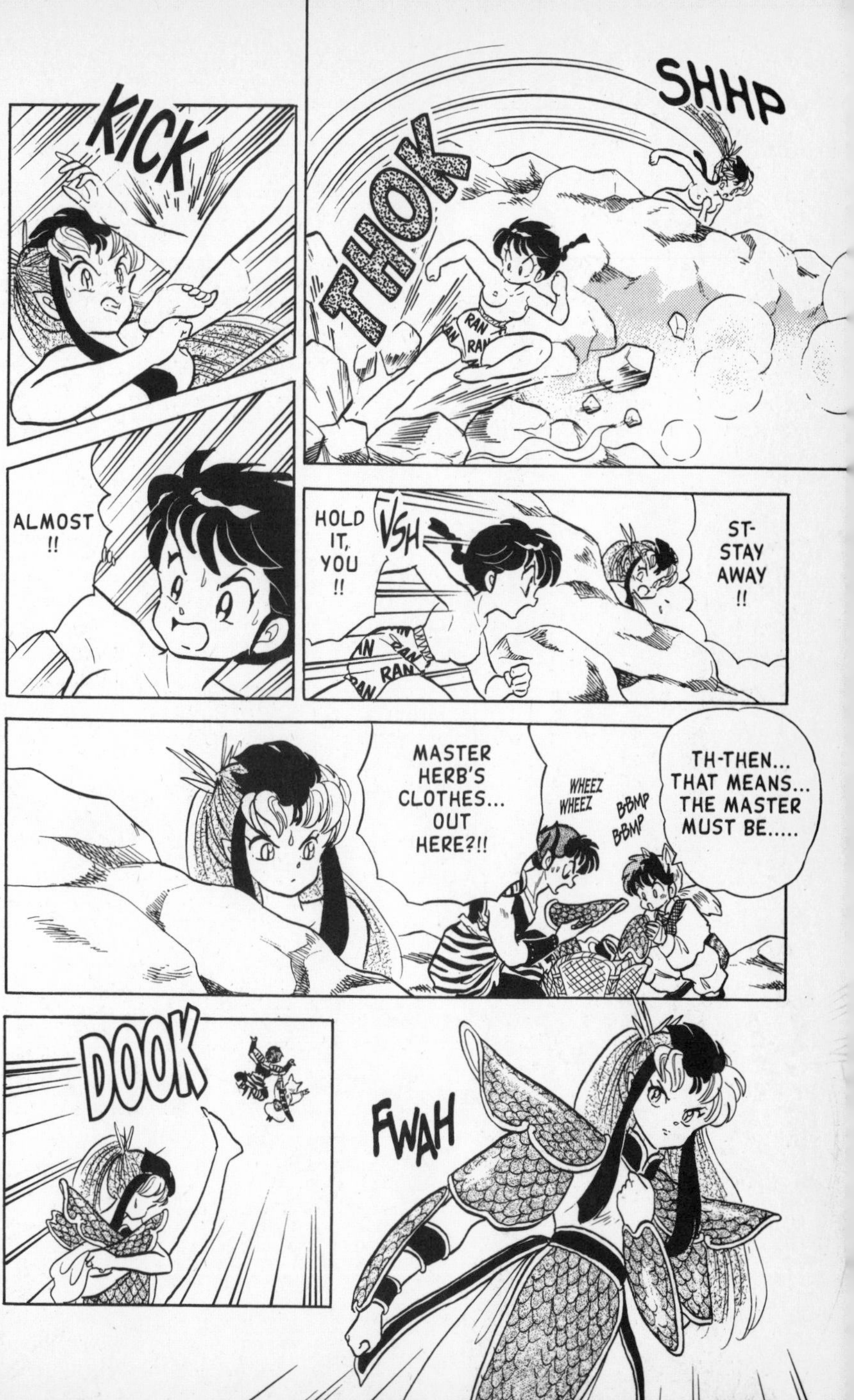
KICK
SHHP
THOK
RAN RAN RAN
ALMOST !!
HOLD IT, YOU !!
VSH
ST-STAY AWAY !!
RAN RAN RAN
MASTER HERB'S CLOTHES... OUT HERE?!!
WHEEZ WHEEZ
B-BMP B-BMP
TH-THEN... THAT MEANS... THE MASTER MUST BE.....
DOOK
FWAH

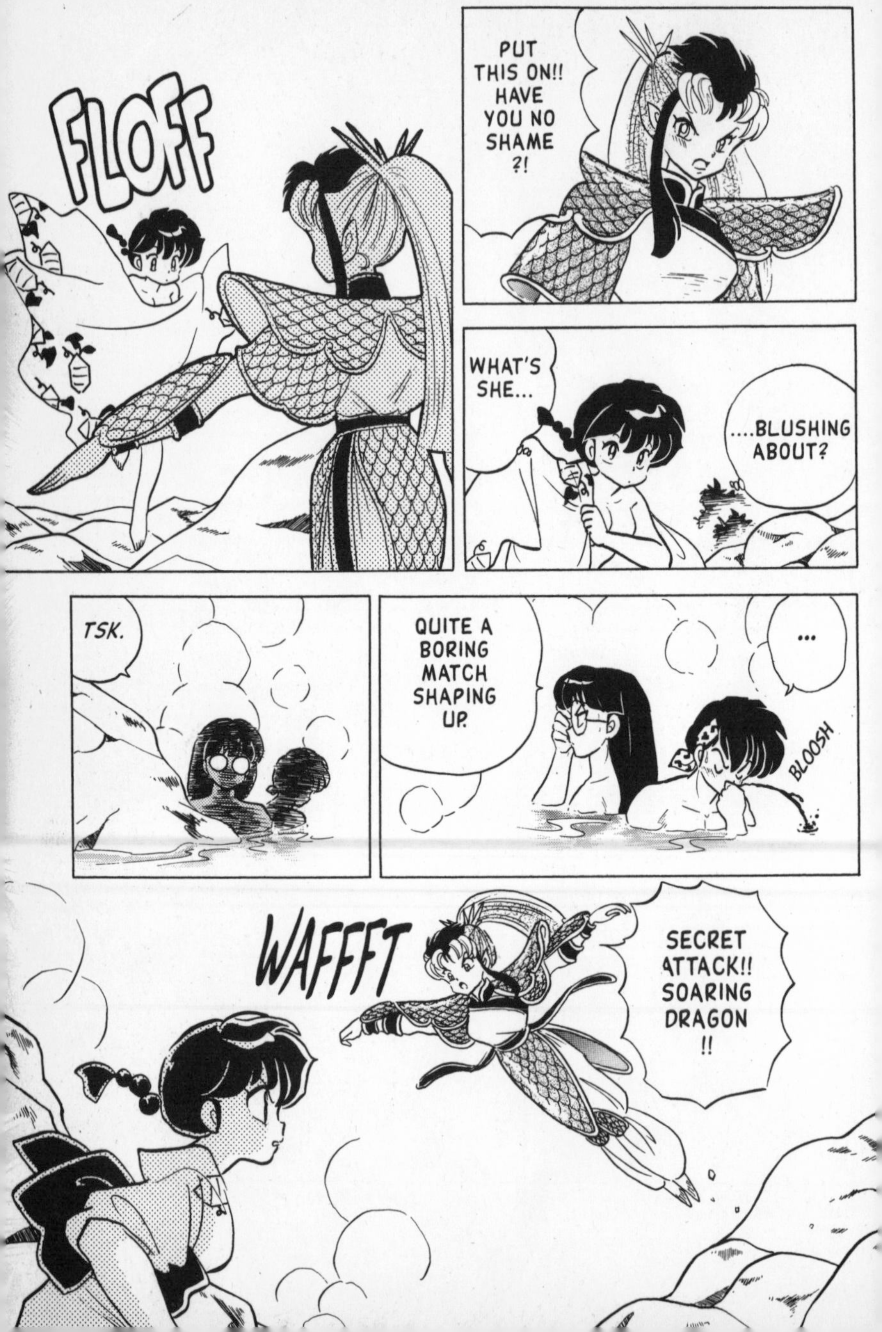
FLOFF
PUT THIS ON!! HAVE YOU NO SHAME ?!
WHAT'S SHE...
....BLUSHING ABOUT?
TSK.
QUITE A BORING MATCH SHAPING UP.
...
BLOOSH
WAFFFT
SECRET ATTACK!! SOARING DRAGON !!

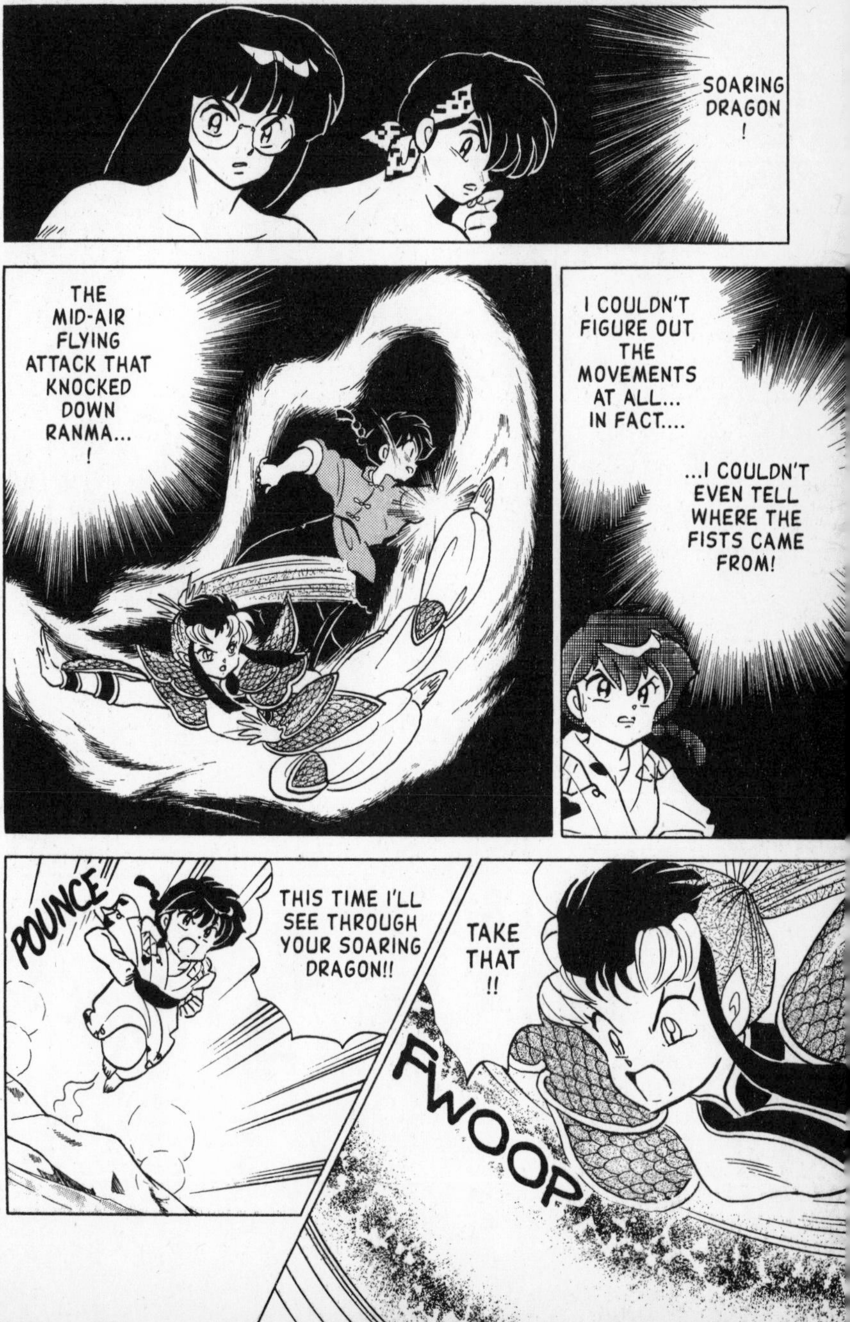
SOARING DRAGON !
THE MID-AIR FLYING ATTACK THAT KNOCKED DOWN RANMA... !
I COULDN'T FIGURE OUT THE MOVEMENTS AT ALL... IN FACT....
...I COULDN'T EVEN TELL WHERE THE FISTS CAME FROM!
POUNCE
THIS TIME I'LL SEE THROUGH YOUR SOARING DRAGON!!
TAKE THAT !!
FWOOP

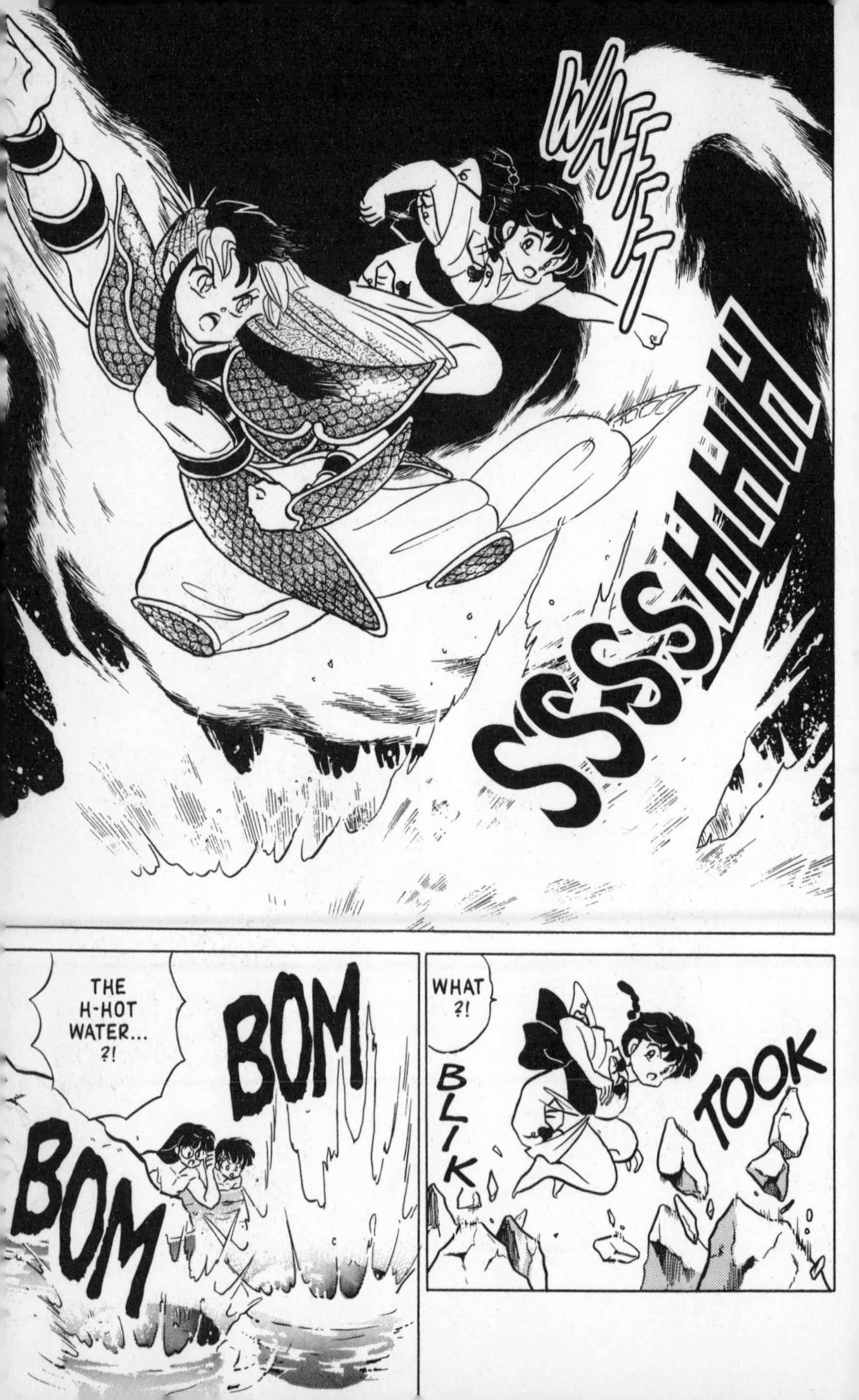
WAFFEET
SSSSHHHH
THE H-HOT WATER... ?!
BOM
BOM
BOM
WHAT ?!
BLIK
TOOK

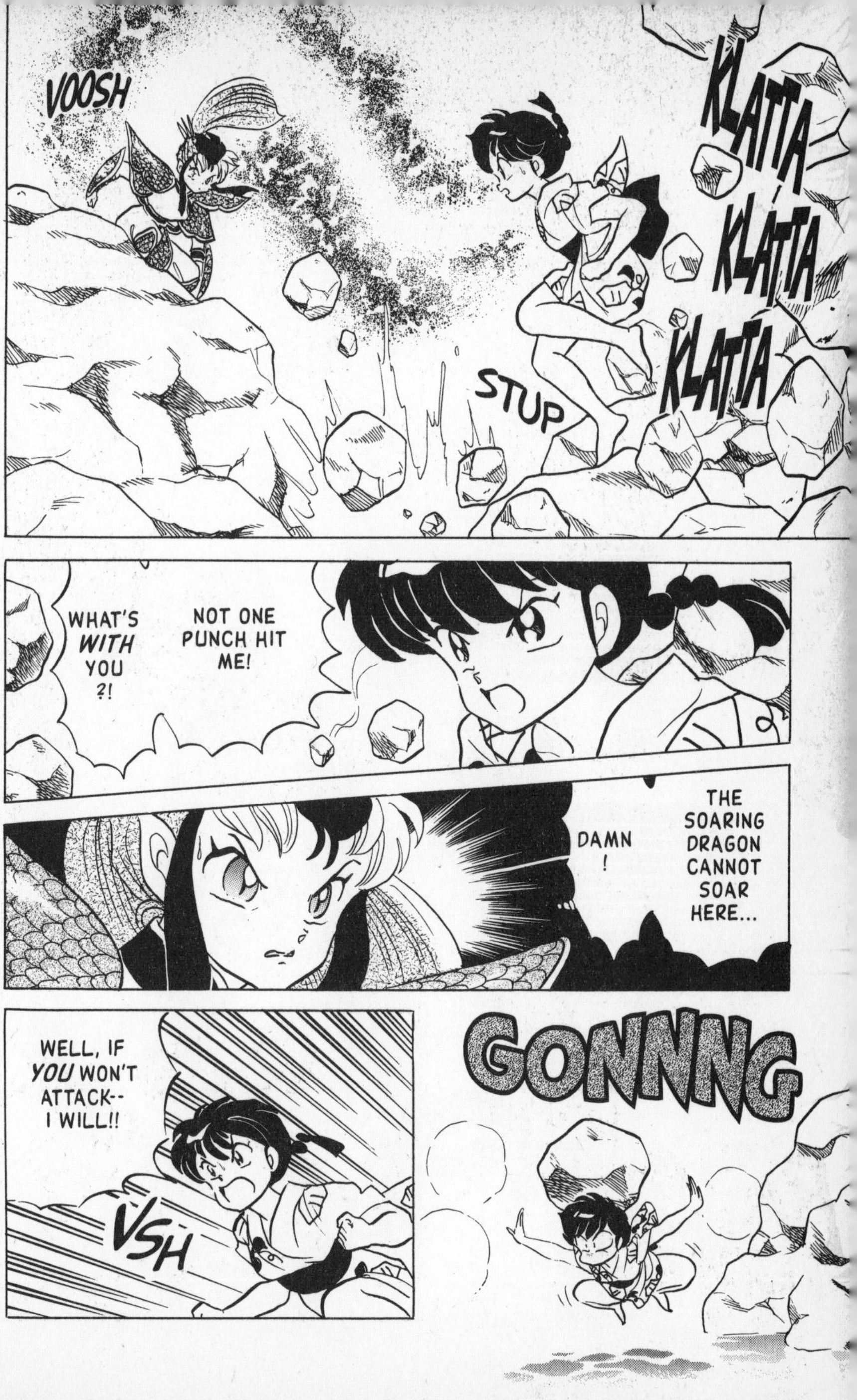
VOOSH
KLATTA KLATTA KLATTA
STUP
WHAT'S *WITH* YOU ?!
NOT ONE PUNCH HIT ME!
DAMN !
THE SOARING DRAGON CANNOT SOAR HERE...
WELL, IF *YOU* WON'T ATTACK-- I WILL!!
VSH
GONNNG

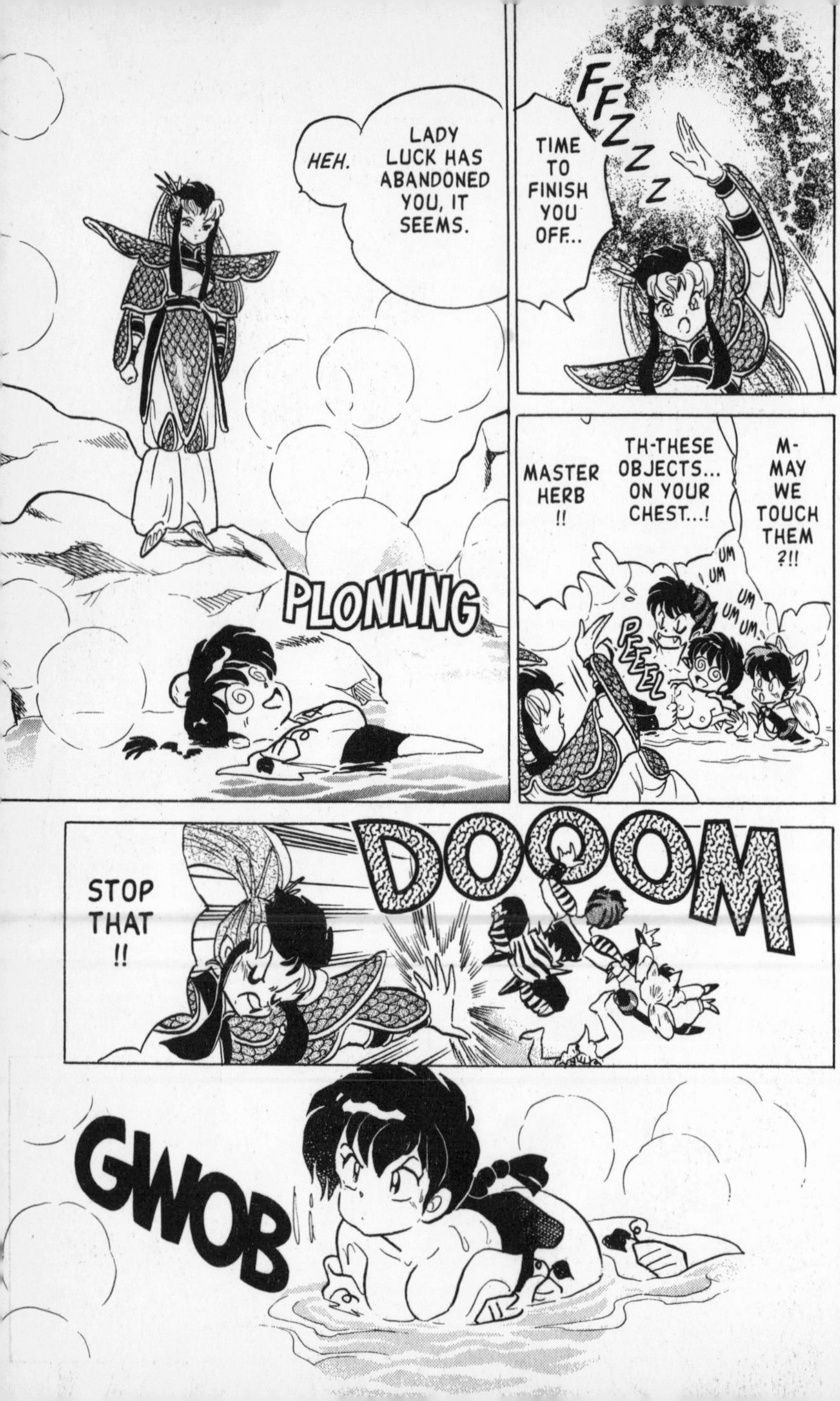
HEH.
LADY LUCK HAS ABANDONED YOU, IT SEEMS.
PLONNNG
FFZZZZ
TIME TO FINISH YOU OFF...
MASTER HERB !!
TH-THESE OBJECTS... ON YOUR CHEST...!
M-MAY WE TOUCH THEM ?!!
UM UM UM UM UM
PEEEL
STOP THAT !!
DOOOM
GWOB

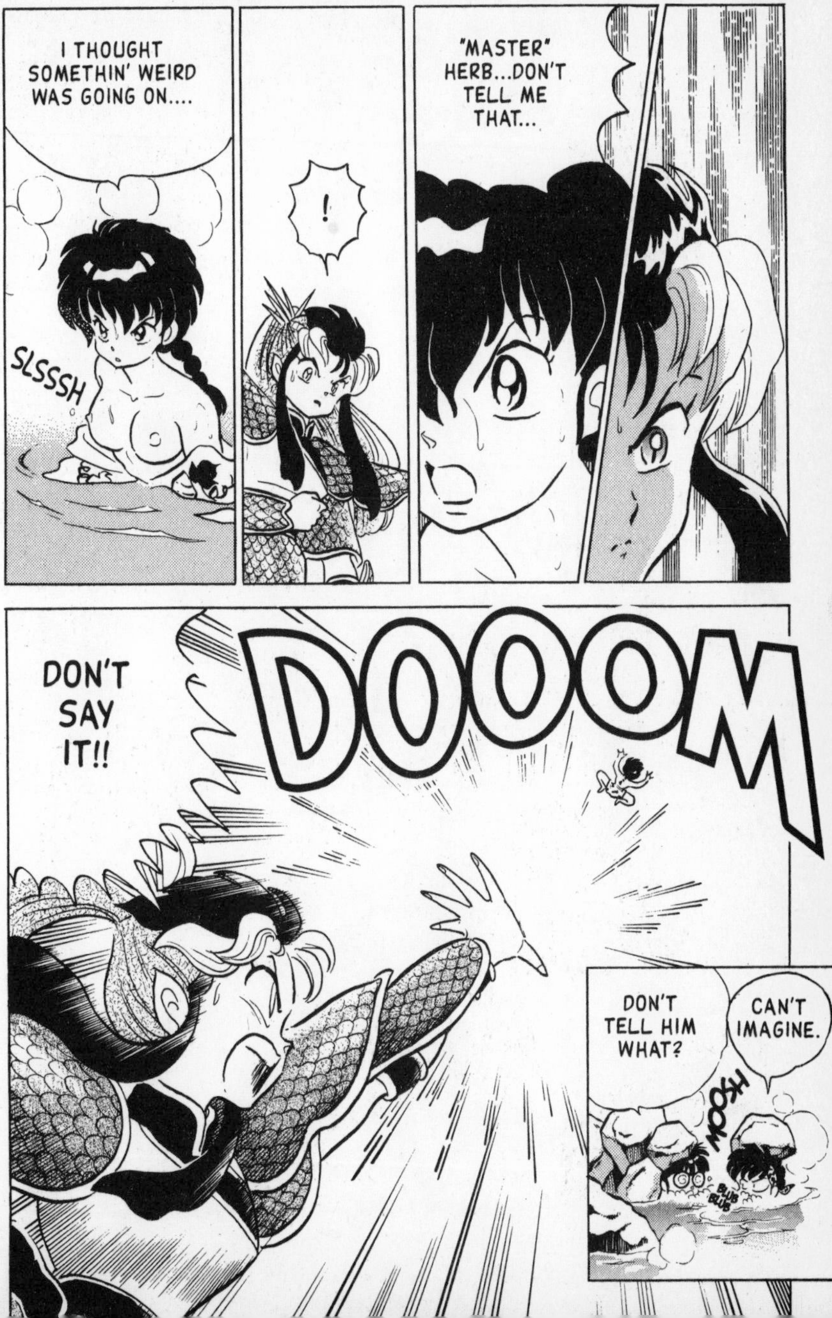
I THOUGHT SOMETHIN' WEIRD WAS GOING ON....
SLSSSH
!
"MASTER" HERB...DON'T TELL ME THAT...
DON'T SAY IT!!
DOOOM
DON'T TELL HIM WHAT?
CAN'T IMAGINE.
WOOSH
BLUB BLUB

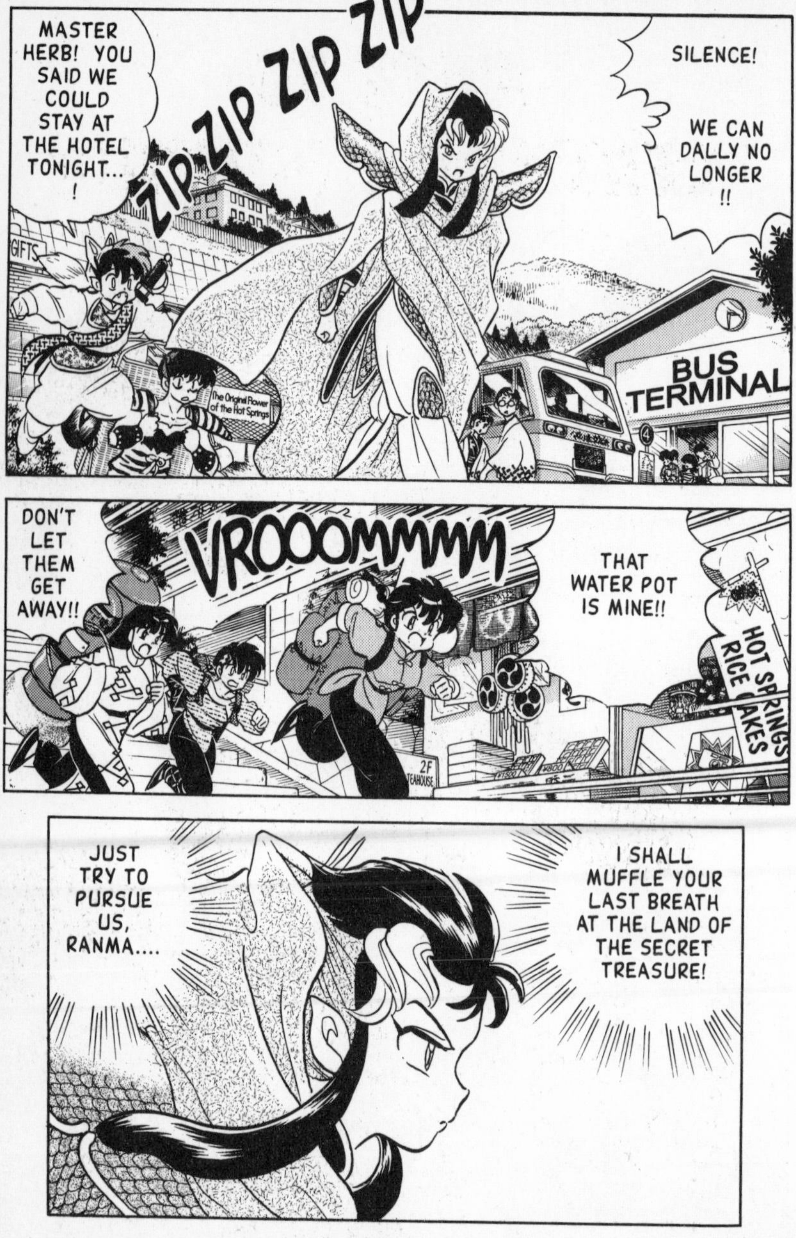
MASTER HERB! YOU SAID WE COULD STAY AT THE HOTEL TONIGHT... !
ZIP ZIP ZIP ZIP
GIFTS
The Original Flower of the Hot Springs
SILENCE!
WE CAN DALLY NO LONGER !!
BUS TERMINAL
DON'T LET THEM GET AWAY!!
VROOOMMMM
THAT WATER POT IS MINE!!
HOT SPRINGS RICE CAKES
2F TEAHOUSE
JUST TRY TO PURSUE US, RANMA....
I SHALL MUFFLE YOUR LAST BREATH AT THE LAND OF THE SECRET TREASURE!

Part 5

RACE TO TREASURE MOUNTAIN

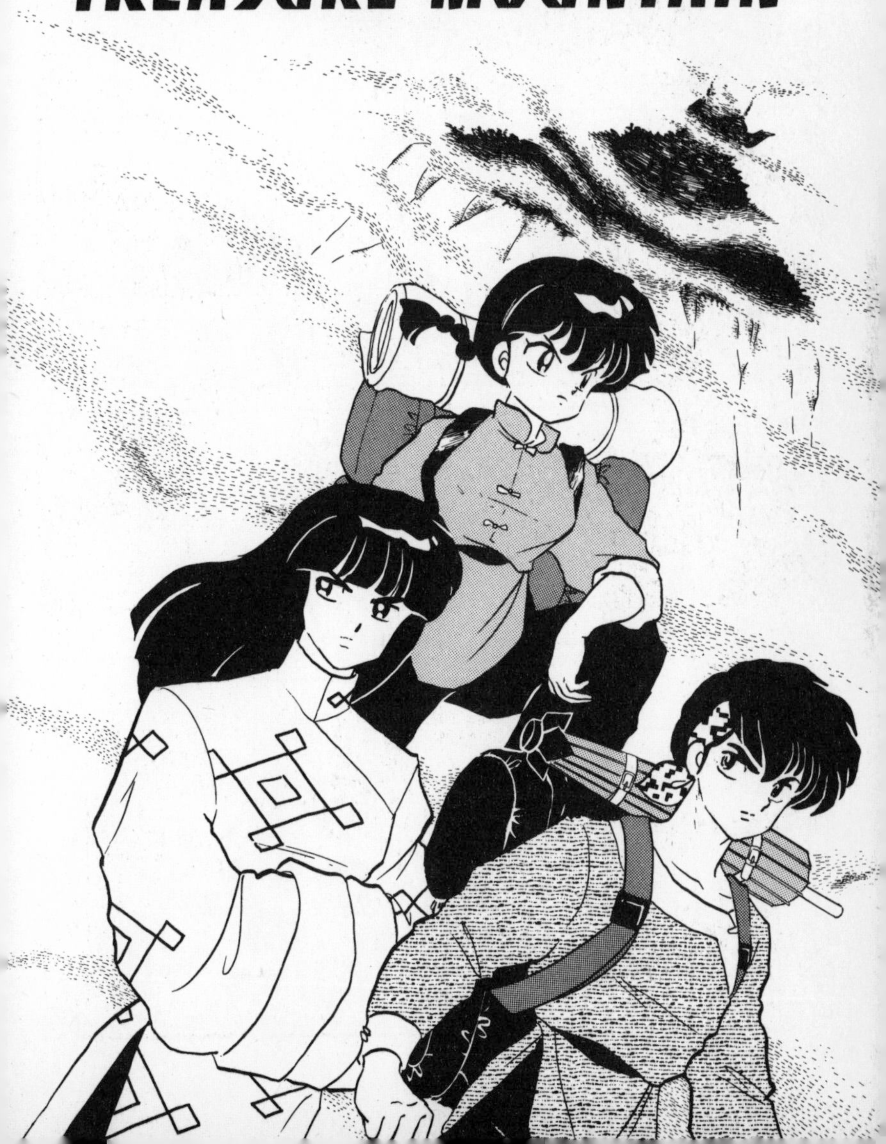

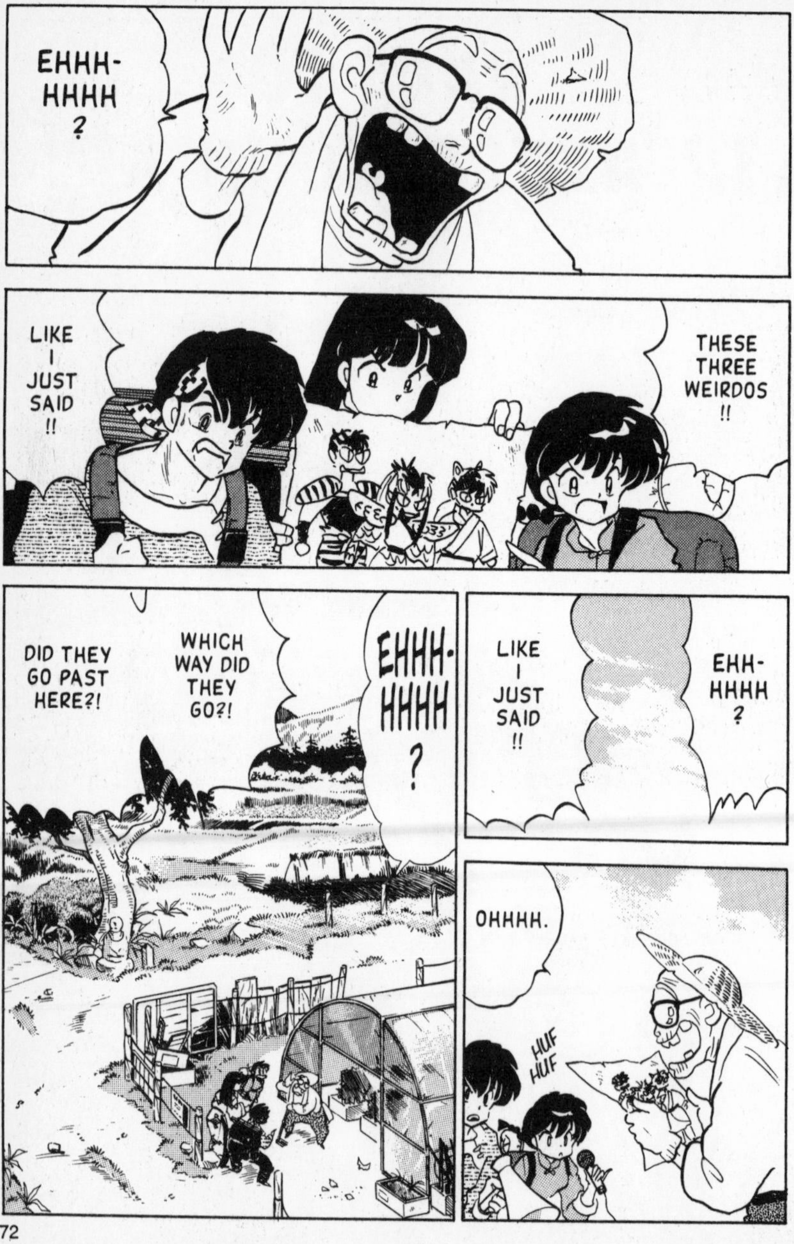
EHHH-HHHH?
LIKE I JUST SAID!!
THESE THREE WEIRDOS!!
DID THEY GO PAST HERE?!
WHICH WAY DID THEY GO?!
EHHH-HHHH?
LIKE I JUST SAID!!
EHH-HHHH?
OHHHH.
HUF HUF

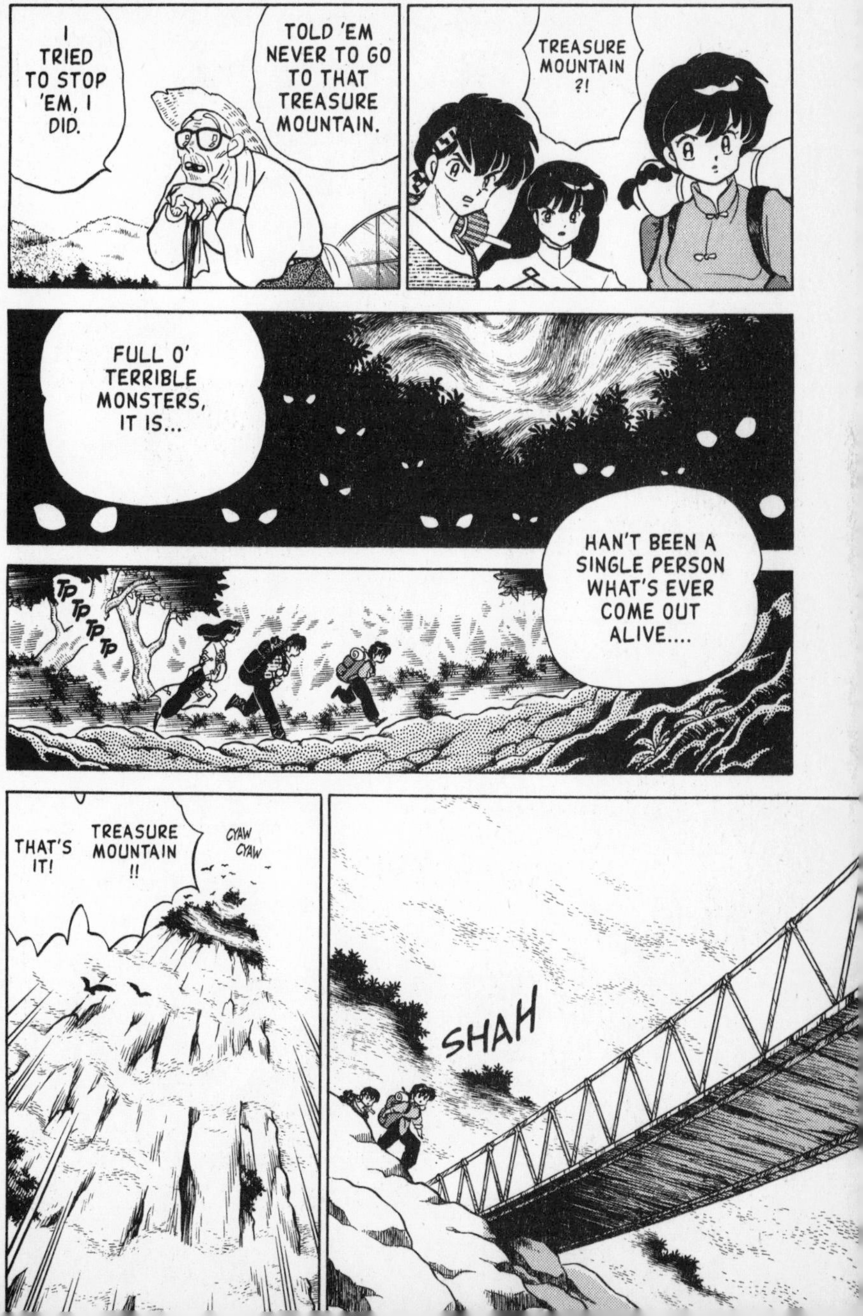
I TRIED TO STOP 'EM, I DID.
TOLD 'EM NEVER TO GO TO THAT TREASURE MOUNTAIN.
TREASURE MOUNTAIN ?!
FULL O' TERRIBLE MONSTERS, IT IS...
TP TP TP TP
HAN'T BEEN A SINGLE PERSON WHAT'S EVER COME OUT ALIVE....
THAT'S IT!
TREASURE MOUNTAIN !!
CYAW CYAW
SHAH

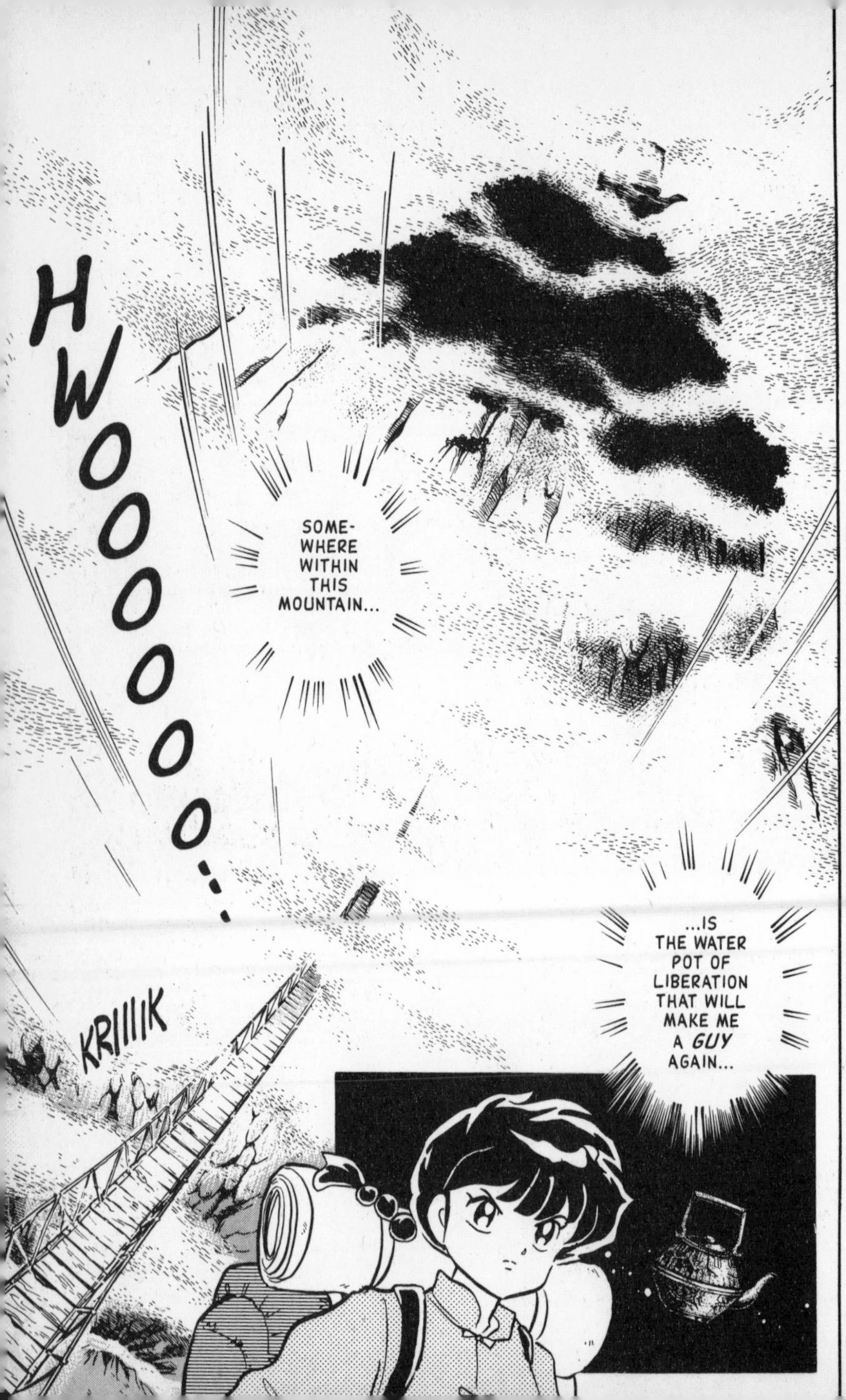
HWOOOOOOO...
SOME-WHERE WITHIN THIS MOUNTAIN...
KRIIIIK
...IS THE WATER POT OF LIBERATION THAT WILL MAKE ME A *GUY* AGAIN...

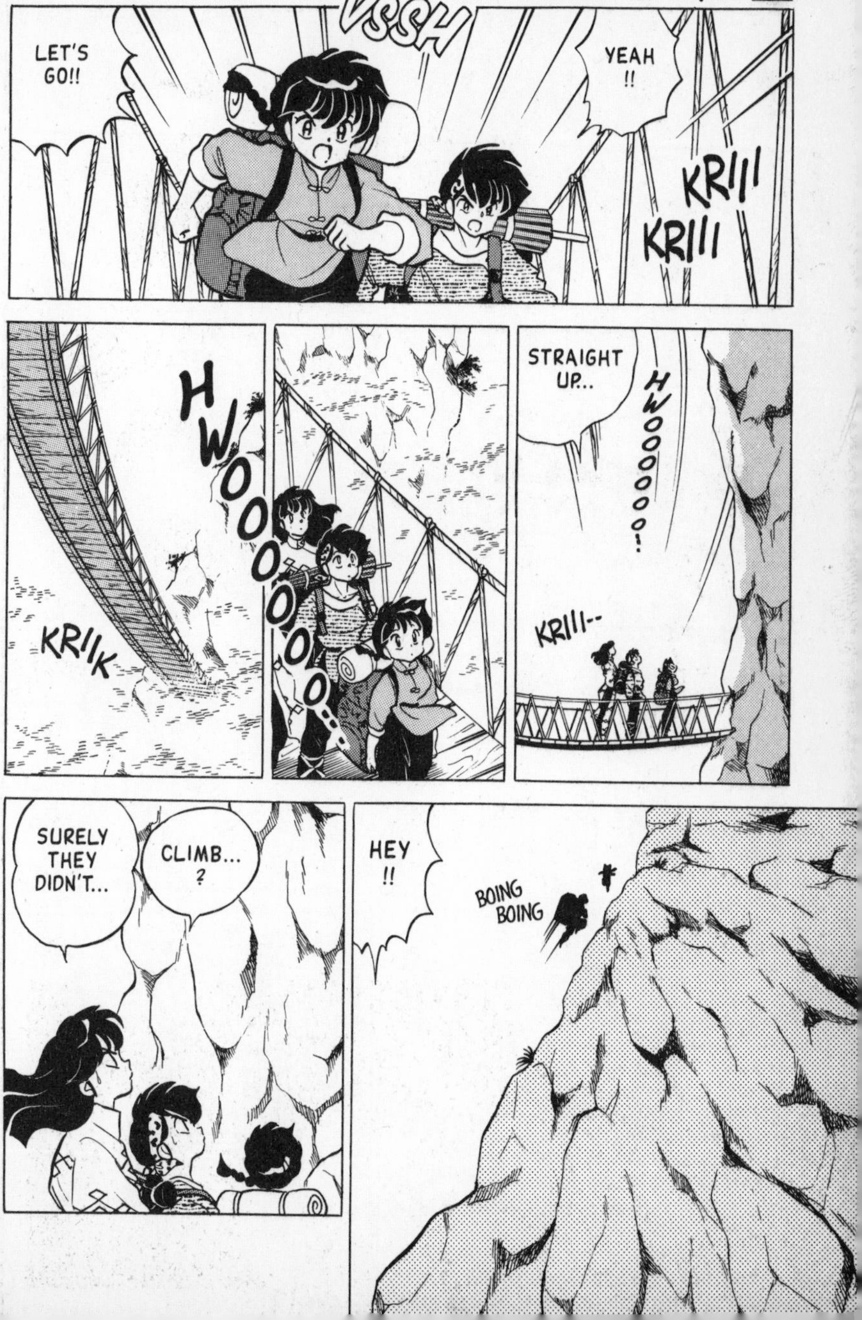
LET'S GO!!
VSSH
YEAH !!
KRIII
KRIII
HWOOOOOOOO...
KRIIK
STRAIGHT UP...
HWOOOOOOO!
KRIII--
SURELY THEY DIDN'T...
CLIMB... ?
HEY !!
BOING BOING

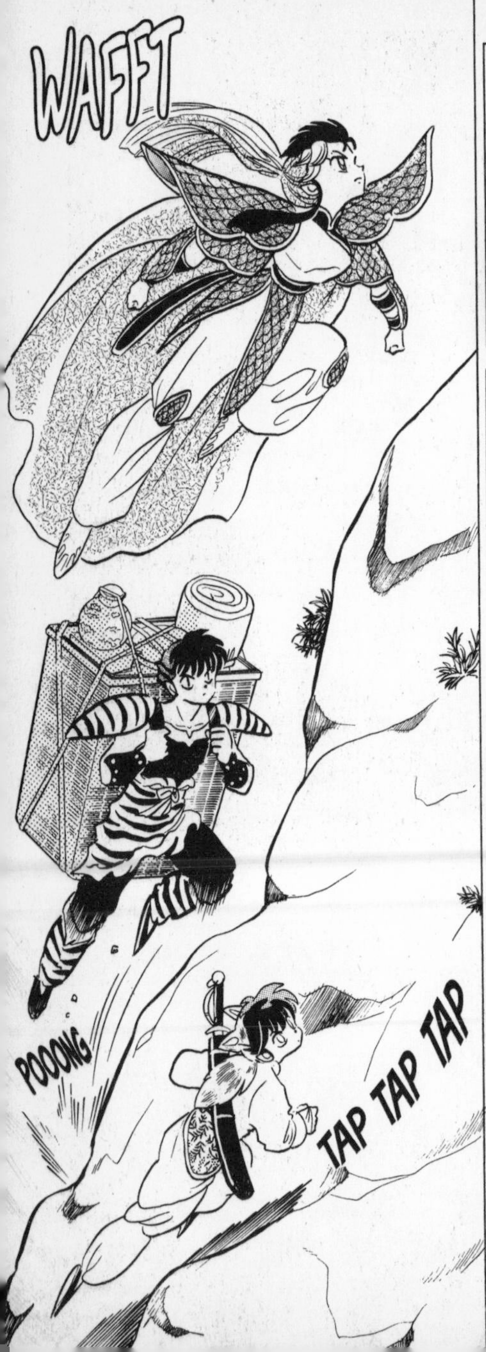
WAFFT
POOONG
TAP TAP TAP

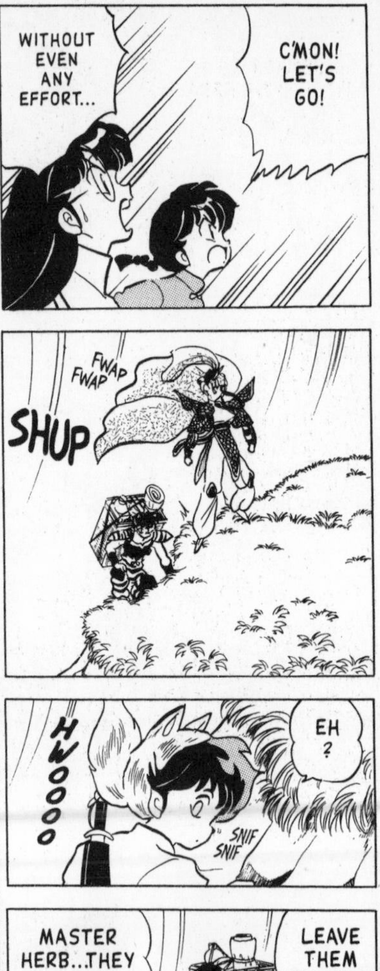
WITHOUT EVEN ANY EFFORT...
C'MON! LET'S GO!
FWAP FWAP
SHUP
HWOOOOO
EH?
SNIF SNIF
MASTER HERB...THEY ARE FOLLOWING US.
LEAVE THEM BE FOR NOW.

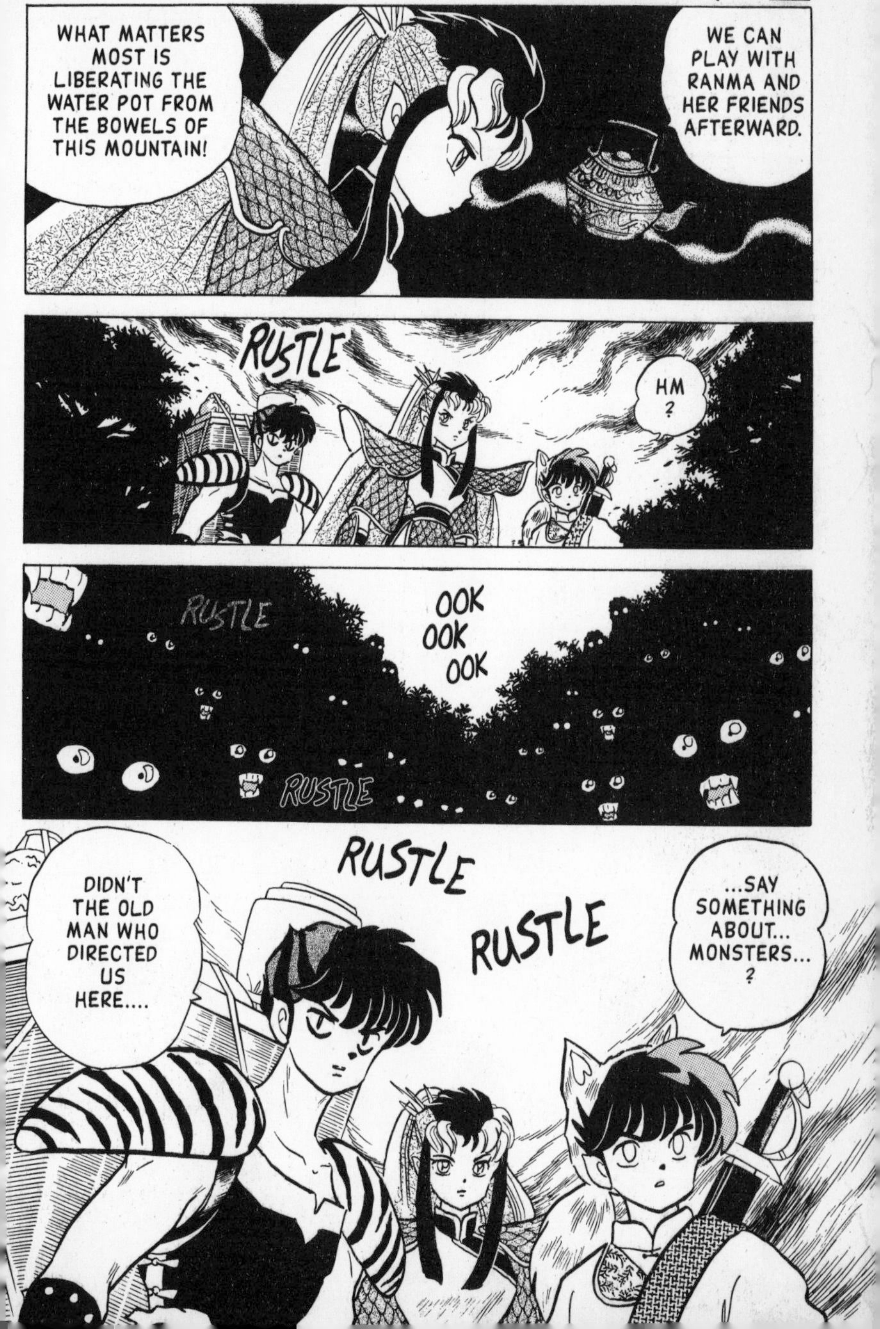
WHAT MATTERS MOST IS LIBERATING THE WATER POT FROM THE BOWELS OF THIS MOUNTAIN!
WE CAN PLAY WITH RANMA AND HER FRIENDS AFTERWARD.
RUSTLE
HM ?
RUSTLE
OOK OOK OOK
RUSTLE
RUSTLE
DIDN'T THE OLD MAN WHO DIRECTED US HERE....
RUSTLE
...SAY SOMETHING ABOUT... MONSTERS... ?

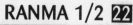

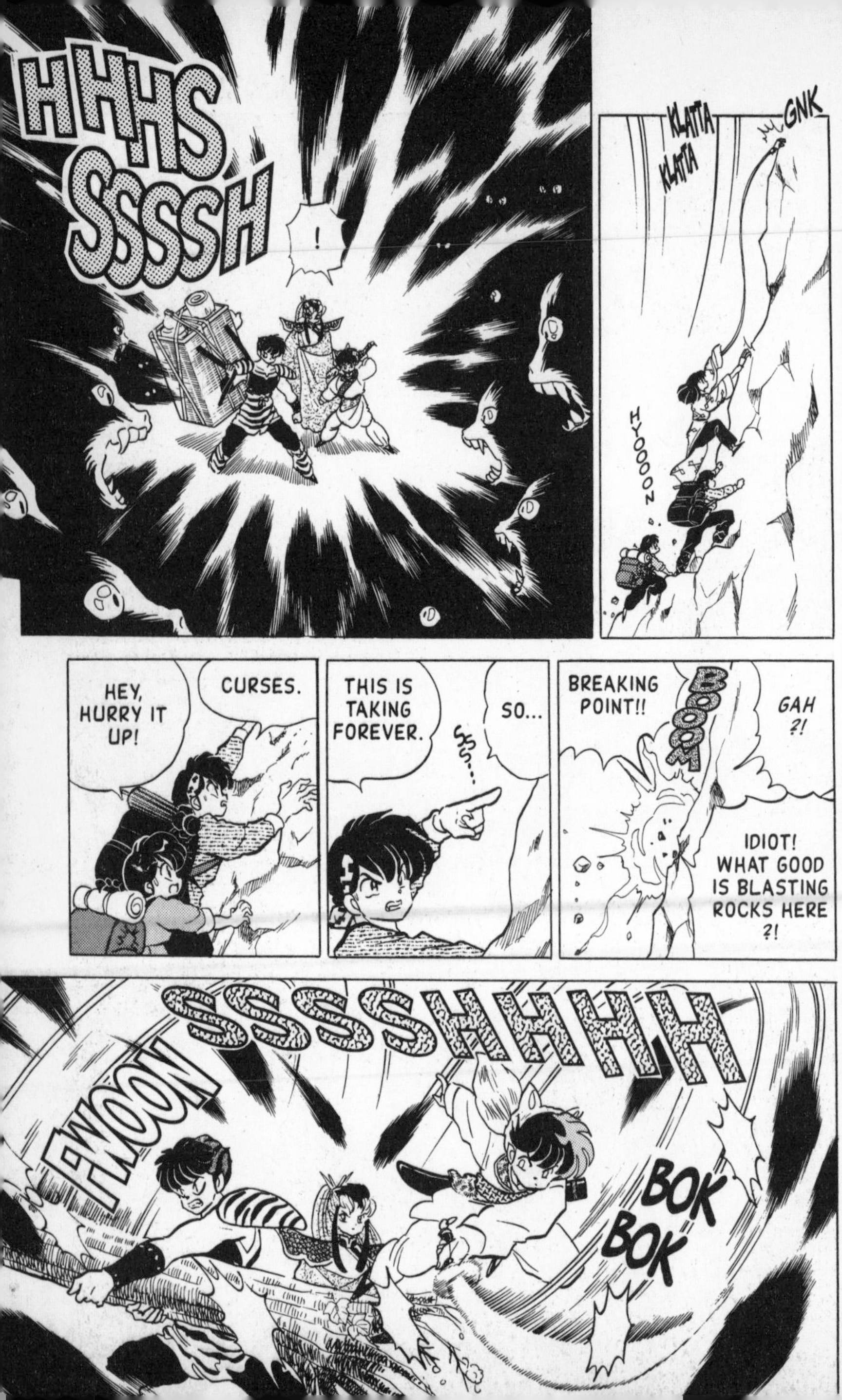
HHHS SSSSH
!
KLATTA KLATTA
GNK
HYOOOON
HEY, HURRY IT UP!
CURSES.
THIS IS TAKING FOREVER.
SO...
BREAKING POINT!!
BOOOM
GAH ?!
IDIOT! WHAT GOOD IS BLASTING ROCKS HERE ?!
AWOOOON
SSSSSHHHHH
BOK BOK

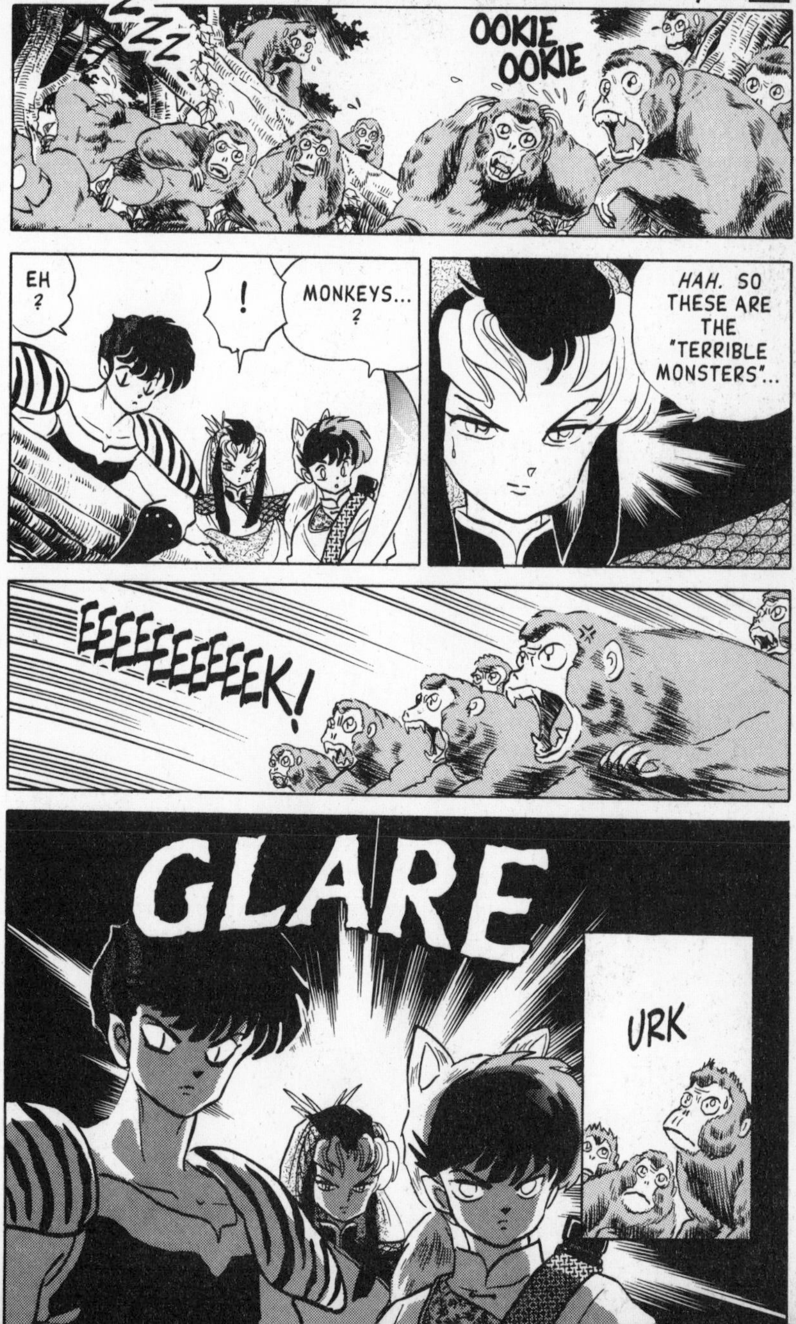
ZZZZ
OOKIE OOKIE
EH ?
!
MONKEYS... ?
HAH. SO THESE ARE THE "TERRIBLE MONSTERS"...
EEEEEEEEEEEK!
GLARE
URK

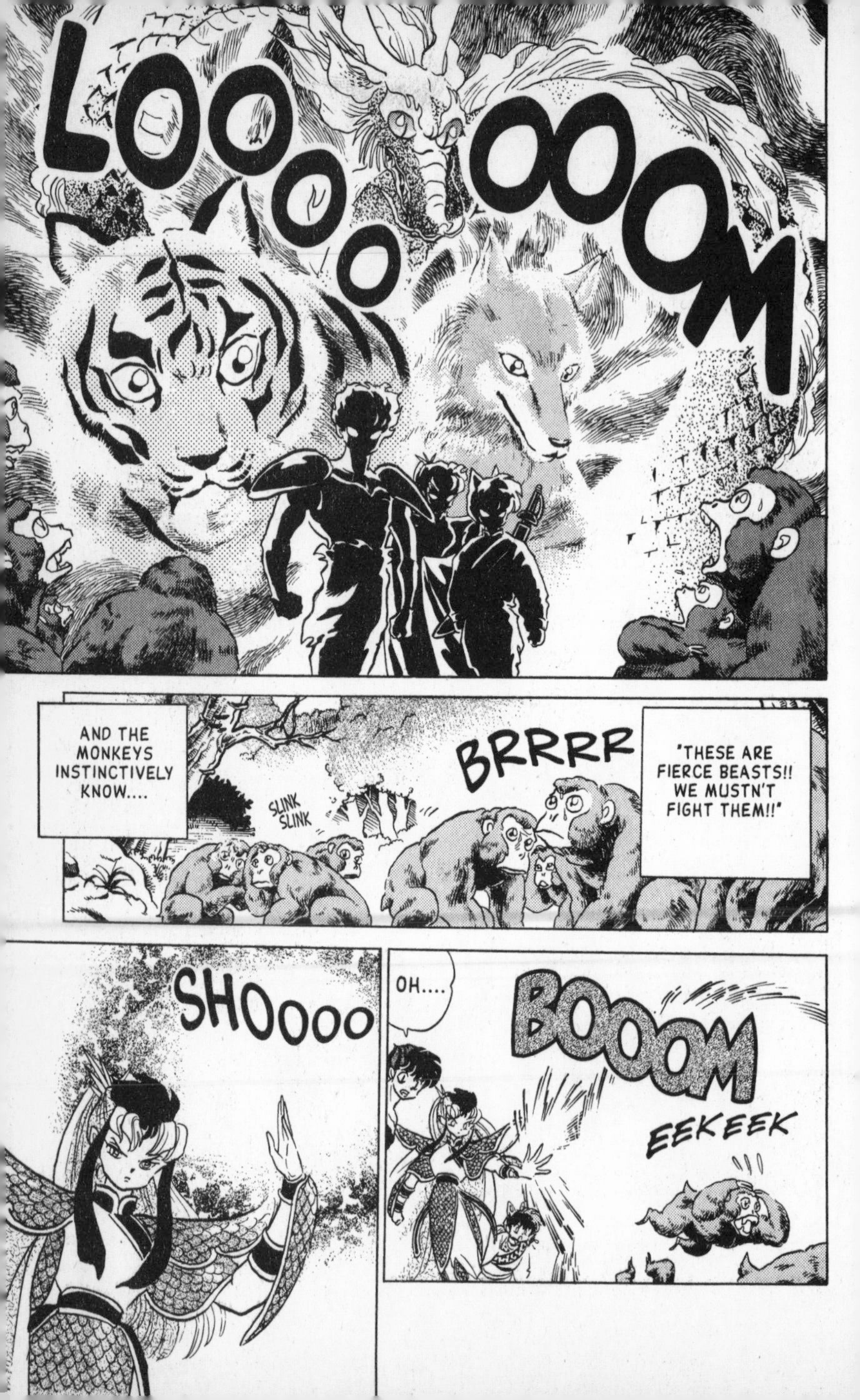
LOOOOOOOOOM
AND THE MONKEYS INSTINCTIVELY KNOW....
SLINK SLINK
BRRRR
"THESE ARE FIERCE BEASTS!! WE MUSTN'T FIGHT THEM!!"
SHOOOOO
OH....
BOOOM
EEKEEK

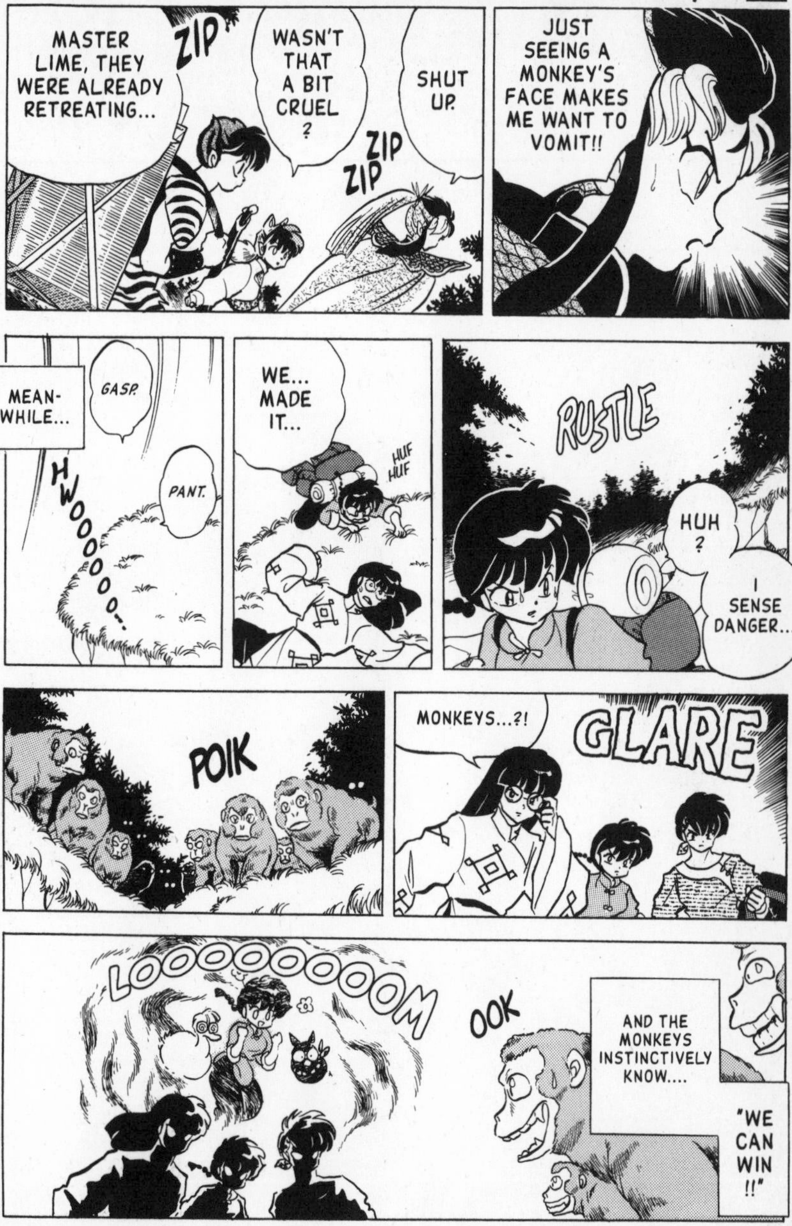
MASTER LIME, THEY WERE ALREADY RETREATING...
ZIP
WASN'T THAT A BIT CRUEL?
SHUT UP.
ZIP ZIP
JUST SEEING A MONKEY'S FACE MAKES ME WANT TO VOMIT!!
MEAN-WHILE...
GASP.
PANT.
HWOOOOOOO...
WE... MADE IT...
HUF HUF
RUSTLE
HUH?
I SENSE DANGER...
POIK
MONKEYS...?!
GLARE
LOOOOOOOOOM
OOK
AND THE MONKEYS INSTINCTIVELY KNOW....
"WE CAN WIN!!"

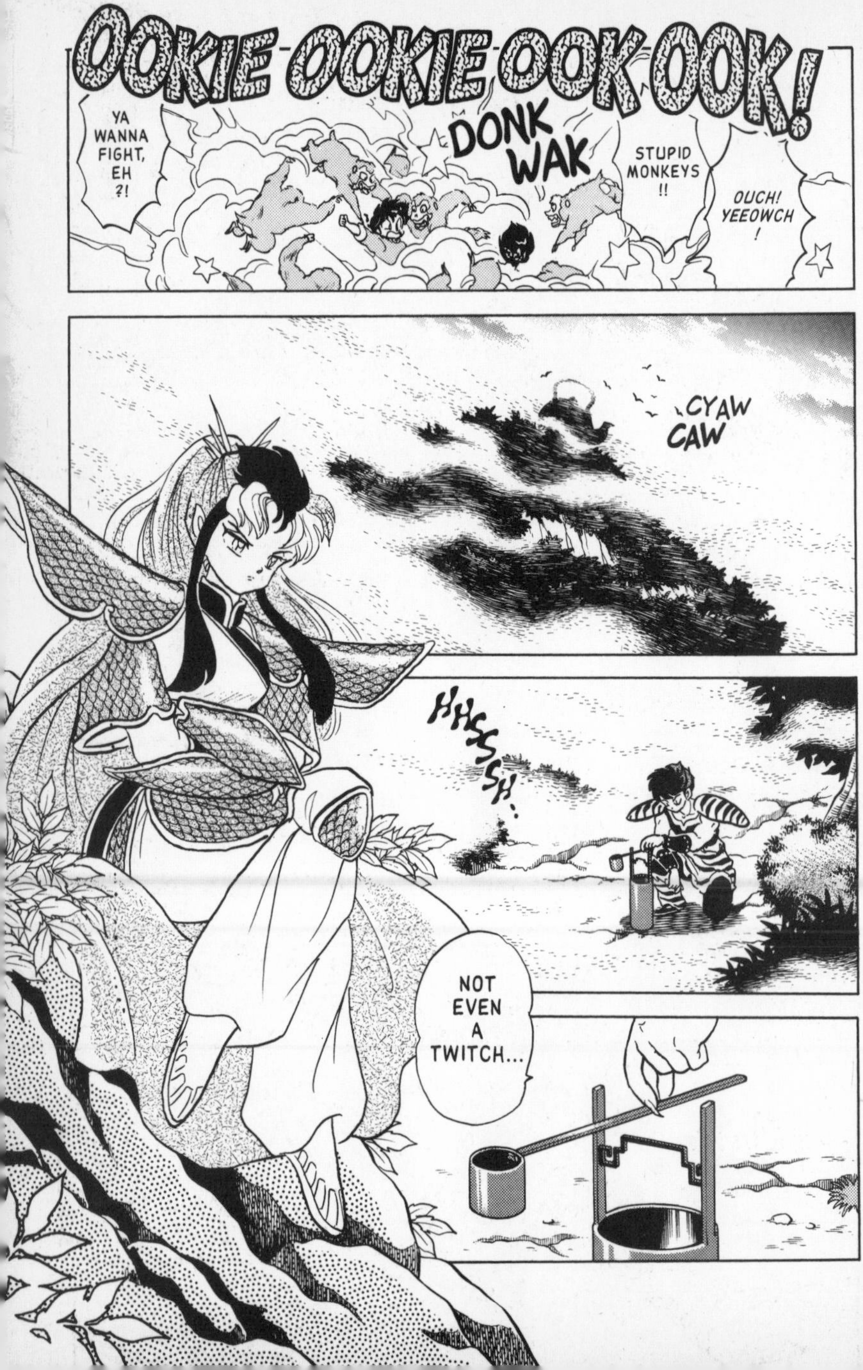
OOKIE OOKIE OOK OOK!
YA WANNA FIGHT, EH ?!
DONK
WAK
STUPID MONKEYS !!
OUCH! YEEOWCH !
CYAW CAW
HHSSSH...
NOT EVEN A TWITCH...

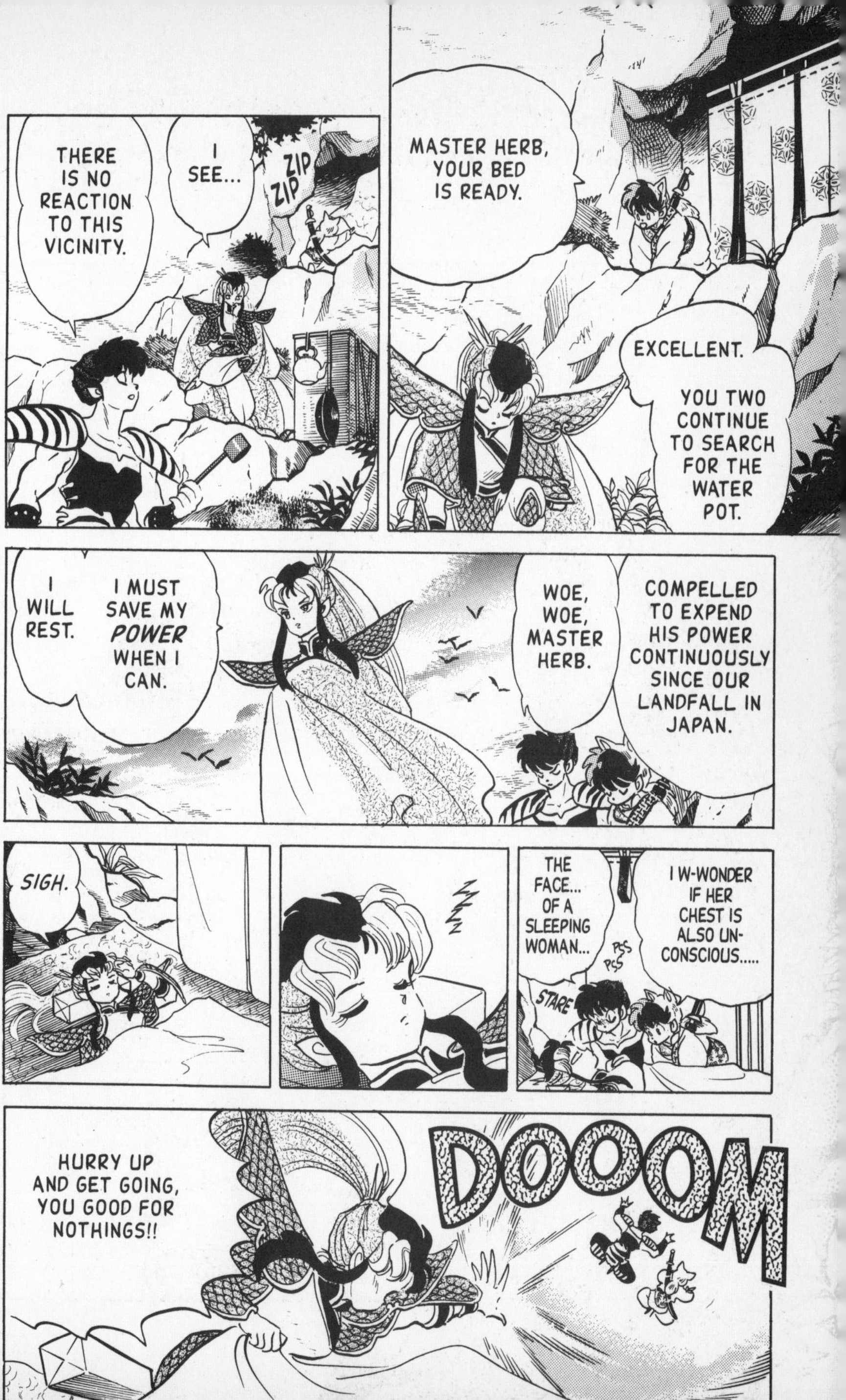
THERE IS NO REACTION TO THIS VICINITY.
I SEE...
ZIP ZIP
MASTER HERB, YOUR BED IS READY.
EXCELLENT.
YOU TWO CONTINUE TO SEARCH FOR THE WATER POT.
I WILL REST.
I MUST SAVE MY *POWER* WHEN I CAN.
WOE, WOE, MASTER HERB.
COMPELLED TO EXPEND HIS POWER CONTINUOUSLY SINCE OUR LANDFALL IN JAPAN.
SIGH.
THE FACE... OF A SLEEPING WOMAN...
PSS PSS
I W-WONDER IF HER CHEST IS ALSO UN-CONSCIOUS.....
STARE
HURRY UP AND GET GOING, YOU GOOD FOR NOTHINGS!!
DOOOOM

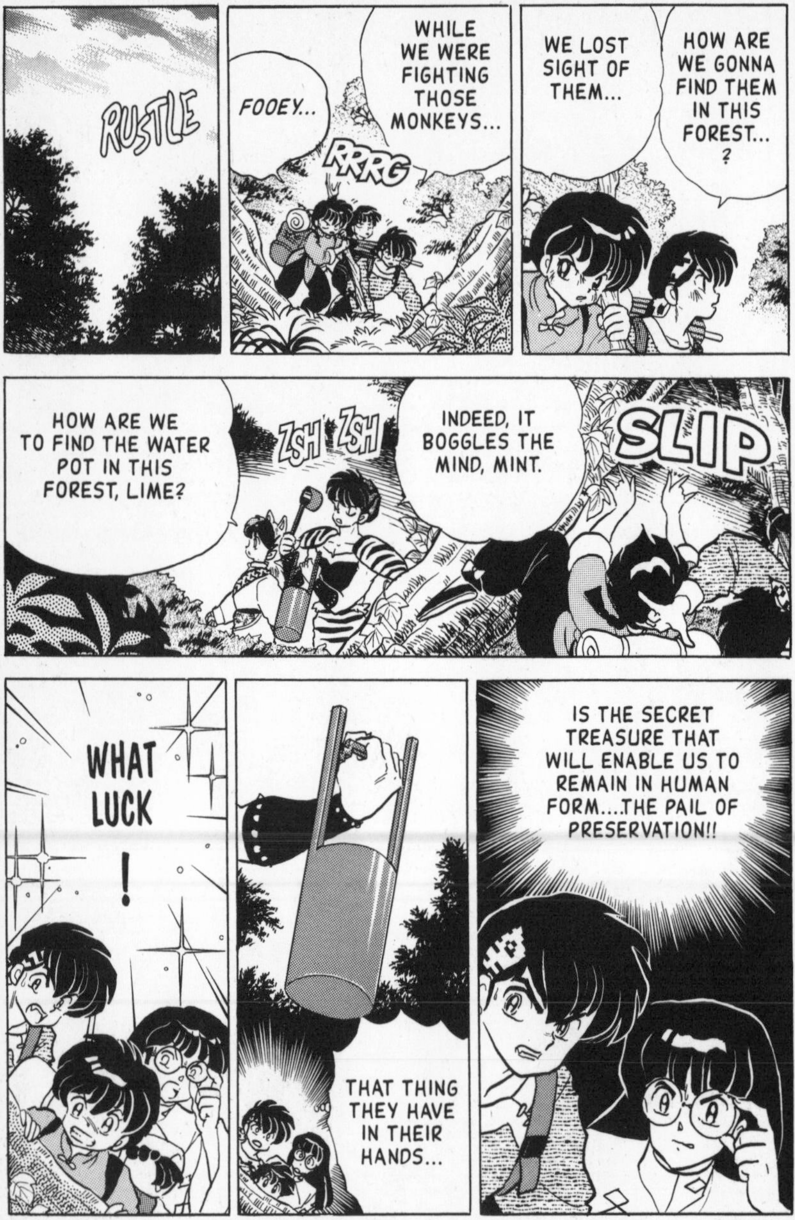

RUSTLE
FOOEY...
WHILE WE WERE FIGHTING THOSE MONKEYS...
RRRG
WE LOST SIGHT OF THEM...
HOW ARE WE GONNA FIND THEM IN THIS FOREST...?
HOW ARE WE TO FIND THE WATER POT IN THIS FOREST, LIME?
ZSH ZSH
INDEED, IT BOGGLES THE MIND, MINT.
SLIP
WHAT LUCK!
THAT THING THEY HAVE IN THEIR HANDS...
IS THE SECRET TREASURE THAT WILL ENABLE US TO REMAIN IN HUMAN FORM....THE PAIL OF PRESERVATION!!

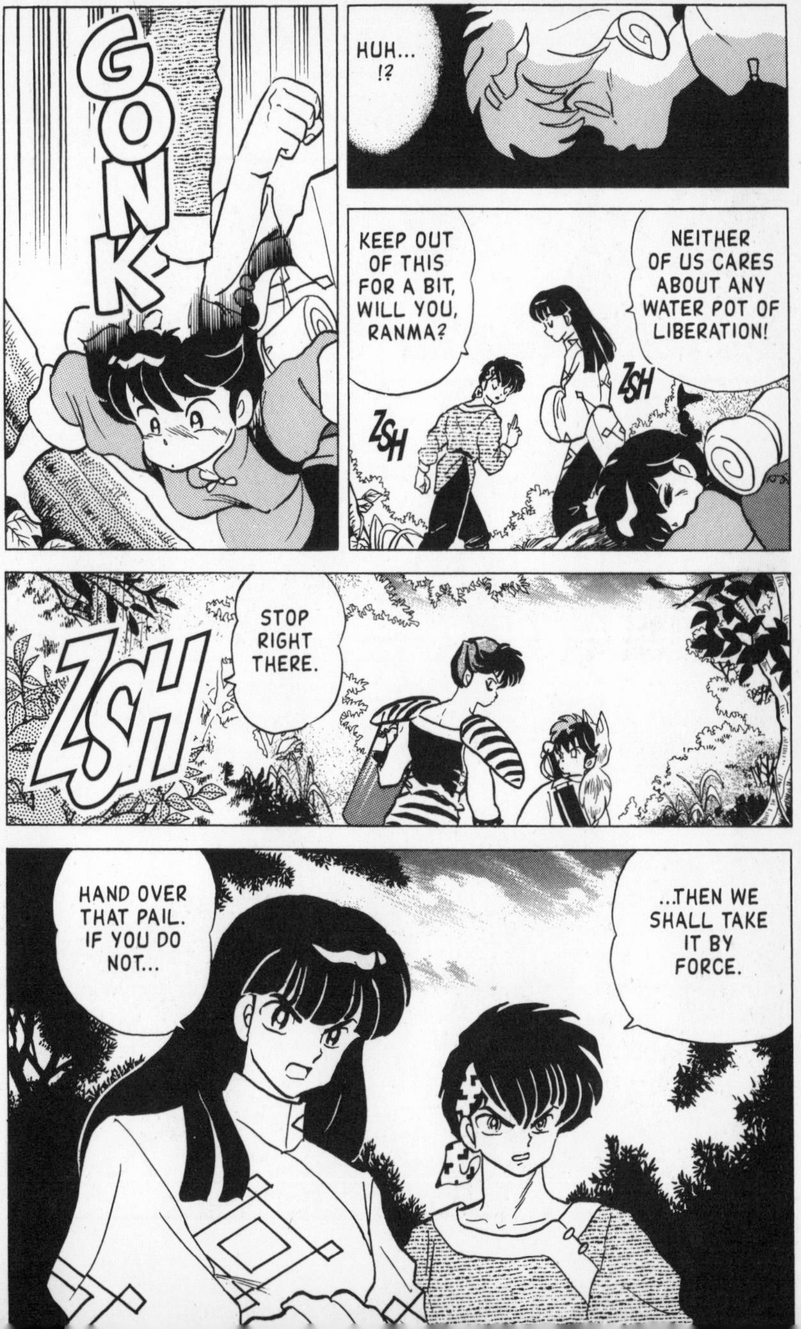
GONK
HUH... !?
KEEP OUT OF THIS FOR A BIT, WILL YOU, RANMA?
ZSH
NEITHER OF US CARES ABOUT ANY WATER POT OF LIBERATION!
ZSH
ZSH
STOP RIGHT THERE.
HAND OVER THAT PAIL. IF YOU DO NOT...
...THEN WE SHALL TAKE IT BY FORCE.

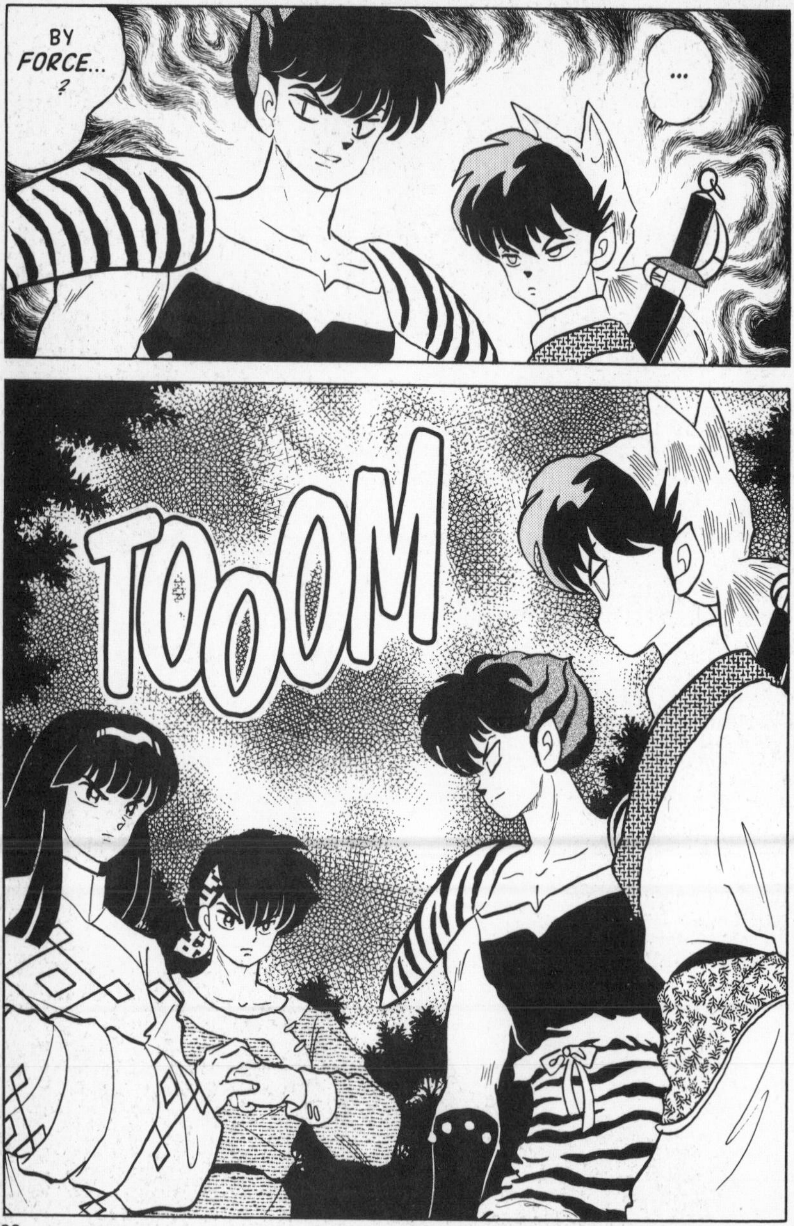
BY FORCE... ?
...
TOOOM

Part 6

DEATH ON TREASURE MOUNTAIN

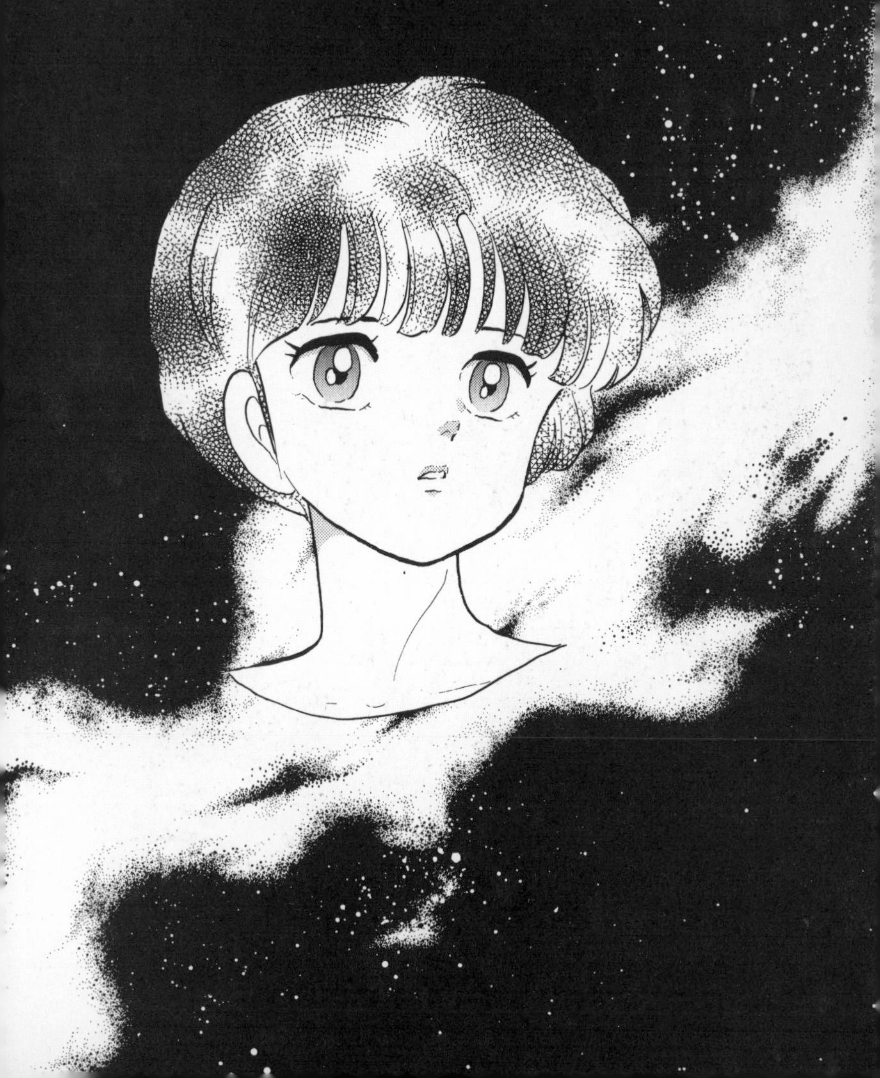

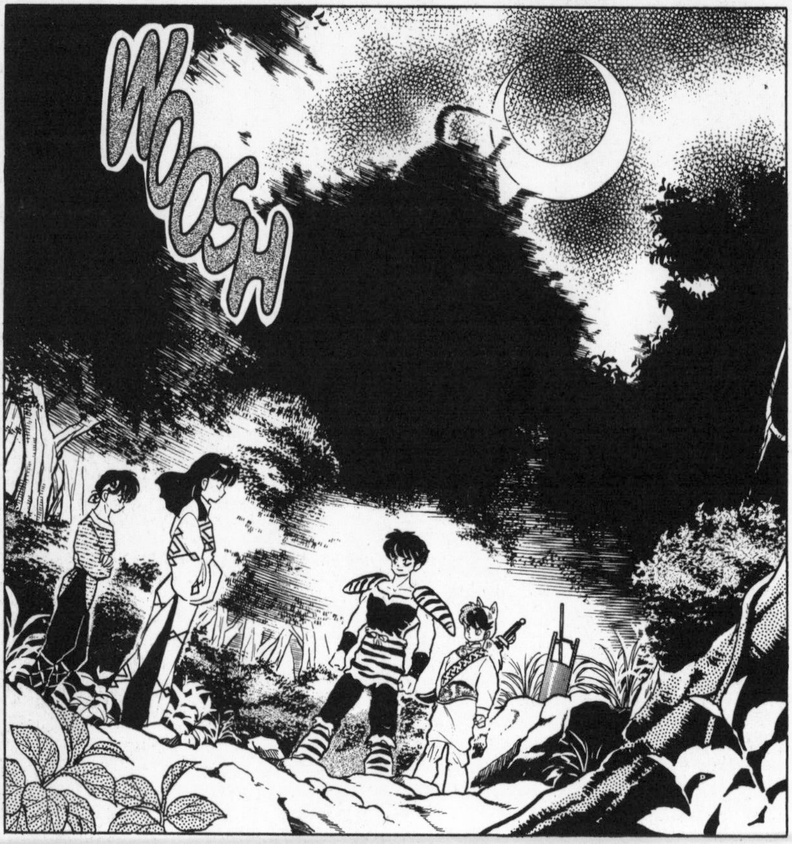
WOOSH

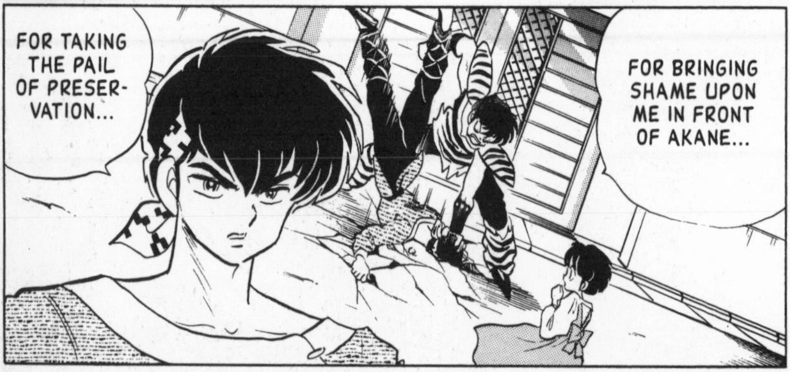
FOR TAKING THE PAIL OF PRESER-VATION...
FOR BRINGING SHAME UPON ME IN FRONT OF AKANE...

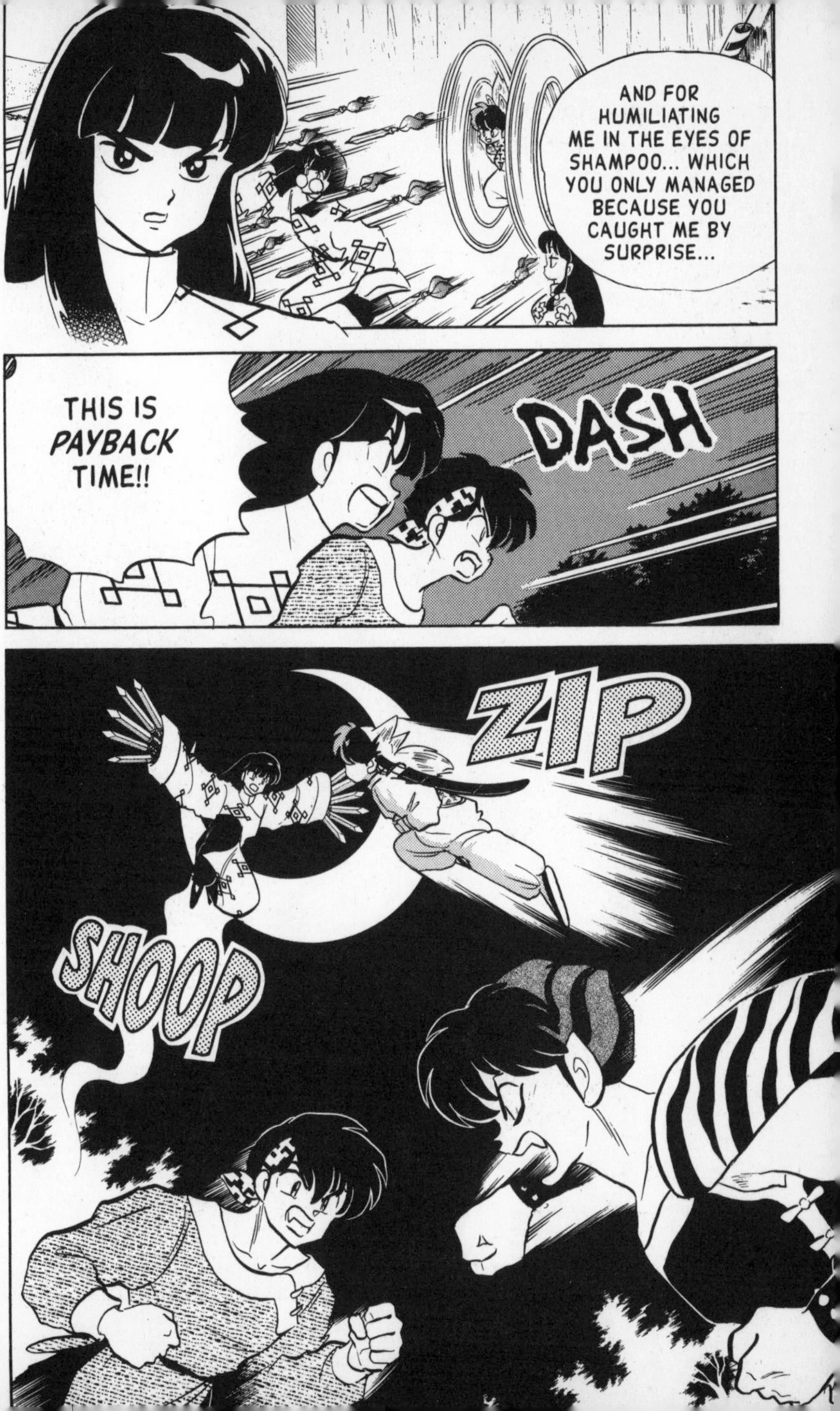
AND FOR HUMILIATING ME IN THE EYES OF SHAMPOO... WHICH YOU ONLY MANAGED BECAUSE YOU CAUGHT ME BY SURPRISE...
THIS IS *PAYBACK* TIME!!
DASH
ZIP
SHOOP

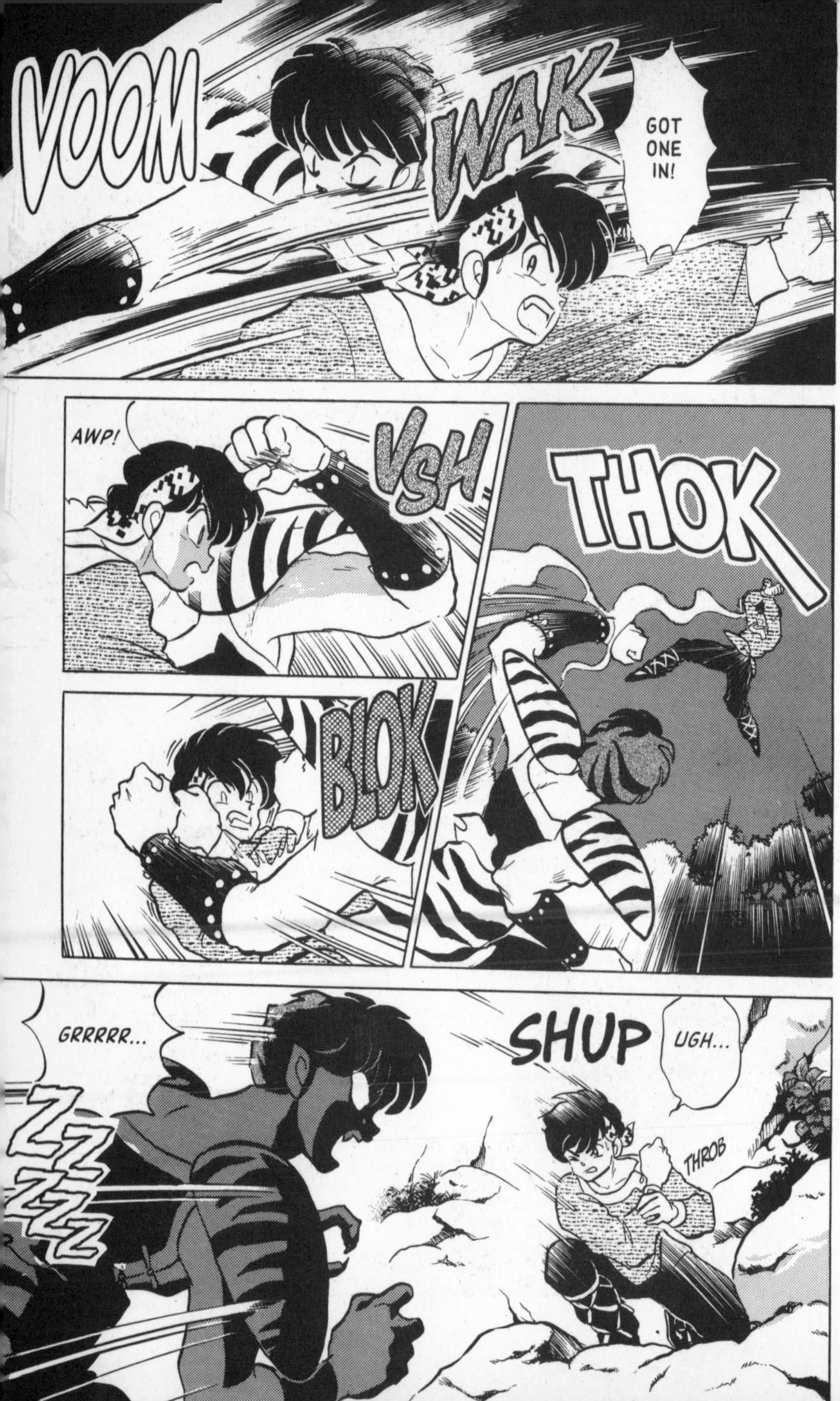
VOOM
WAK
GOT ONE IN!
AWP!
VSH
BLOK
THOK
GRRRRR...
ZZZZZZ
SHUP
UGH...
THROB

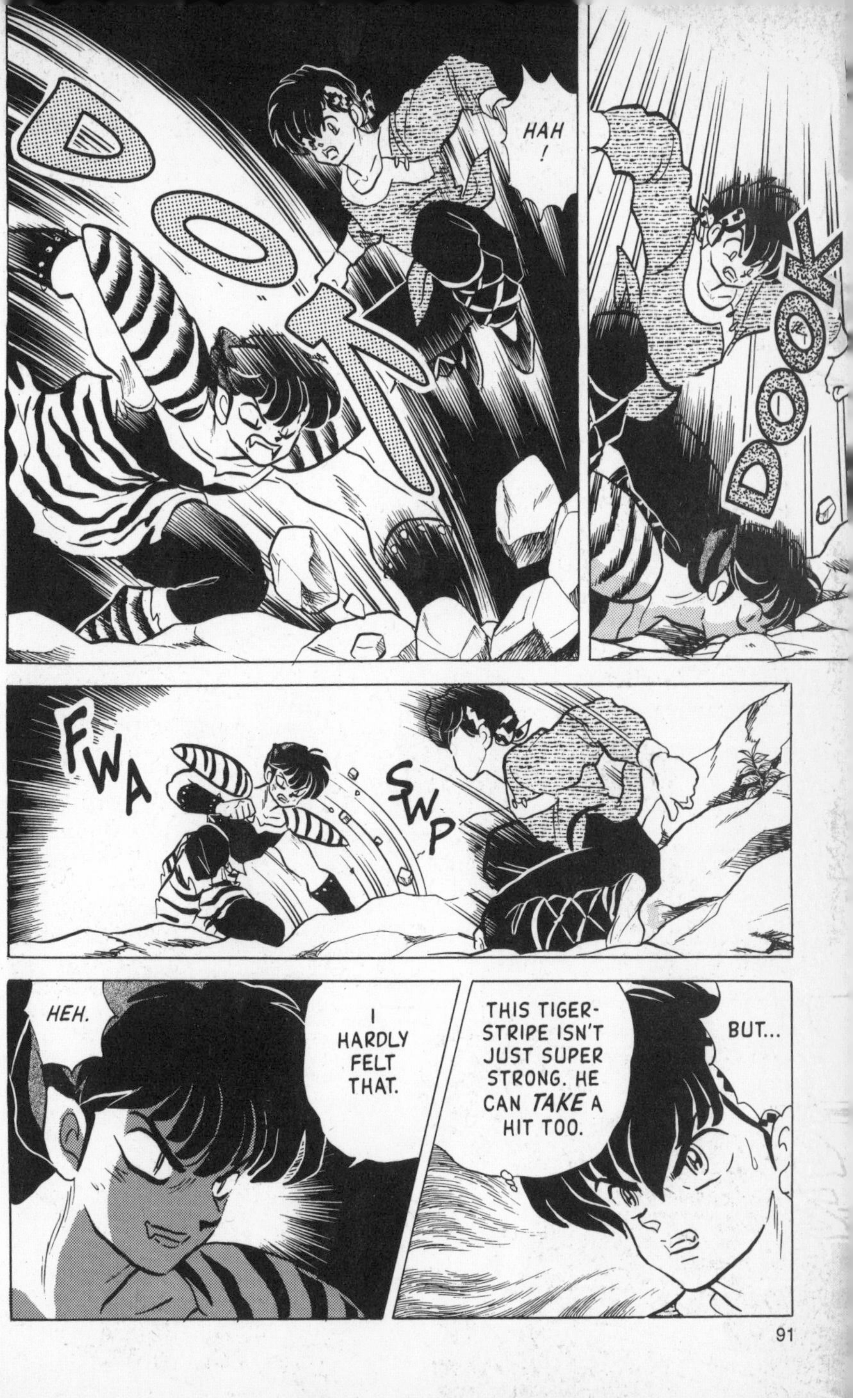
DOOM
HAH !
DOOK
FWA
SWP
HEH.
I HARDLY FELT THAT.
THIS TIGER-STRIPE ISN'T JUST SUPER STRONG. HE CAN *TAKE* A HIT TOO.
BUT...

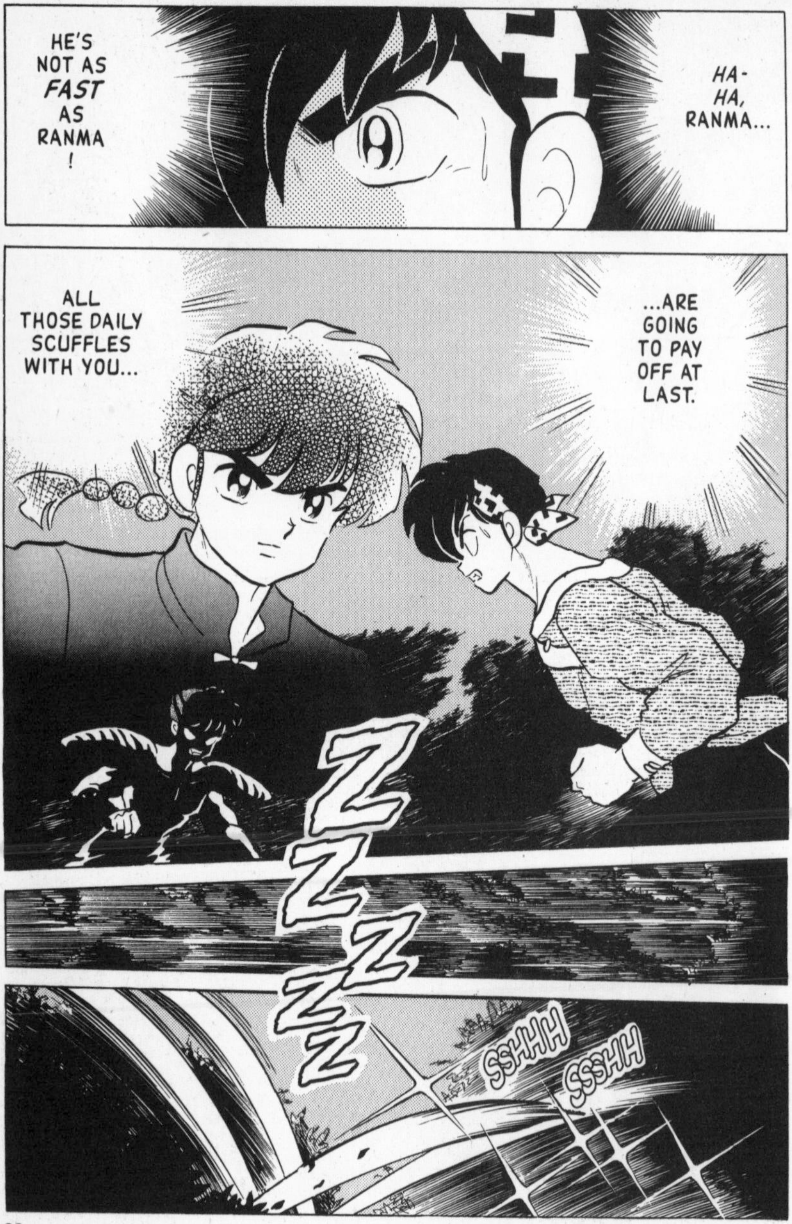
HE'S NOT AS *FAST* AS RANMA!
HA-HA, RANMA...
ALL THOSE DAILY SCUFFLES WITH YOU...
...ARE GOING TO PAY OFF AT LAST.
ZZZZZ
SSHHH
SSSHH

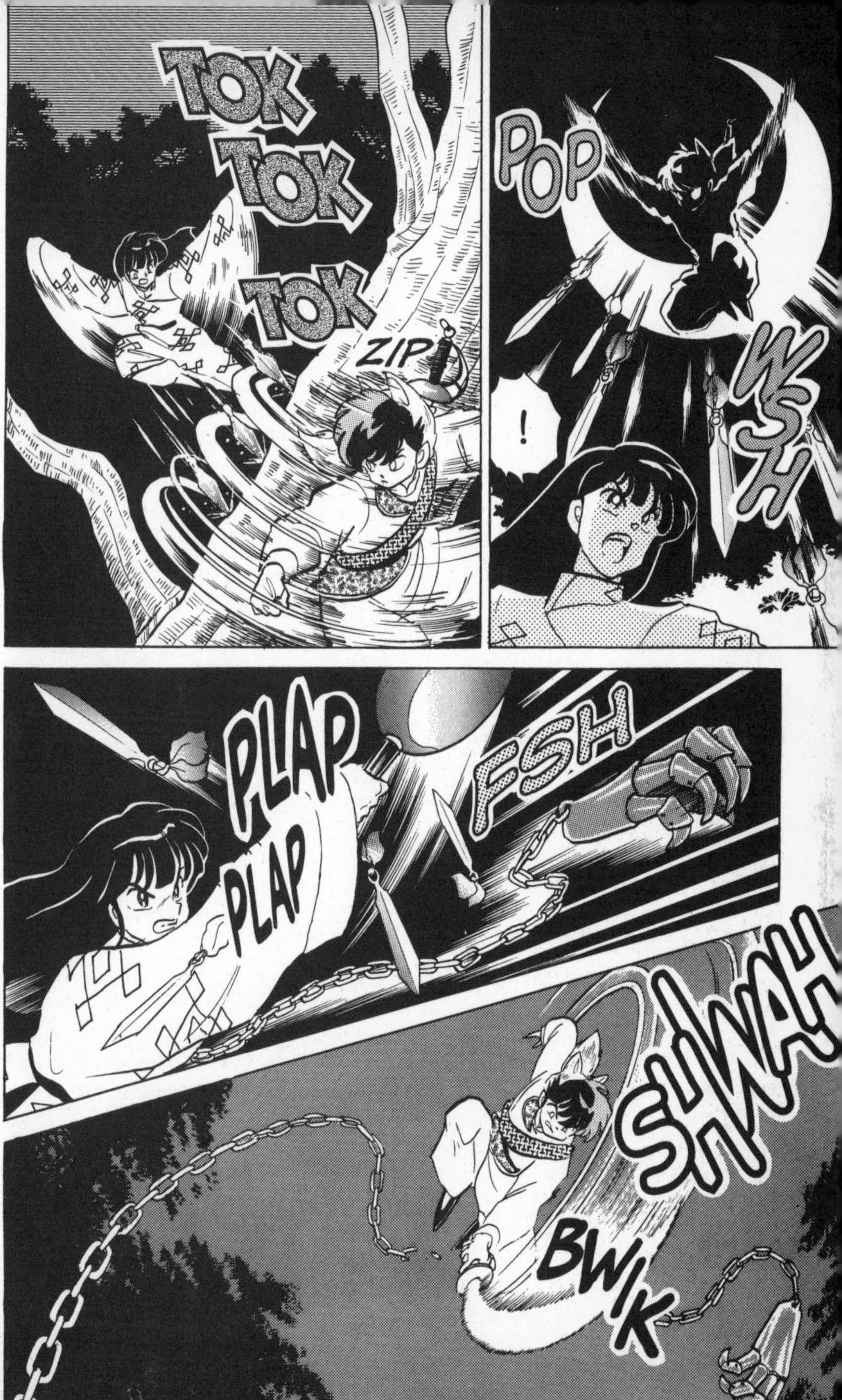
TOK
TOK
TOK
ZIP
POP
!
WSH
PLAP
PLAP
FSH
SHWAH
BWIK

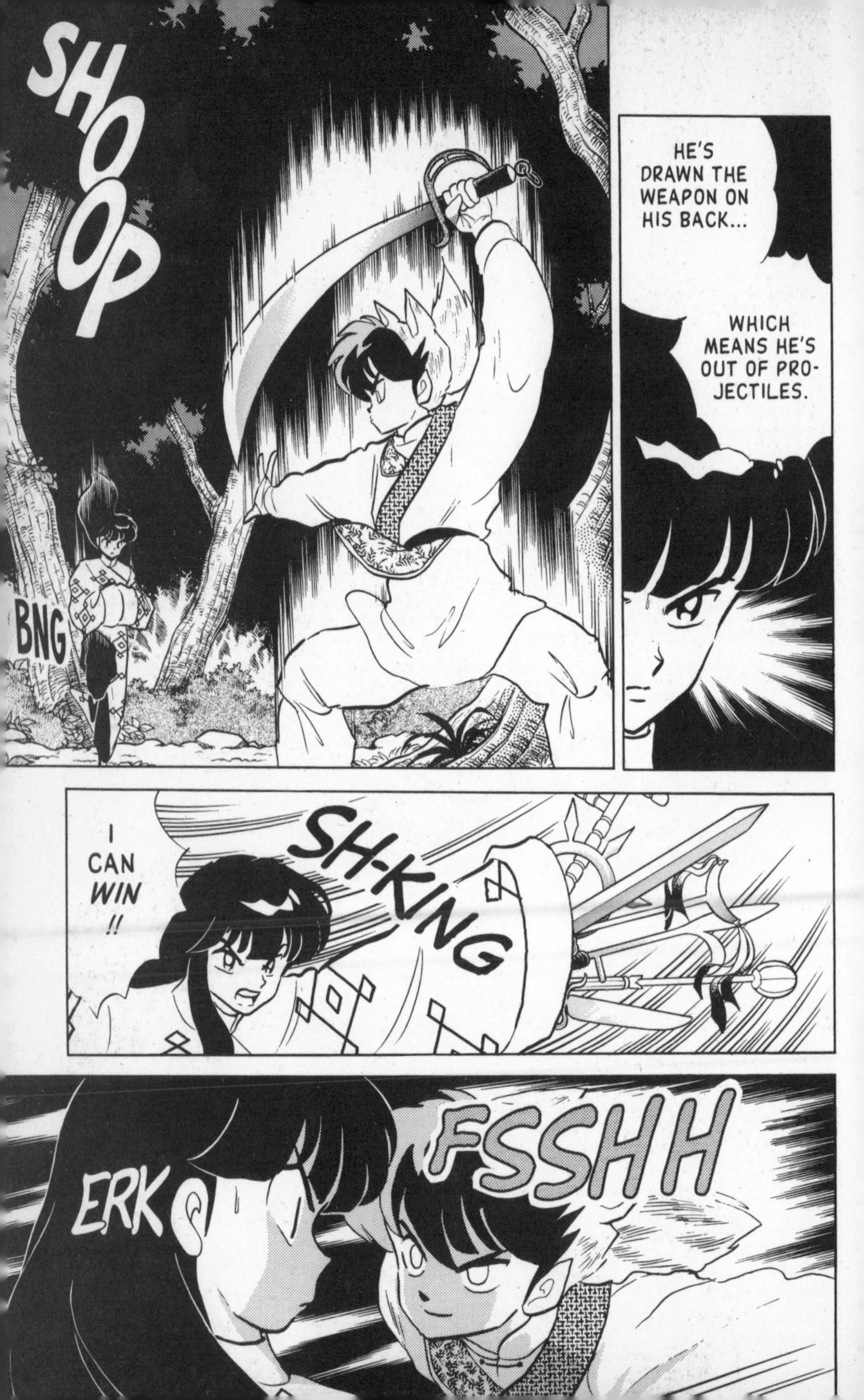
SHOOP
BNG
HE'S DRAWN THE WEAPON ON HIS BACK...
WHICH MEANS HE'S OUT OF PRO-JECTILES.
I CAN *WIN* !!
SH-KING
ERK
FSSHH

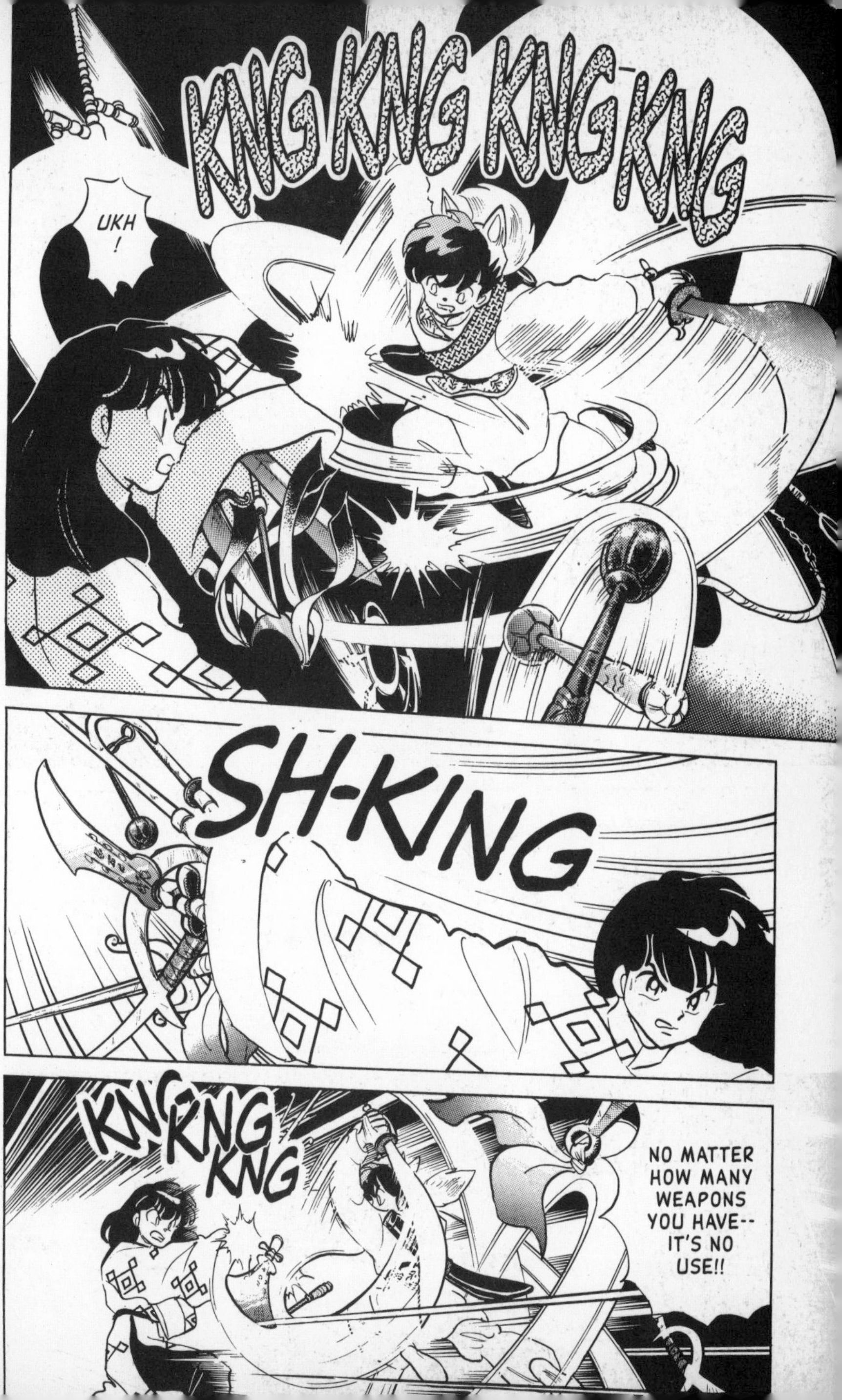
KNG KNG KNG KNG
UKH!
SH-KING
KNG KNG KNG
NO MATTER HOW MANY WEAPONS YOU HAVE-- IT'S NO USE!!

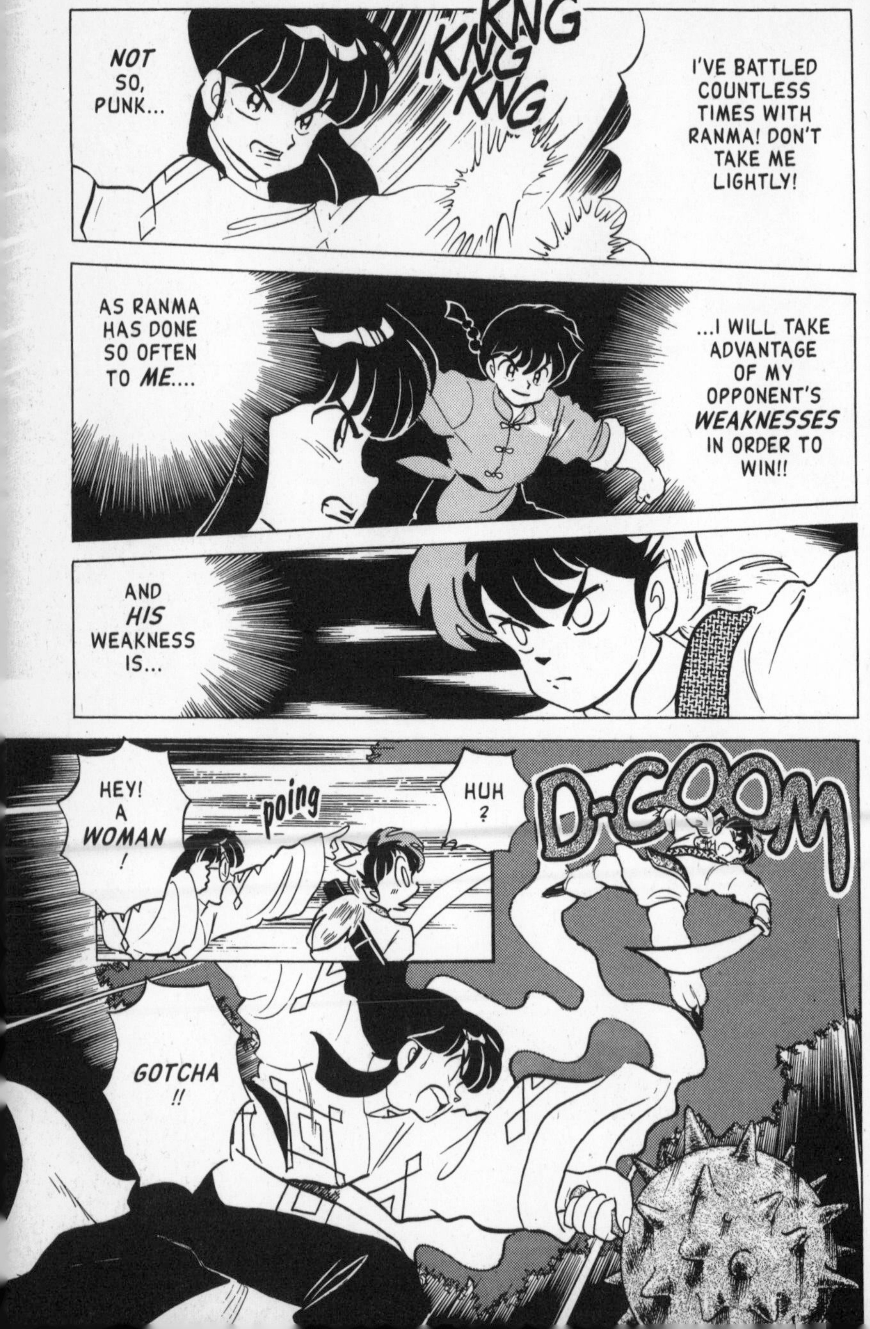
NOT SO, PUNK...
KNG KNG KNG KNG
I'VE BATTLED COUNTLESS TIMES WITH RANMA! DON'T TAKE ME LIGHTLY!
AS RANMA HAS DONE SO OFTEN TO ME....
...I WILL TAKE ADVANTAGE OF MY OPPONENT'S WEAKNESSES IN ORDER TO WIN!!
AND HIS WEAKNESS IS...
HEY! A WOMAN!
poing
HUH?
D-COOM
GOTCHA!!

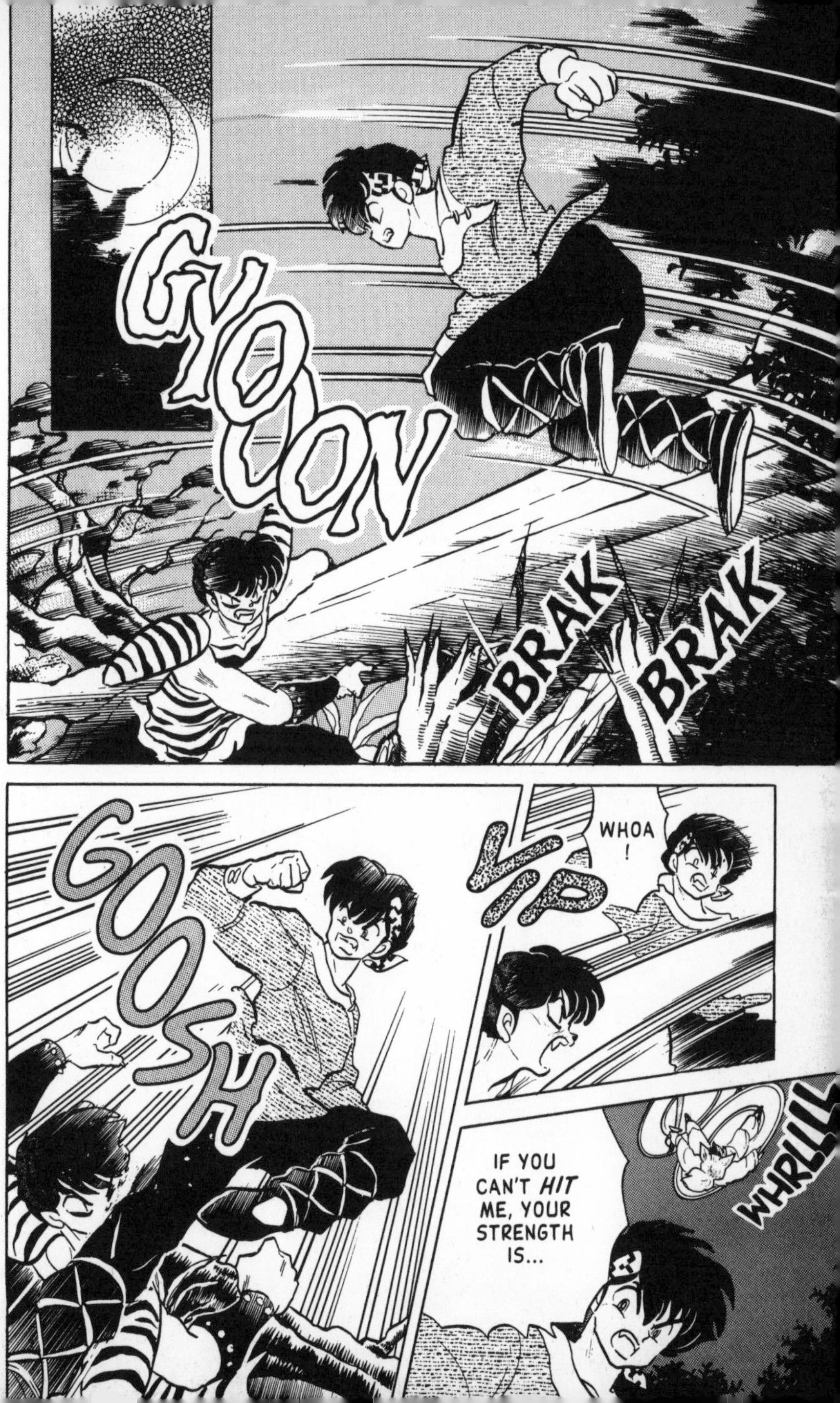
GYOOON
BRAK
BRAK
WHOA!
YIP
IF YOU CAN'T *HIT* ME, YOUR STRENGTH IS...
WHRLLL
GOOSH

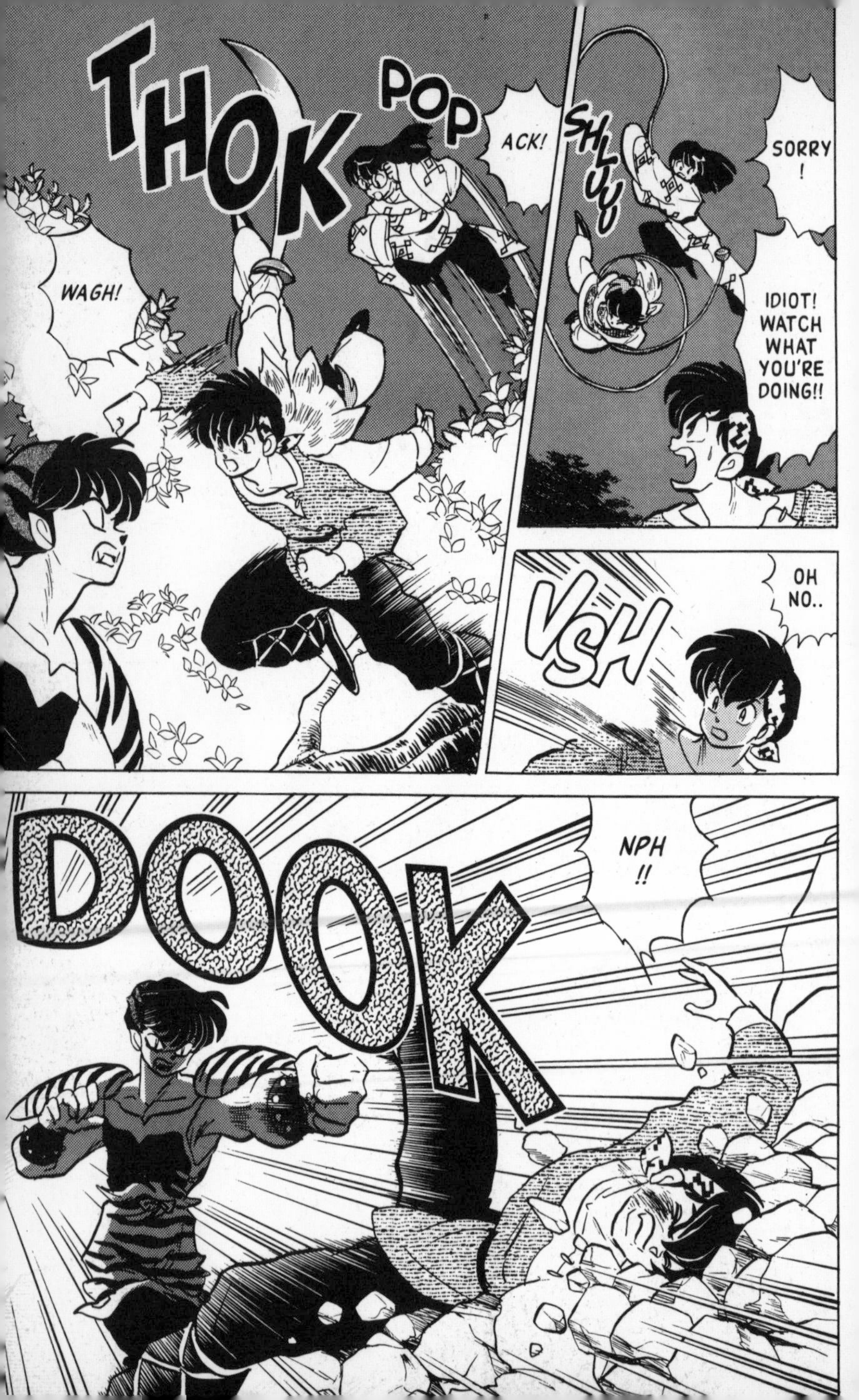
THOK
POP
ACK!
WAGH!
SHLUUU
SORRY!
IDIOT! WATCH WHAT YOU'RE DOING!!
VSH
OH NO..
DOOK
NPH!!

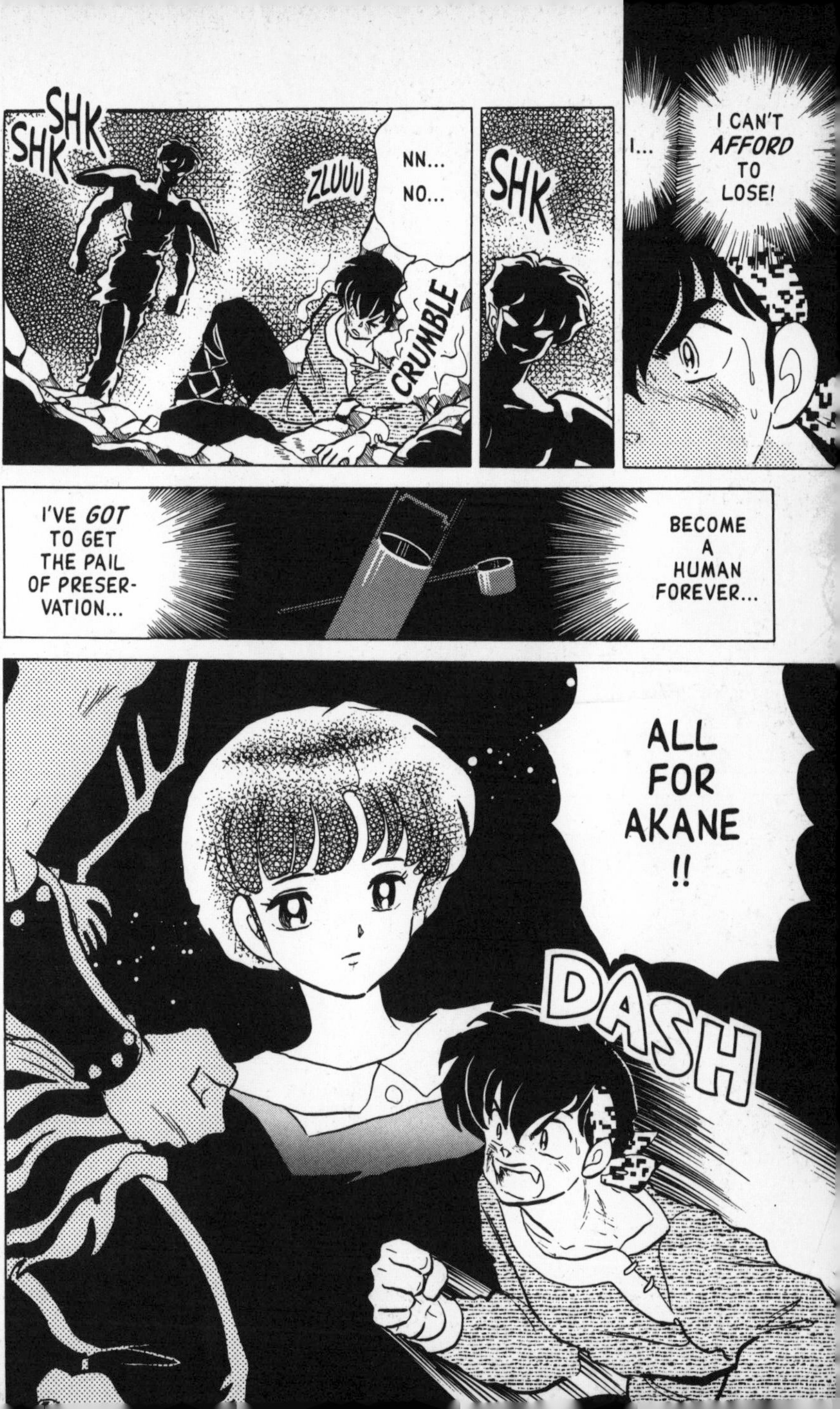
SHK SHK
ZLUUU
NN... NO...
CRUMBLE
SHK
I...
I CAN'T *AFFORD* TO LOSE!
I'VE *GOT* TO GET THE PAIL OF PRESER-VATION...
BECOME A HUMAN FOREVER...
ALL FOR AKANE !!
DASH

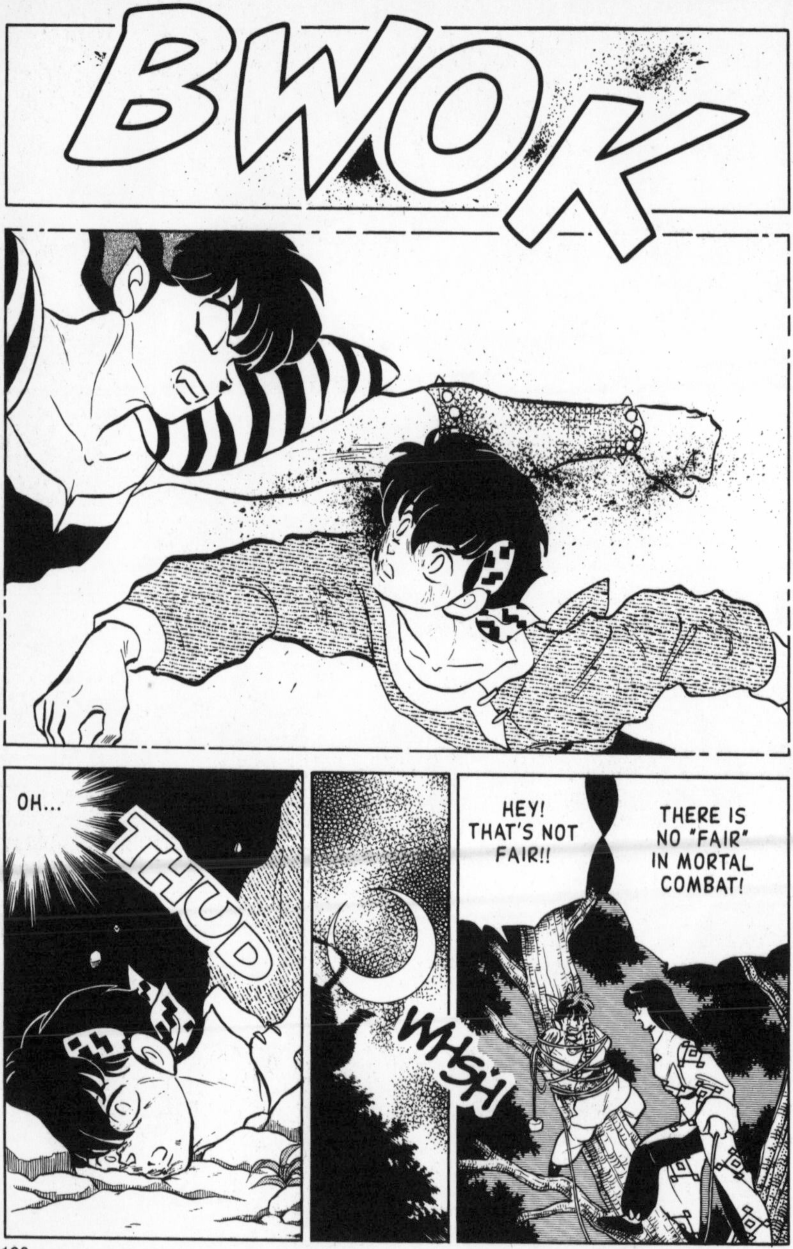
BWOK
OH...
THUD
WHSH
HEY! THAT'S NOT FAIR!!
THERE IS NO "FAIR" IN MORTAL COMBAT!

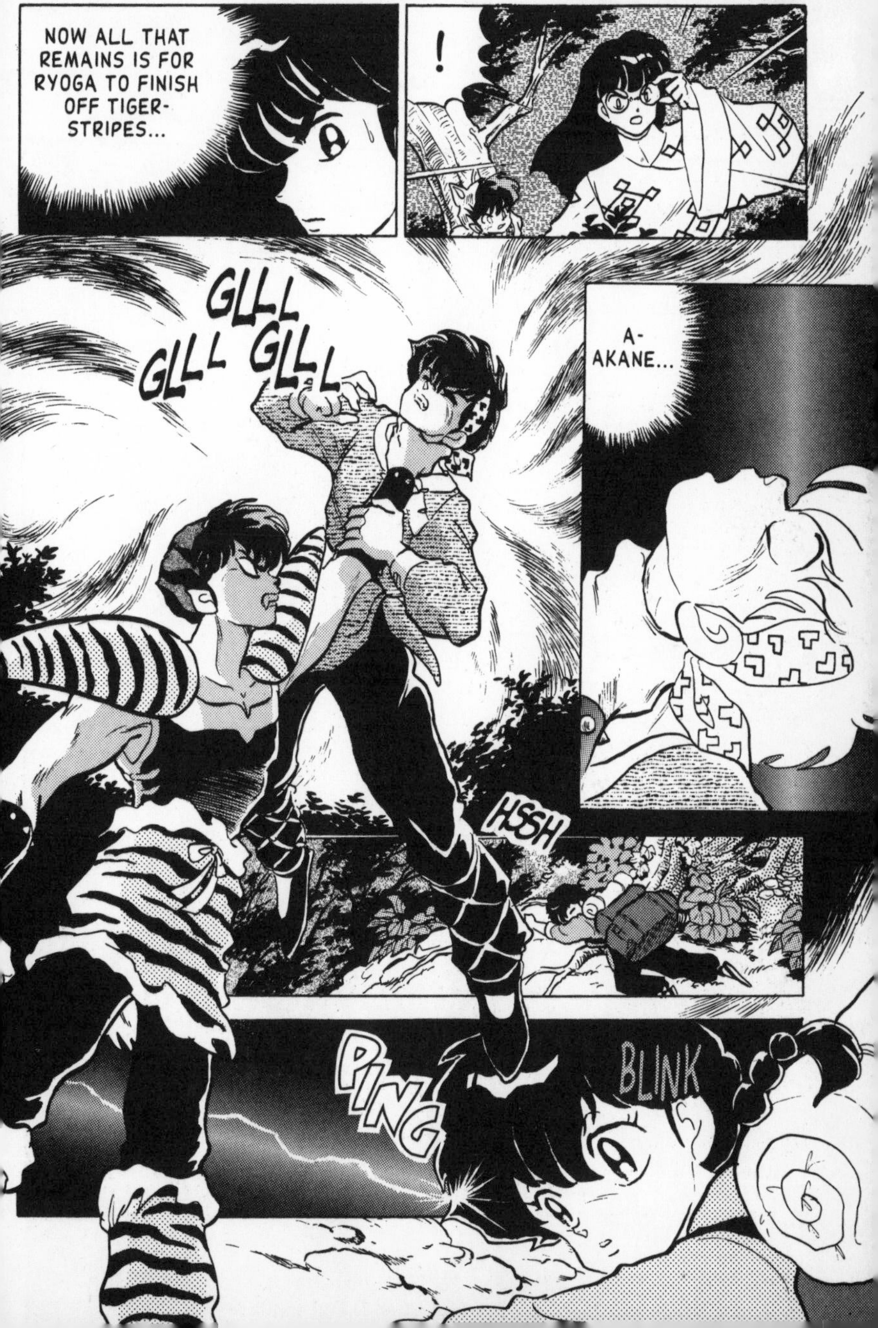
NOW ALL THAT REMAINS IS FOR RYOGA TO FINISH OFF TIGER-STRIPES...
!
GLLL GLLL GLLL
A- AKANE...
HSSH
PING
BLINK

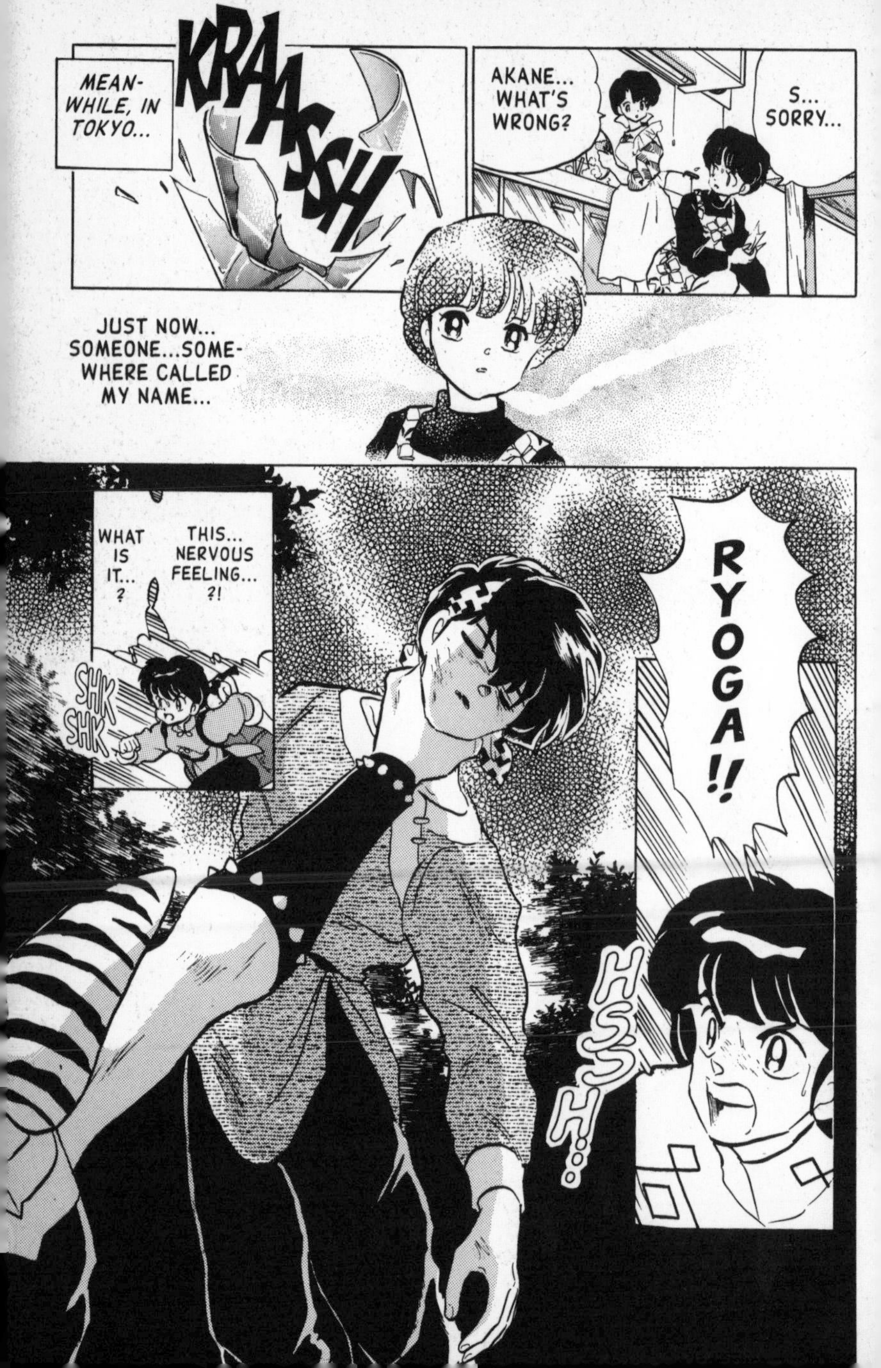
MEAN-
WHILE, IN
TOKYO...
KRAASSH
AKANE...
WHAT'S
WRONG?
S...
SORRY...
JUST NOW...
SOMEONE...SOME-
WHERE CALLED
MY NAME...
WHAT
IS
IT...
?
THIS...
NERVOUS
FEELING...
?!
SHK
SHK
RYOGA!!
HSSH...

THE TRAGEDY OF THE PAIL

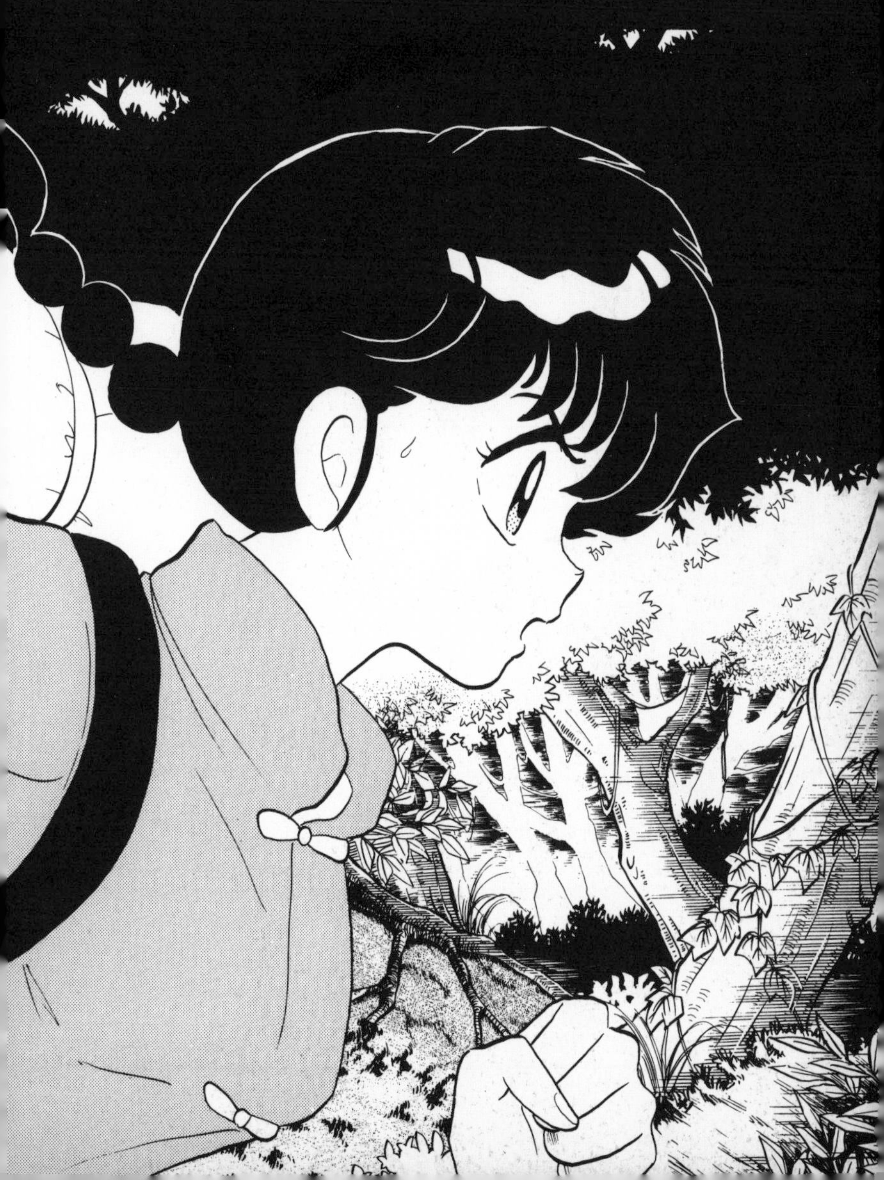

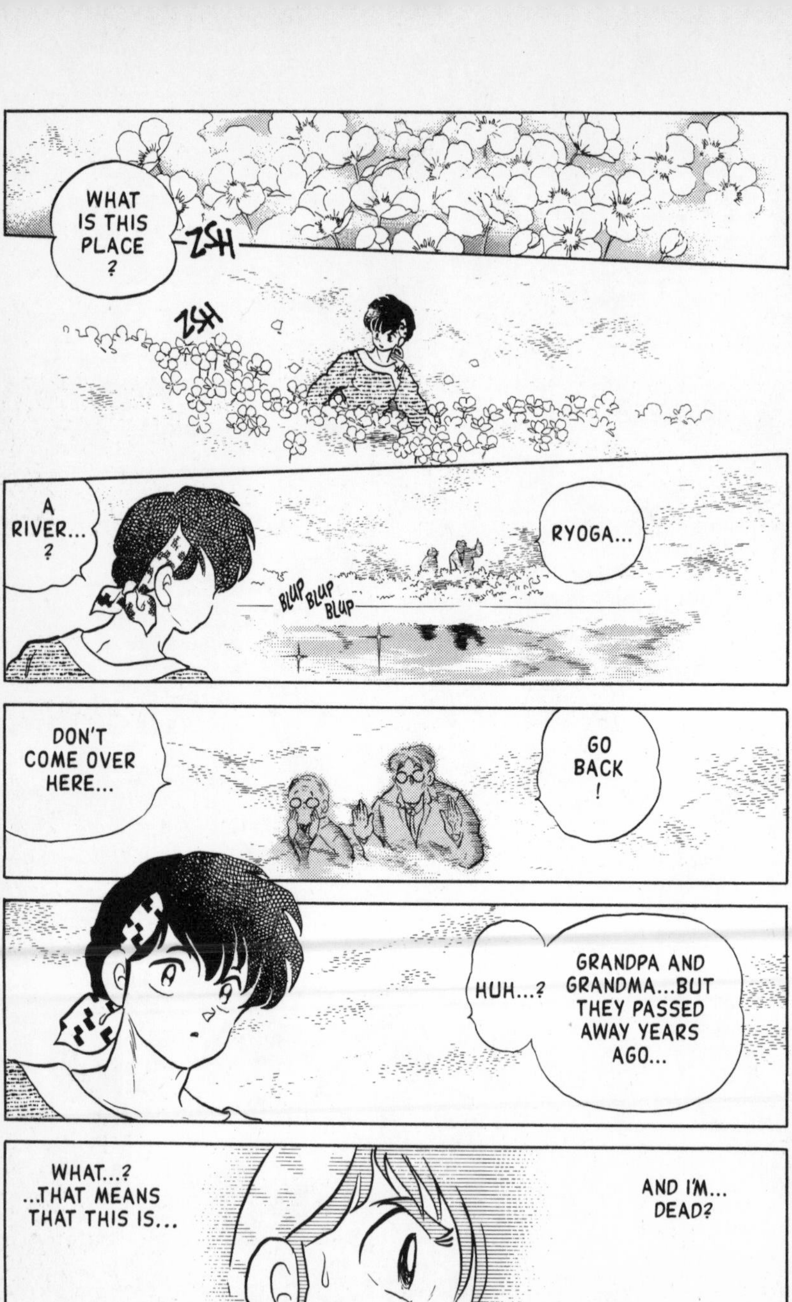
WHAT IS THIS PLACE ?
ZSH
ZSH
A RIVER... ?
RYOGA...
BLUP BLUP BLUP
DON'T COME OVER HERE...
GO BACK !
GRANDPA AND GRANDMA...BUT THEY PASSED AWAY YEARS AGO...
HUH...?
WHAT...? ...THAT MEANS THAT THIS IS...
AND I'M... DEAD?

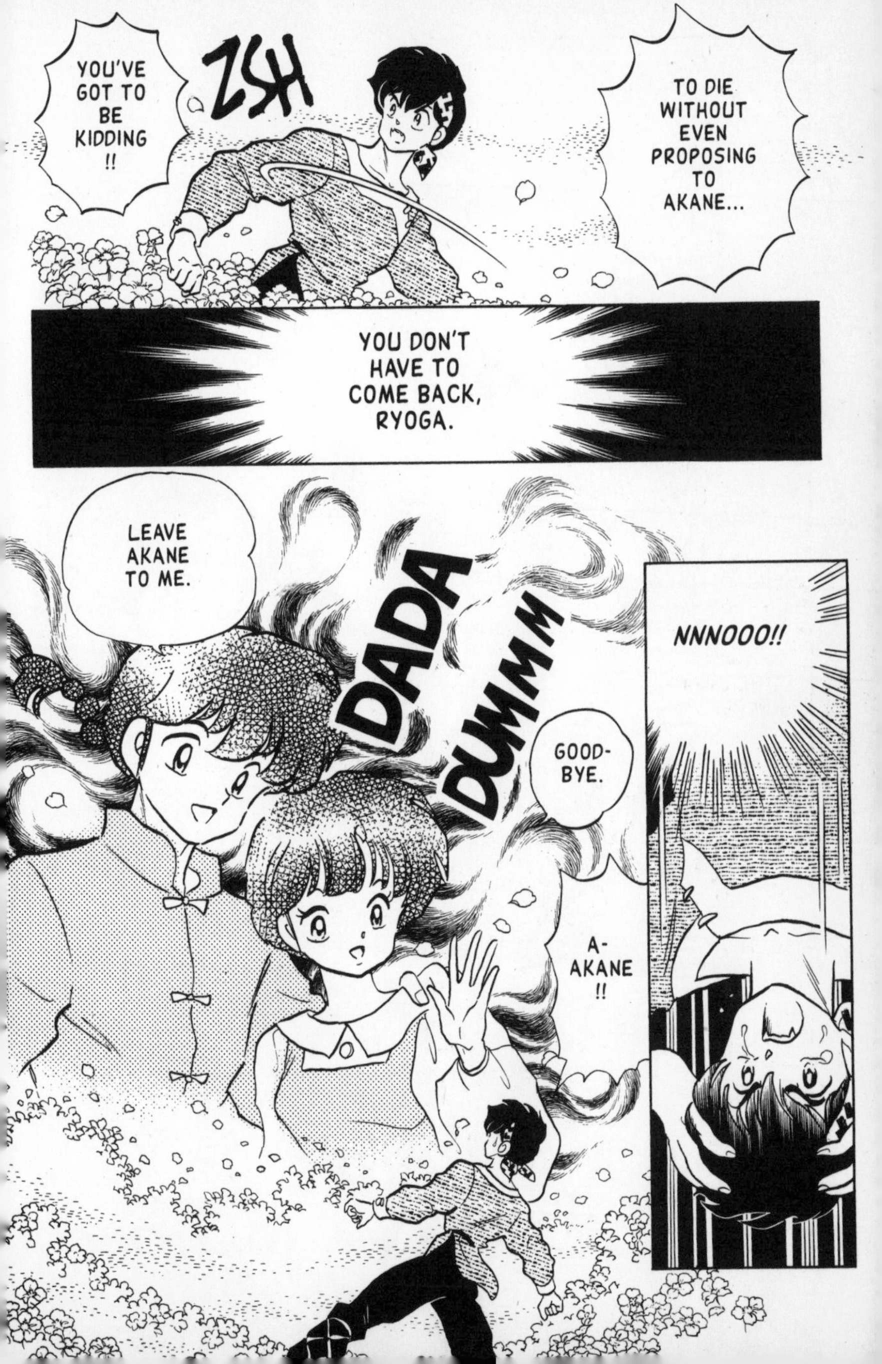
YOU'VE GOT TO BE KIDDING !!
ZSH
TO DIE WITHOUT EVEN PROPOSING TO AKANE...
YOU DON'T HAVE TO COME BACK, RYOGA.
LEAVE AKANE TO ME.
DADA DUMM
GOOD-BYE.
A-AKANE !!
NNNOOO!!

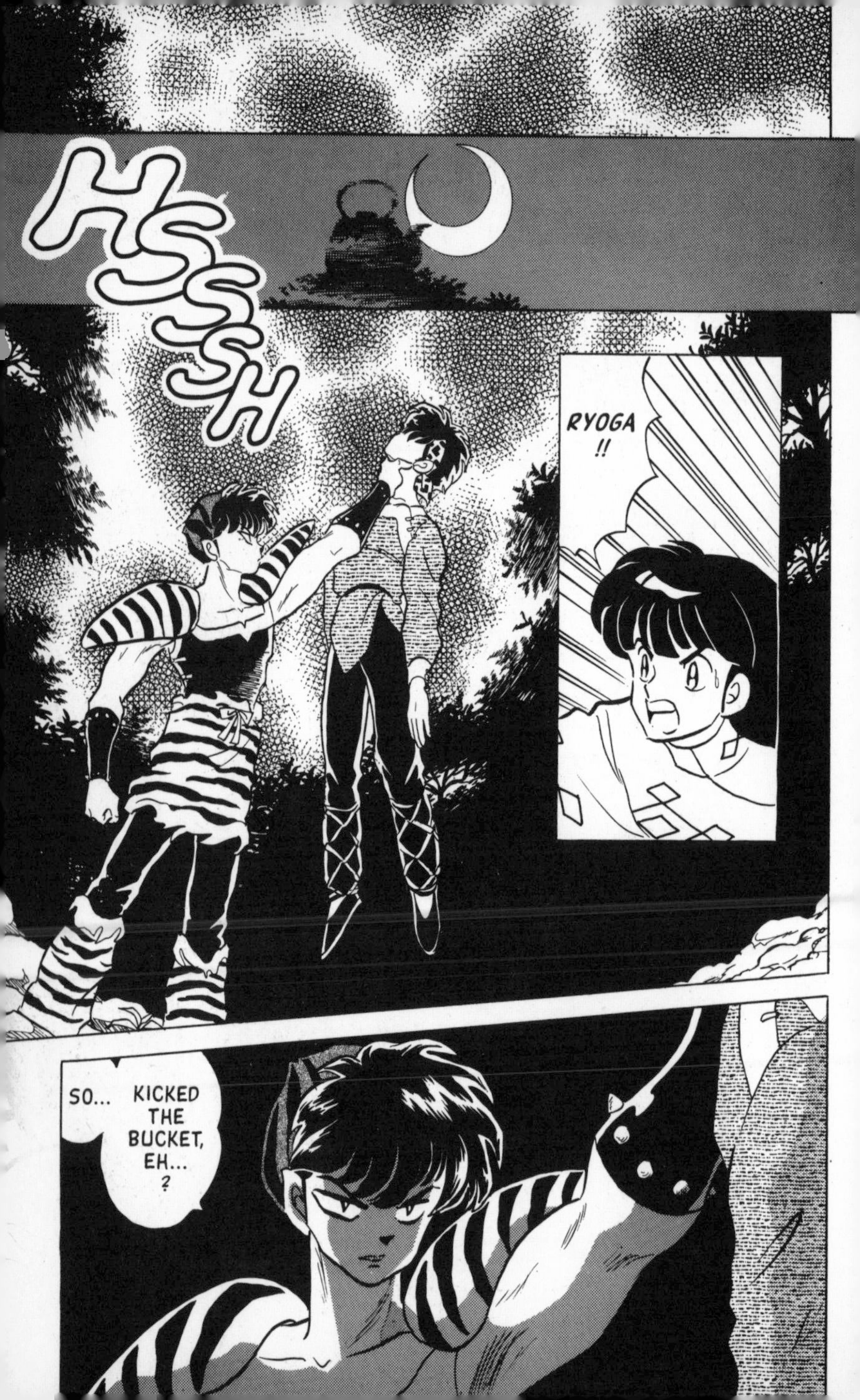
HSSSSH
RYOGA !!
SO... KICKED THE BUCKET, EH... ?

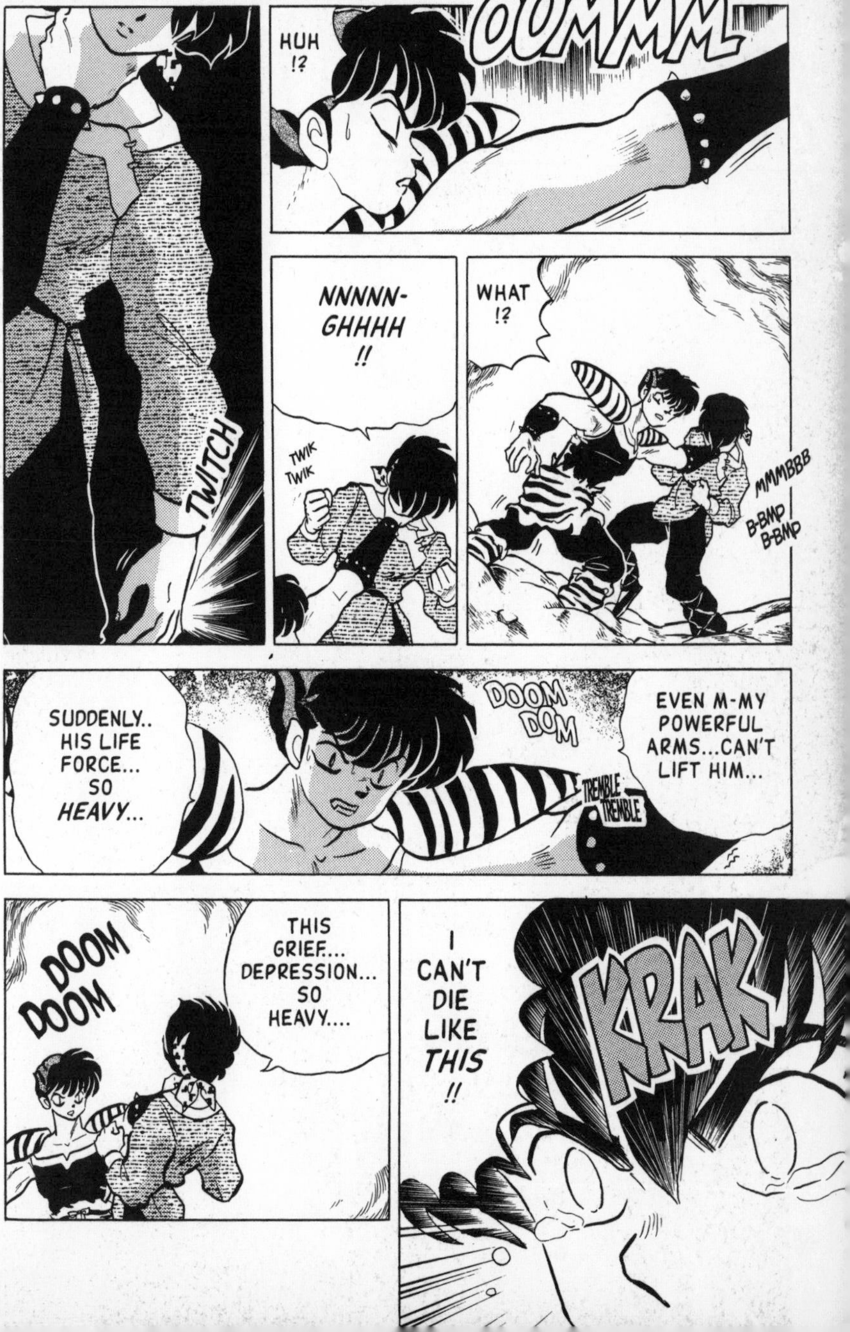
TWITCH
HUH !?
OOMMMM
NNNNN- GHHHH !!
TWIK TWIK
WHAT !?
MMMBBB
B-BMP B-BMP
SUDDENLY.. HIS LIFE FORCE... SO HEAVY...
DOOM DOM
TREMBLE TREMBLE
EVEN M-MY POWERFUL ARMS...CAN'T LIFT HIM...
DOOM DOOM
THIS GRIEF.... DEPRESSION... SO HEAVY....
I CAN'T DIE LIKE THIS !!
KRAK

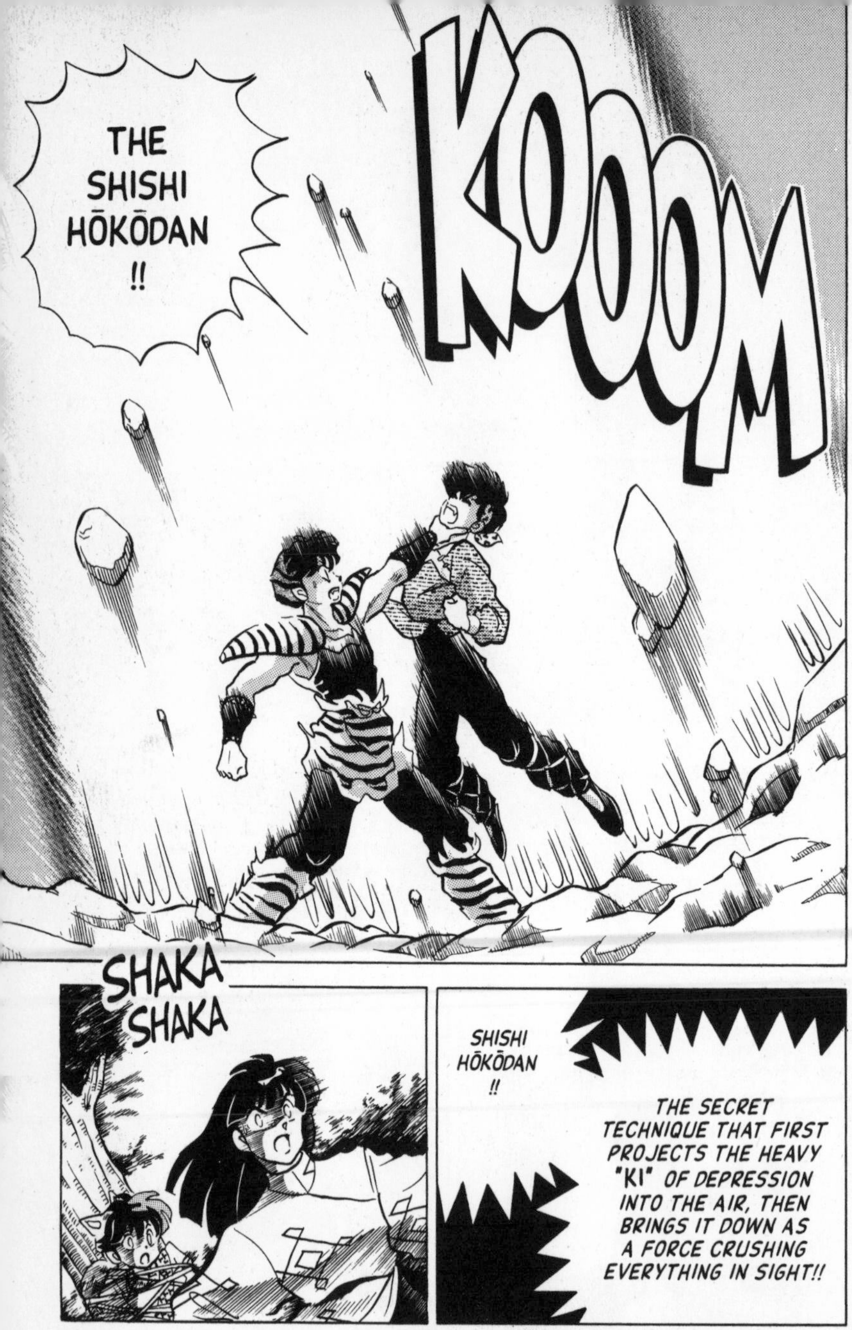
THE SHISHI HŌKŌDAN !!
KOOOOM
SHAKA SHAKA
SHISHI HŌKŌDAN !!
THE SECRET TECHNIQUE THAT FIRST PROJECTS THE HEAVY "KI" OF DEPRESSION INTO THE AIR, THEN BRINGS IT DOWN AS A FORCE CRUSHING EVERYTHING IN SIGHT!!

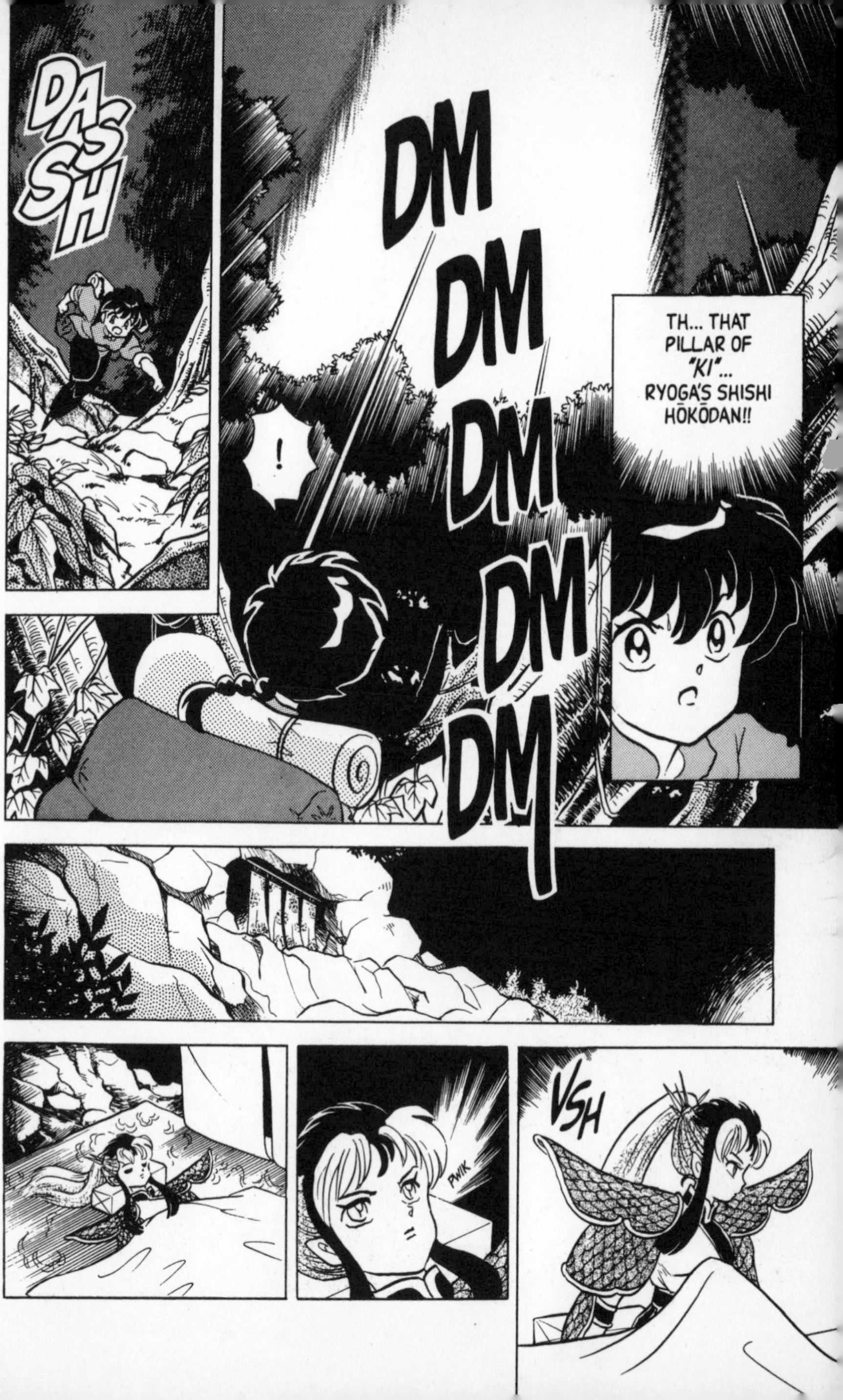
DASH
!
DM DM DM DM DM DM
TH... THAT PILLAR OF "KI"... RYOGA'S SHISHI HŌKŌDAN!!
PWIK
VSH

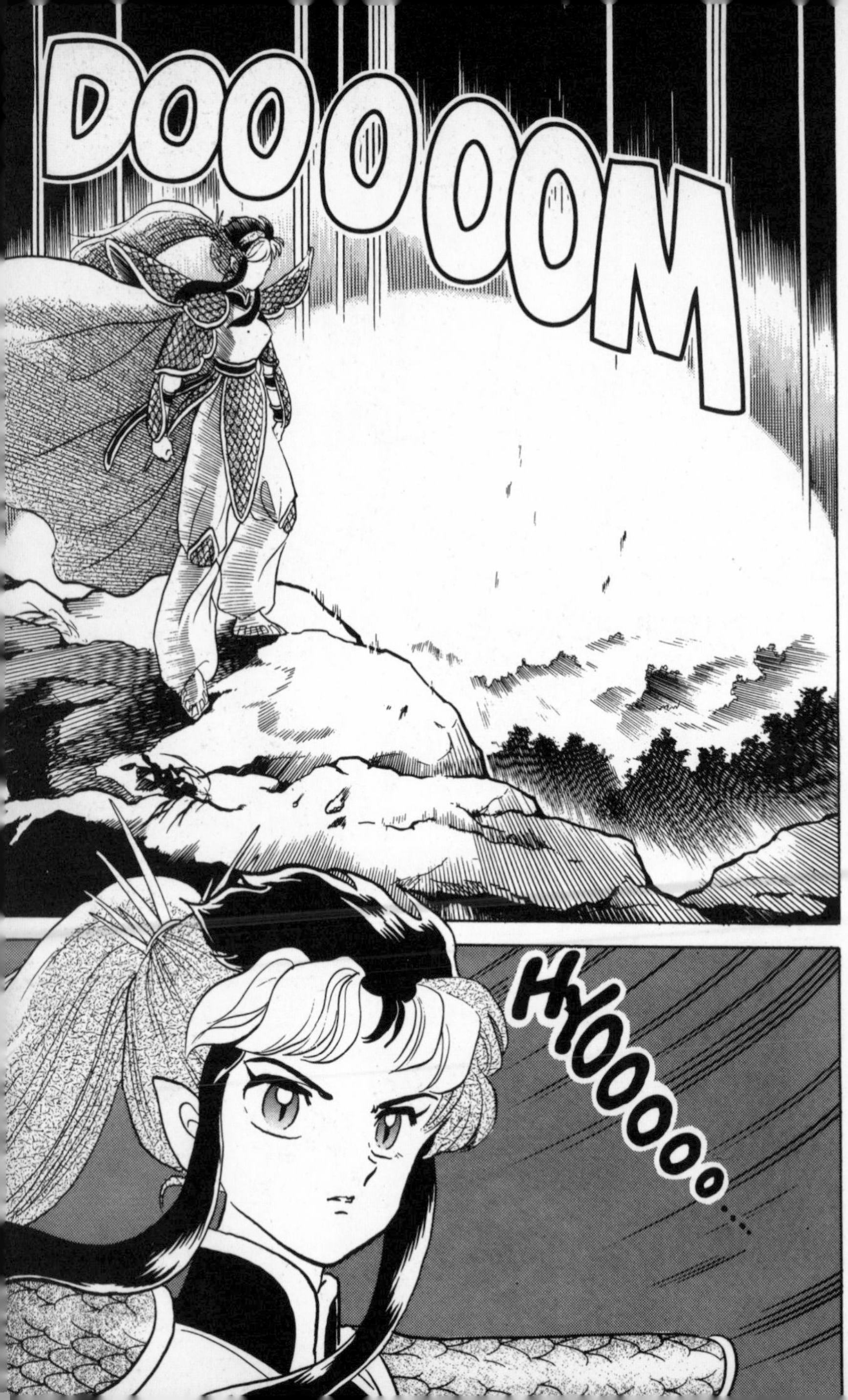
DOOOOOM
HYOOOOO.....

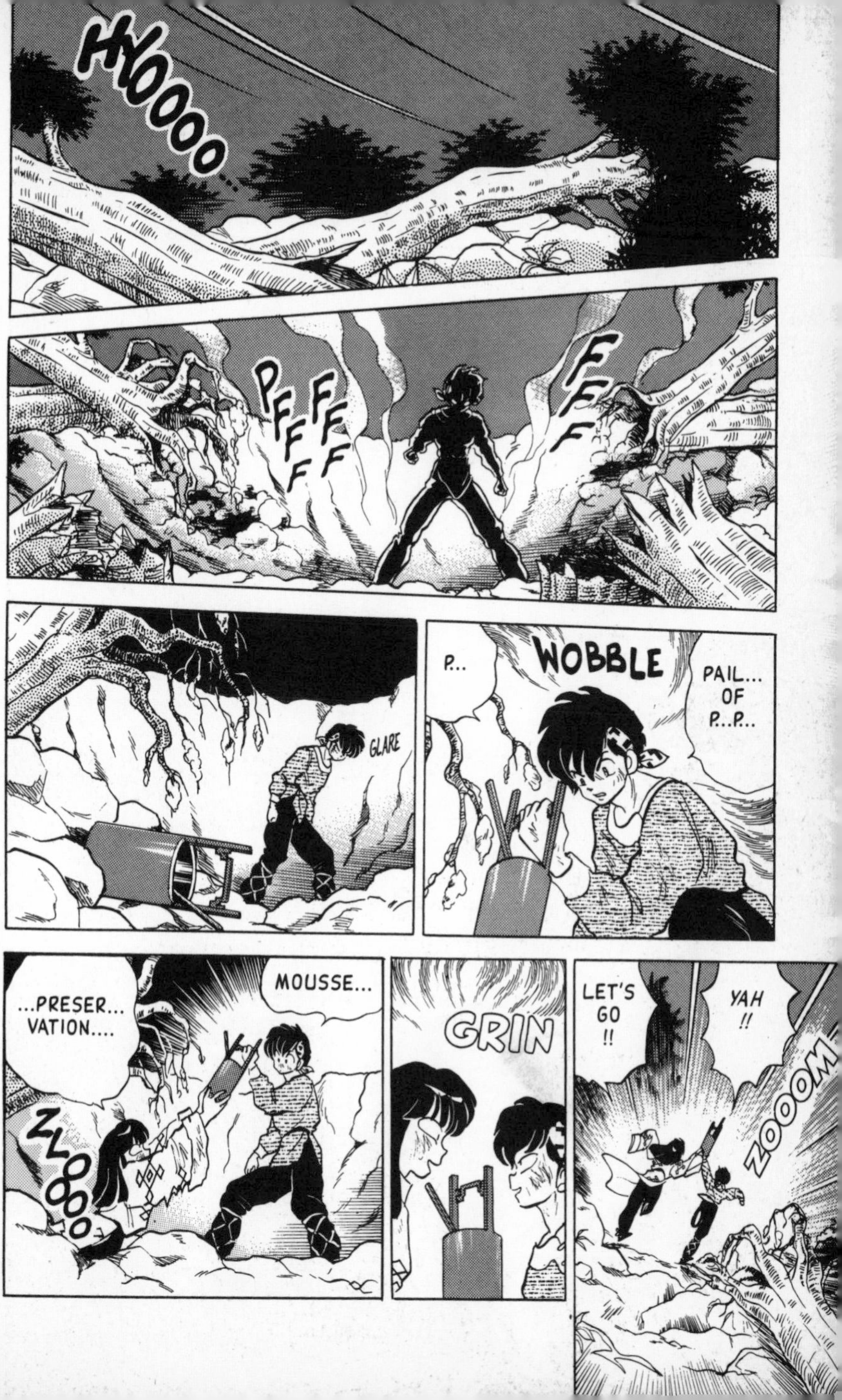
HYOOOO...
PFFFF
FFFF
FFF
GLARE
P...
WOBBLE
PAIL... OF P...P...
...PRESER... VATION....
MOUSSE...
ZZOOOO
GRIN
LET'S GO !!
YAH !!
ZOOOM

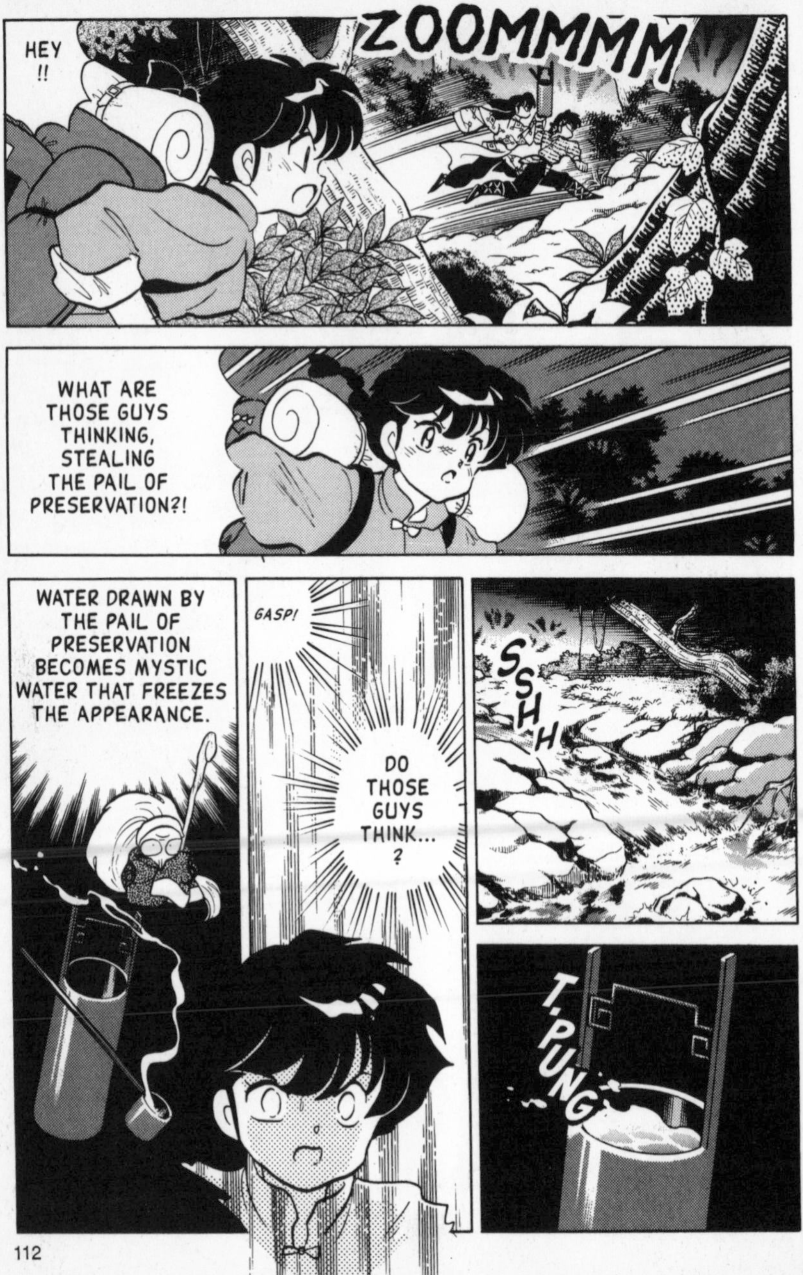
HEY !!
ZOOMMMM
WHAT ARE THOSE GUYS THINKING, STEALING THE PAIL OF PRESERVATION?!
WATER DRAWN BY THE PAIL OF PRESERVATION BECOMES MYSTIC WATER THAT FREEZES THE APPEARANCE.
GASP!
DO THOSE GUYS THINK... ?
SSHH
T.PUNG

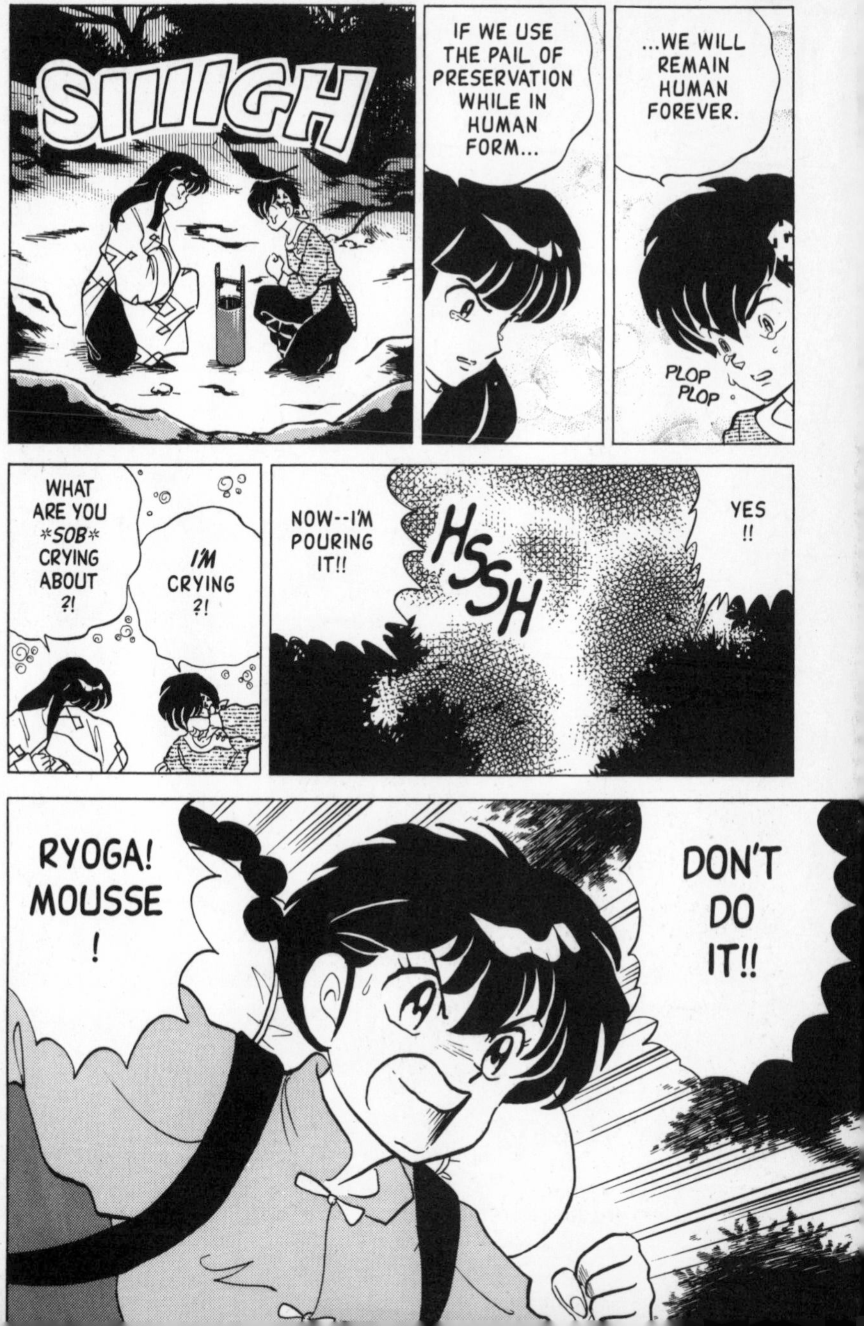
SIIIIGH
IF WE USE THE PAIL OF PRESERVATION WHILE IN HUMAN FORM...
...WE WILL REMAIN HUMAN FOREVER.
PLOP PLOP
WHAT ARE YOU *SOB* CRYING ABOUT ?!
I'M CRYING ?!
NOW--I'M POURING IT!!
HSSSH
YES !!
RYOGA! MOUSSE !
DON'T DO IT!!

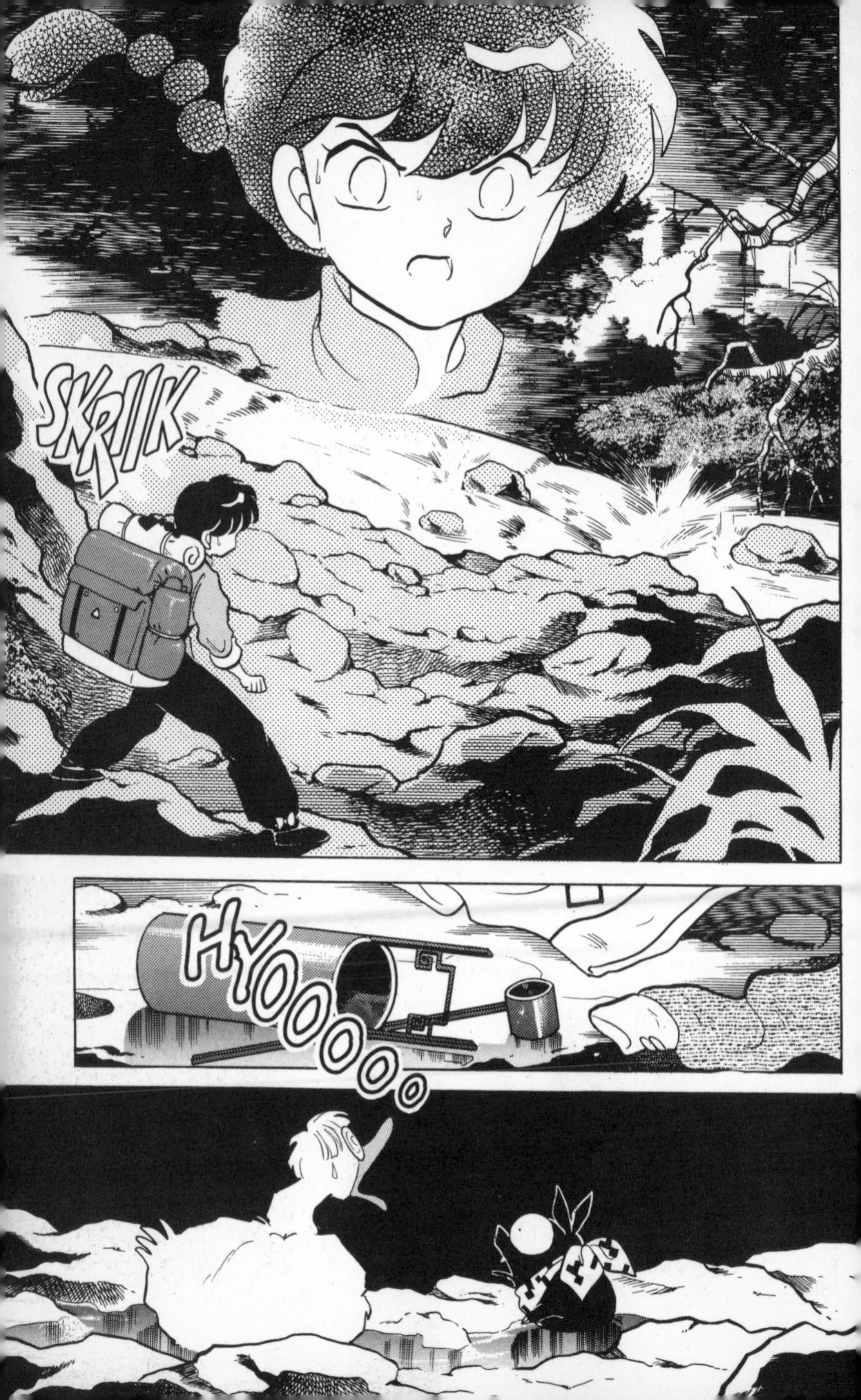
SKRIIK
HYOOOOO

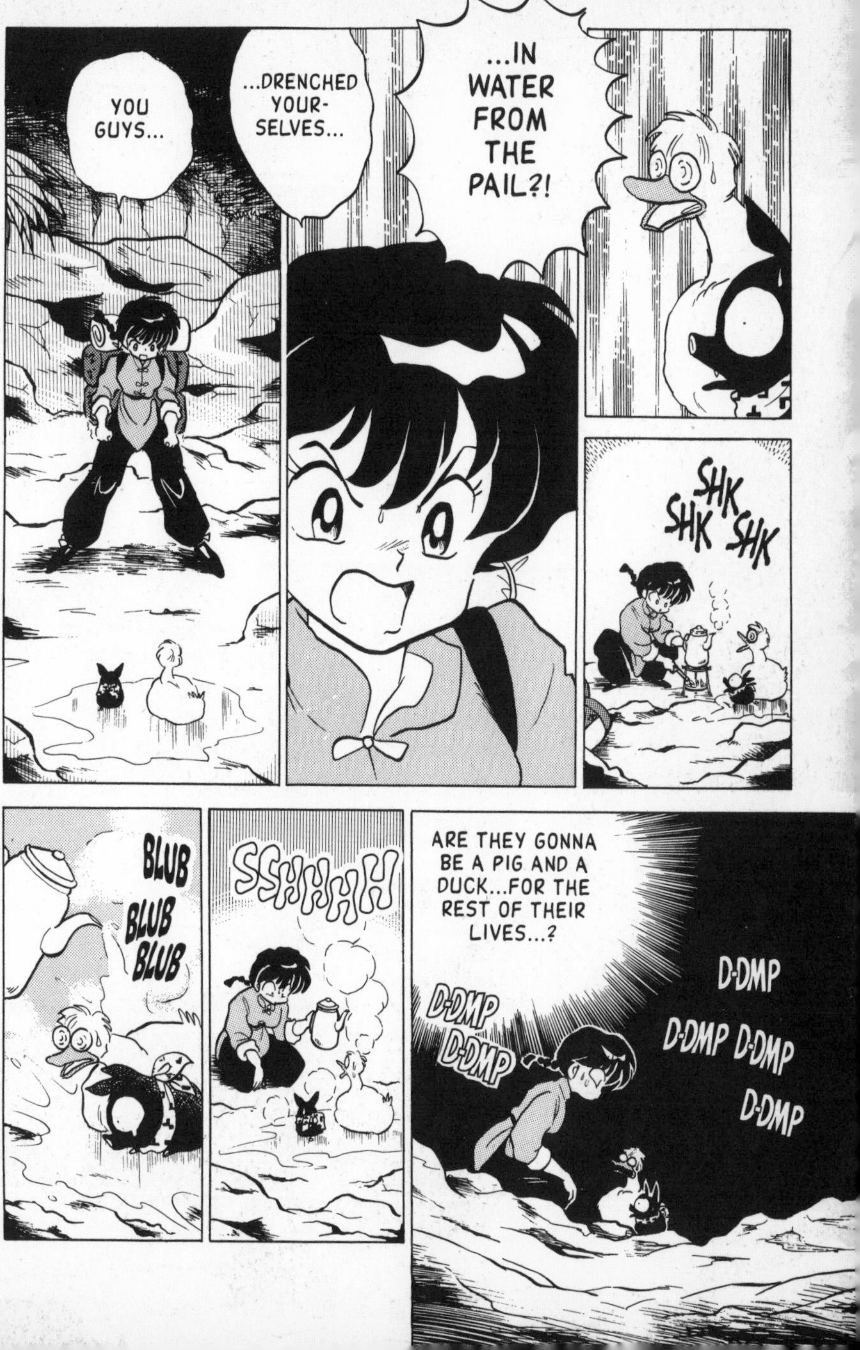
YOU GUYS...
...DRENCHED YOUR-SELVES...
...IN WATER FROM THE PAIL?!
SHK SHK SHK
BLUB BLUB BLUB
SSHHHHH
ARE THEY GONNA BE A PIG AND A DUCK...FOR THE REST OF THEIR LIVES...?
D-DMP D-DMP
D-DMP
D-DMP D-DMP
D-DMP

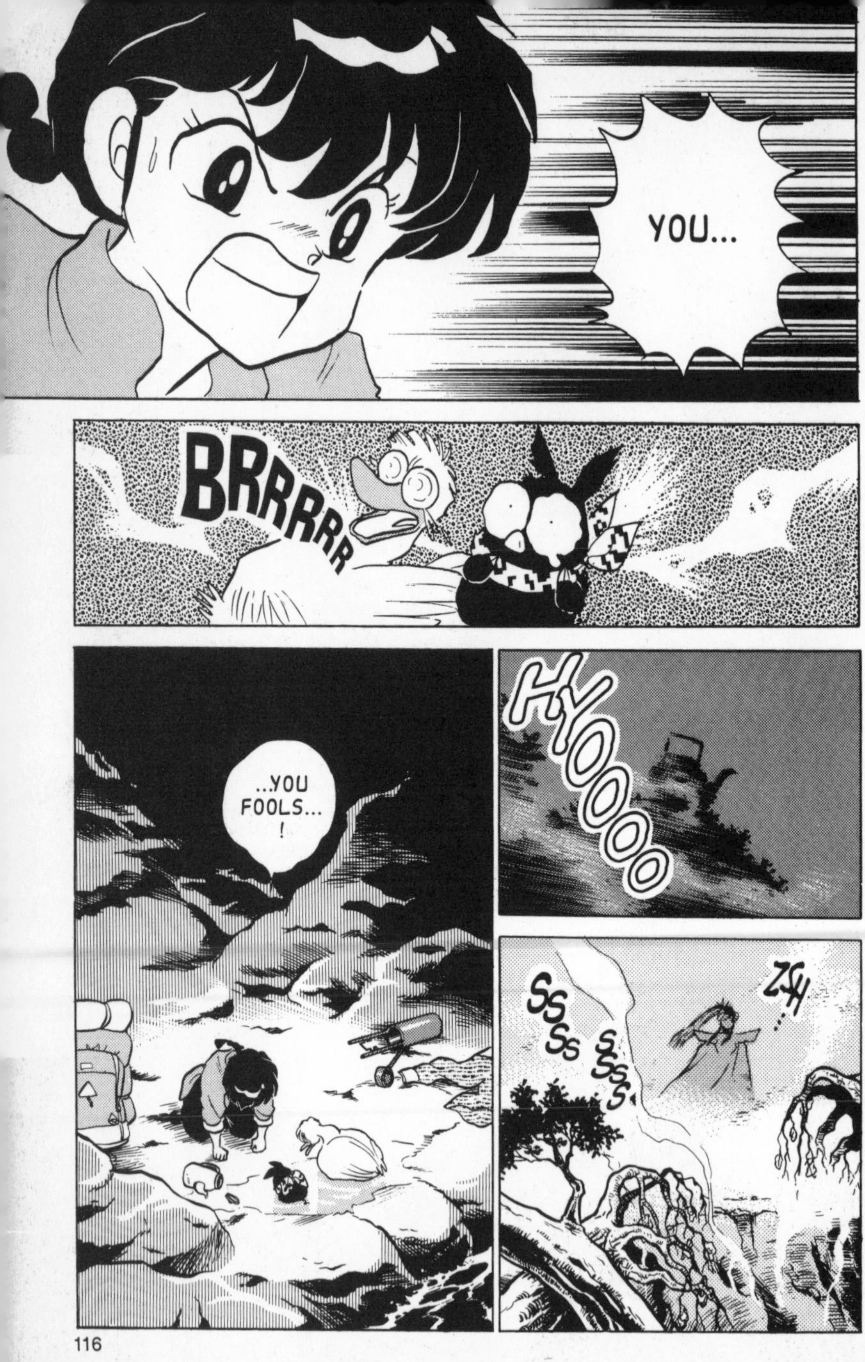
YOU...
BRRRRRR
...YOU FOOLS... !
HYOOOO
SSSS
SSSS
ZSH

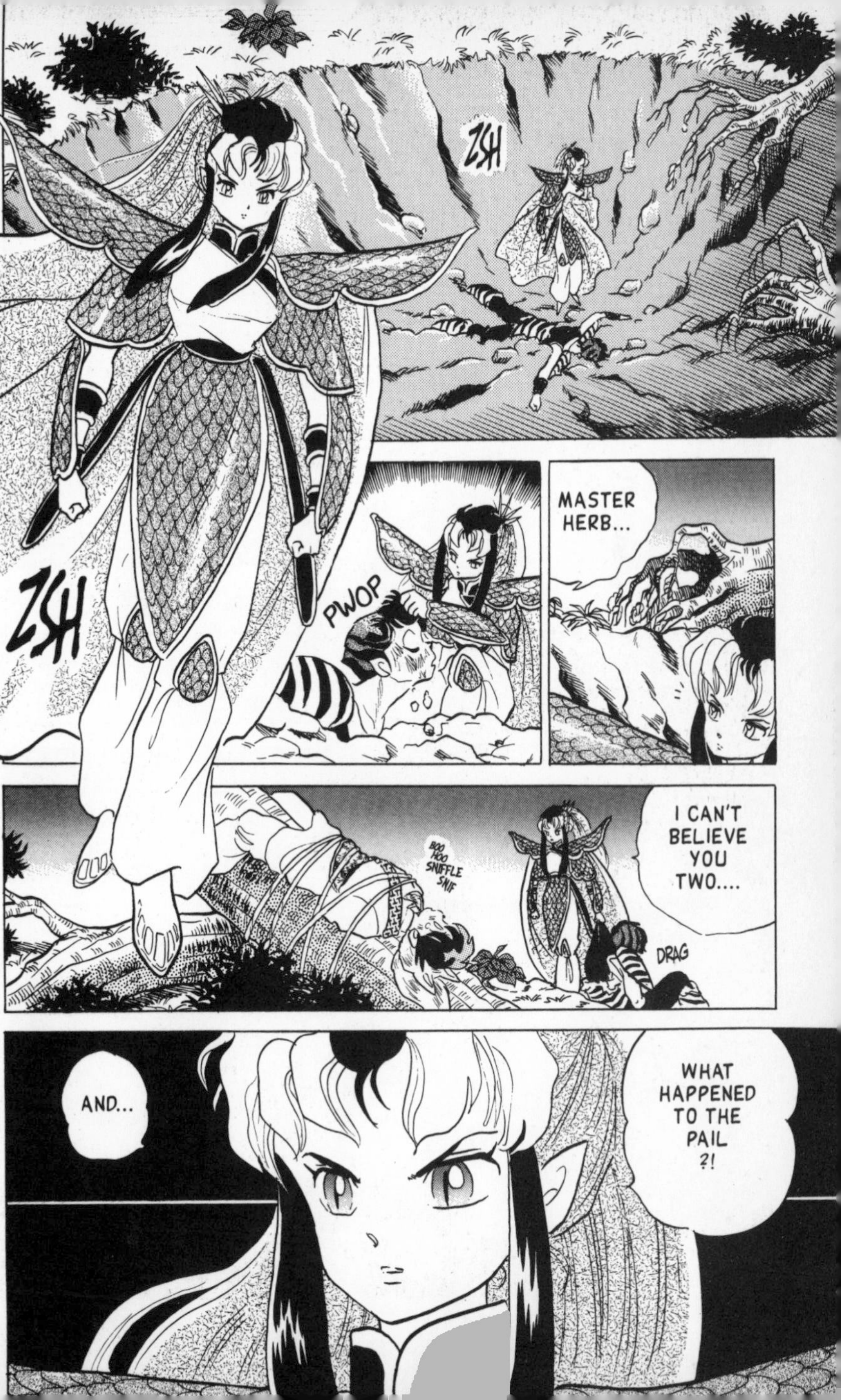
ZSH
ZSH
PWOP
MASTER HERB...
BOO HOO SNIFFLE SNIF
I CAN'T BELIEVE YOU TWO....
DRAG
AND...
WHAT HAPPENED TO THE PAIL ?!

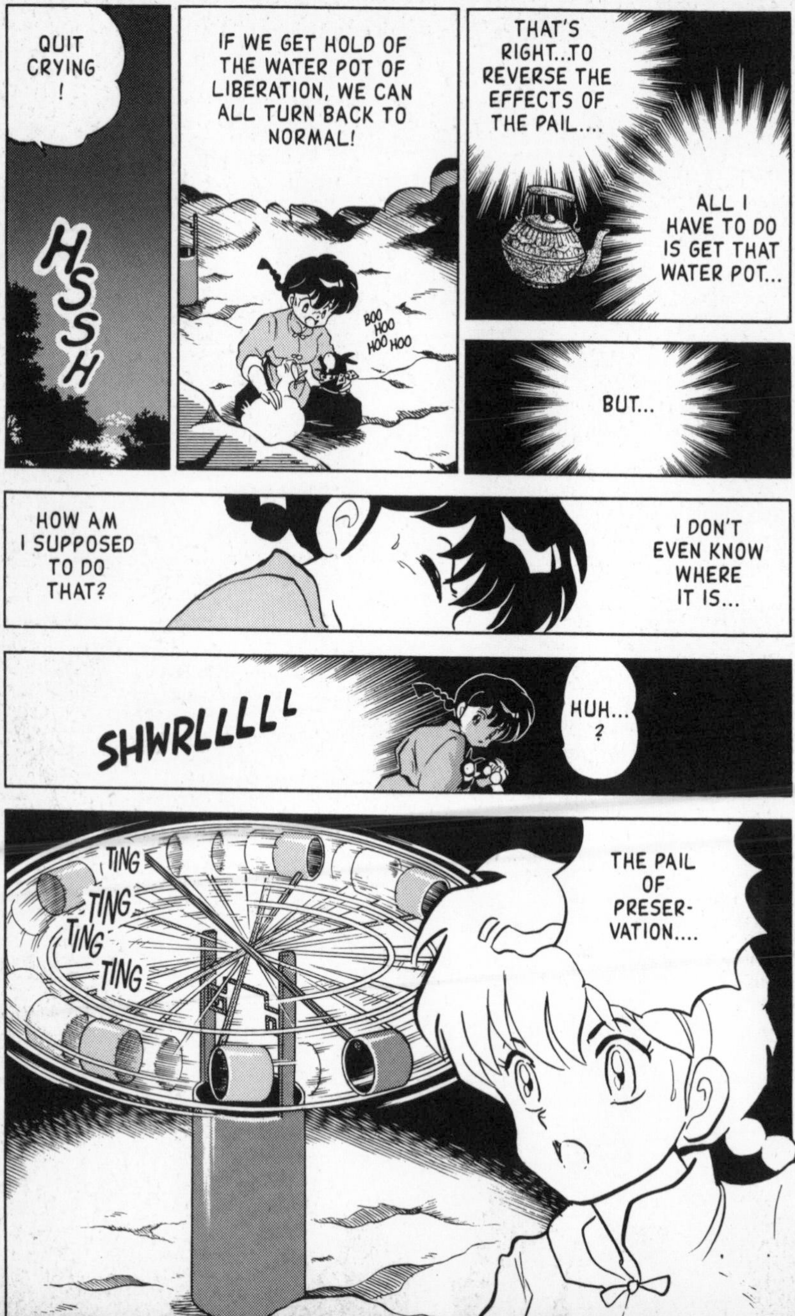
QUIT CRYING!
HSSH
IF WE GET HOLD OF THE WATER POT OF LIBERATION, WE CAN ALL TURN BACK TO NORMAL!
BOO HOO HOO HOO
THAT'S RIGHT...TO REVERSE THE EFFECTS OF THE PAIL....
ALL I HAVE TO DO IS GET THAT WATER POT...
BUT...
HOW AM I SUPPOSED TO DO THAT?
I DON'T EVEN KNOW WHERE IT IS...
SHWRLLLLL
HUH...?
TING
TING
TING
TING
THE PAIL OF PRESER-VATION....

Part 8

THE WATERFALL OF SECRET TREAUSURE REVEALED!

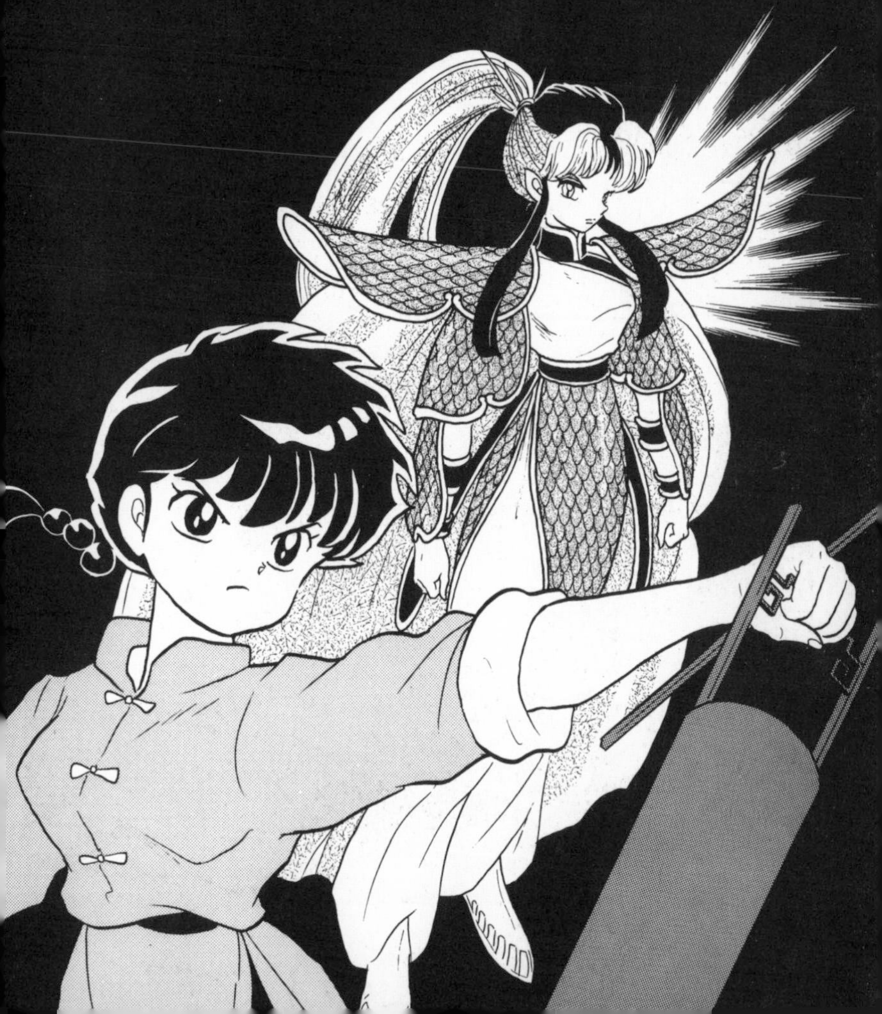

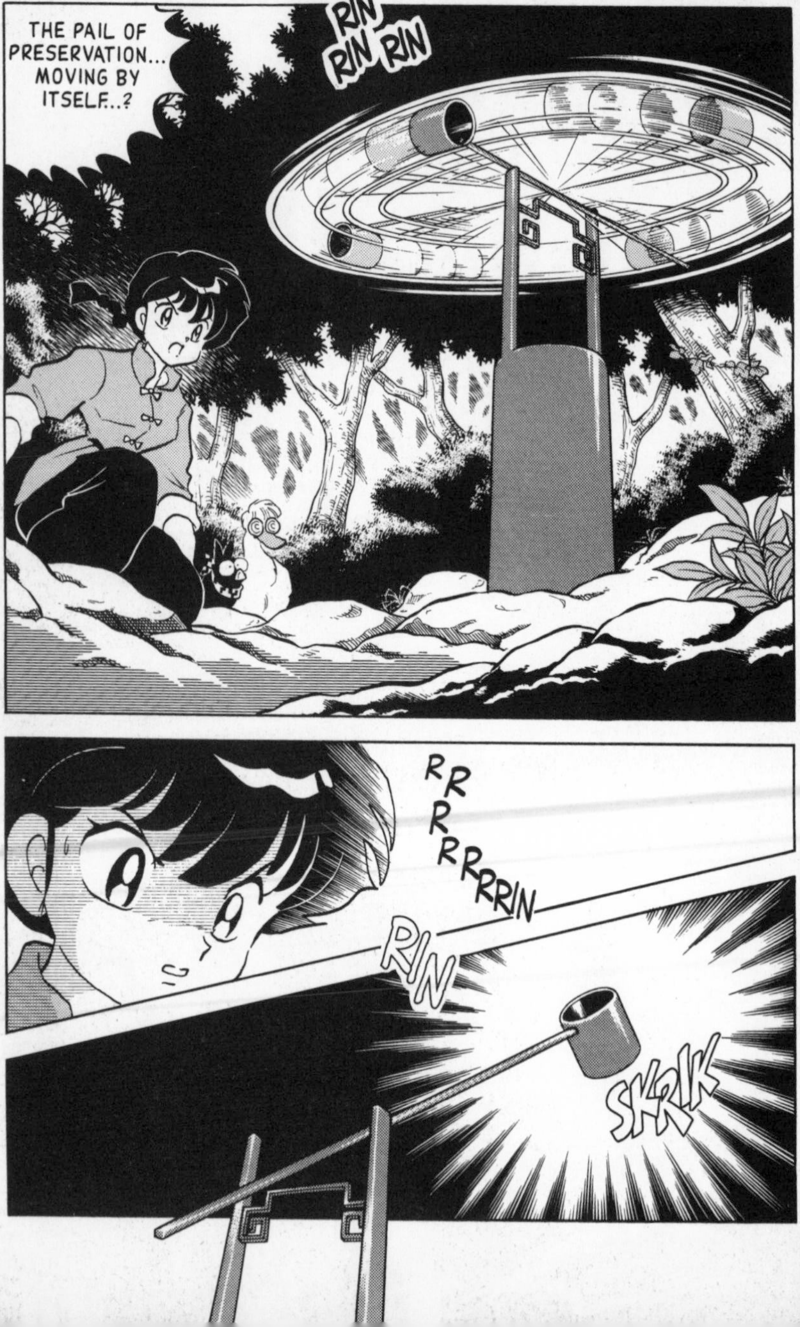
THE PAIL OF PRESERVATION... MOVING BY ITSELF...?
RIN RIN RIN
RRRRRRRIN
RIN
SKRIK

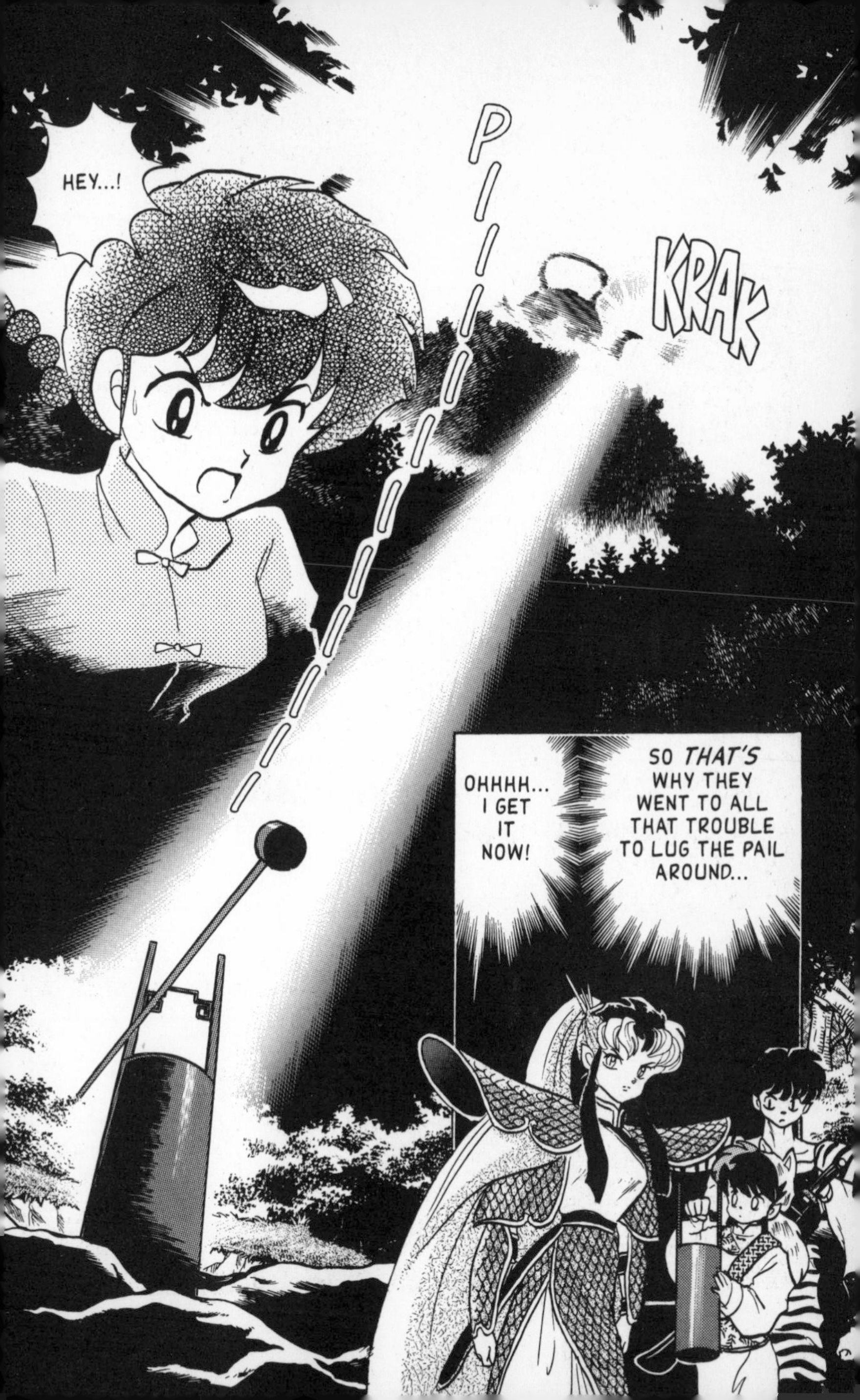
HEY...!
PIIIIIIIIIIIIIII
KRAK
OHHHH... I GET IT NOW!
SO *THAT'S* WHY THEY WENT TO ALL THAT TROUBLE TO LUG THE PAIL AROUND...

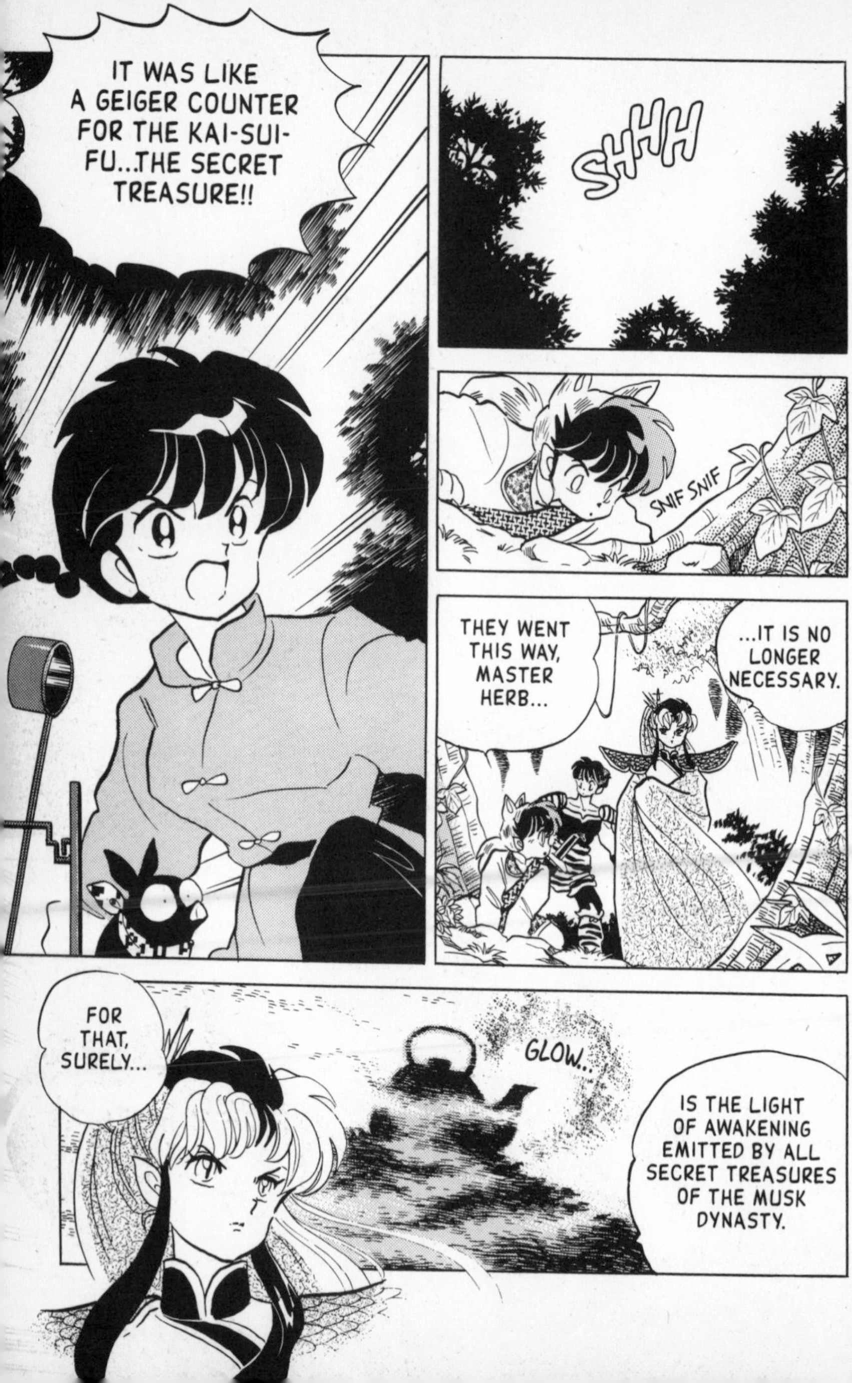
IT WAS LIKE A GEIGER COUNTER FOR THE KAI-SUI-FU...THE SECRET TREASURE!!
SHHH
SNIF SNIF
THEY WENT THIS WAY, MASTER HERB...
...IT IS NO LONGER NECESSARY.
FOR THAT, SURELY...
GLOW...
IS THE LIGHT OF AWAKENING EMITTED BY ALL SECRET TREASURES OF THE MUSK DYNASTY.

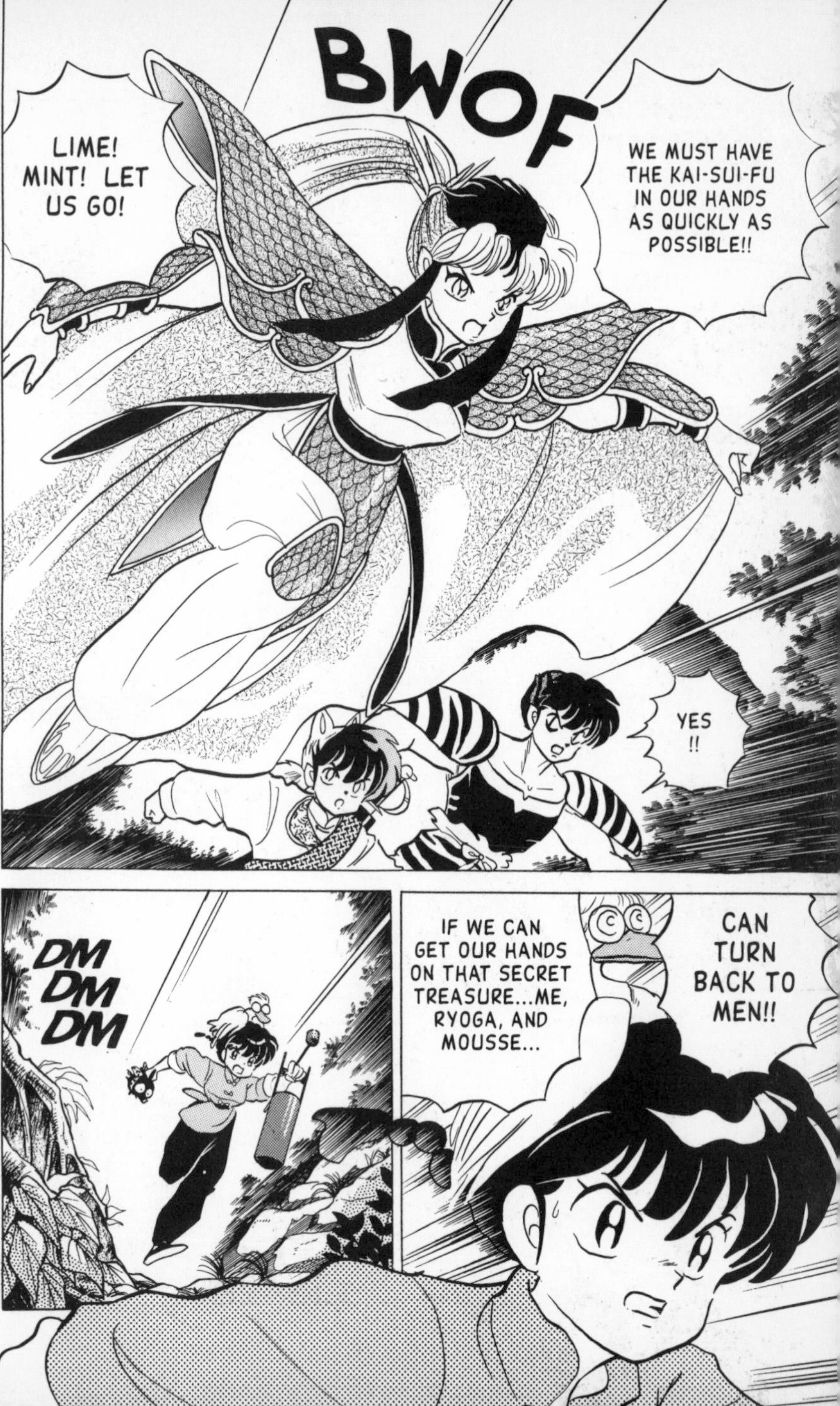
BWOF
LIME! MINT! LET US GO!
WE MUST HAVE THE KAI-SUI-FU IN OUR HANDS AS QUICKLY AS POSSIBLE!!
YES !!
DM DM DM
IF WE CAN GET OUR HANDS ON THAT SECRET TREASURE...ME, RYOGA, AND MOUSSE...
CAN TURN BACK TO MEN!!

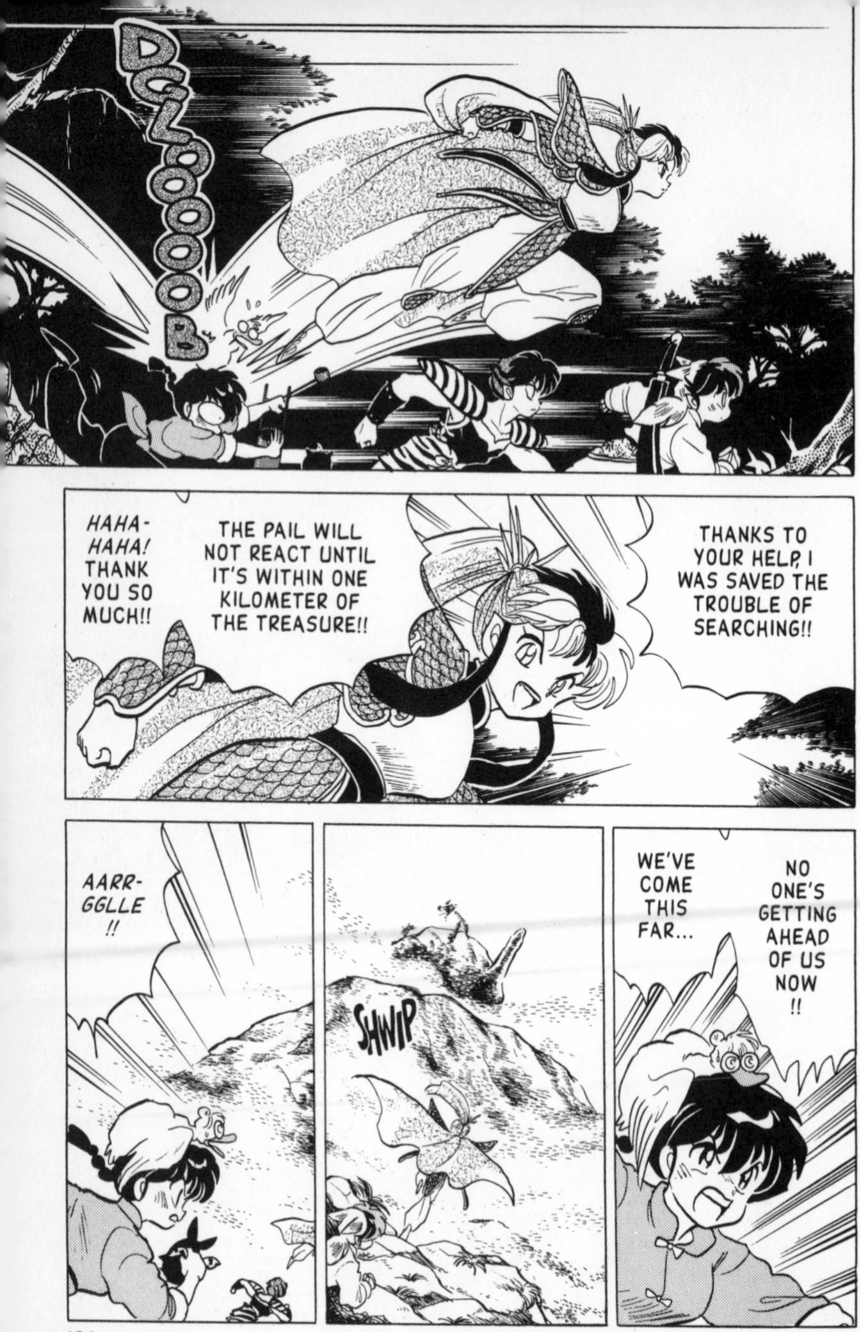
DGLOOOOOB
HAHA-HAHA! THANK YOU SO MUCH!!
THE PAIL WILL NOT REACT UNTIL IT'S WITHIN ONE KILOMETER OF THE TREASURE!!
THANKS TO YOUR HELP, I WAS SAVED THE TROUBLE OF SEARCHING!!
AARR-GGLLE !!
SHWIP
WE'VE COME THIS FAR...
NO ONE'S GETTING AHEAD OF US NOW !!

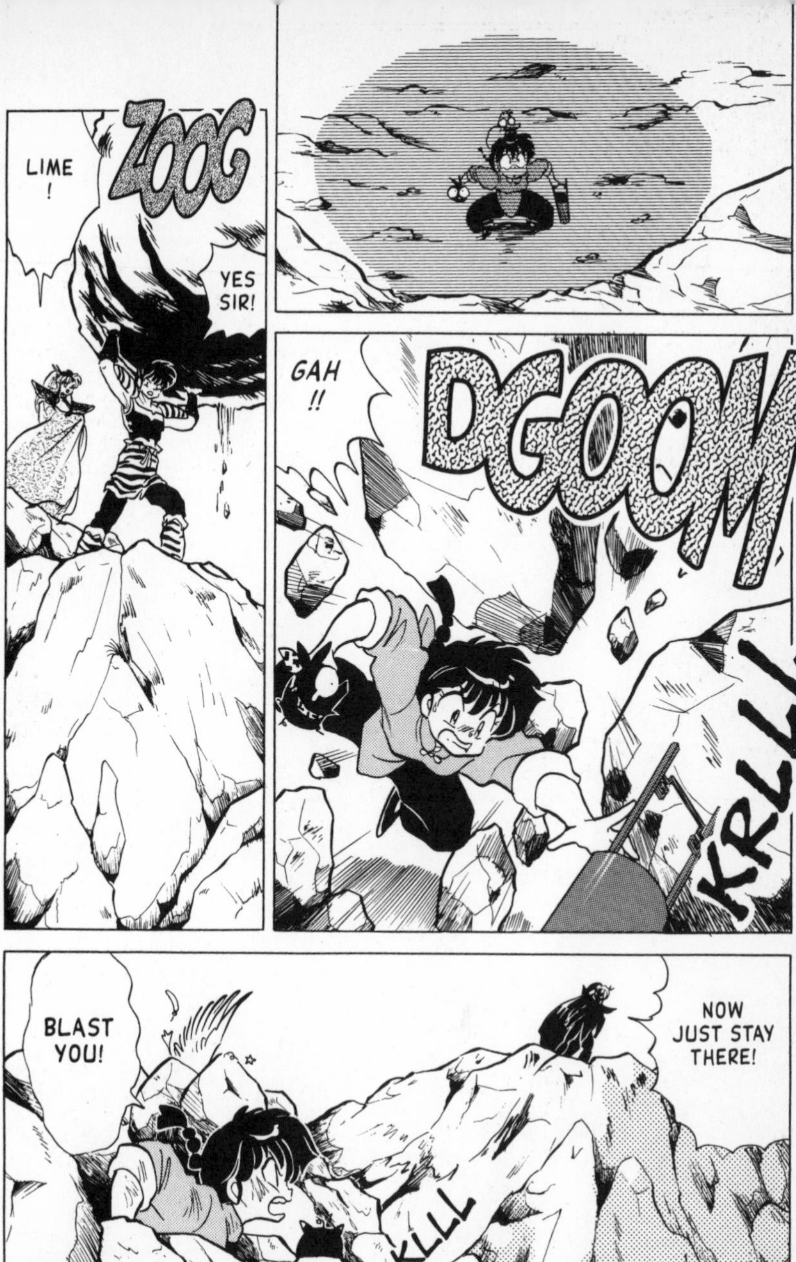
LIME!
ZOOG
YES SIR!
GAH!!
DGOOM
KRLLL
BLAST YOU!
KLLL
NOW JUST STAY THERE!

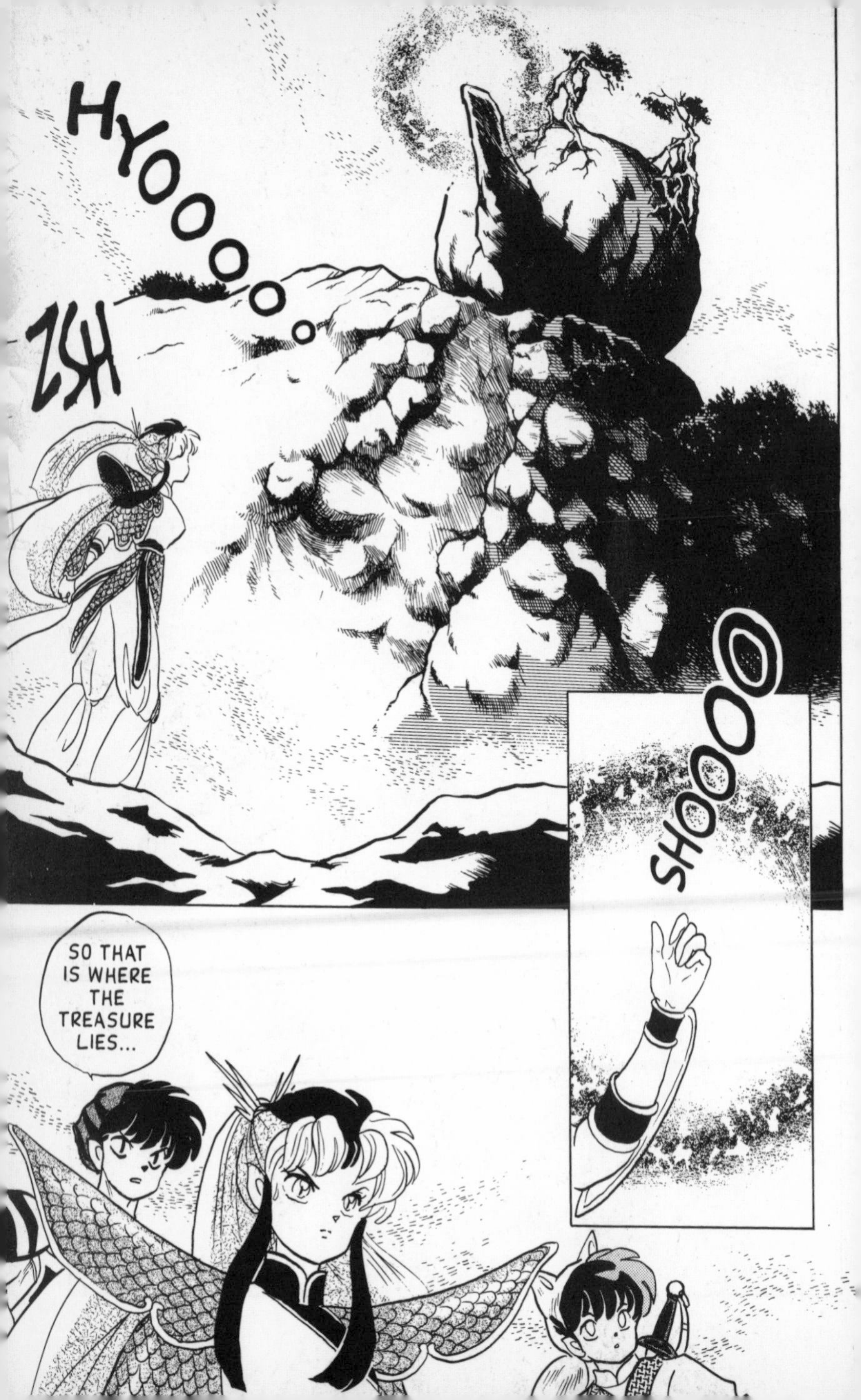
HYOOOOO...
ZSH
SHOOOOO
SO THAT IS WHERE THE TREASURE LIES...

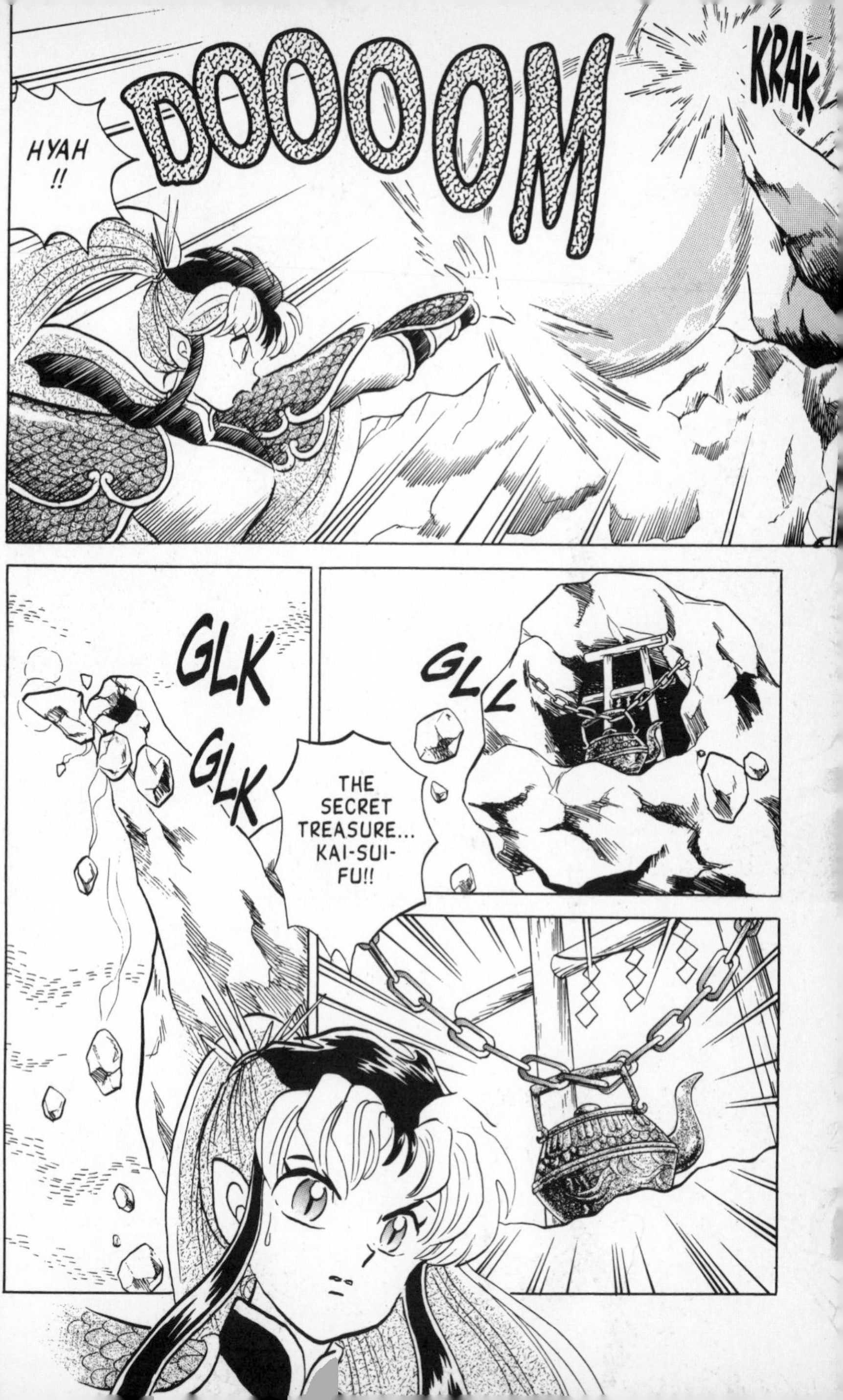
HYAH !!
DOOOOOM
KRAK
GLK
GLK
GLL
THE SECRET TREASURE... KAI-SUI-FU!!

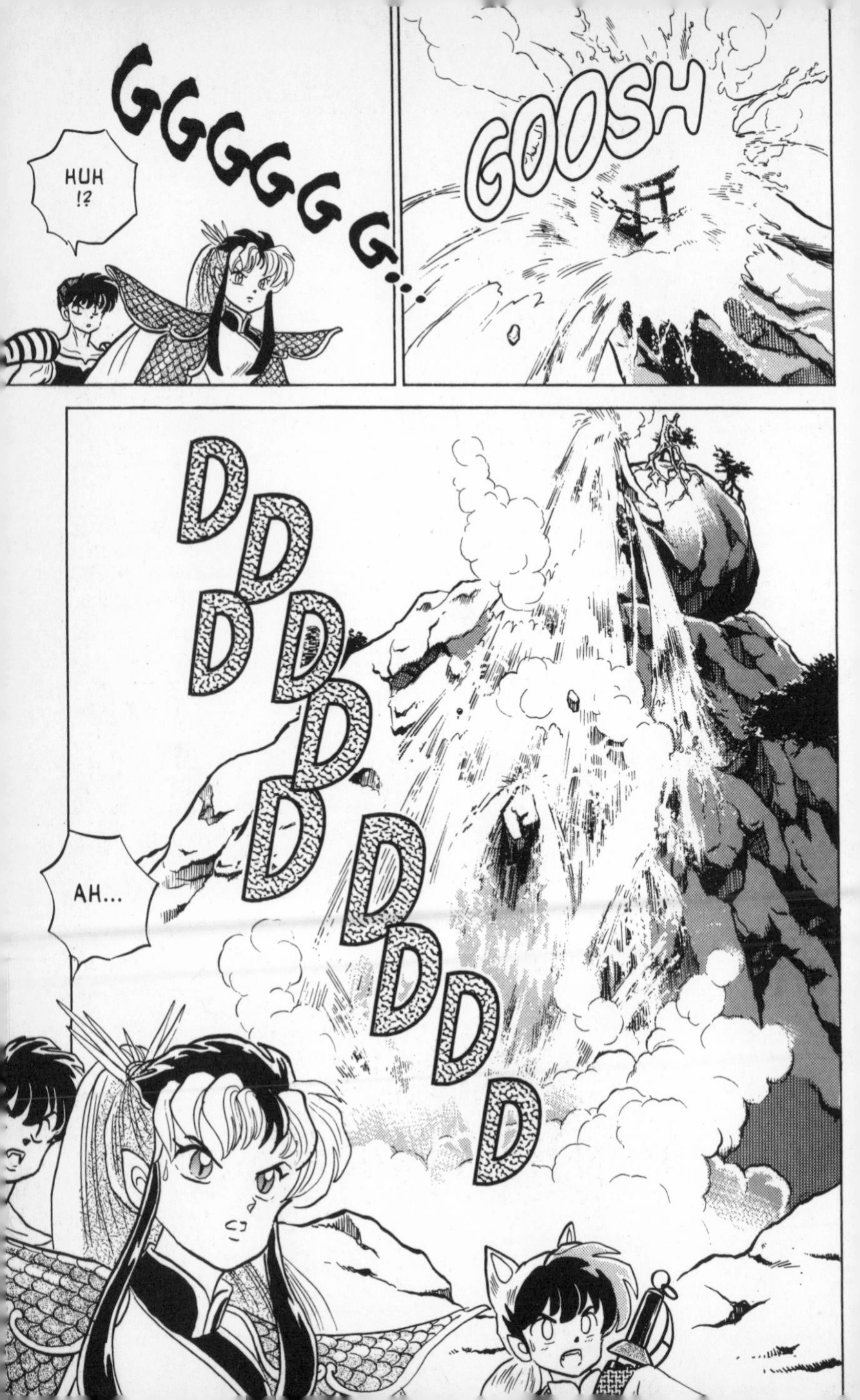

GGGGGG...
HUH !?
GOOSH
DDDDDDDDDDD
AH...

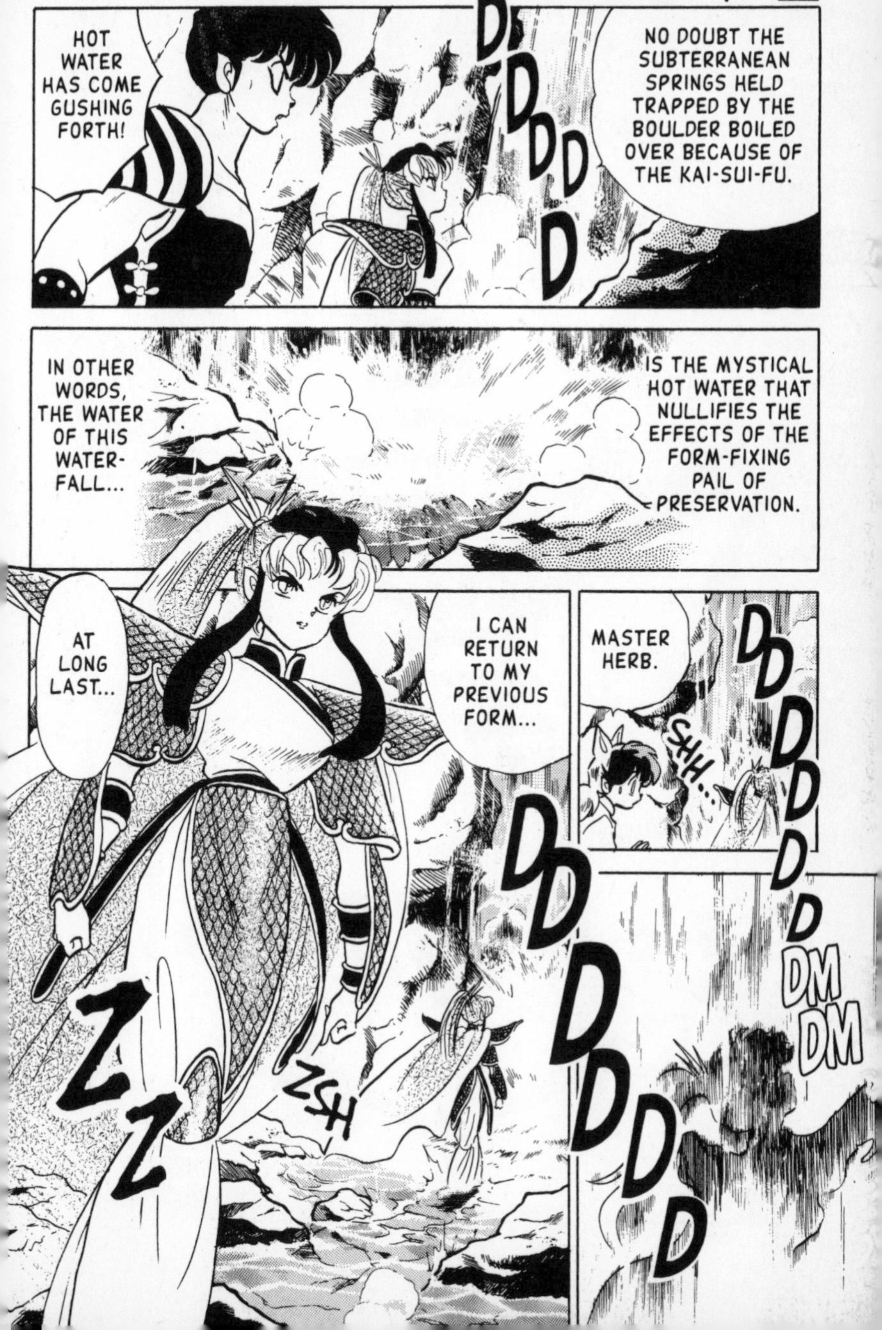
HOT WATER HAS COME GUSHING FORTH!
DDDDDD
NO DOUBT THE SUBTERRANEAN SPRINGS HELD TRAPPED BY THE BOULDER BOILED OVER BECAUSE OF THE KAI-SUI-FU.
IN OTHER WORDS, THE WATER OF THIS WATER-FALL...
IS THE MYSTICAL HOT WATER THAT NULLIFIES THE EFFECTS OF THE FORM-FIXING PAIL OF PRESERVATION.
AT LONG LAST...
I CAN RETURN TO MY PREVIOUS FORM...
ZZZ
ZSH
DDDDDDD
MASTER HERB.
SHH...
DDDDDDDD
DM DM

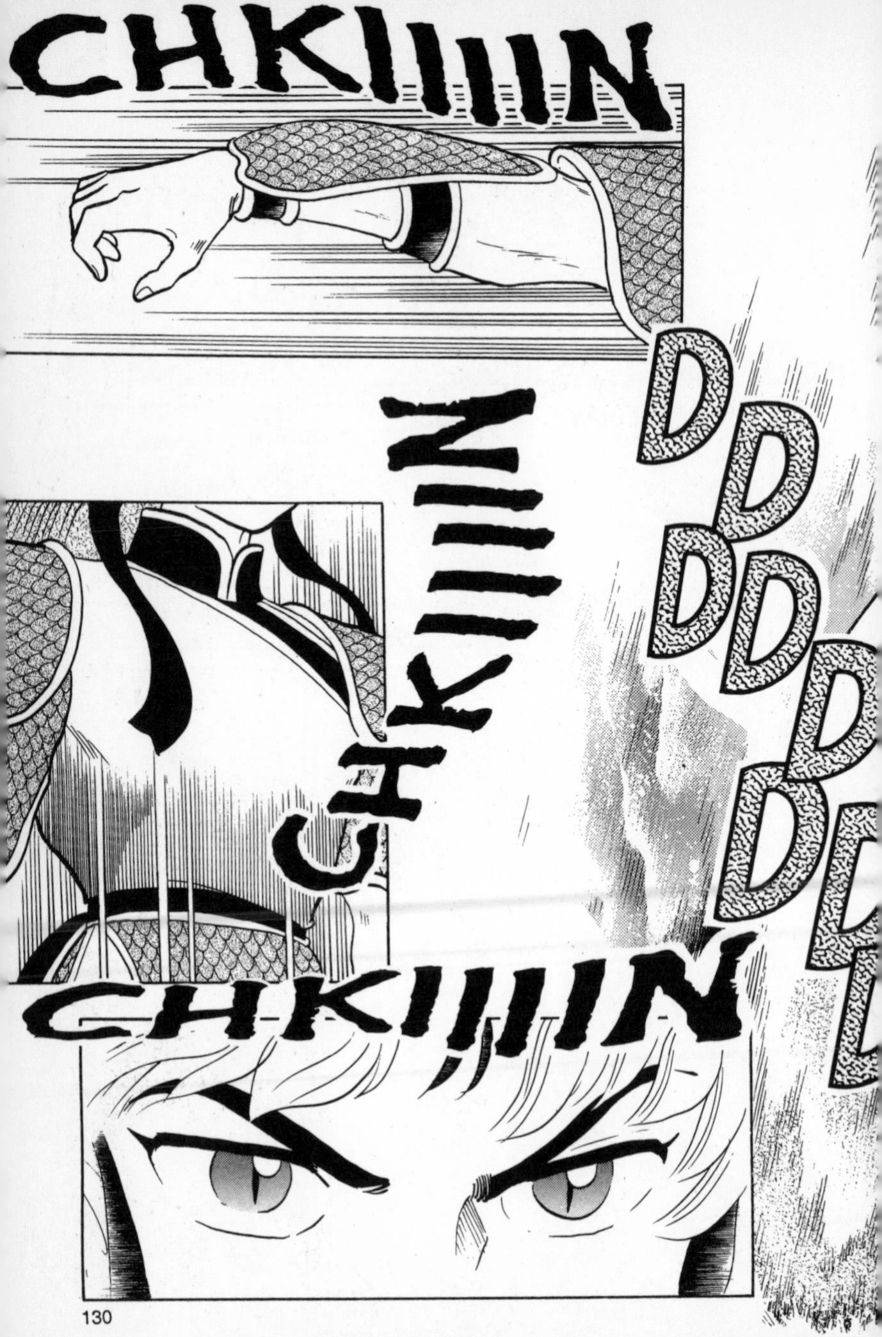
CHKIIIIN
DDDDDDDDD
CHKIIIIN
CHKIIIIN

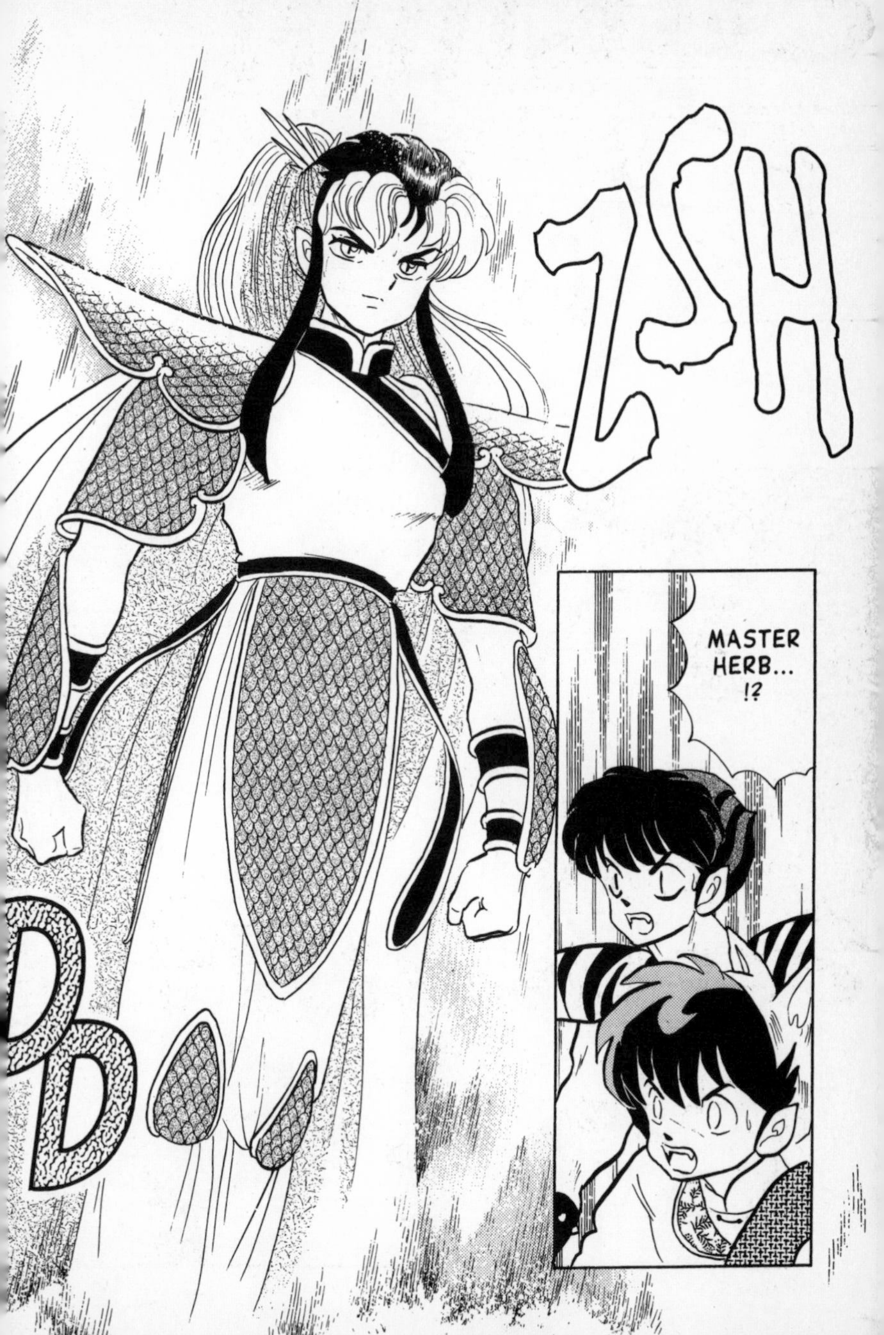
ZSH
DOD
MASTER HERB... !?

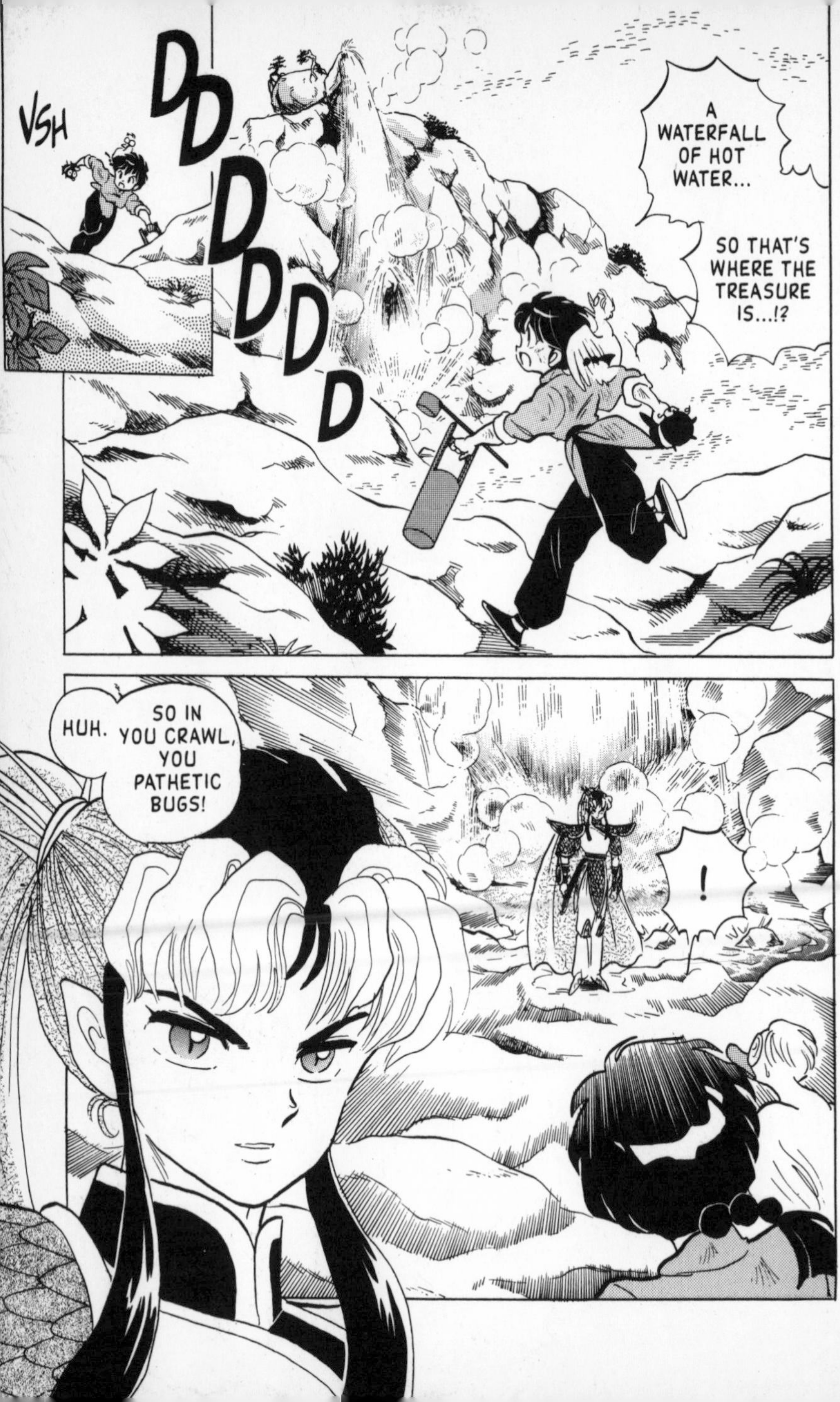
VSH
DDDDDD
A WATERFALL OF HOT WATER...
SO THAT'S WHERE THE TREASURE IS...!?
HUH. SO IN YOU CRAWL, YOU PATHETIC BUGS!
!

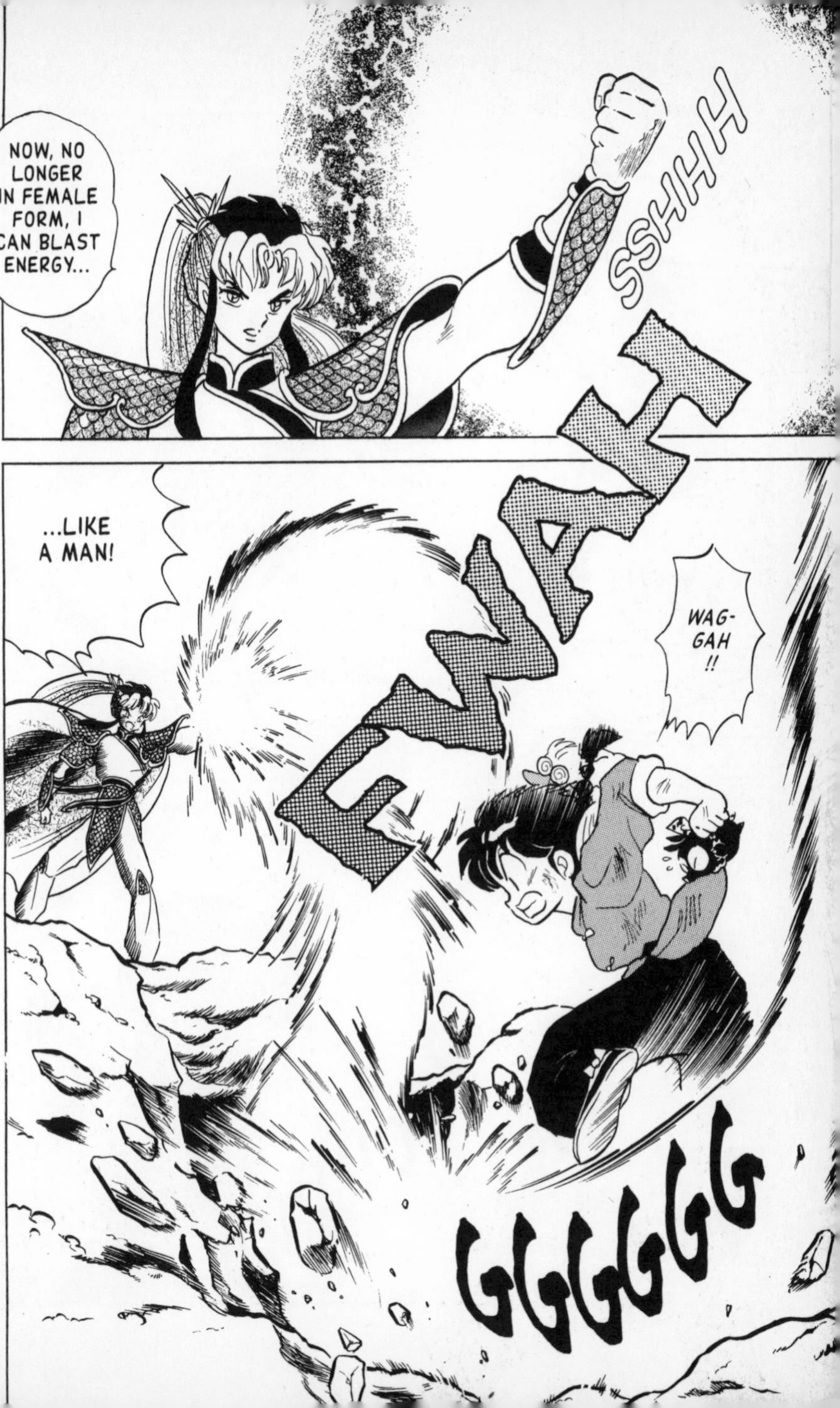
NOW, NO LONGER IN FEMALE FORM, I CAN BLAST ENERGY...
SSHHH
...LIKE A MAN!
FWAH
WAG-GAH !!
GGGGGG

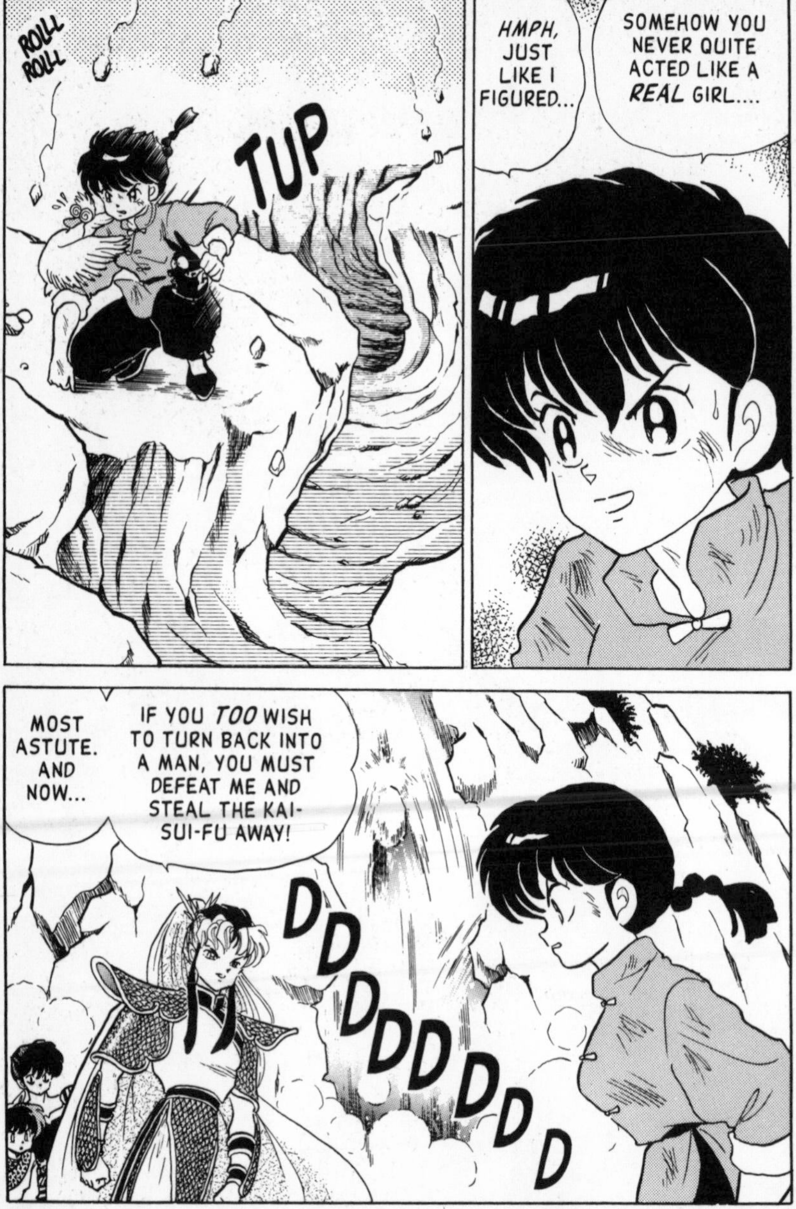
ROLL ROLL
TUP
HMPH, JUST LIKE I FIGURED...
SOMEHOW YOU NEVER QUITE ACTED LIKE A *REAL* GIRL....
MOST ASTUTE. AND NOW...
IF YOU *TOO* WISH TO TURN BACK INTO A MAN, YOU MUST DEFEAT ME AND STEAL THE KAI-SUI-FU AWAY!
DDDDDDDDDDD

Part 9

AN EVER-ELUSIVE TREASURE

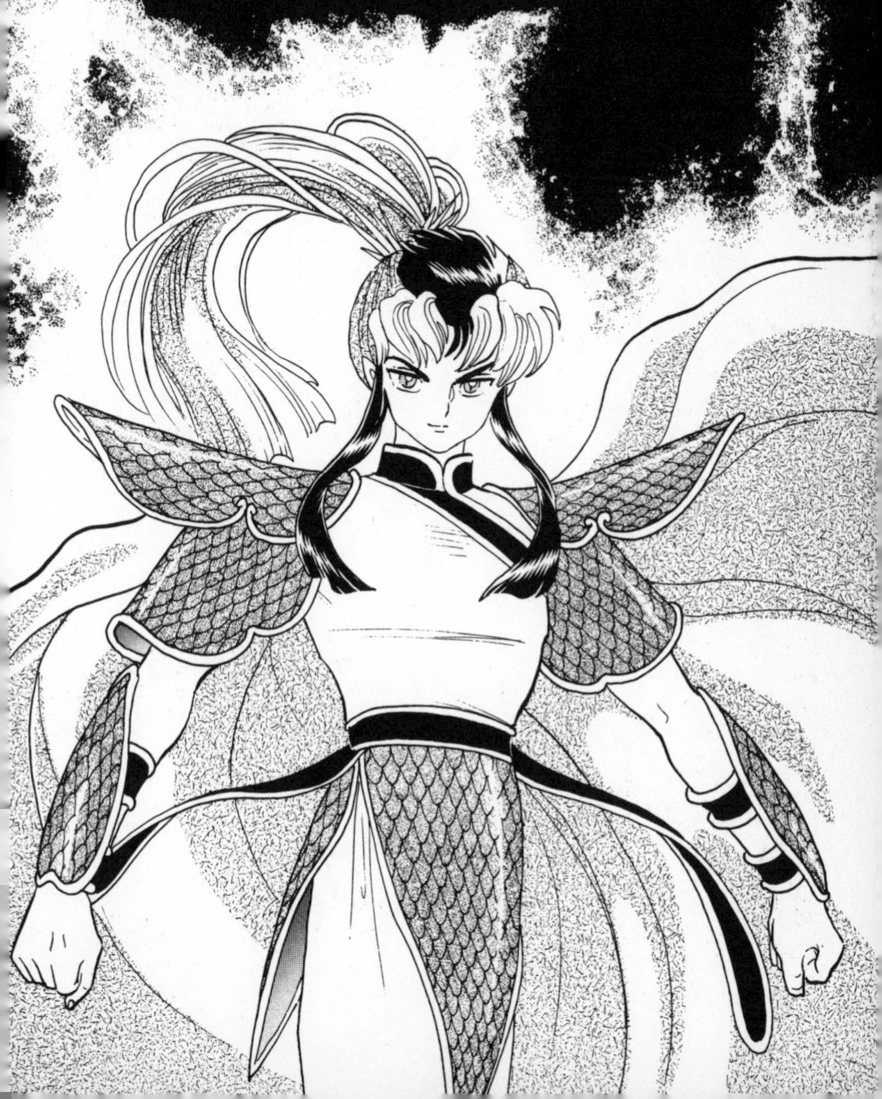

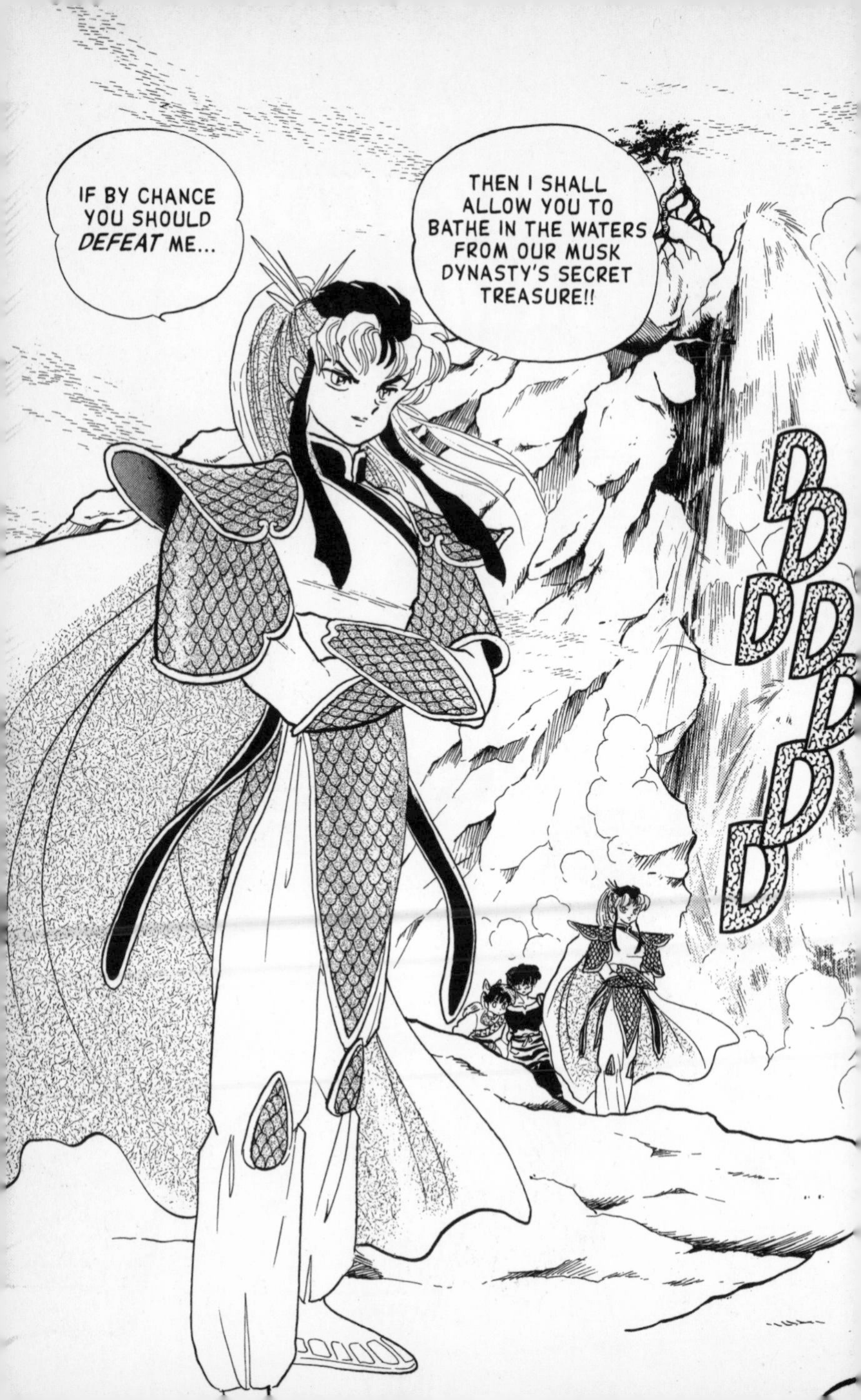
IF BY CHANCE YOU SHOULD *DEFEAT* ME...
THEN I SHALL ALLOW YOU TO BATHE IN THE WATERS FROM OUR MUSK DYNASTY'S SECRET TREASURE!!
DDDDDDDD

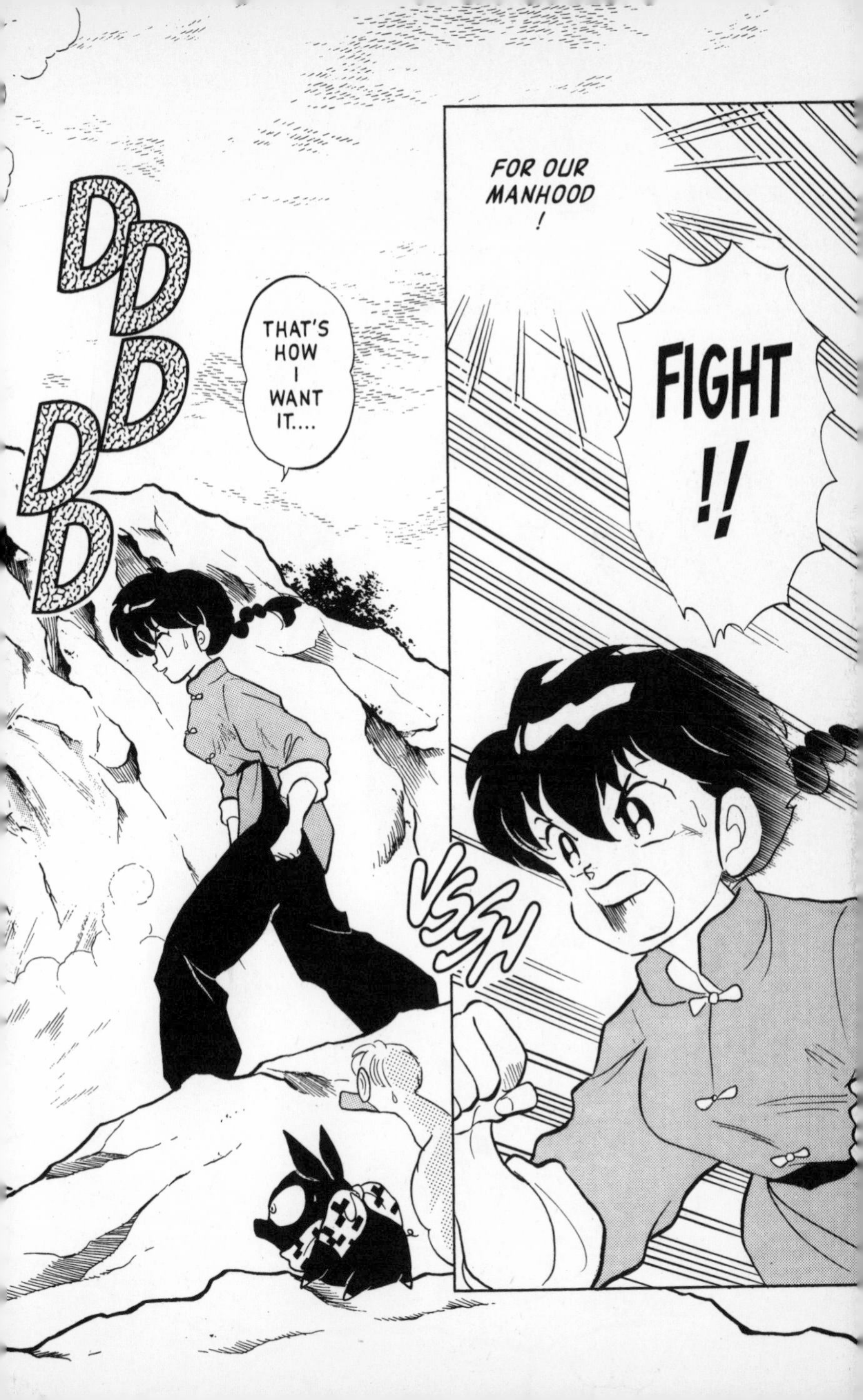
FOR OUR MANHOOD!
FIGHT!!
VSSH
DDDDD
THAT'S HOW I WANT IT....

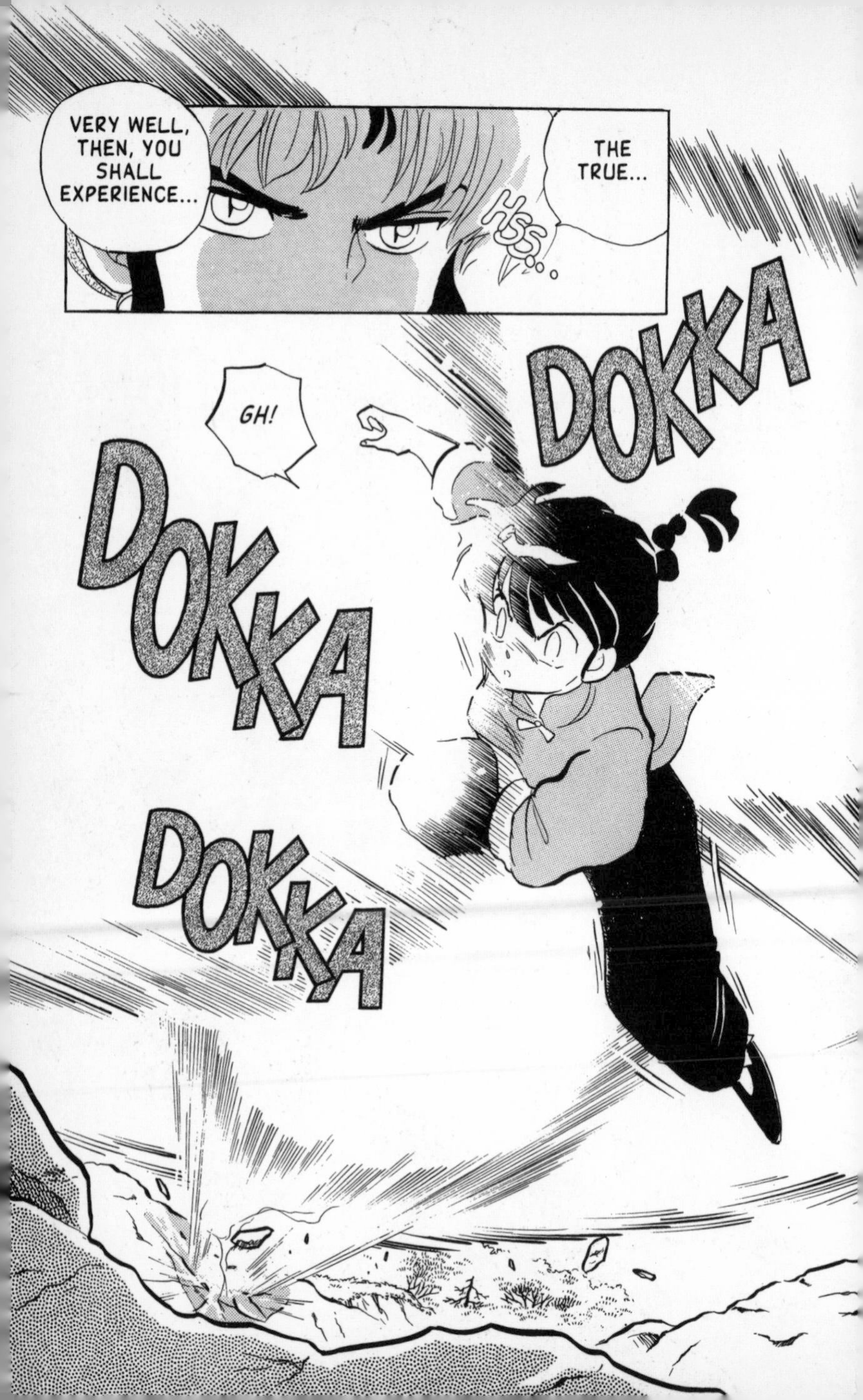
VERY WELL, THEN, YOU SHALL EXPERIENCE...
THE TRUE...
HSS...
GH!
DOKKA
DOKKA
DOKKA

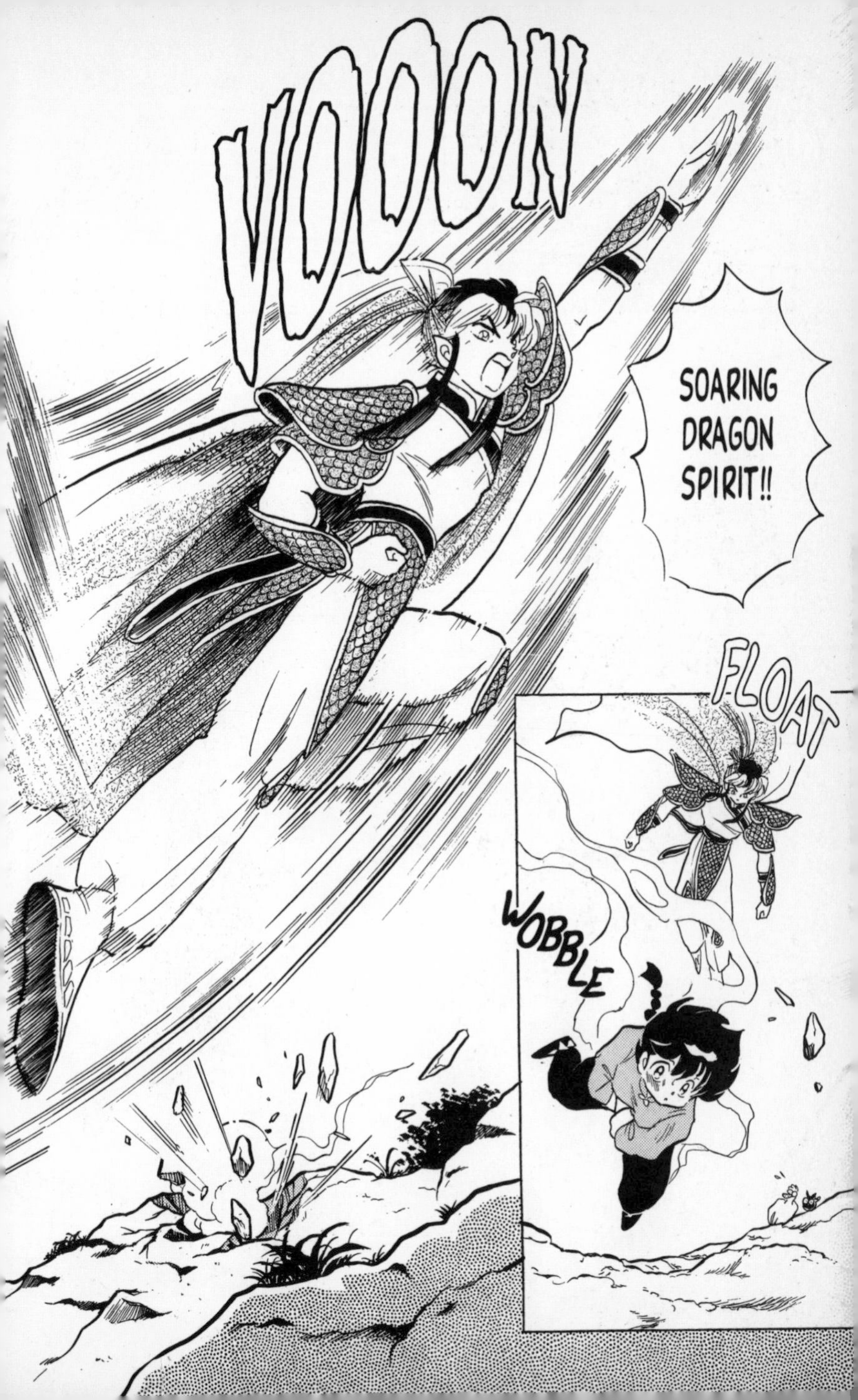
VOOON
SOARING DRAGON SPIRIT!!
FLOAT
WOBBLE

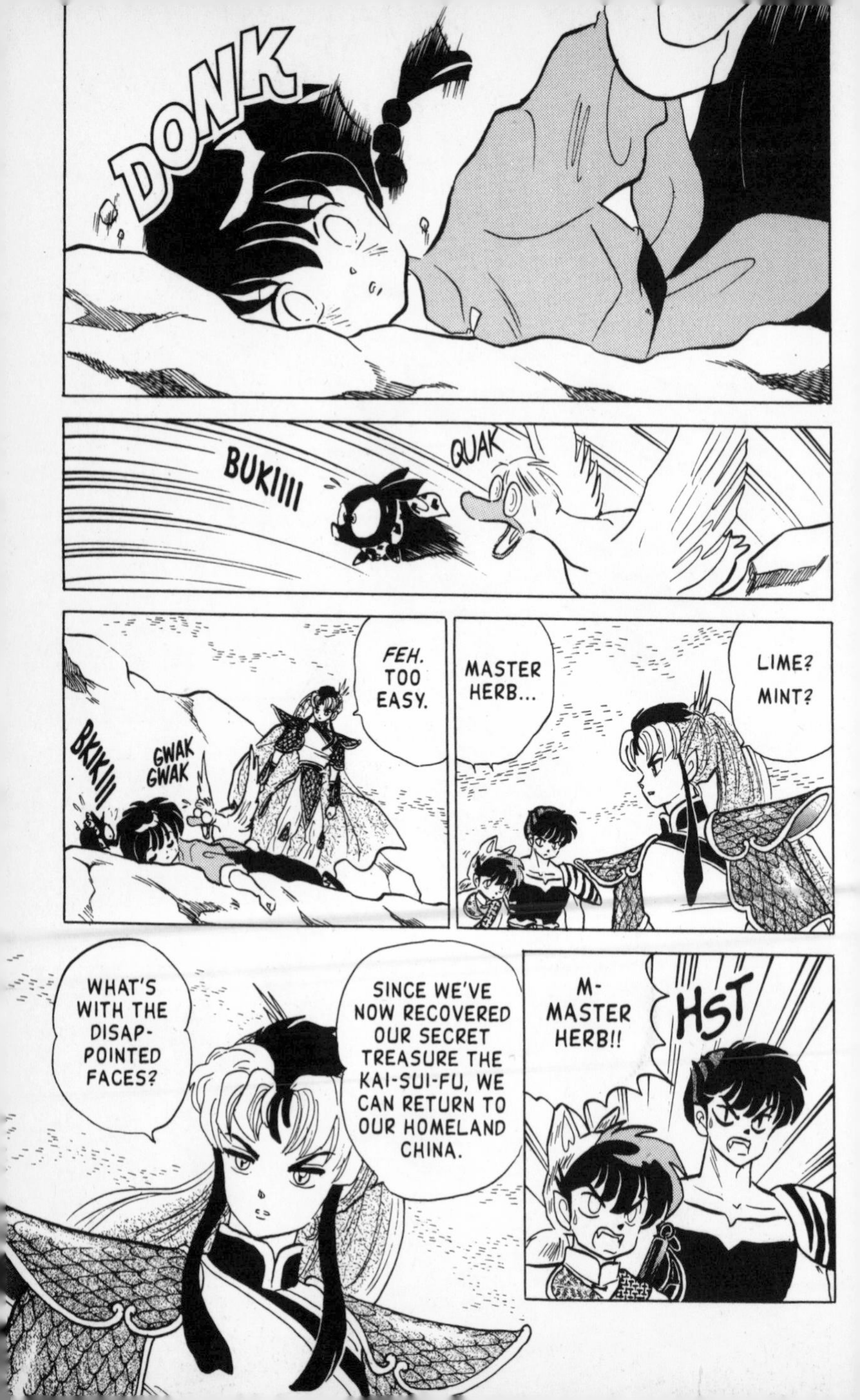
DONK
BUKIIII
QUAK
BKIKIII
GWAK GWAK
FEH. TOO EASY.
MASTER HERB...
LIME? MINT?
WHAT'S WITH THE DISAP-POINTED FACES?
SINCE WE'VE NOW RECOVERED OUR SECRET TREASURE THE KAI-SUI-FU, WE CAN RETURN TO OUR HOMELAND CHINA.
M-MASTER HERB!!
HST

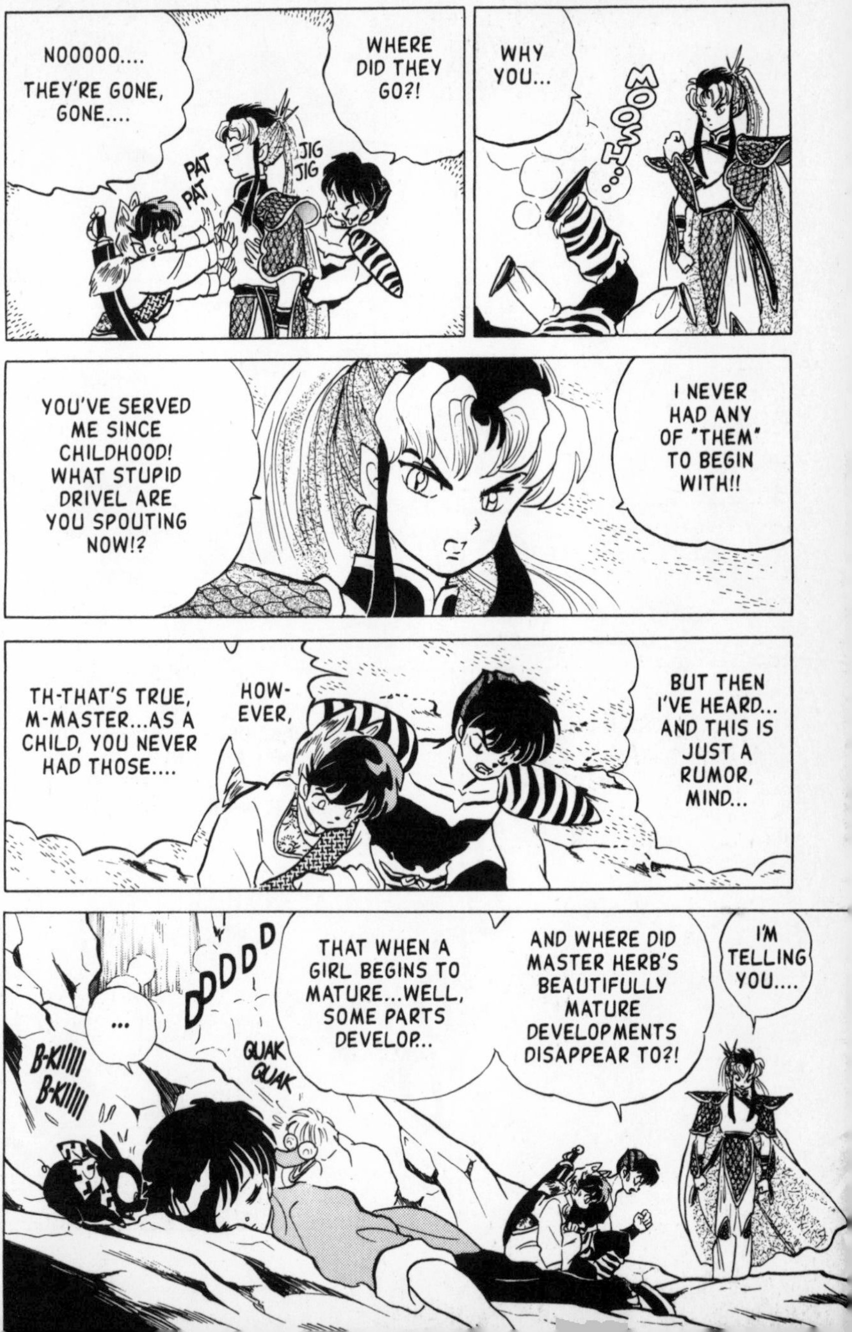
NOOOOO....
THEY'RE GONE, GONE....
PAT PAT
WHERE DID THEY GO?!
JIG JIG
WHY YOU...
MOOSH...
YOU'VE SERVED ME SINCE CHILDHOOD! WHAT STUPID DRIVEL ARE YOU SPOUTING NOW!?
I NEVER HAD ANY OF "THEM" TO BEGIN WITH!!
TH-THAT'S TRUE, M-MASTER...AS A CHILD, YOU NEVER HAD THOSE....
HOW-EVER,
BUT THEN I'VE HEARD... AND THIS IS JUST A RUMOR, MIND...
...
B-KIIIII B-KIIIII
DDDDD
QUAK QUAK
THAT WHEN A GIRL BEGINS TO MATURE...WELL, SOME PARTS DEVELOP...
AND WHERE DID MASTER HERB'S BEAUTIFULLY MATURE DEVELOPMENTS DISAPPEAR TO?!
I'M TELLING YOU....

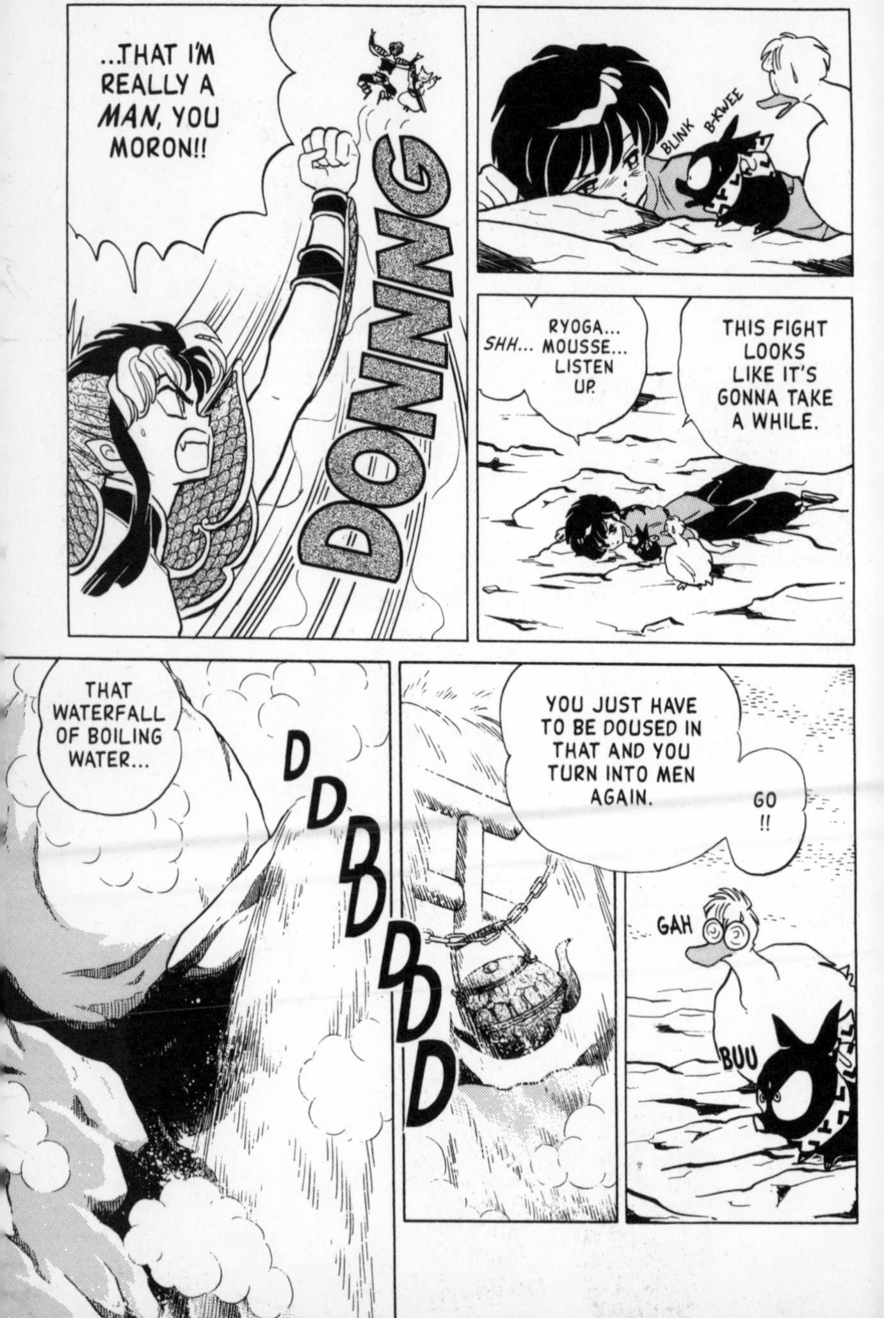

...THAT I'M REALLY A *MAN*, YOU MORON!!
DOWNG
BLINK
B-KWEE
SHH...
RYOGA... MOUSSE... LISTEN UP.
THIS FIGHT LOOKS LIKE IT'S GONNA TAKE A WHILE.
THAT WATERFALL OF BOILING WATER...
DDBDDDD
YOU JUST HAVE TO BE DOUSED IN THAT AND YOU TURN INTO MEN AGAIN.
GO !!
GAH
BUU

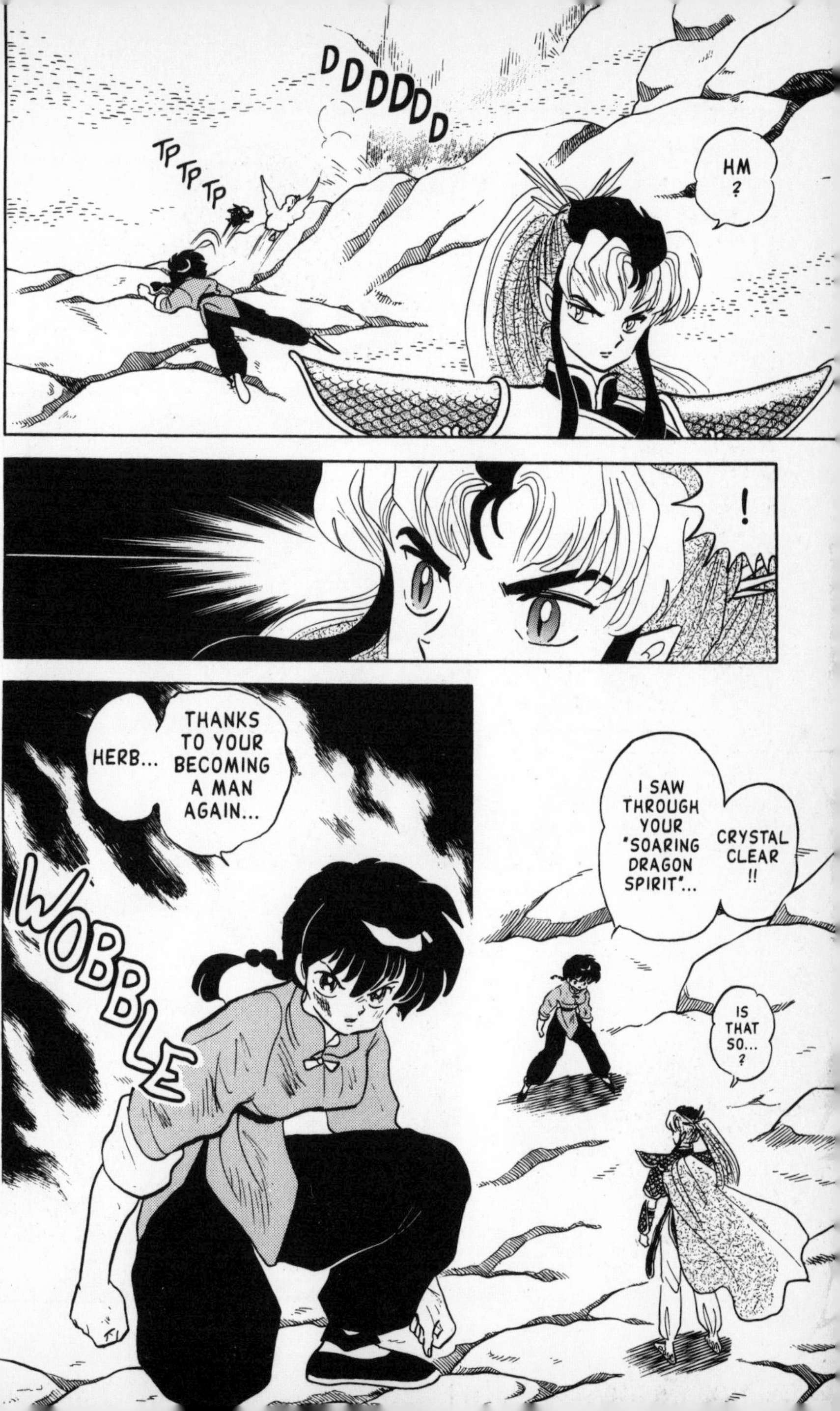
DDDDDDD
TP TP TP TP
HM ?
!
HERB... THANKS TO YOUR BECOMING A MAN AGAIN...
WOBBLE
I SAW THROUGH YOUR "SOARING DRAGON SPIRIT"...
CRYSTAL CLEAR !!
IS THAT SO... ?

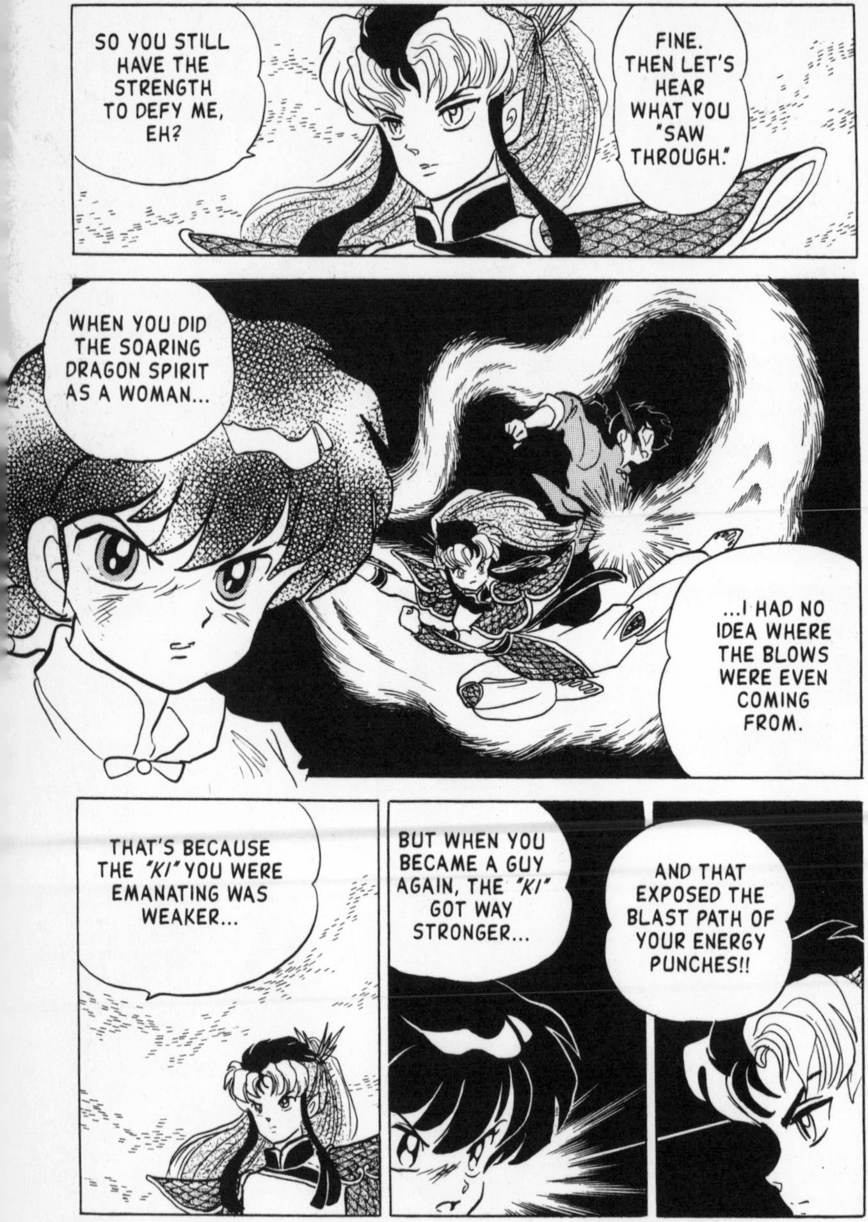
SO YOU STILL HAVE THE STRENGTH TO DEFY ME, EH?
FINE. THEN LET'S HEAR WHAT YOU "SAW THROUGH."
WHEN YOU DID THE SOARING DRAGON SPIRIT AS A WOMAN...
...I HAD NO IDEA WHERE THE BLOWS WERE EVEN COMING FROM.
THAT'S BECAUSE THE "KI" YOU WERE EMANATING WAS WEAKER...
BUT WHEN YOU BECAME A GUY AGAIN, THE "KI" GOT WAY STRONGER...
AND THAT EXPOSED THE BLAST PATH OF YOUR ENERGY PUNCHES!!

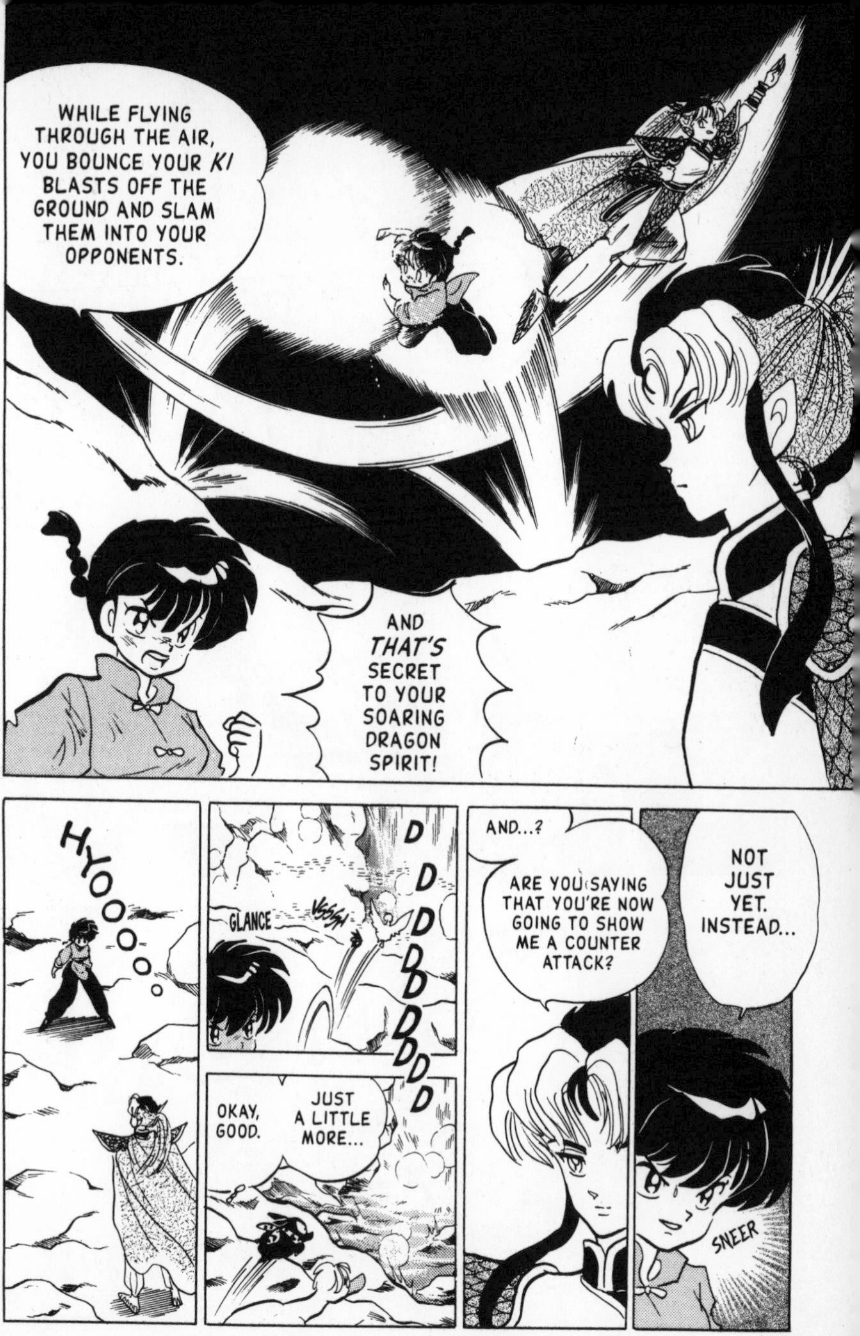
WHILE FLYING THROUGH THE AIR, YOU BOUNCE YOUR *KI* BLASTS OFF THE GROUND AND SLAM THEM INTO YOUR OPPONENTS.
AND *THAT'S* SECRET TO YOUR SOARING DRAGON SPIRIT!
HYOOOOOO
GLANCE
VSSSH
DDDDDDDDDD
OKAY, GOOD.
JUST A LITTLE MORE...
AND...?
ARE YOU SAYING THAT YOU'RE NOW GOING TO SHOW ME A COUNTER ATTACK?
NOT JUST YET. INSTEAD...
SNEER

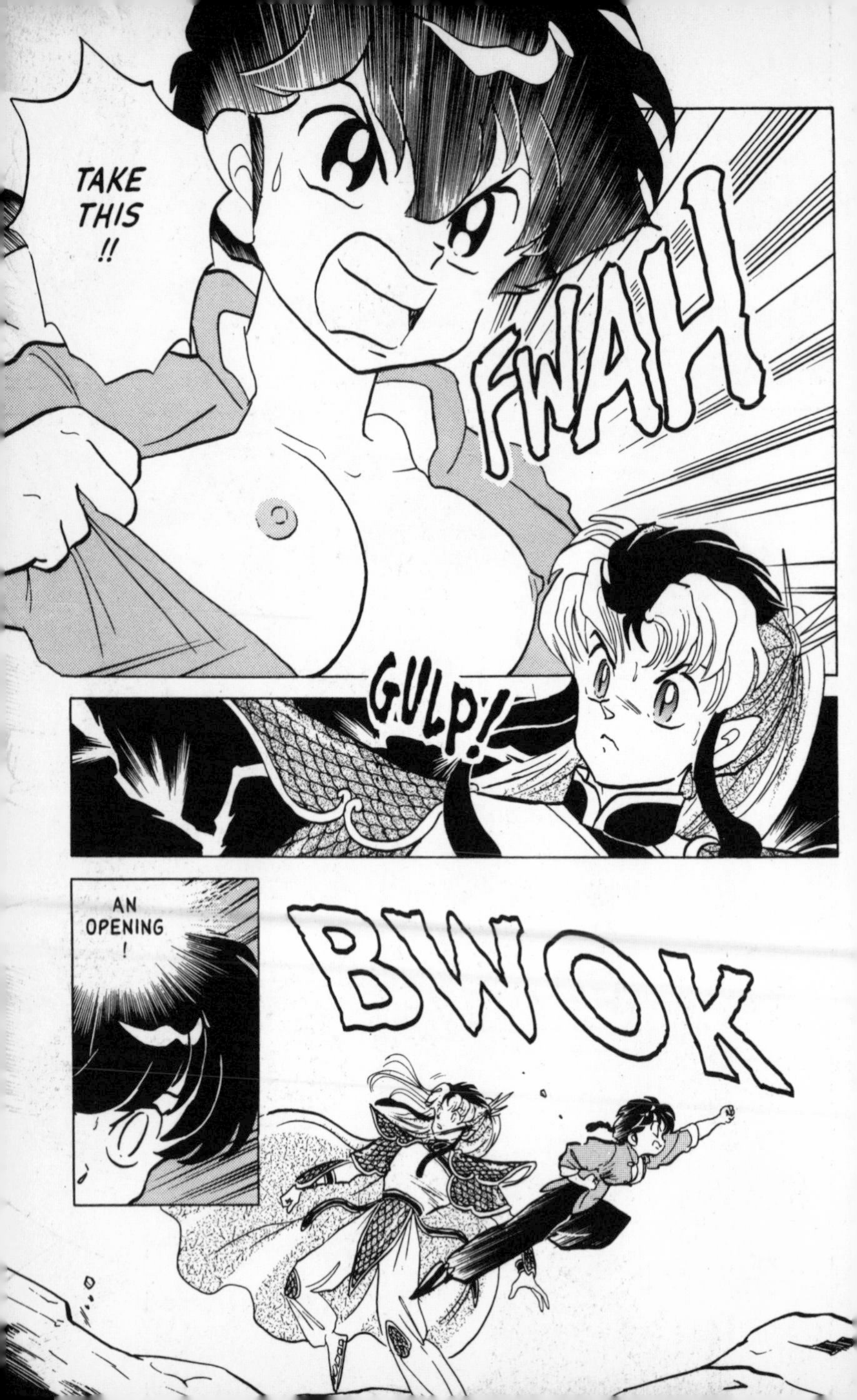

TAKE THIS !!
FWAH
GULP!
AN OPENING !
BWOK

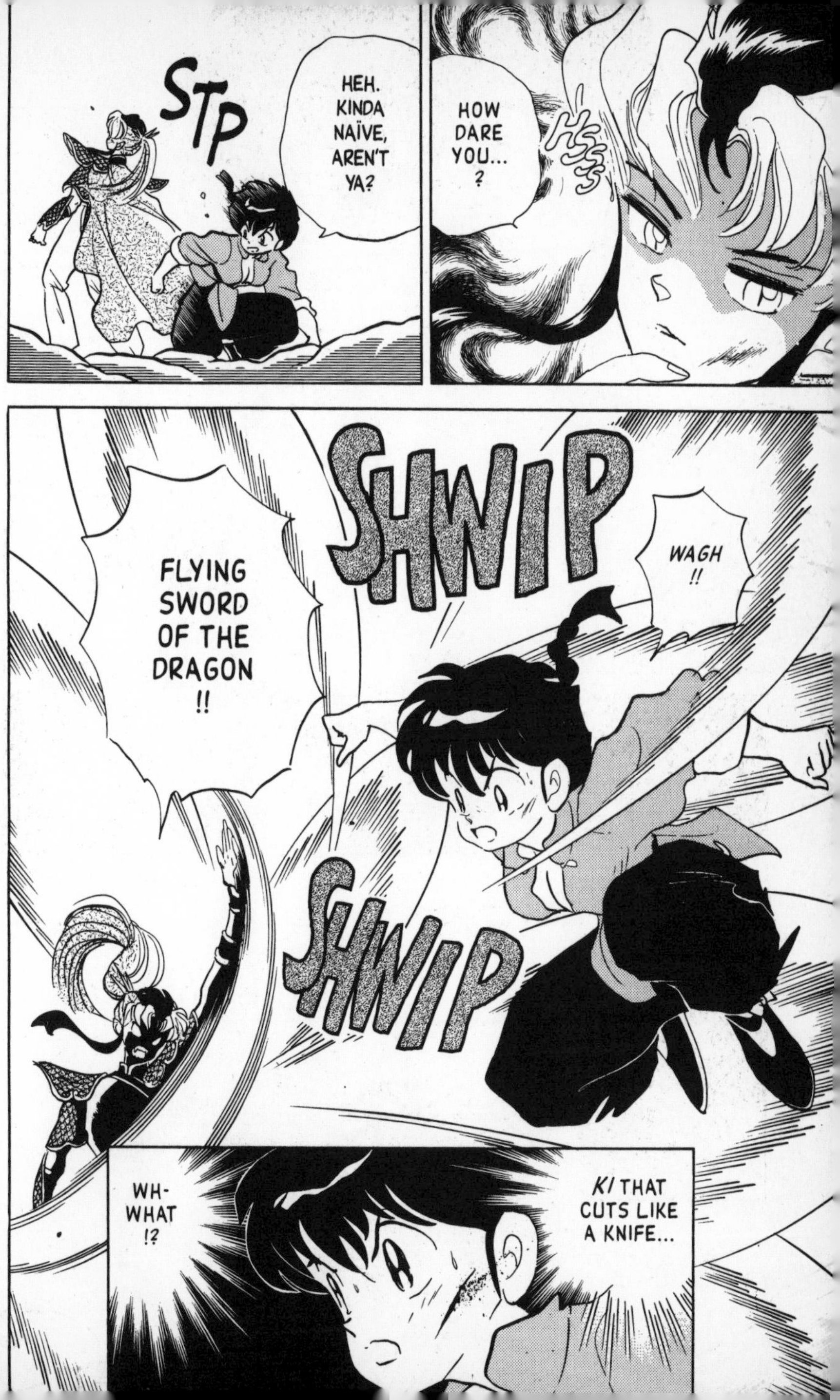
STP
HEH. KINDA NAÏVE, AREN'T YA?
HOW DARE YOU...?
HSSS
FLYING SWORD OF THE DRAGON!!
SHWIP
WAGH!!
SHWIP
WH- WHAT!?
KI THAT CUTS LIKE A KNIFE...

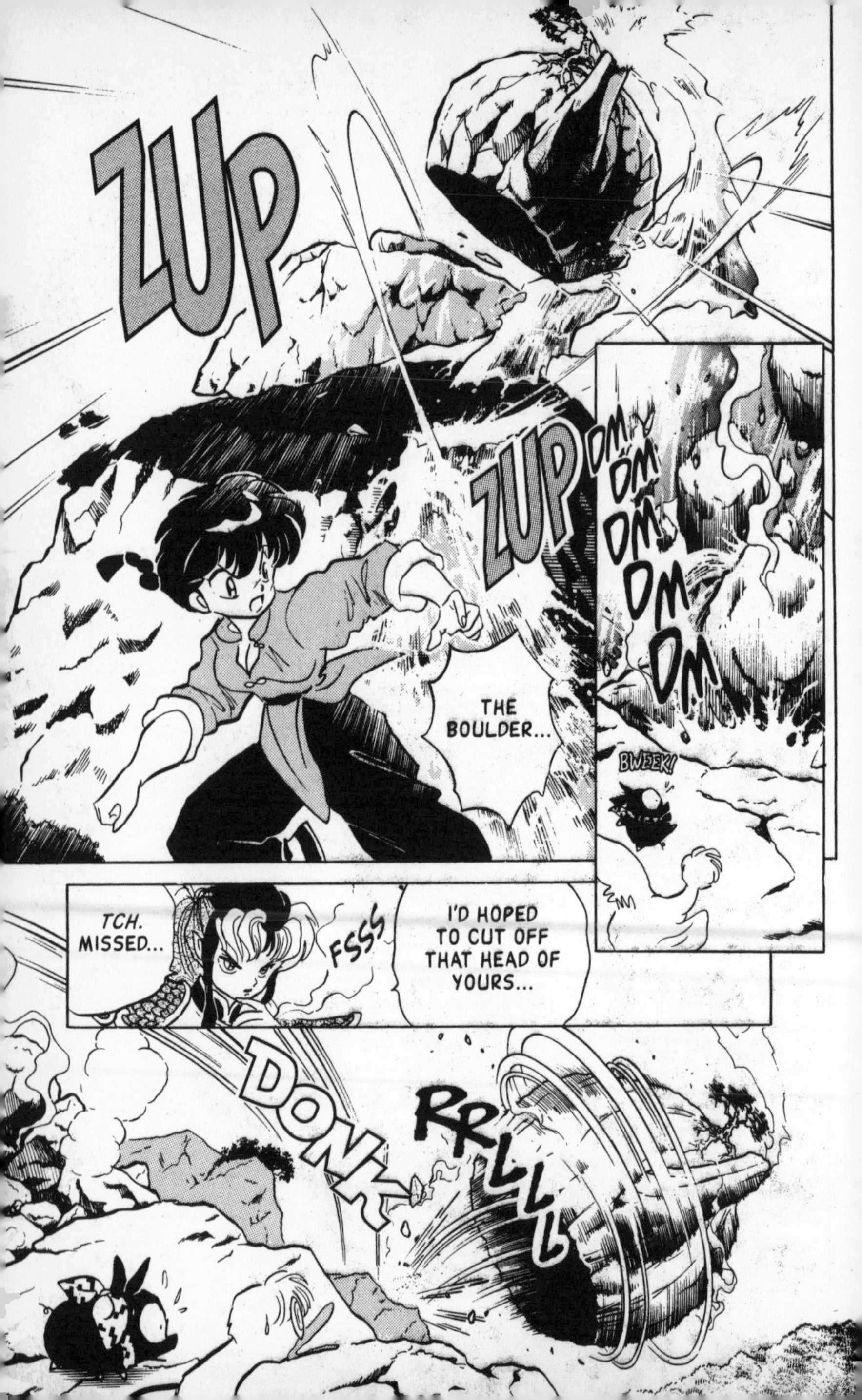
ZUP
ZUP
THE BOULDER...
DM DM DM DM DM DM
BWEEK!
TCH. MISSED...
FSSS
I'D HOPED TO CUT OFF THAT HEAD OF YOURS...
DONK
RRLLLL

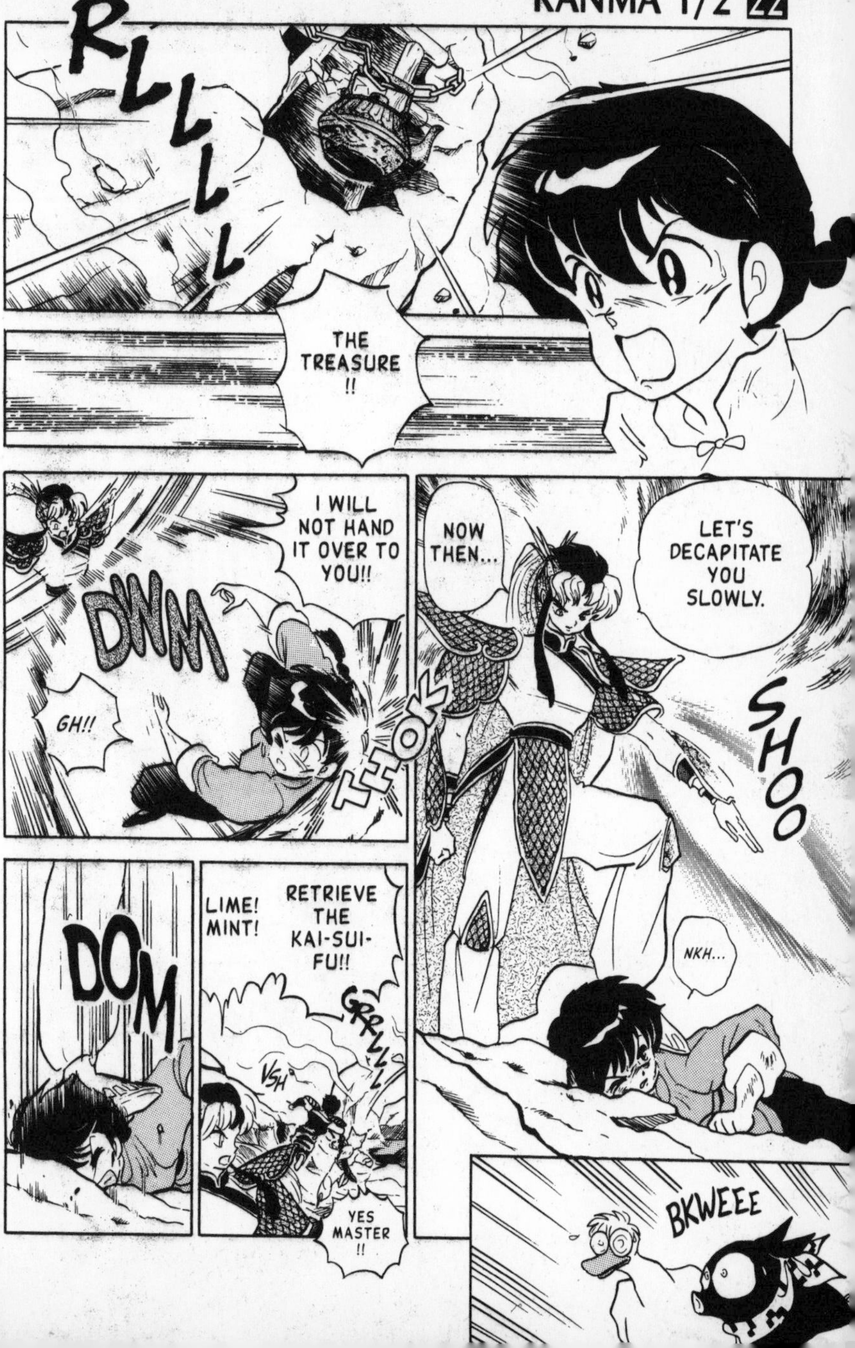
RLLLLL
THE TREASURE !!
I WILL NOT HAND IT OVER TO YOU!!
DNM
GH!!
THOK
DOM
LIME! MINT!
RETRIEVE THE KAI-SUI-FU!!
GRRLLL
VSH
YES MASTER !!
NOW THEN...
LET'S DECAPITATE YOU SLOWLY.
SHOO
NKH...
BKWEEE

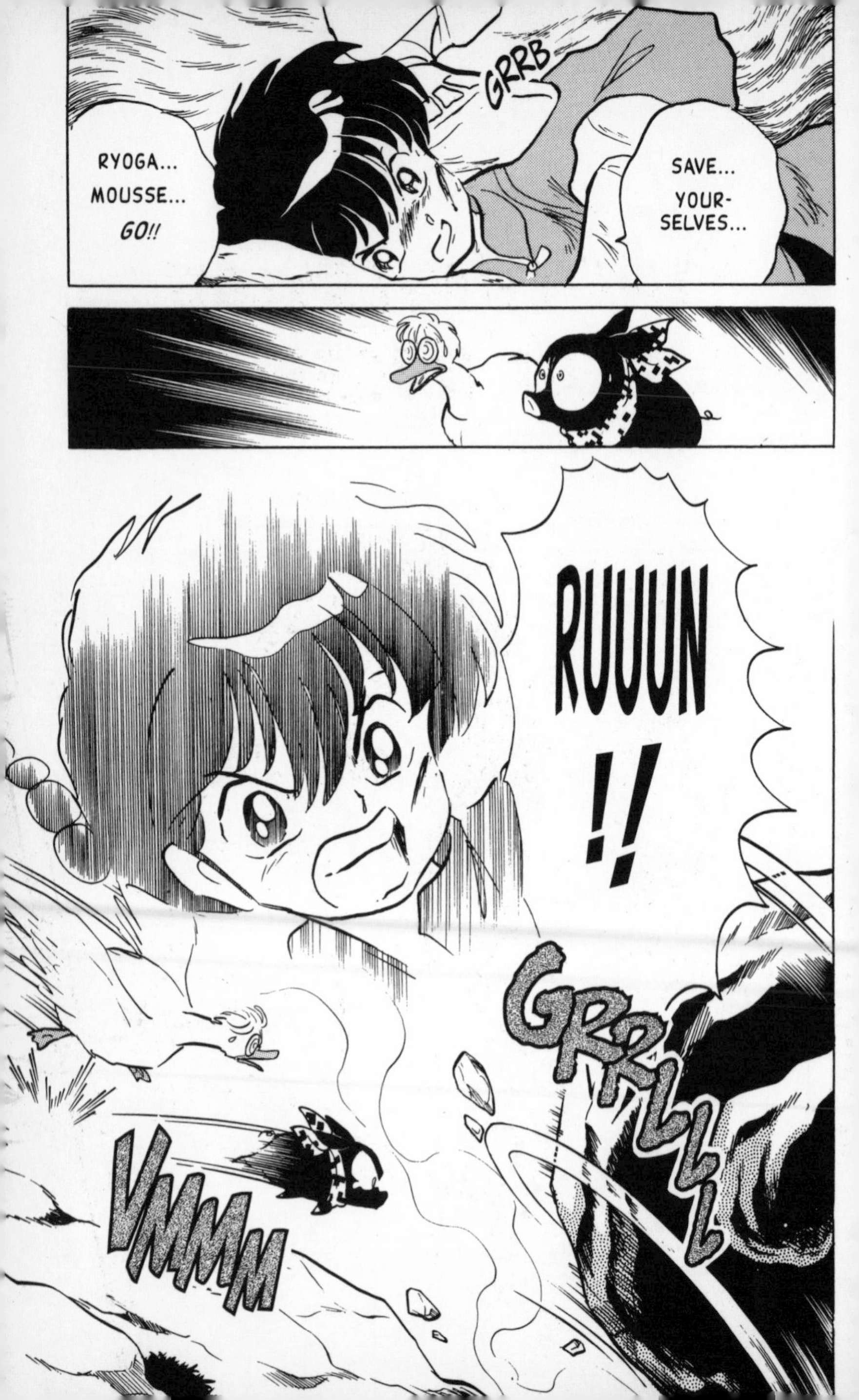
GRRB
RYOGA... MOUSSE... GO!!
SAVE... YOUR-SELVES...
RUUUN!!
GRRLLL
VMMM

Part 10

THE CONFESSION OF RAGE!

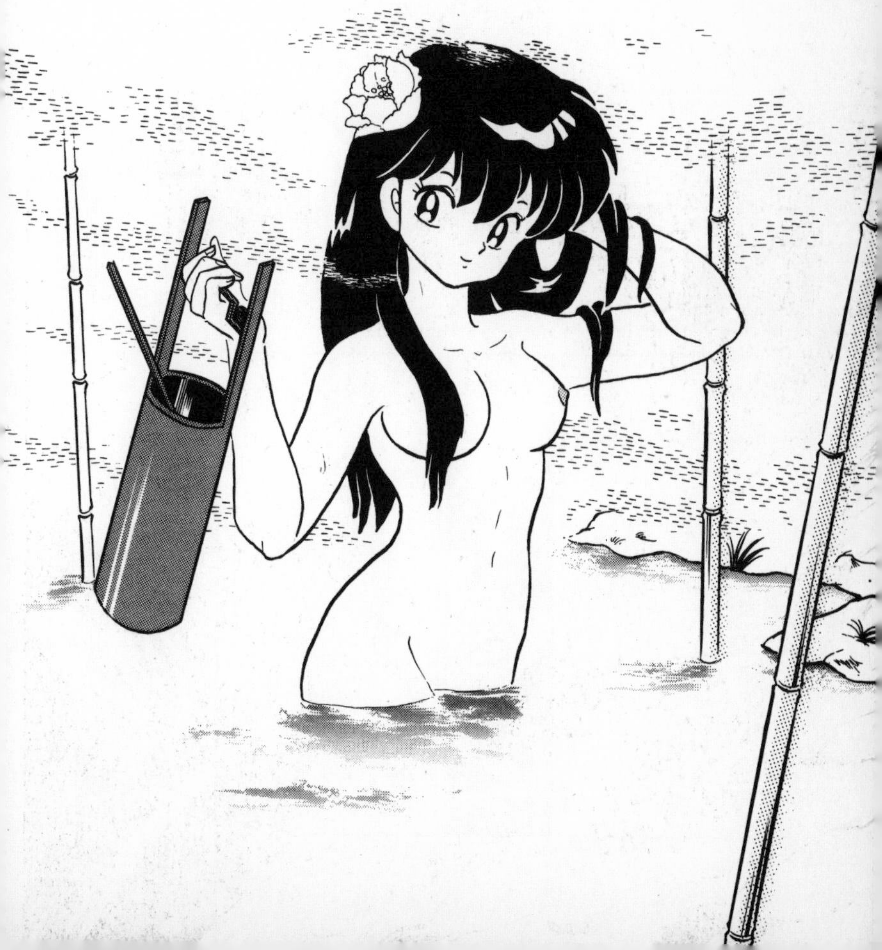

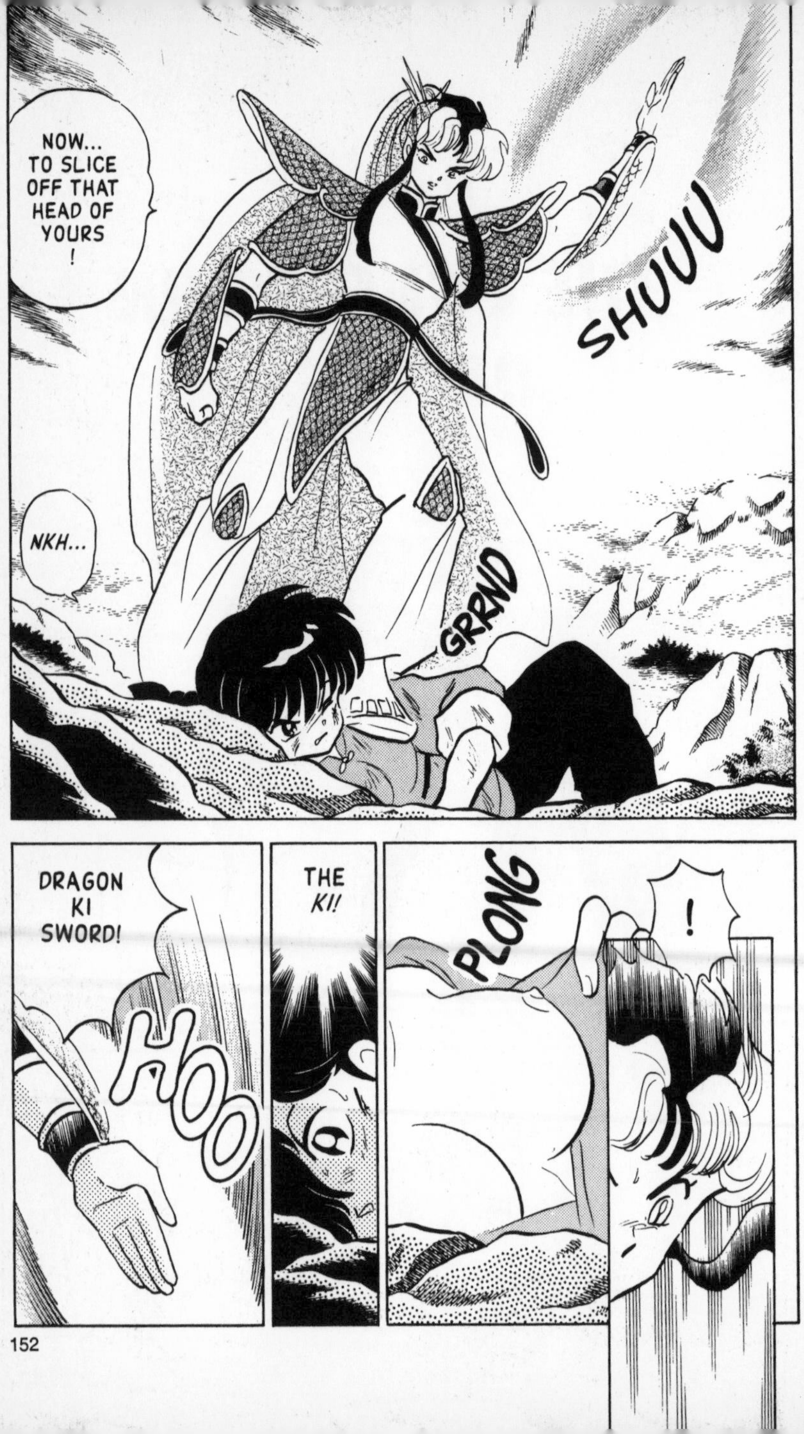
NOW... TO SLICE OFF THAT HEAD OF YOURS !
SHUUU
NKH...
GRRND
DRAGON KI SWORD!
HOO
THE KI!
PLONG
!

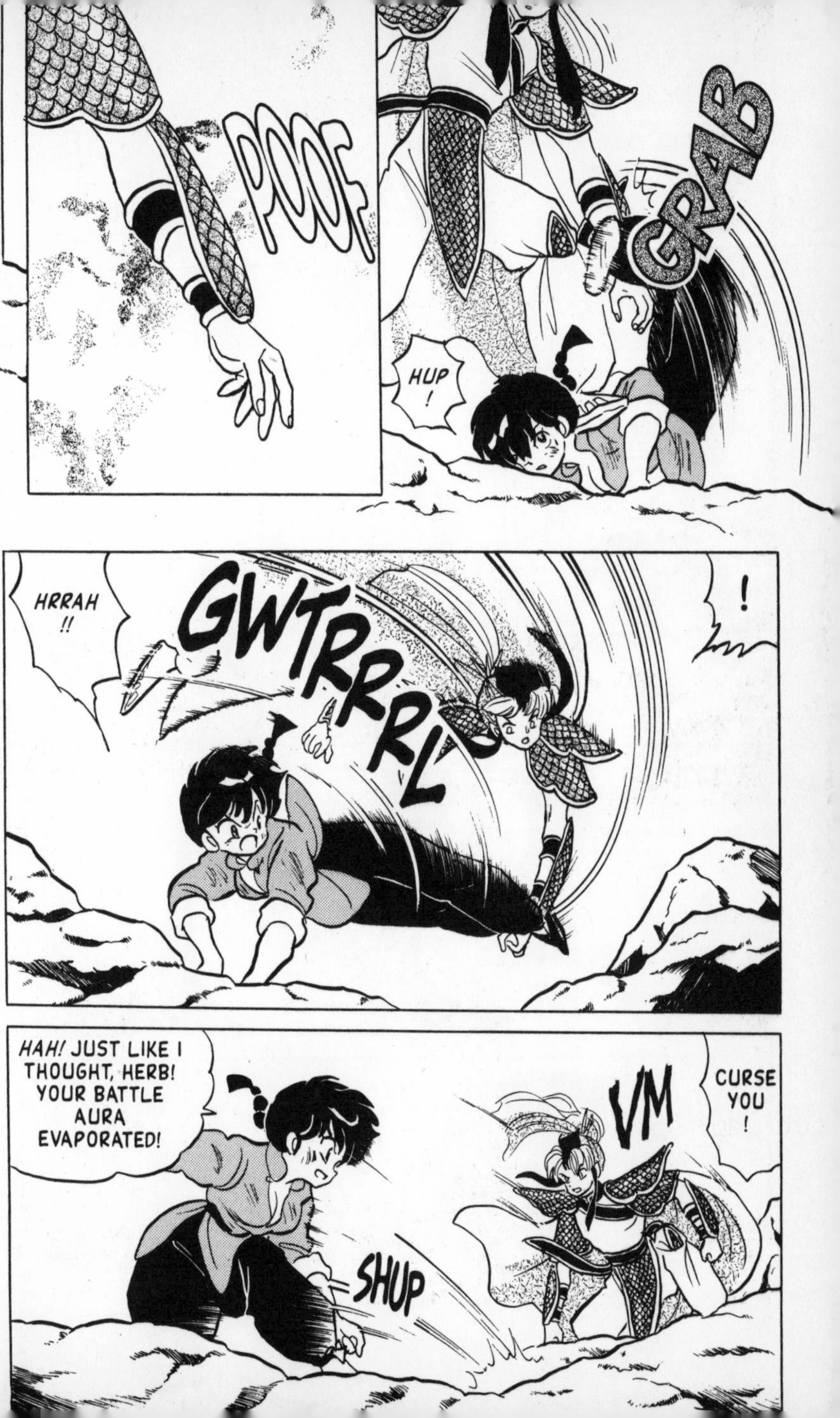
POOF
GRAB
HUP!
HRRAH!!
GWTRRRL
!
HAH! JUST LIKE I THOUGHT, HERB! YOUR BATTLE AURA EVAPORATED!
SHUP
VM
CURSE YOU!

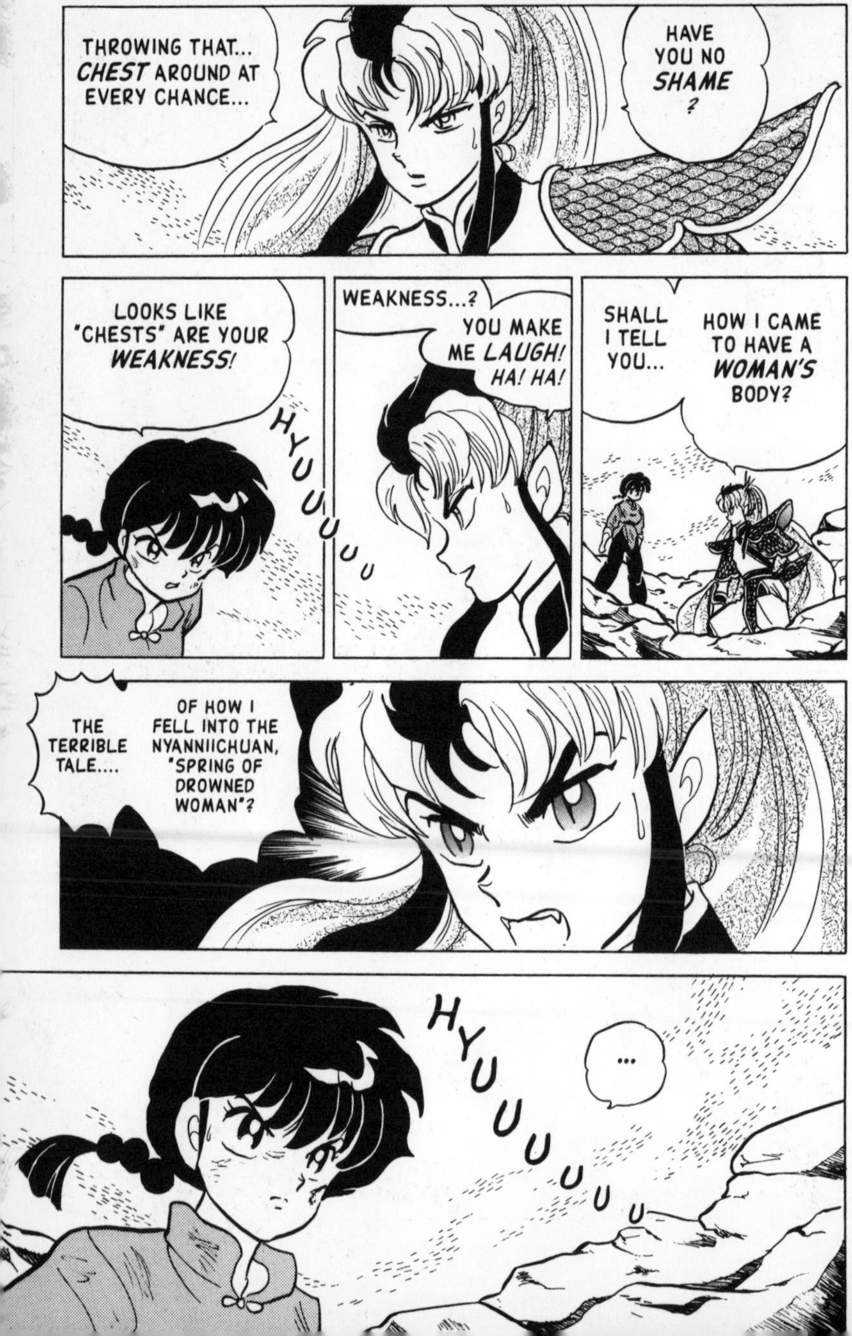
THROWING THAT... CHEST AROUND AT EVERY CHANCE...
HAVE YOU NO SHAME ?
LOOKS LIKE "CHESTS" ARE YOUR WEAKNESS!
HYUUUUUU
WEAKNESS...?
YOU MAKE ME LAUGH! HA! HA!
SHALL I TELL YOU...
HOW I CAME TO HAVE A WOMAN'S BODY?
THE TERRIBLE TALE....
OF HOW I FELL INTO THE NYANNIICHUAN, "SPRING OF DROWNED WOMAN"?
HYUUUUUUUU
...

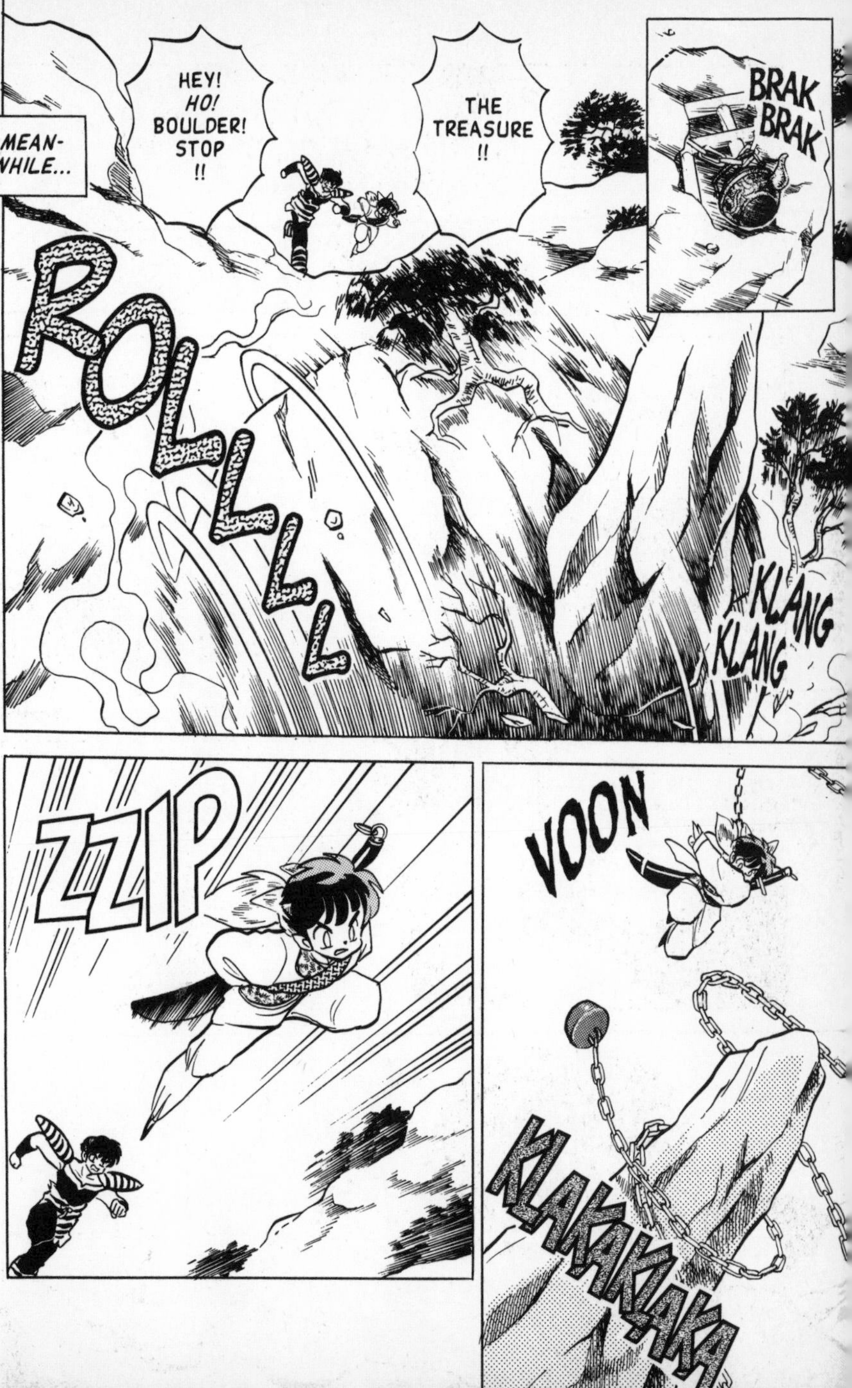
MEAN-WHILE...
HEY! HO! BOULDER! STOP !!
THE TREASURE !!
ROLLLLL
BRAK BRAK
KLANG KLANG
ZZIP
VOON
KLAKAKAKA

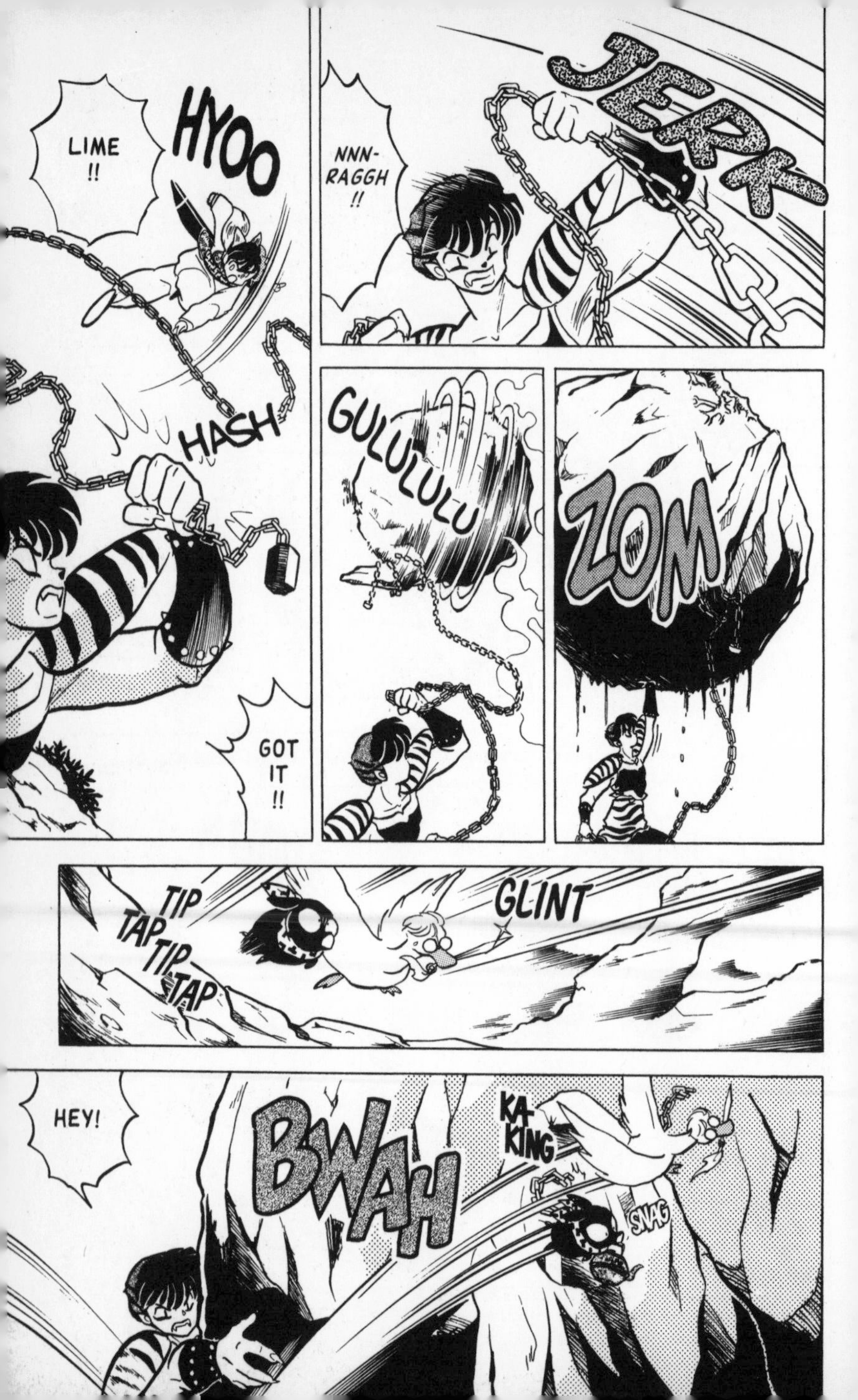

LIME !!
HYOO
HASH
GOT IT !!
NNN-RAGGH !!
JERK
GULULULU
ZOM
TIP TAP TIP TAP
GLINT
HEY!
BWAH
KA-KING
SNAG

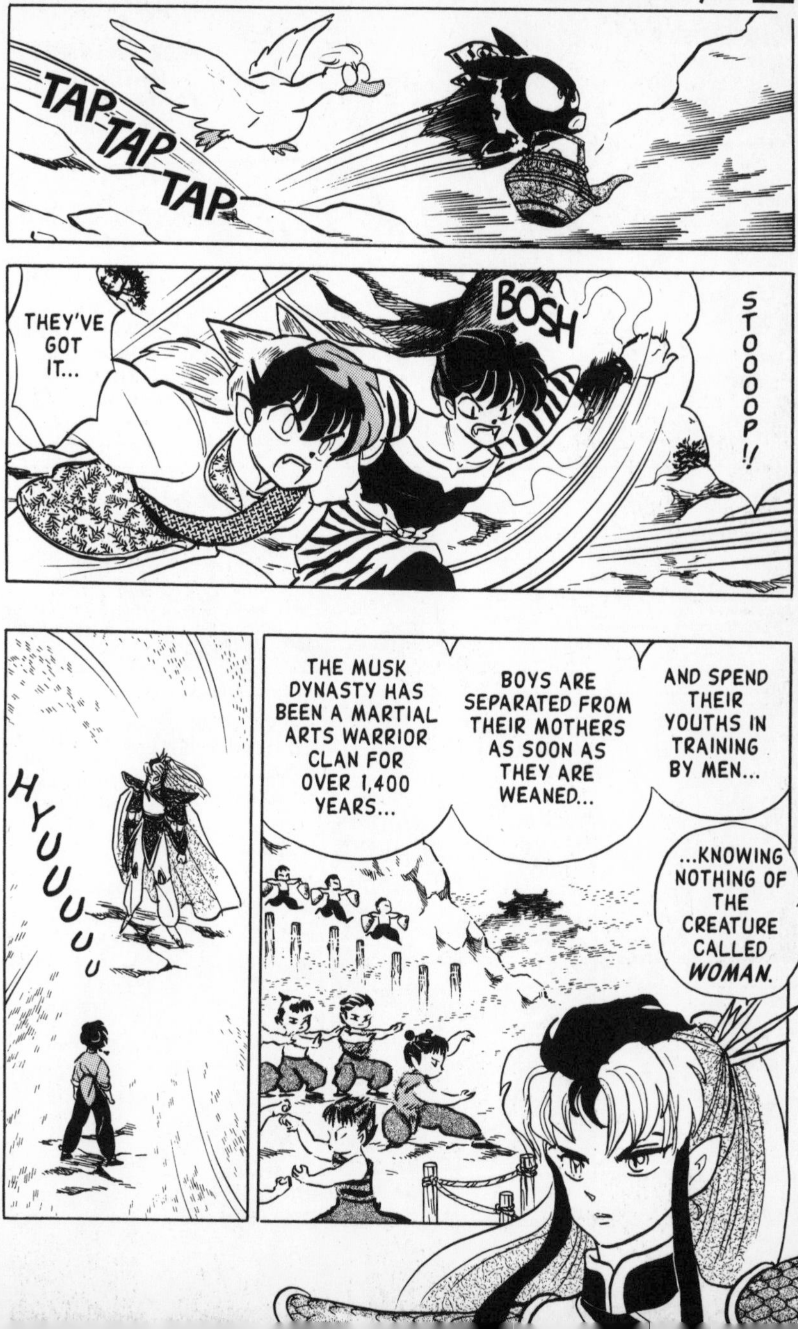
TAP TAP TAP
THEY'VE GOT IT...
BOSH
STOOOOOP!!
HYUUUUUU
THE MUSK DYNASTY HAS BEEN A MARTIAL ARTS WARRIOR CLAN FOR OVER 1,400 YEARS...
BOYS ARE SEPARATED FROM THEIR MOTHERS AS SOON AS THEY ARE WEANED...
AND SPEND THEIR YOUTHS IN TRAINING BY MEN...
...KNOWING NOTHING OF THE CREATURE CALLED *WOMAN*.

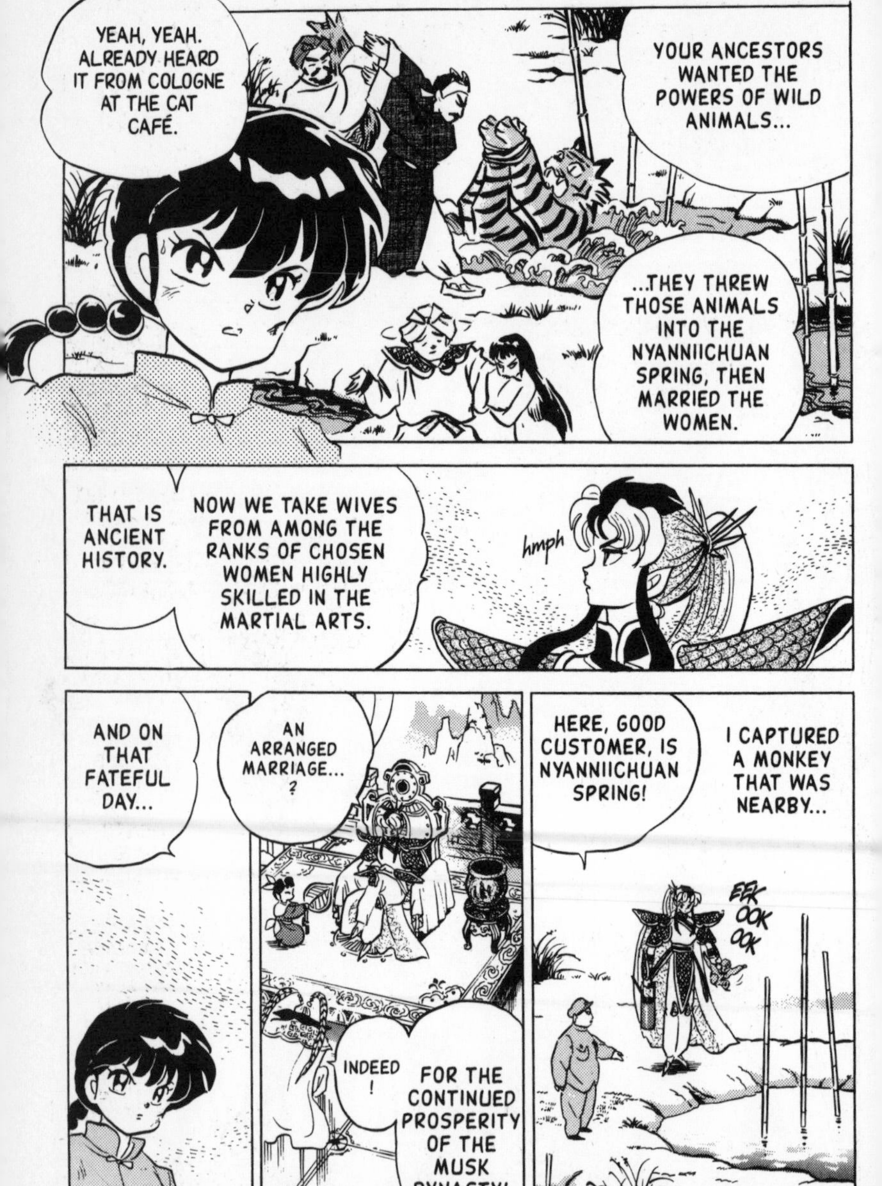
YEAH, YEAH. ALREADY HEARD IT FROM COLOGNE AT THE CAT CAFÉ.
YOUR ANCESTORS WANTED THE POWERS OF WILD ANIMALS...
...THEY THREW THOSE ANIMALS INTO THE NYANNIICHUAN SPRING, THEN MARRIED THE WOMEN.
THAT IS ANCIENT HISTORY.
NOW WE TAKE WIVES FROM AMONG THE RANKS OF CHOSEN WOMEN HIGHLY SKILLED IN THE MARTIAL ARTS.
hmph
AND ON THAT FATEFUL DAY...
AN ARRANGED MARRIAGE...?
INDEED!
FOR THE CONTINUED PROSPERITY OF THE MUSK DYNASTY!
HERE, GOOD CUSTOMER, IS NYANNIICHUAN SPRING!
I CAPTURED A MONKEY THAT WAS NEARBY...
EEK OOK OOK

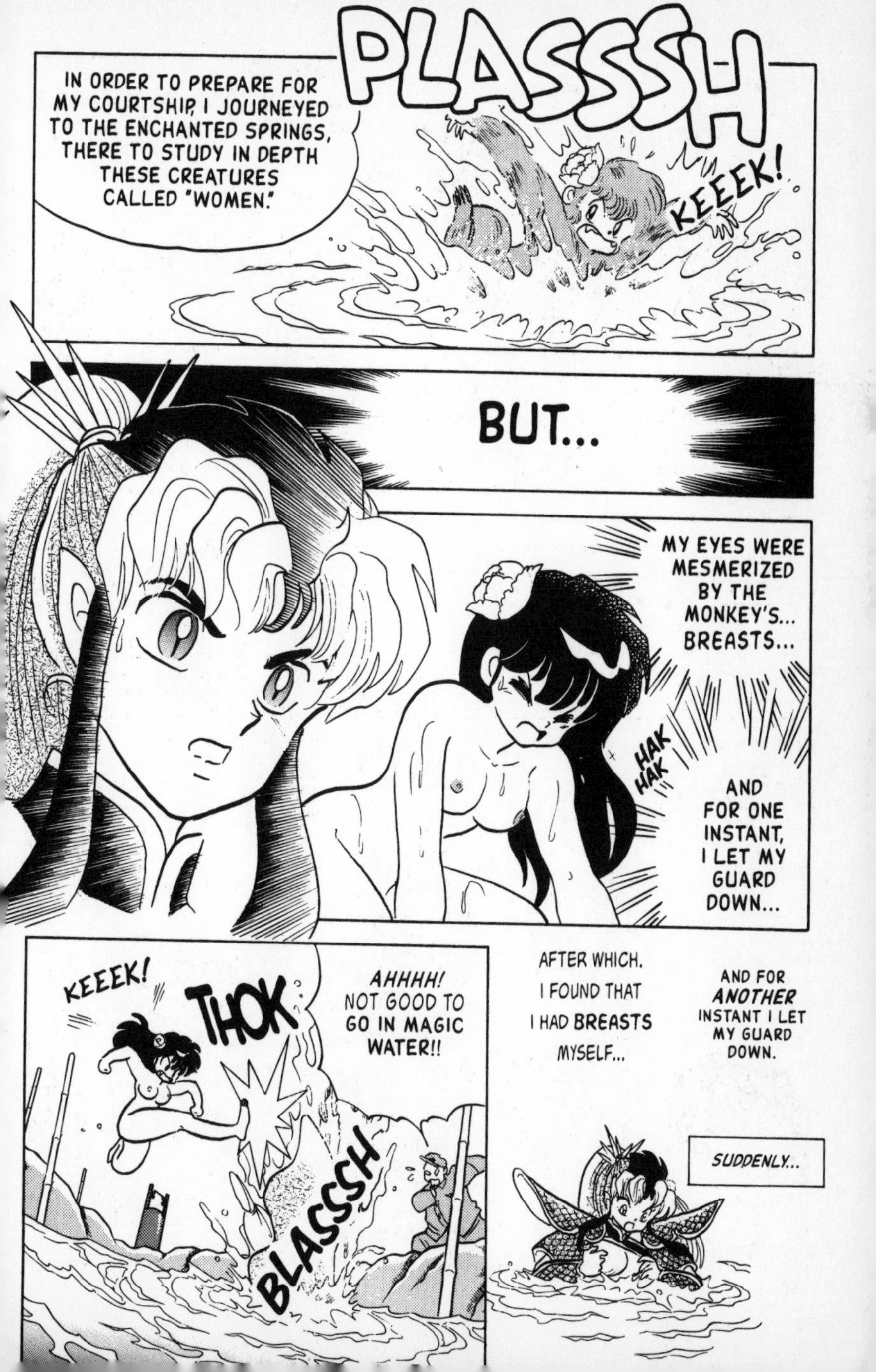
PLASSSH
IN ORDER TO PREPARE FOR MY COURTSHIP, I JOURNEYED TO THE ENCHANTED SPRINGS, THERE TO STUDY IN DEPTH THESE CREATURES CALLED "WOMEN."
KEEEK!
BUT...
MY EYES WERE MESMERIZED BY THE MONKEY'S... BREASTS...
HAK HAK
AND FOR ONE INSTANT, I LET MY GUARD DOWN...
KEEEK!
THOK
AHHHH! NOT GOOD TO GO IN MAGIC WATER!!
BLASSSH
AFTER WHICH, I FOUND THAT I HAD BREASTS MYSELF...
AND FOR ANOTHER INSTANT I LET MY GUARD DOWN.
SUDDENLY...

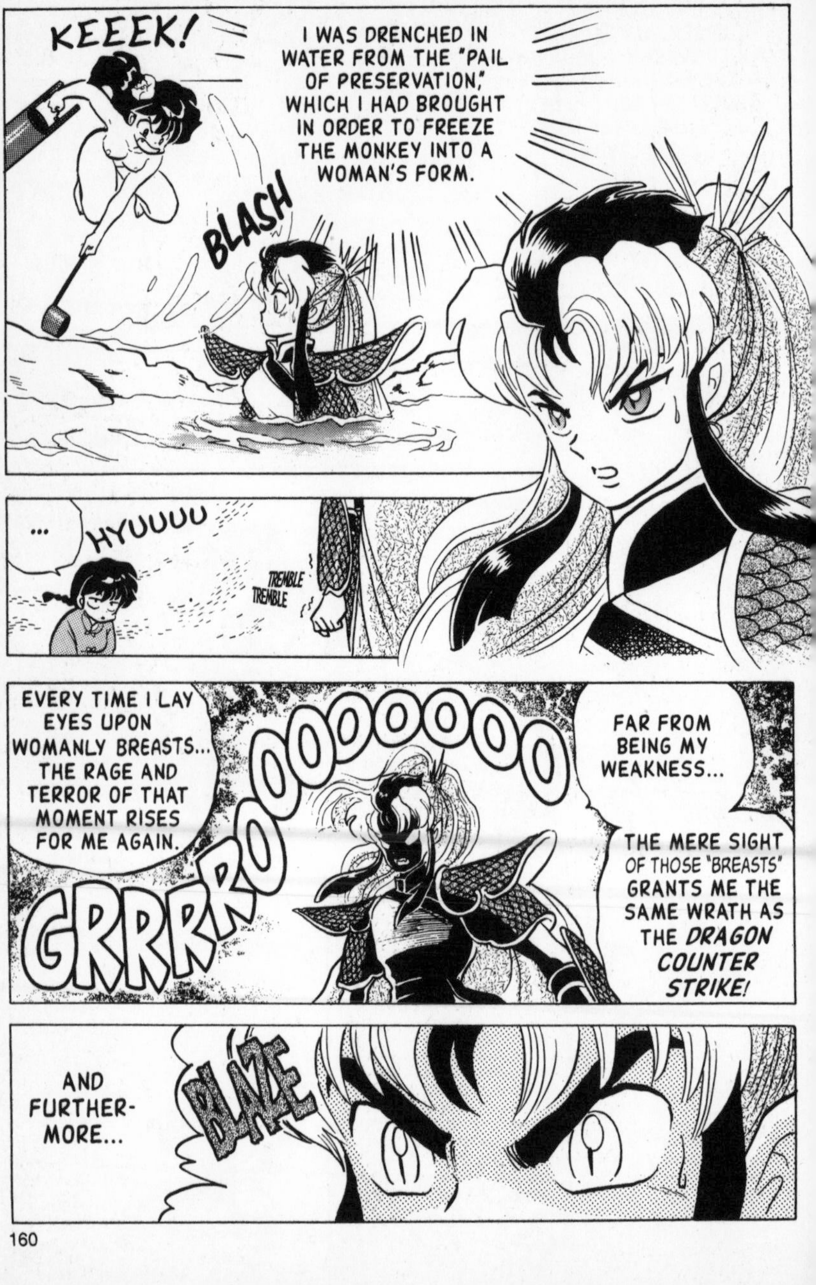
KEEEK!
I WAS DRENCHED IN WATER FROM THE "PAIL OF PRESERVATION," WHICH I HAD BROUGHT IN ORDER TO FREEZE THE MONKEY INTO A WOMAN'S FORM.
BLASH
...
HYUUUU
TREMBLE TREMBLE
EVERY TIME I LAY EYES UPON WOMANLY BREASTS... THE RAGE AND TERROR OF THAT MOMENT RISES FOR ME AGAIN.
GRRRROOOOOOOOOO
FAR FROM BEING MY WEAKNESS...
THE MERE SIGHT OF THOSE "BREASTS" GRANTS ME THE SAME WRATH AS THE *DRAGON COUNTER STRIKE!*
AND FURTHER-MORE...
BLAZE

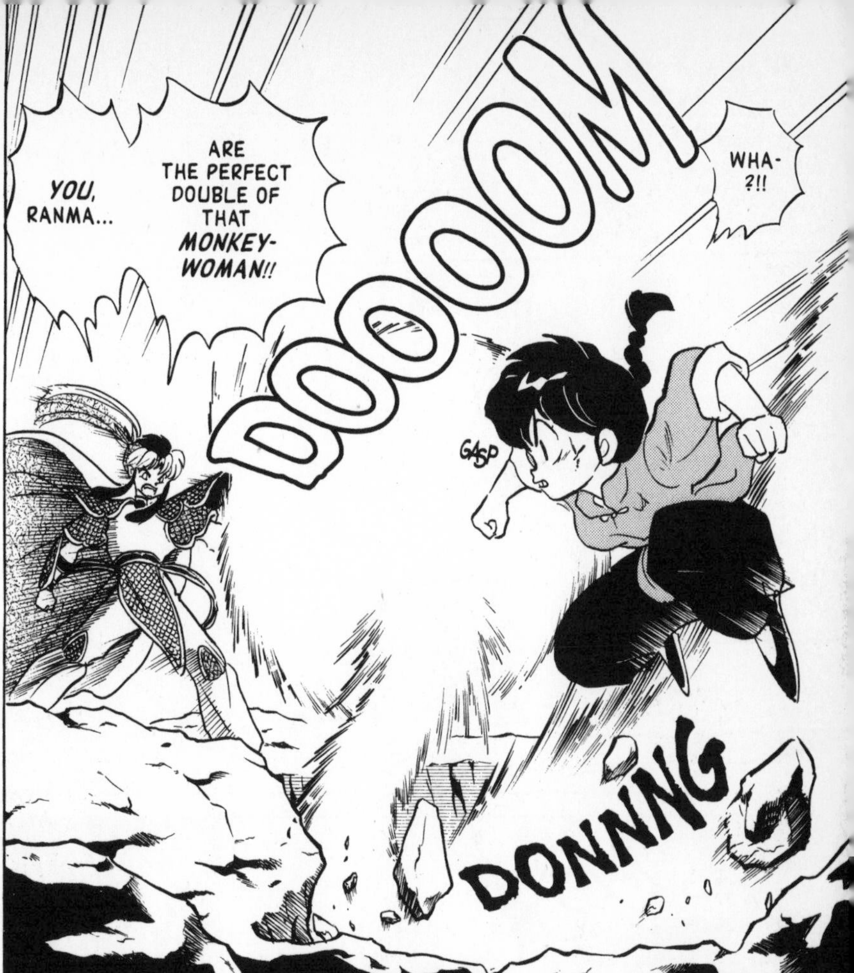
YOU, RANMA...
ARE THE PERFECT DOUBLE OF THAT MONKEY-WOMAN!!
DOOOOOM
WHA-?!!
GASP
DONNNG

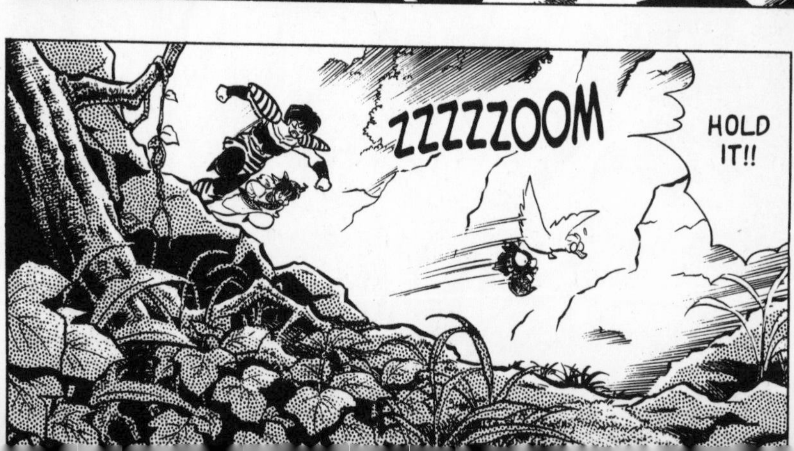
ZZZZZOOM
HOLD IT!!

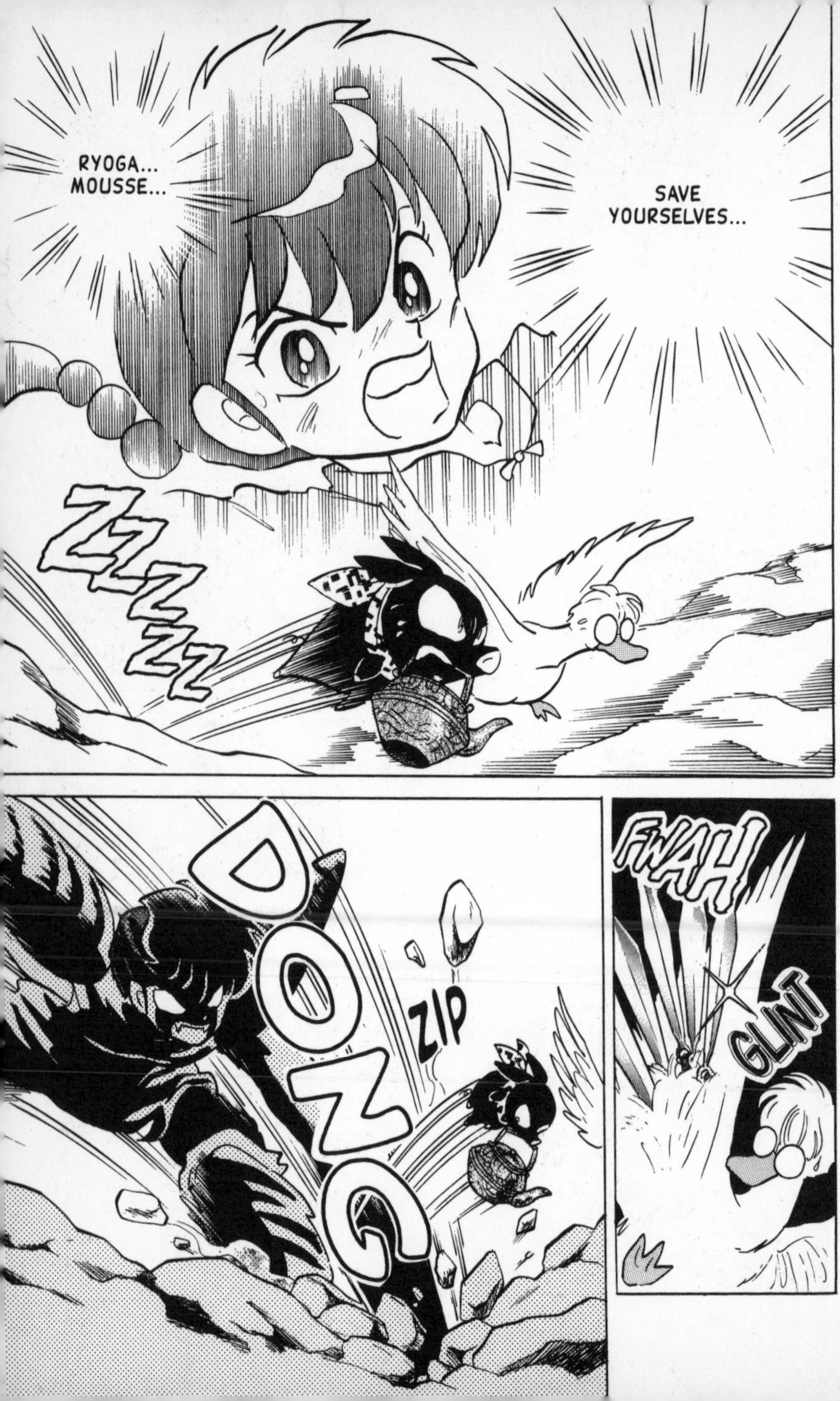
RYOGA... MOUSSE...
SAVE YOURSELVES...
ZZZZZ
DOONG
ZIP
FWAH
GLINT

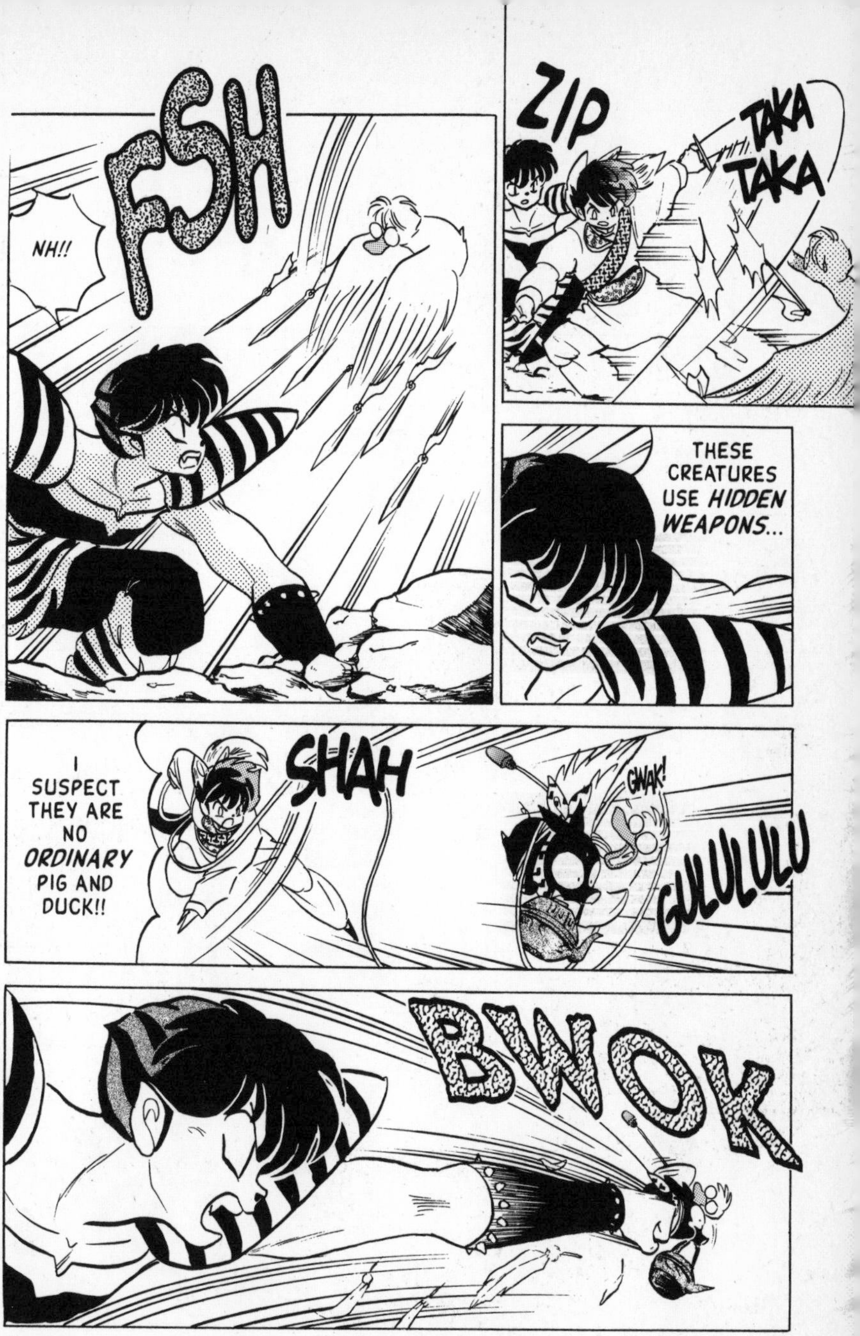
FSH
NH!!
ZIP
TAKA TAKA
THESE CREATURES USE *HIDDEN WEAPONS*...
I SUSPECT THEY ARE NO *ORDINARY* PIG AND DUCK!!
SHAH
GWAK!
GULULULU
BWOK

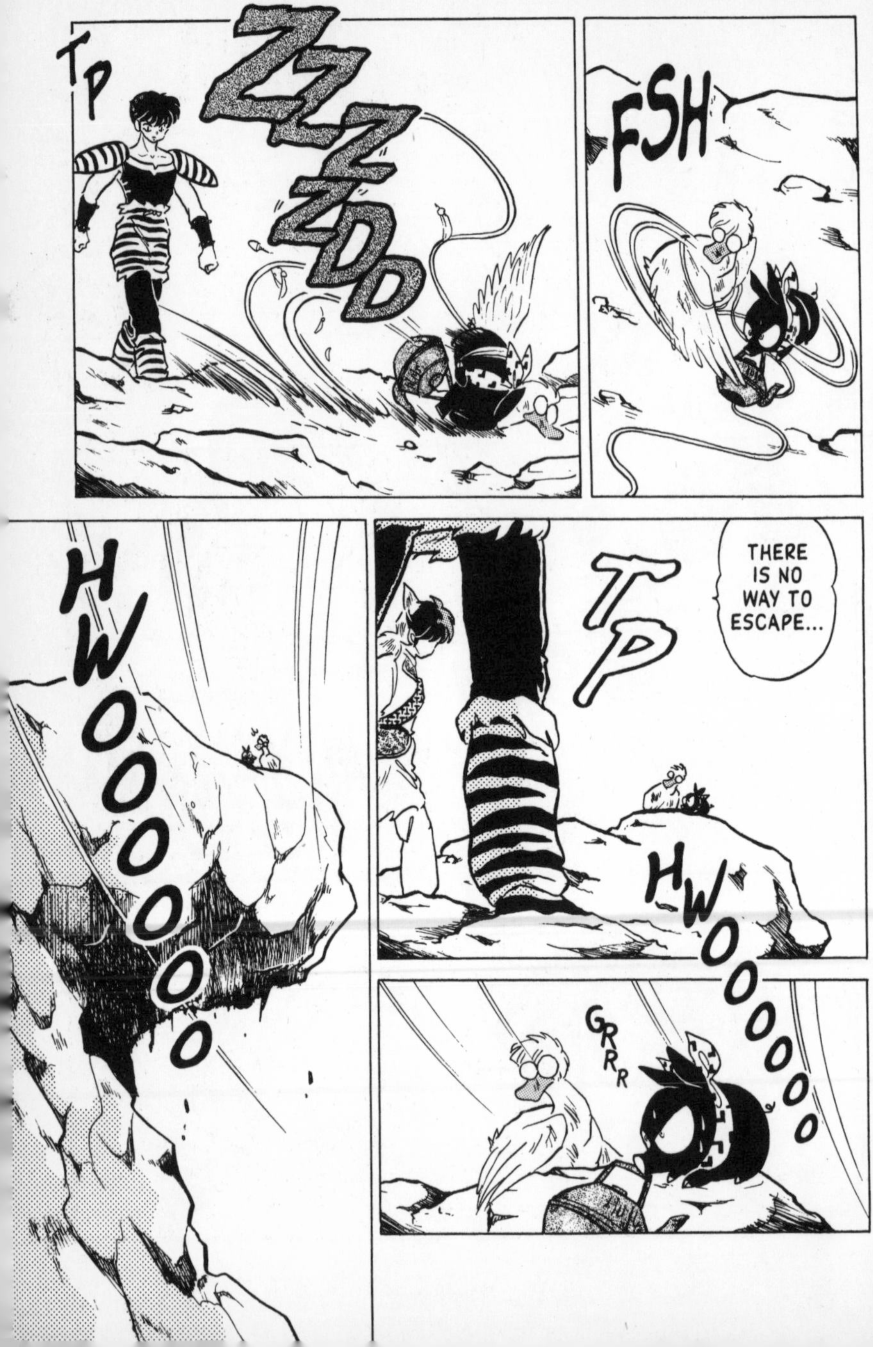
TP
ZZZZDD
FSH
HWOOOOOO
TP
THERE IS NO WAY TO ESCAPE...
HWOOOOOOOO
GRRR

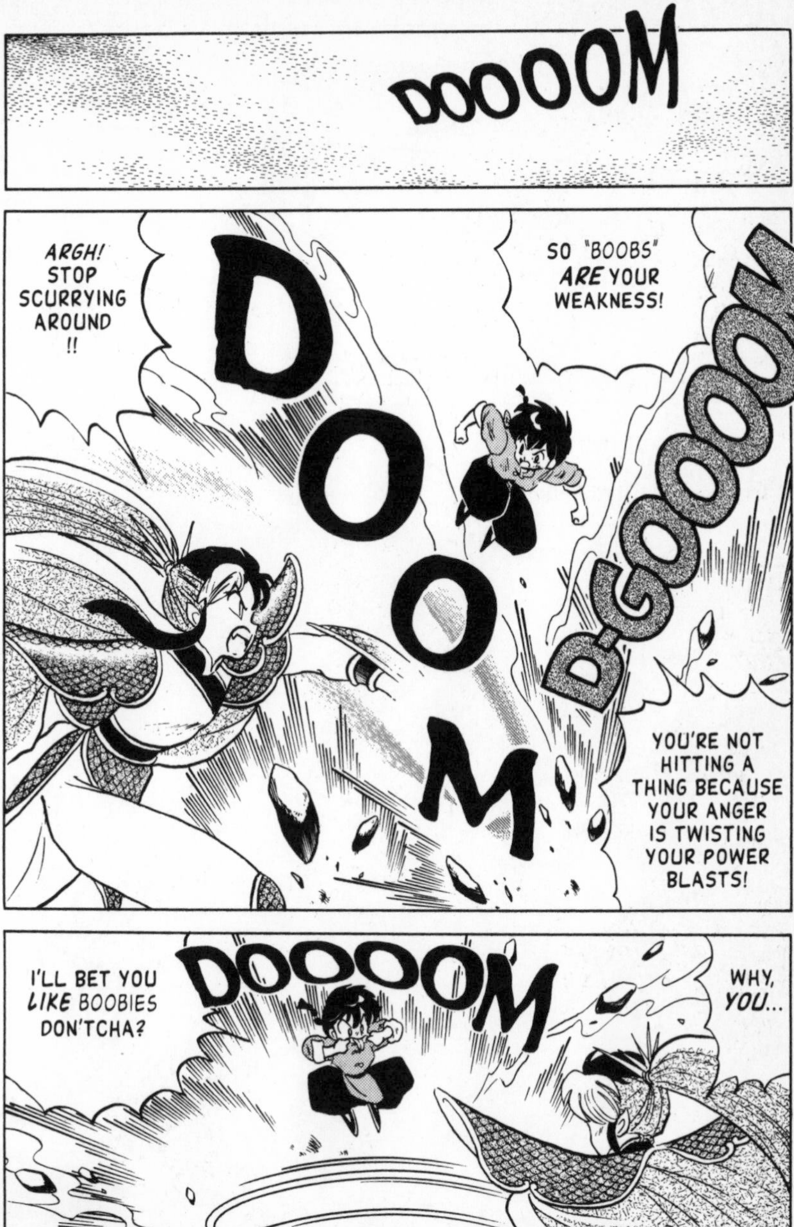
DOOOOM
ARGH! STOP SCURRYING AROUND !!
DOOM
SO "BOOBS" ARE YOUR WEAKNESS!
D-GOOOOOM
YOU'RE NOT HITTING A THING BECAUSE YOUR ANGER IS TWISTING YOUR POWER BLASTS!
I'LL BET YOU LIKE BOOBIES DON'TCHA?
DOOOOOM
WHY, YOU...

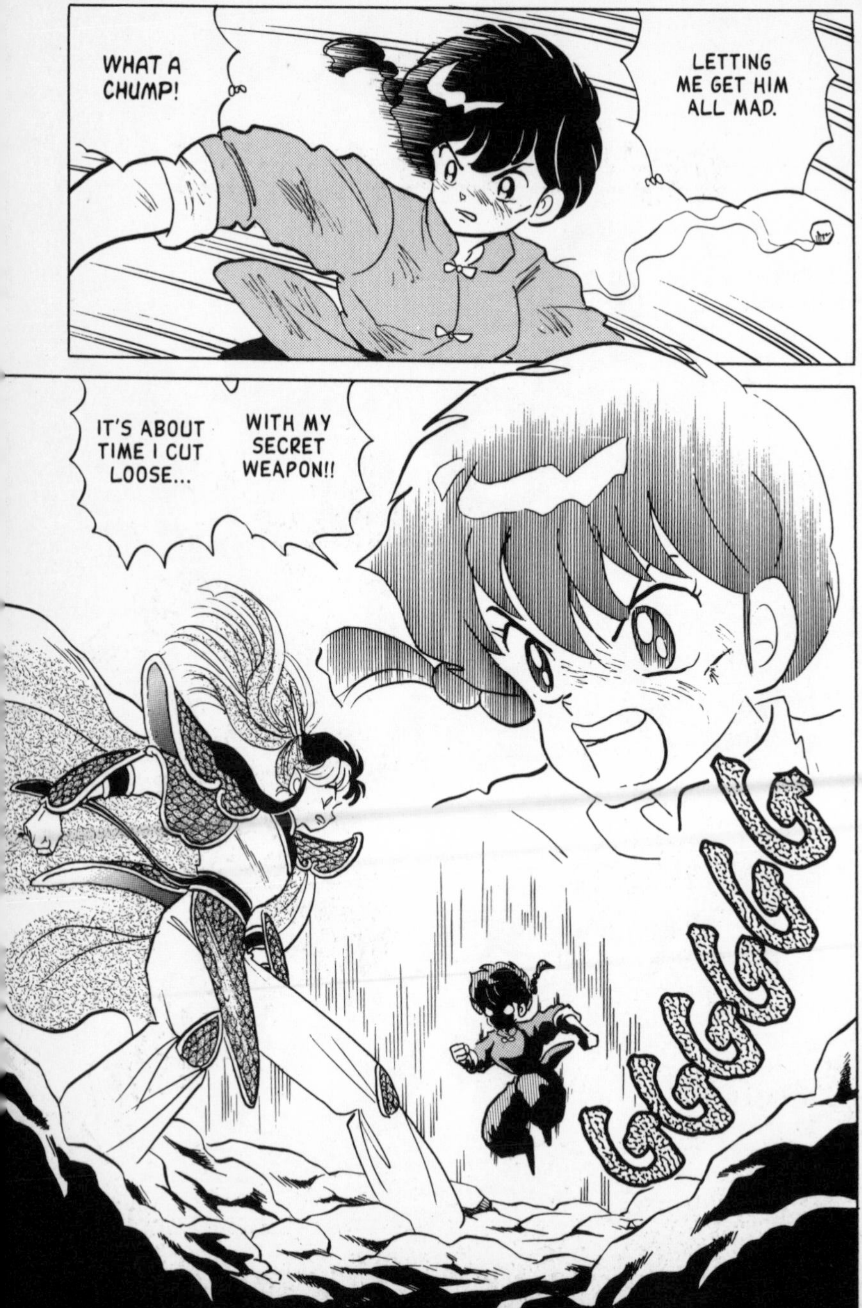
WHAT A CHUMP!
LETTING ME GET HIM ALL MAD.
IT'S ABOUT TIME I CUT LOOSE...
WITH MY SECRET WEAPON!!

Part 11

RISE UP, RANMA!

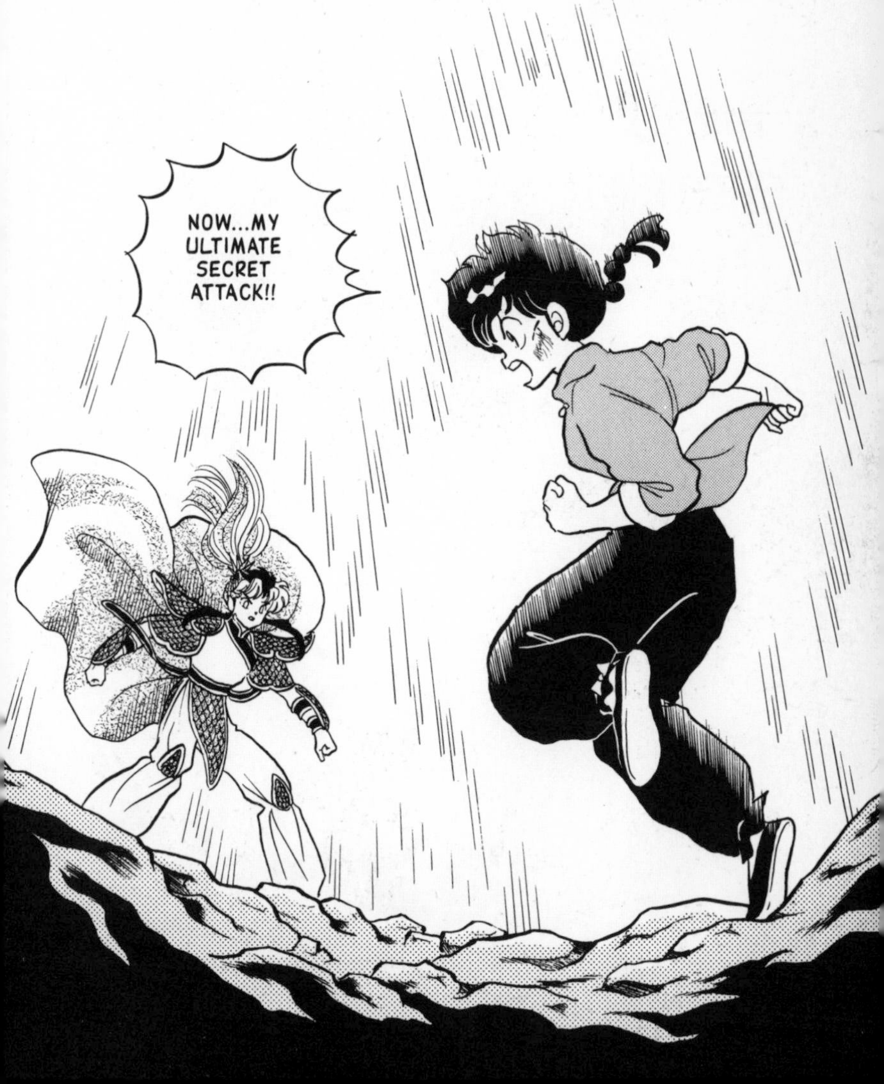
NOW...MY ULTIMATE SECRET ATTACK!!

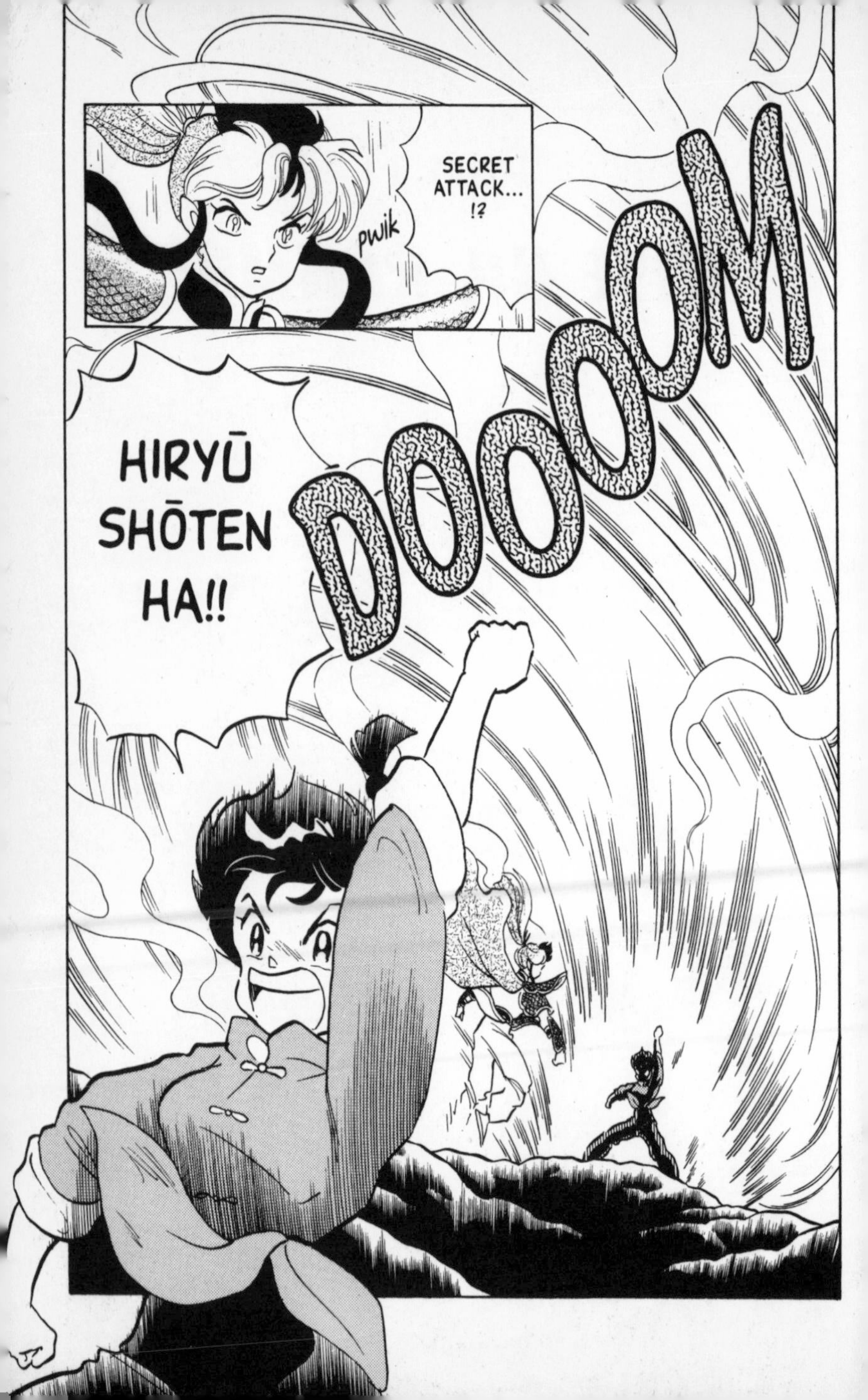

pwik
SECRET ATTACK... !?
HIRYŪ SHŌTEN HA!!
DOOOOOM

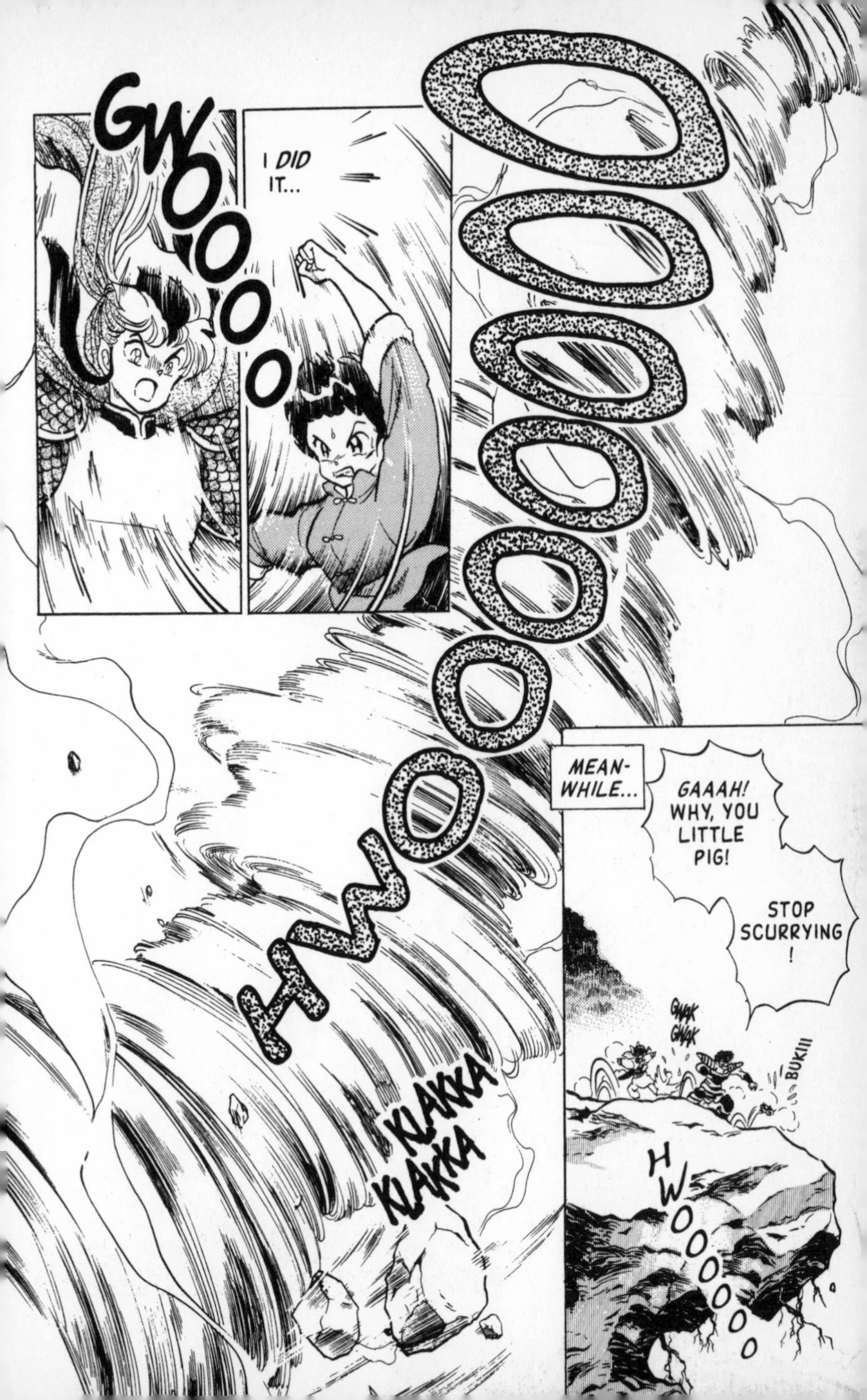
GWOOOOO
I DID IT...
HWOOOOOOOO
KLAKKA KLAKKA
MEAN-WHILE...
GAAAH! WHY, YOU LITTLE PIG!
STOP SCURRYING!
GWAK GWAK
BUKIII
HWOOOOOOO

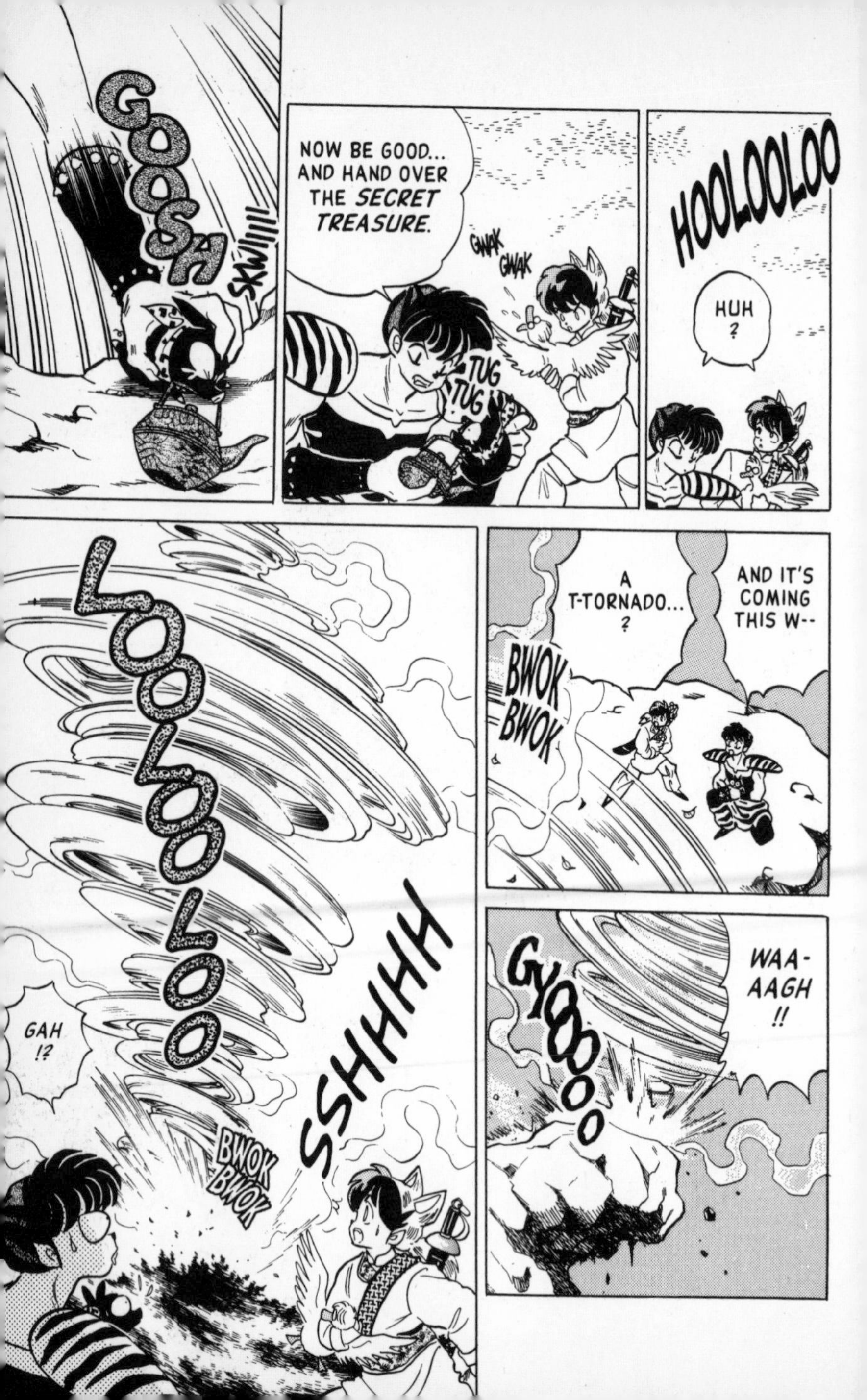
GOOSH
SKWIIII!!
NOW BE GOOD... AND HAND OVER THE SECRET TREASURE.
GWAK GWAK
TUG TUG
HOOLOOLOO
HUH ?
LOOLOOLOO
SSHHHH
GAH !?
BWOK BWOK
A T-TORNADO... ?
AND IT'S COMING THIS W--
BWOK BWOK
GYOOOOO
WAA-AAGH !!

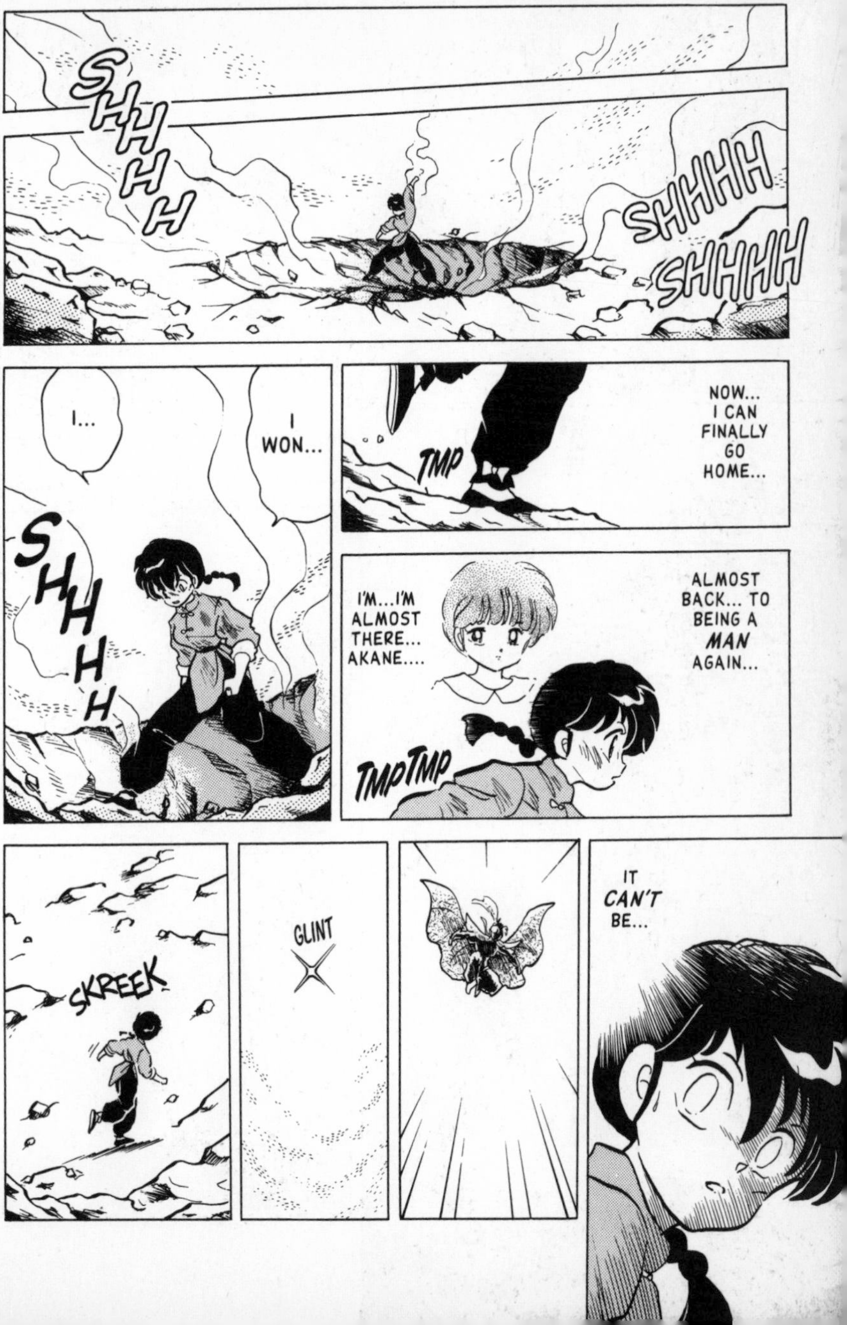
SHHHH
SHHHH
SHHHH
I...
I WON...
SHHHH
NOW... I CAN FINALLY GO HOME...
TMP
I'M...I'M ALMOST THERE... AKANE....
ALMOST BACK... TO BEING A MAN AGAIN...
TMPTMP
SKREEK
GLINT
IT CAN'T BE...

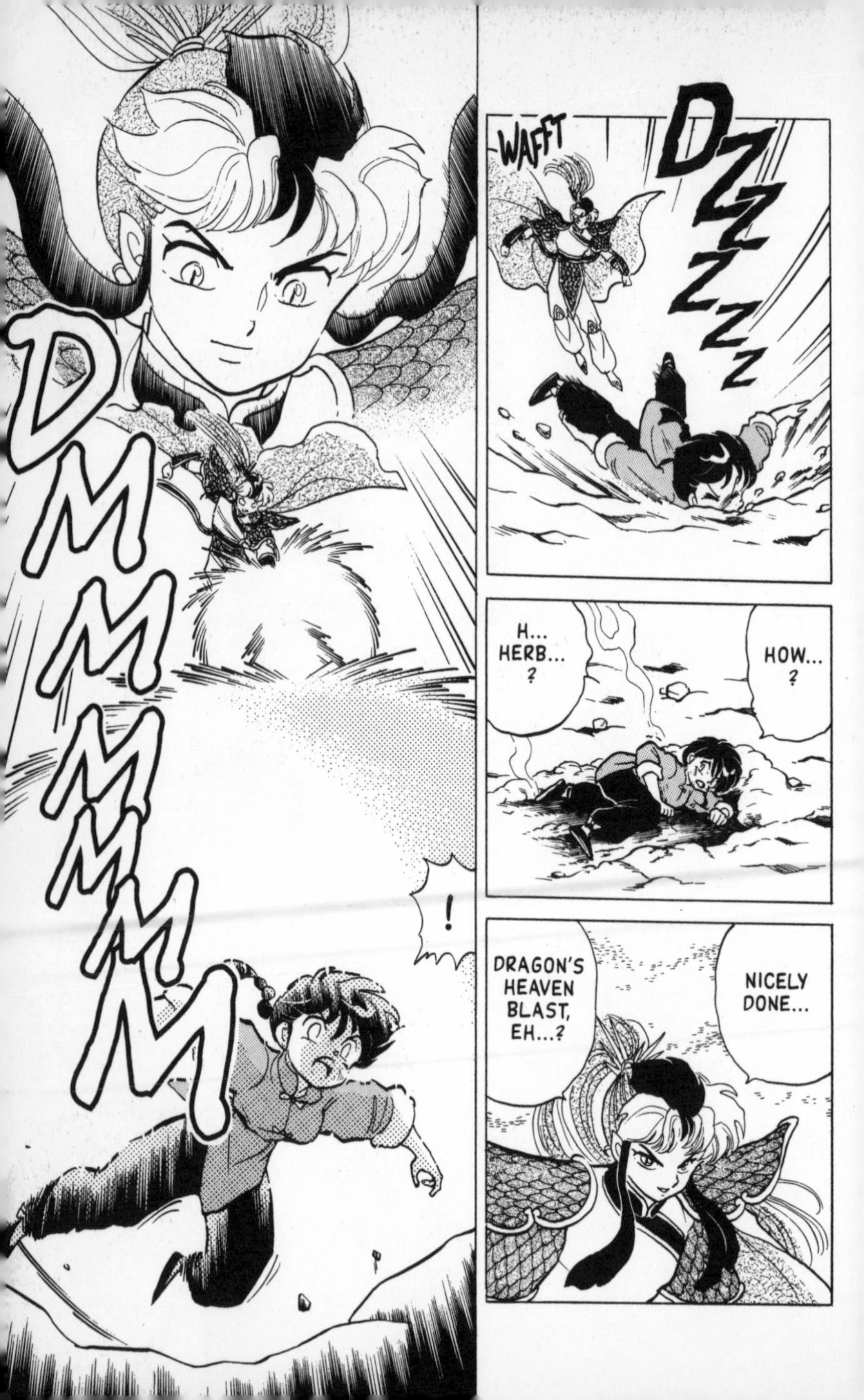
DMMMMMM
!
WAFFT
DZZZZZ
H... HERB...?
HOW...?
DRAGON'S HEAVEN BLAST, EH...?
NICELY DONE...

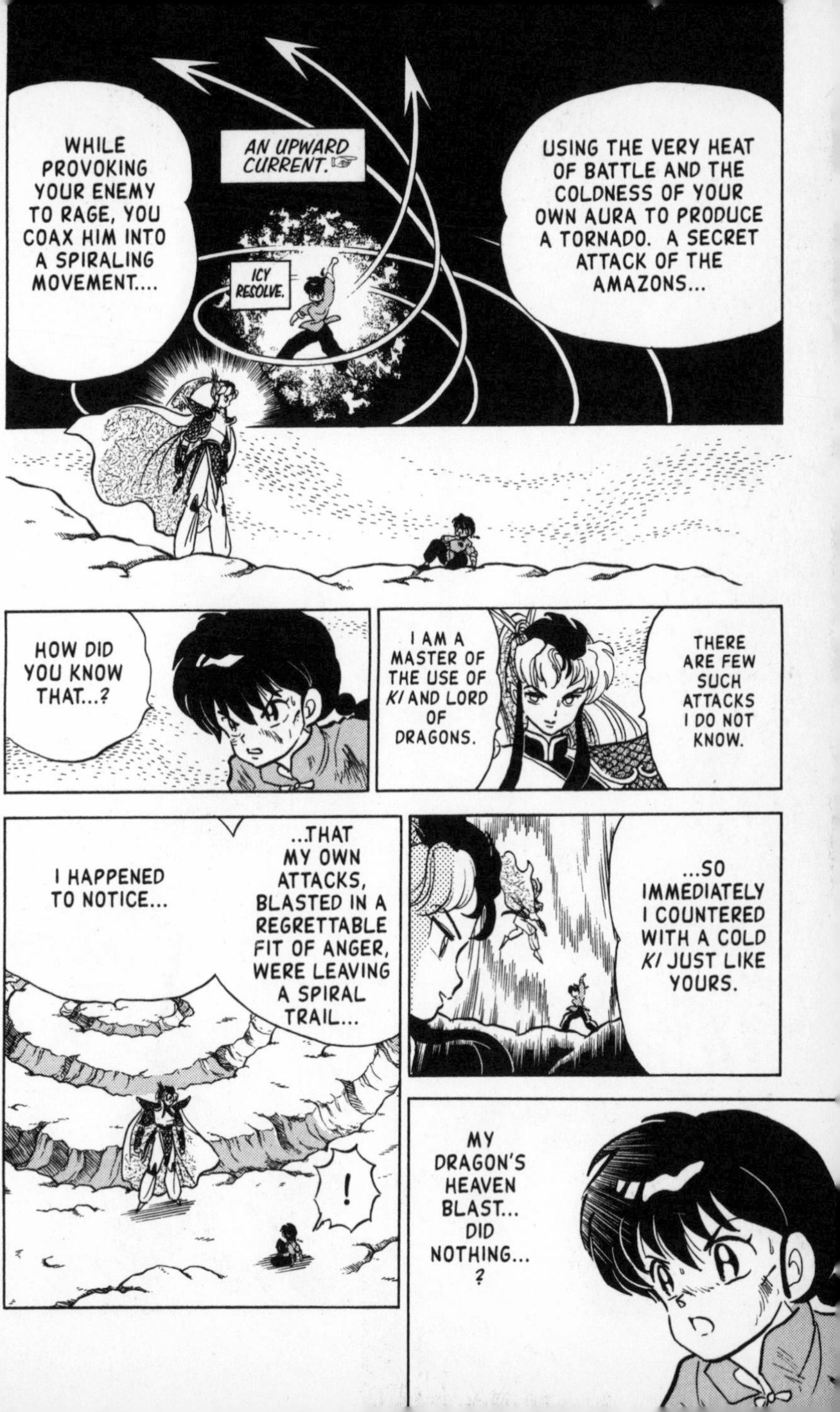
WHILE PROVOKING YOUR ENEMY TO RAGE, YOU COAX HIM INTO A SPIRALING MOVEMENT....
AN UPWARD CURRENT.
ICY RESOLVE.
USING THE VERY HEAT OF BATTLE AND THE COLDNESS OF YOUR OWN AURA TO PRODUCE A TORNADO. A SECRET ATTACK OF THE AMAZONS...
HOW DID YOU KNOW THAT...?
I AM A MASTER OF THE USE OF KI AND LORD OF DRAGONS.
THERE ARE FEW SUCH ATTACKS I DO NOT KNOW.
I HAPPENED TO NOTICE...
...THAT MY OWN ATTACKS, BLASTED IN A REGRETTABLE FIT OF ANGER, WERE LEAVING A SPIRAL TRAIL...
!
...SO IMMEDIATELY I COUNTERED WITH A COLD KI JUST LIKE YOURS.
MY DRAGON'S HEAVEN BLAST... DID NOTHING...?

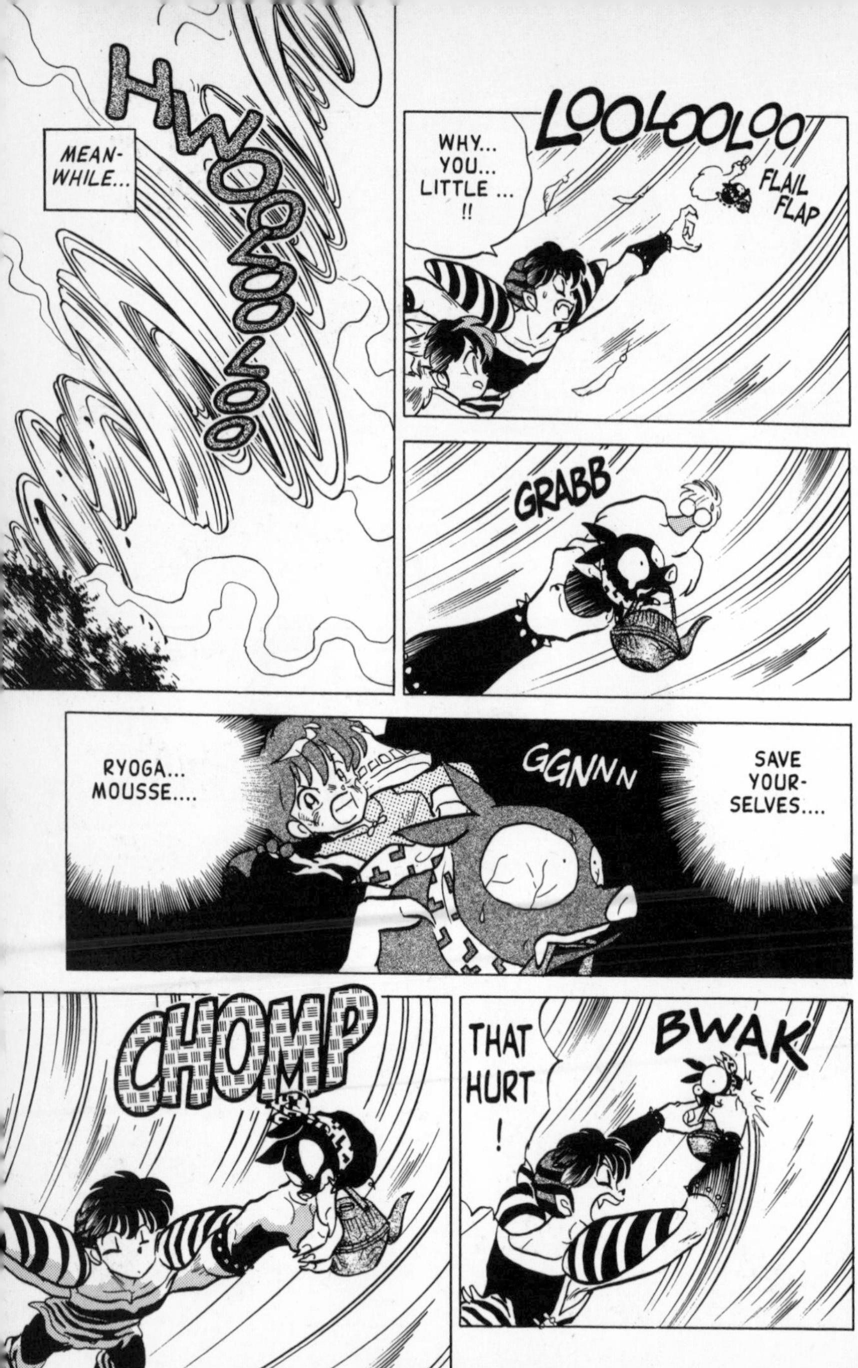
MEAN-WHILE...
HWOOOOOOOLOO
WHY... YOU... LITTLE ... !!
LOOLOOLOO
FLAIL FLAP
GRABB
RYOGA... MOUSSE....
GGNNNN
SAVE YOUR-SELVES....
CHOMP
THAT HURT !
BWAK

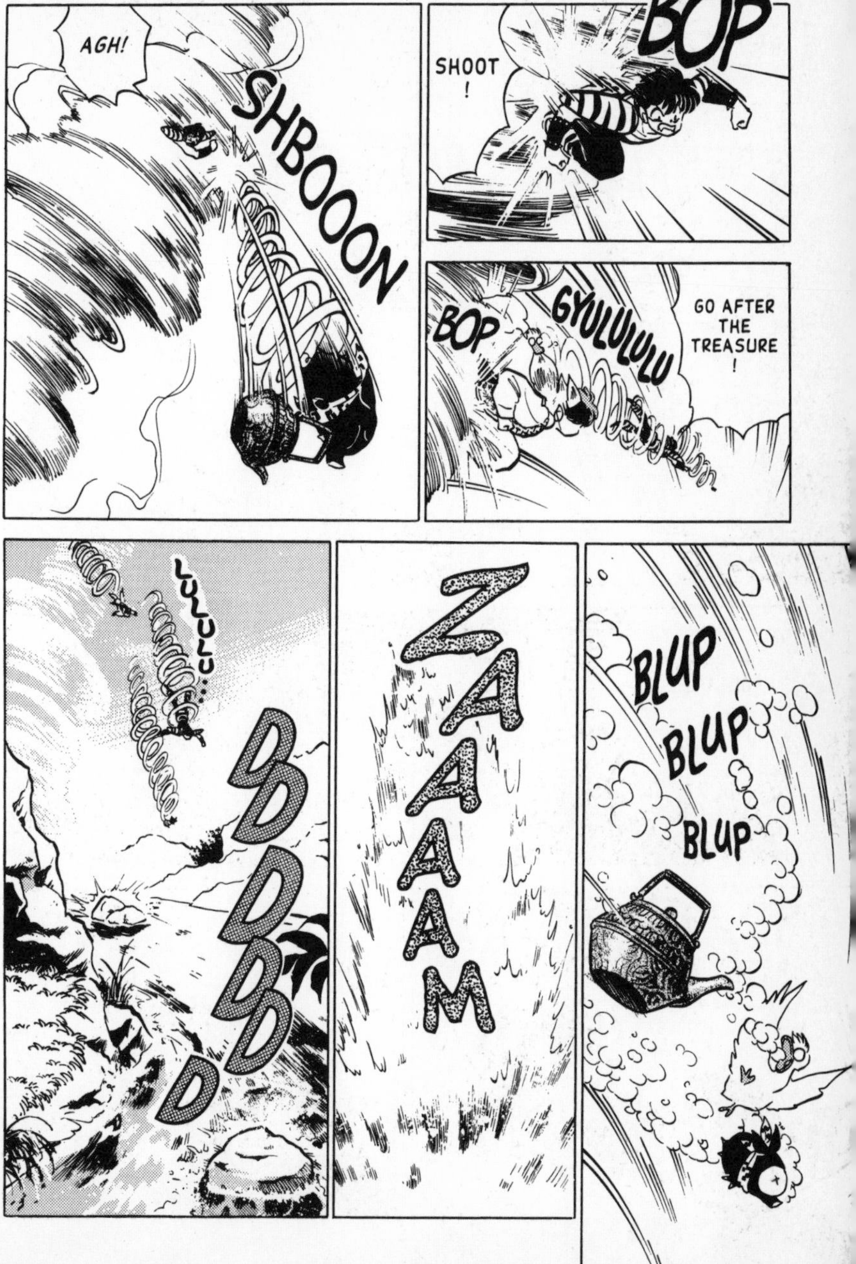
AGH!
SHBOOON
SHOOT!
BOP
BOP
GYULULULU
GO AFTER THE TREASURE!
LULULULU...
DDDDDD
ZAAAAM
BLUP
BLUP
BLUP

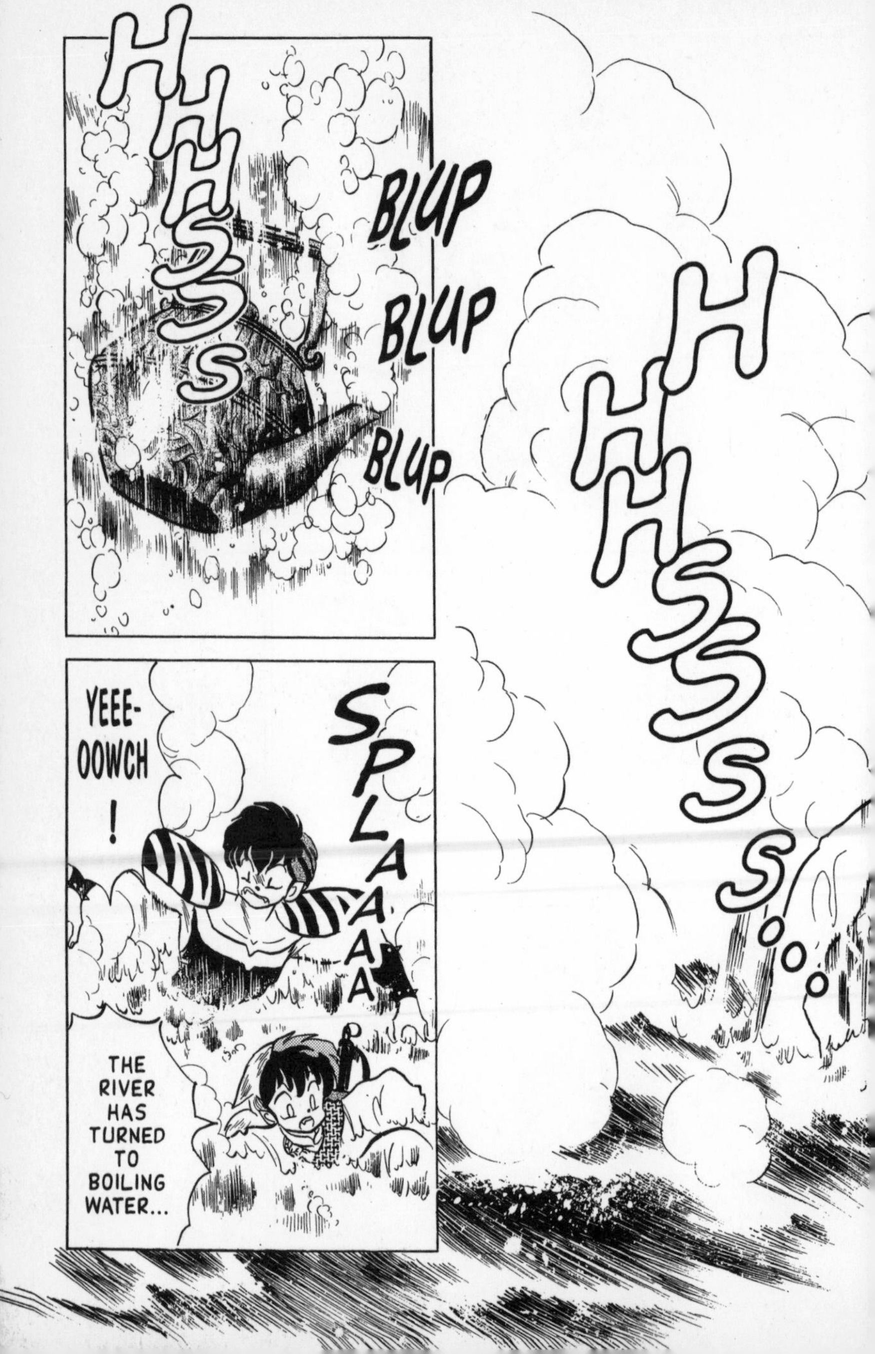

HHHSSS
BLUP
BLUP
BLUP
HHHHSSSSS...
SPLAAAAA
YEEE-OOWCH!
THE RIVER HAS TURNED TO BOILING WATER...

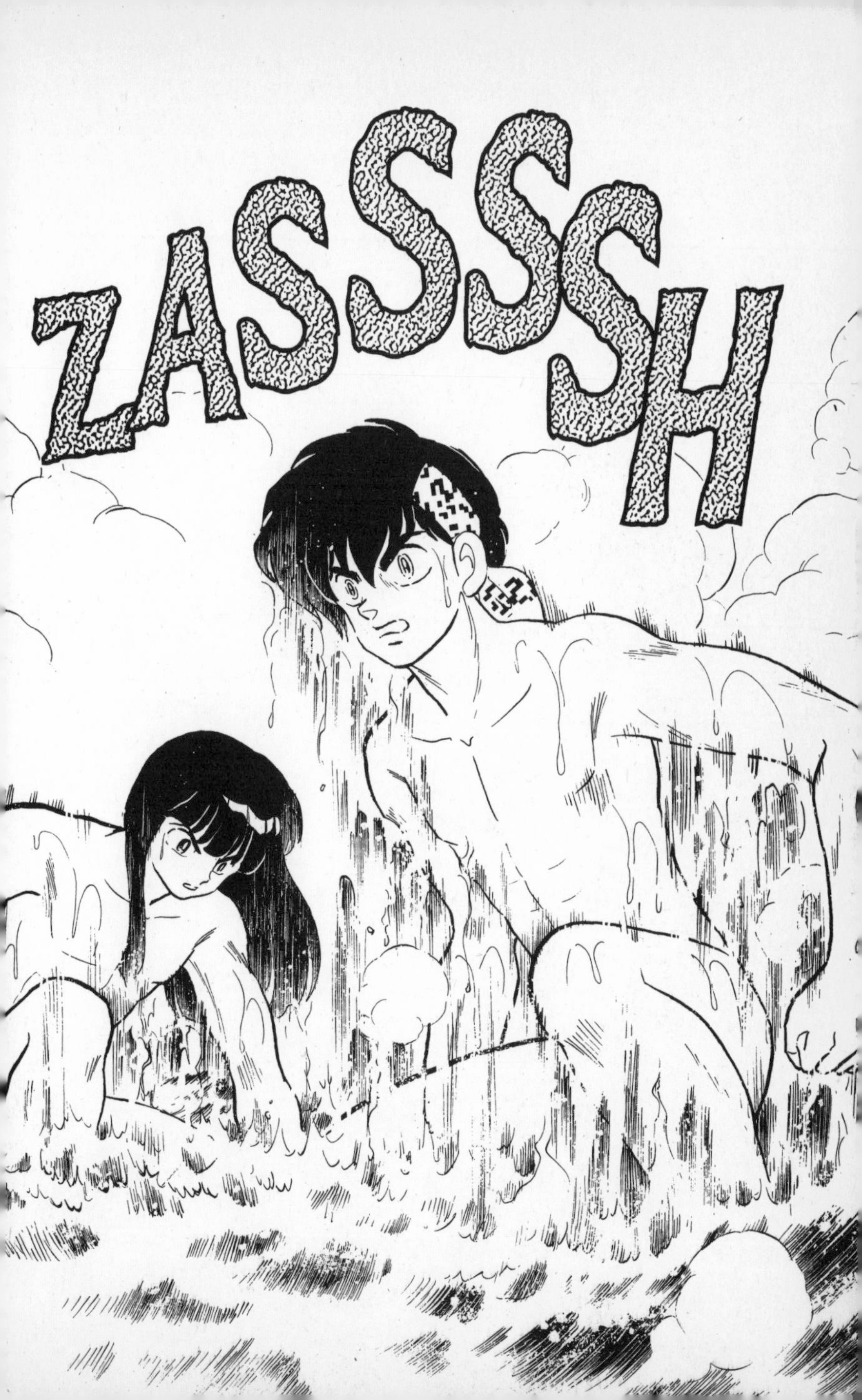
ZASSSH

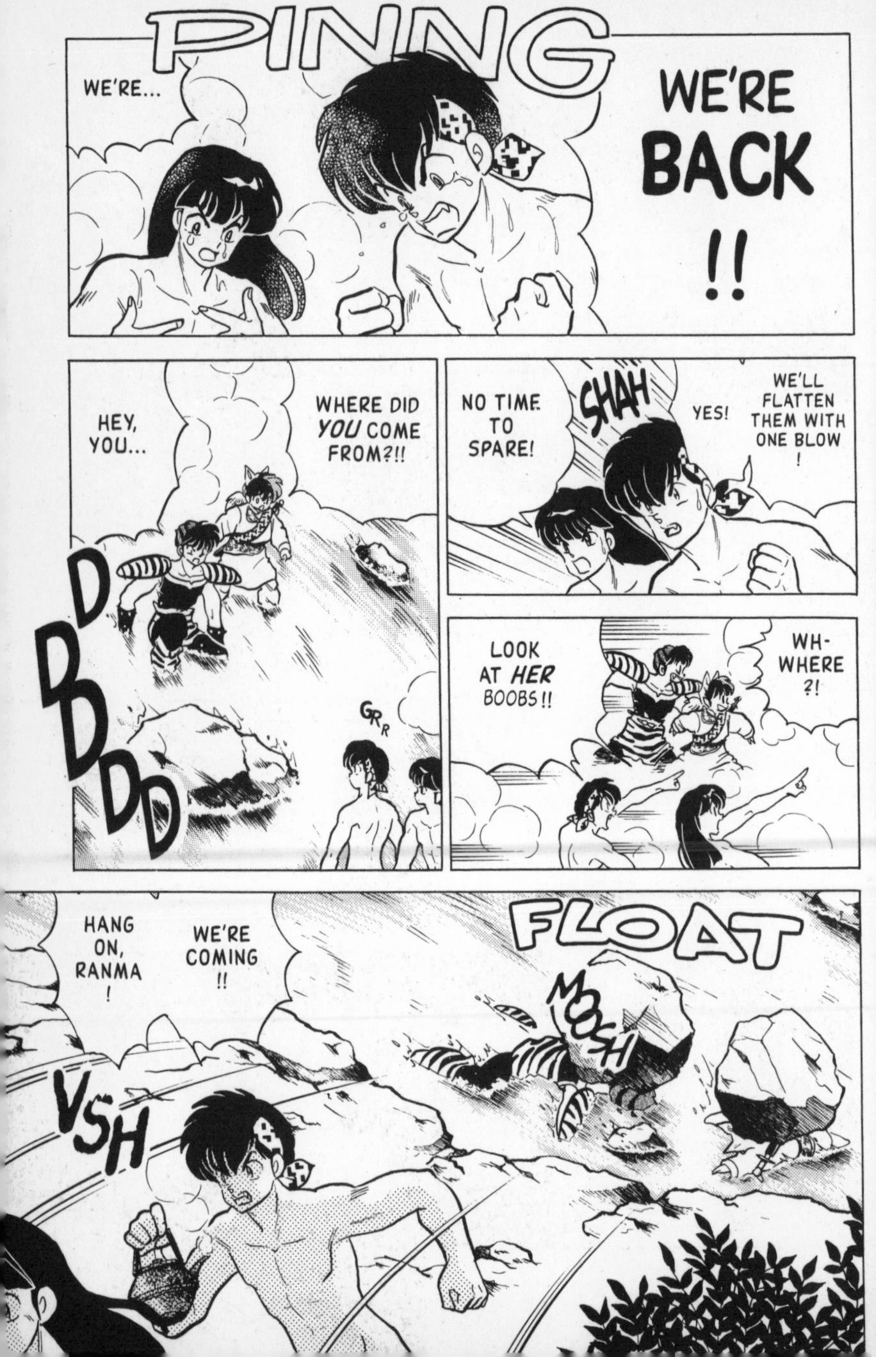
PINNG
WE'RE...
WE'RE BACK !!
HEY, YOU...
WHERE DID *YOU* COME FROM?!!
DDDD
GRR
NO TIME TO SPARE!
SHAH
YES!
WE'LL FLATTEN THEM WITH ONE BLOW !
LOOK AT *HER* BOOBS !!
WH-WHERE ?!
HANG ON, RANMA !
WE'RE COMING !!
FLOAT
MOOSH
VSH

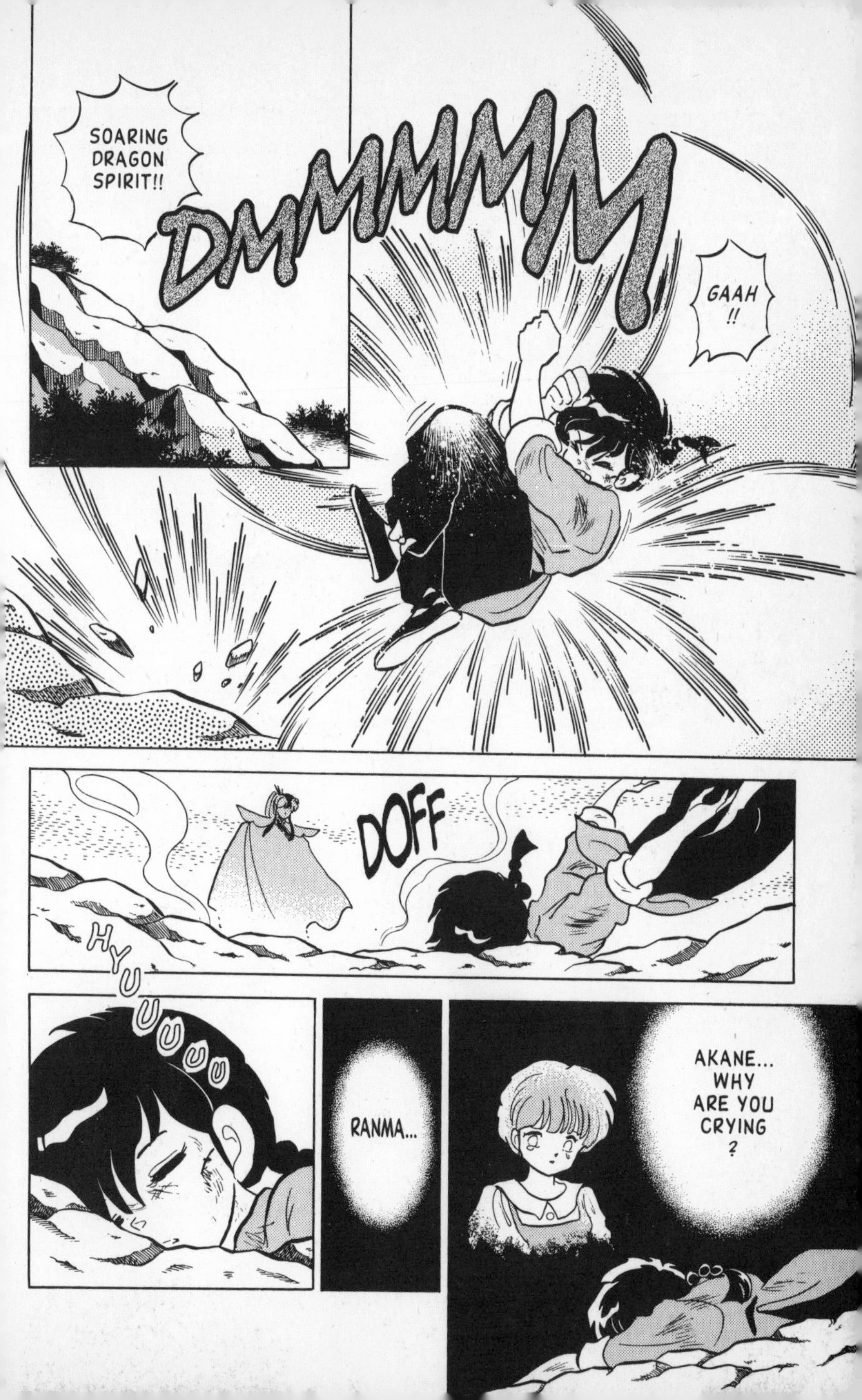
SOARING DRAGON SPIRIT!!
DMMMMM
GAAH !!
DOFF
HYUUUUUU
RANMA...
AKANE... WHY ARE YOU CRYING ?

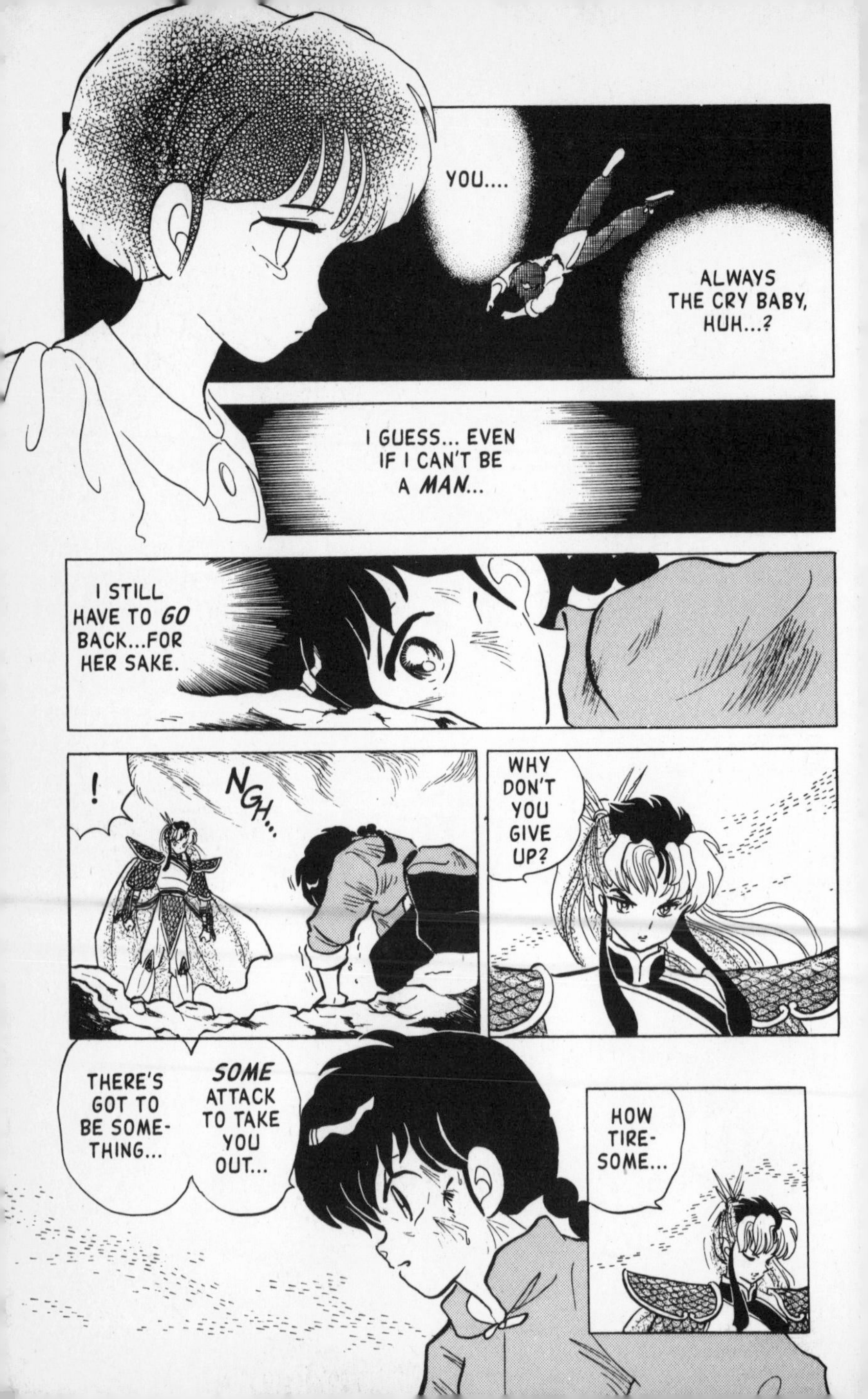
YOU....
ALWAYS THE CRY BABY, HUH...?
I GUESS... EVEN IF I CAN'T BE A *MAN*...
I STILL HAVE TO *GO* BACK...FOR HER SAKE.
!
NGH...
WHY DON'T YOU GIVE UP?
THERE'S GOT TO BE SOME-THING...
SOME ATTACK TO TAKE YOU OUT...
HOW TIRE-SOME...

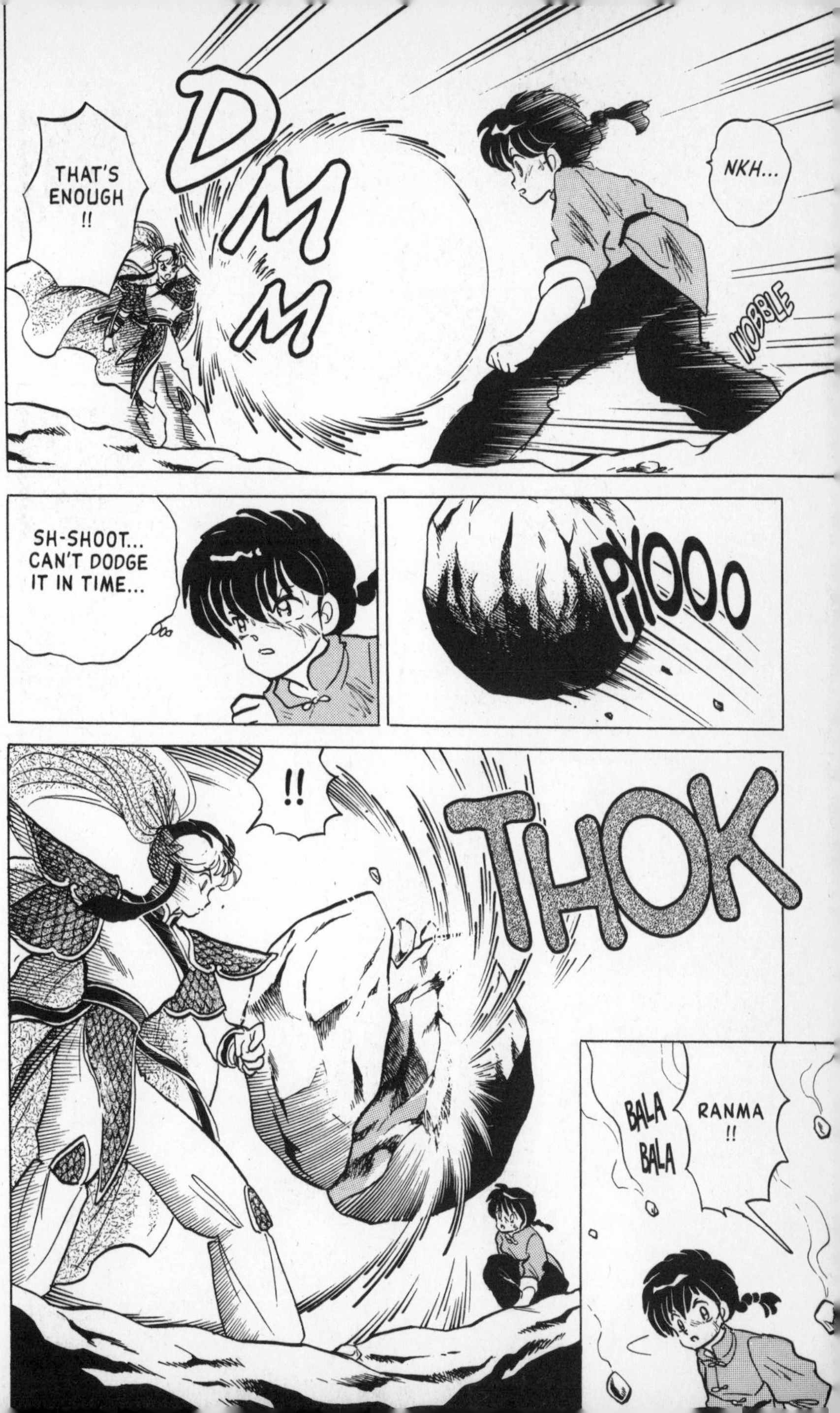
THAT'S ENOUGH !!
DMM
NKH...
WOBBLE
SH-SHOOT... CAN'T DODGE IT IN TIME...
PYOOO
!!
THOK
BALA BALA
RANMA !!

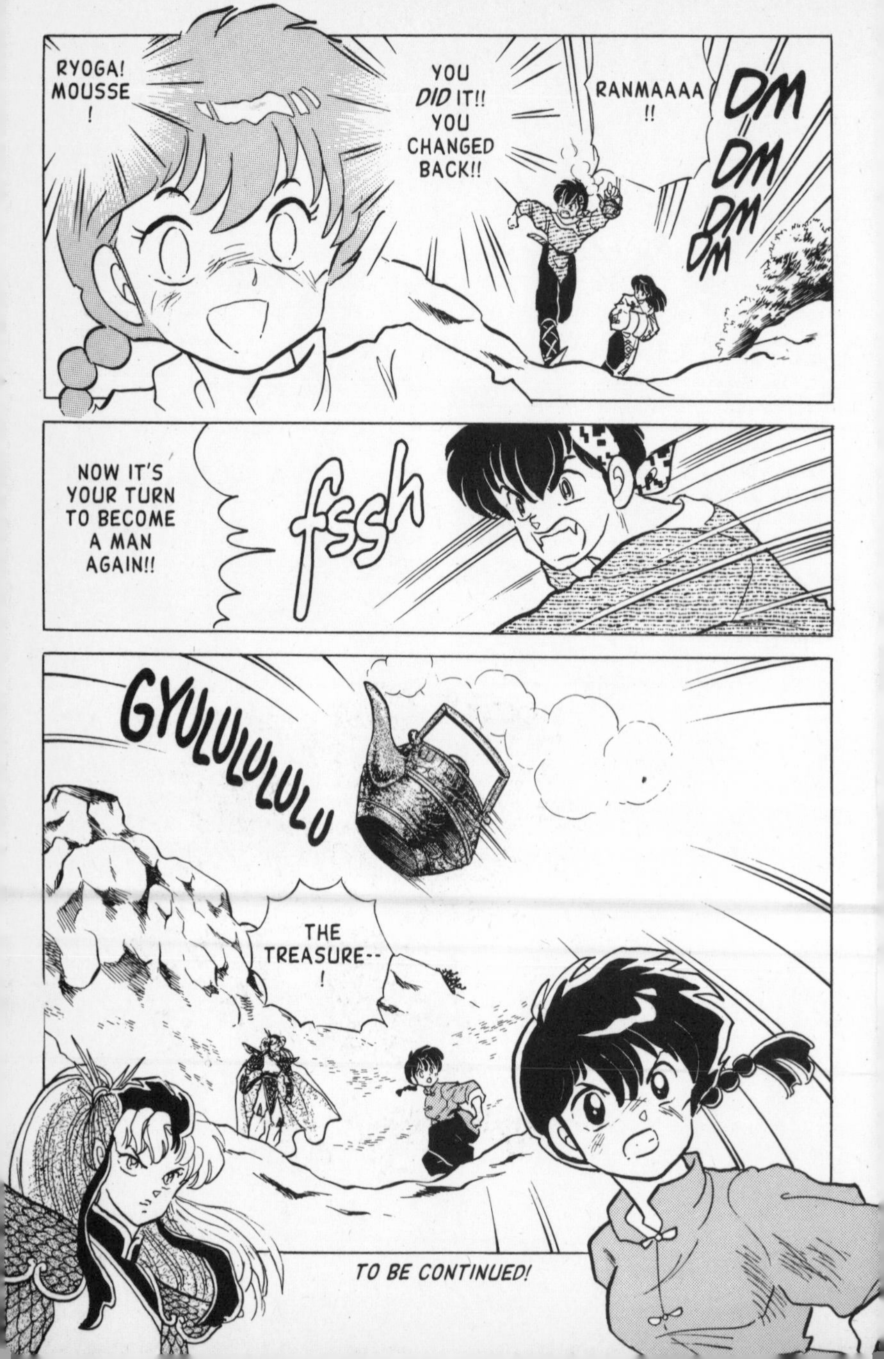
RYOGA! MOUSSE !
YOU *DID* IT!! YOU CHANGED BACK!!
RANMAAAA !!
DM DM DM DM
NOW IT'S YOUR TURN TO BECOME A MAN AGAIN!!
fssh
GYULULULULU
THE TREASURE-- !
TO BE CONTINUED!

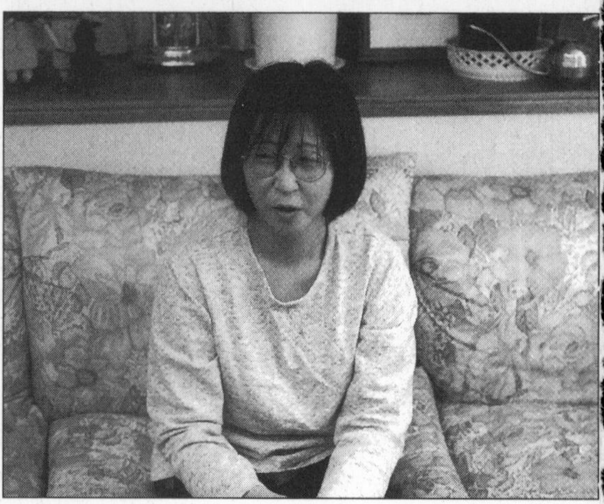

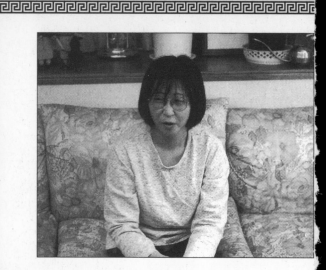

About Rumiko Takahashi

Born in 1957 in Niigata, Japan, Rumiko Takahashi attended women college in Tokyo, where she began studying comics with Kazuo Koik author of *Crying Freeman*. She later became an assistant to horror-r artist Kazuo Umezu (*Orochi*). In 1978, she won a prize in Shogakuka annual "New Comic Artist Contest," and in that same year her boy meets-alien comedy series *Urusei Yatsura* began appearing in the manga magazine *Shônen Sunday*. This phenomenally successful se ran for nine years and sold over 22 million copies. Takahashi's late *Ranma 1/2* series enjoyed even greater popularity.

Takahashi is considered by many to be one of the world's mo popular manga artists. With the publication of Volume 34 of her *Ra 1/2* series in Japan, Takahashi's total sales passed *one hundred m* copies of her compiled works.

Takahashi's serial titles include *Urusei Yatsura, Ranma 1/2, On Pound Gospel, Maison Ikkoku* and *InuYasha*. Additionally, Takahashi drawn many short stories which have been published in America the title "Rumic Theater," and several installments of a saga know her "Mermaid" series. Most of Takahashi's major stories have als animated, and are widely available in translation worldwide. *InuY* her most recent serial story, first published in *Shônen Sunday* in 19